Latin American Masses and Minorities:
Their Images and Realities

Two volumes

SALALM Secretariat
Memorial Library
University of Wisconsin--Madison

LATIN AMERICAN MASSES AND
MINORITIES: THEIR IMAGES
AND REALITIES

VOLUME I

Papers of the Thirtieth Annual Meeting of the
SEMINAR ON THE ACQUISITION OF
LATIN AMERICAN LIBRARY MATERIALS

Princeton University
Princeton, New Jersey
June 19 - 23, 1985

Dan C. Hazen
Editor

SALALM Secretariat
Memorial Library, University of Wisconsin--Madison

ISBN 0-917617-11-8

SALALM XXX

and

the <u>Papers</u> of SALALM XXX

are dedicated to the memory of

Marietta Daniels Shepard

(1913 – 1984)

C O N T E N T S

Part Two.   Sample Inquiries into Latin
American Masses and Minorities

Part Three.   Images and Realities
in Nontraditional Formats

Outline of Contents in Volume II

PREFACE

The thirtieth annual Seminar on the Acquisition of Latin American Library Materials (SALALM XXX) was held at Princeton University between June 19 and 23, 1985. The meeting focused on the images and realities of Latin American masses and minorities. In addition to the customary array of business sessions, committee meetings, and social events, the conference incorporated some twenty panels and workshops addressing different aspects of the theme. These sessions were particularly designed to tap the substantial Latin Americanist resources of the New York metropolitan region; the "East Coast Committee," chaired by Princeton's Peter T. Johnson, carried out much of the hard work of identifying participants and organizing panels. The conference program, reproduced at the end of these Papers, provides a fairly complete indication of the Princeton activities.

These Papers include a substantial subset of the Conference presentations. The largest group of omissions represents informal workshop presentations, for which a formal manuscript was neither desired nor appropriate. A few papers have been published in other outlets, and have thus been omitted. And a few manuscripts were never forthcoming.

In other words, the thematic patchwork of conference papers on hand does not fully reflect the original conference structure. Consequently, the initial sequence of topics has been recast. These Papers begin with a general reflection on the meeting's theme. Each of the five main sections is introduced, in turn, with a brief statement of background and purpose. The papers are numbered consecutively, but because of their length they are presented in two volumes. Volume I contains sections I through III; Volume II contains sections IV and V.

INTRODUCTION

Latin America's culture of literacy remains, even today, that of a privileged minority. For most, life remains close to subsistence. Its possibilities are defined by the underlying structures of material and psychological survival: the land, the weather, the values traditional to particular groups and subgroups. This life is most directly expressed, and interpreted, through such nonliterary manifestations as domestic architecture, land use, settlement patterns, food, music, folk art, and engrained patterns of behavior and belief. Even politicization and political movements, so frequently taken to prove the penetration of modern, individualistic values, must somehow adjust to the circumstances that define life for the masses. The expressions and documentation most revealing of most Latin Americans, in other words, may take forms unexpected by observers from a postindustrial society.

A few quotations may help establish this context in a somewhat different way. Fernand Braudel, in prefacing the first volume of his massive study <u>Civilization and Capitalism, 15th–18th Century</u>, notes:

> Ever-present, all pervasive, repetitive, material life is run according to routine: people go on sowing wheat as they always have done, planting maize as they always have done, terracing the paddy-fields as they always have done, sailing in the Red Sea as they always have done. The obstinate presence of the past greedily and steadily swallows up the fragile lifetime of men. And this layer of stagnant history is enormous: all rural life, that is 80 to 90% of the world's population, belongs to it for the most part.[1]

> Sometimes a few anecdotes are enough to set up a signal which points to a way of life. . . . I have seen a Japanese costume of the fifteenth century; and found it very like one of the eighteenth; and a Spanish traveller once described his conversation with a Japanese diplomat who was astonished and even shocked to see Europeans appear in such very different clothing at intervals of only a few years. Is the passion for fashion a peculiarly European thing? Is it insignificant? Through little details, travellers' notes, a society stands revealed. The ways people eat, dress, or lodge, at the different levels of that society, are never a matter of indifference.[2]

Braudel's poetry describes an approach that has been challenged as overly economistic and materialistic. François Chevalier, in a recent address before the Conference on Latin American History, more prosaicly notes:

> . . . the purely socio-economic focus is losing part of its attraction among the new generations. This--even when the English edition of Fernand Braudel's three volume Civilisation matérielle . . . is appearing and the author is being incorporated into the French Academy. . . . the purely economic-social perspective is insufficient to account for phenomena that are, at times, essential. . . . the complex phenomena of partial acculturation, deculturation, and reculturation are essential. The topic of religion or religious change, in the broadest sense of the word, is a central problem.[3]

We must ponder both the material and the psychic under-pinnings of society if we want to approach full understanding--and even as our own literate, affluent, urban, technological culture so often resists such perceptiveness. Without understanding these manifestations of the masses, we can neither fully appreciate nor adequately apprehend Latin America, however "successful" our short-term determinations in matters of economic policy or international politics. And we will mark but little progress in our understanding of ourselves and our fellows in the absence of such broadly humanistic endeavor.

Our conference title speaks of Latin America's minorities as well as its masses. The rationale for inclusion is twofold. The working definition of "minority" which we have adopted emphasizes groups marginal to Latin America's elite societies. Some minorities, thus, are virtually indistinguishable from the masses already considered. Certainly, this is the case for the region's indigenous populations, or for economically, politically, and socially peripheral groups like tenant farmers and urban squatters.

Even those politically or socially dissonant groups whose "minority" status is primarily defined by their lack of conformity to the patterns and precepts of elite society--gays, Jews, ideological dissidents, and so forth--very frequently manifest their uniqueness through forms of communication, conduct, and expression analogous to the less self-conscious idiosyncrasies of the "mass minorities" mentioned above. Diet, dress styles, music, and settlement patterns--depending on the specific case--may distinguish these minorities as much as they characterize the larger groups. And, of course, it bears recalling that census definitions through much of the region attribute ethnic identity through precisely such considerations as dress and diet: an Indian is an Indian because he or she wears ojotas (or huaraches), bases his diet on potatoes (or corn), cannot read or write, and so forth.

Our case for including Latin American minorities can be extended as we consider the documentation they produce. Expressions of masses and minorities alike tend to emphasize forms that diverge from the elite's "high" print culture. At times, as with the chapbook literature of Northeastern Brazil, or the mimeographed broadsides and leaflets of political dissidents, we remain close to the traditional core materials of library collections. Our libraries may not always know quite how to handle these materials, but they nonetheless fall into familiar categories. In other cases, the forms or formats are themselves alien. Photographic evidence provides essential documentation of both material culture and ritual. Music, whether transcribed onto paper or recorded--and whether recorded on field equipment or in a sound studio--affords another example. Documenting the material culture of Latin America, as well as the iconographic and symbolic manifestations of popular beliefs, aspirations, frustrations, and preoccupations, requires us to go beyond our customary routine.

A second dimension of the conference theme involves the juxtaposition of image and reality. Here we again face issues common to all scholarship and to the study of all societies and social groups. These issues comprise a broad hierarchy. They originate in the overarching epistemological concerns of knowledge, truth, and reality, and then descend to the more immediate framework set by the research paradigms and priorities of specific disciplines. They subsequently focus on the seemingly humbler but equally significant biases introduced by patterns of documentation, and by the differential availability of particular forms and formats of information.

The librarian, information specialist, or scholar concerned with Latin America must necessarily be concerned with the region's masses and minorities. He or she must with equal necessity confront the adequacy of current acquisition patterns, collecting ideologies, and research paradigms as they affect our ability to improve our understanding. This, in turn, requires us to both define and extend our models for libraries and research.

Five years ago, at SALALM's Albuquerque meeting, we considered the parameters for developing library collections in support of Latin American Studies through the current decade. Two points then merited particular emphasis: the need for cooperation; and the need for librarians to "move beyond our subordinate and dependent status with regard to publishing output and university structures, and toward a broader interaction with the disciplines of research." Among the possible goals was a "renewed vision of librarians as scholars and shapers as well as acceptors and reflectors of research paradigms and disciplinary concerns."[4]

At the Princeton conference, scholars explained their uses of both traditional and nontraditional forms of documentation in studying Latin America's masses and minorities. As we absorb these messages, we look forward to more fully articulating our own role in leading the way for scholarship. By anticipating research needs and possibilities alike, we can play an active role in shaping the studies of tomorrow. We can and, whether we wish it or not, we <u>will</u> help determine whether that scholarship is adequate: whether it truly illuminates and reflects, or merely distorts and caricatures, the peoples it would describe.

Dan C. Hazen

NOTES

1. Fernand Braudel, <u>Civilization and Capitalism</u>, 15th-18th <u>Century</u>, Vol. I, <u>The Structures of Everyday Life: The Limits of the Possible</u> (New York, NY: Harper & Row, 1981), p. 28.

2. Ibid., p. 29.

3. François Chevalier, "New Perspectives and New Focuses on Latin American Research," <u>Newsletter</u>, Conference on Latin American History, 21:1 (April, 1985), 13-14.

4. Dan C. Hazen, "Major Latin American Collections in Private Institutions: New Roles and Responsibilities in the 1980s," in <u>Library Resources on Latin America: New Perspectives for the 1980s. Final Report and Working Papers of the Twenty-Fifth Seminar on the Acquisition of Latin American Library Materials</u> (Madison, WI: SALALM Secretariat, 1981), pp. 241-242.

Latin American Masses and Minorities:
Their Images and Realities

Volume I

Part One

Finding the Truth:
Philosophical and Conceptual Dilemmas
in Latin Americanist Scholarship

INTRODUCTION

The description and analysis of any individual, group, or society assume that the object of study possesses an objective reality. However, and as the metaphysicians have demonstrated all too clearly, "objective reality" is an elusive and perhaps illusory concept. Any perception and any statement filter some event or fact through a human observer's consciousness. The process is necessarily imbued with and, indeed, founded in both overt and unconscious intrusions. The intrusions become ever more complex as researchers attempt to control their own distortions of perceptions which have already been filtered through more immediate observers' cultural and behavioral screens. The problem is ubiquitous and daunting--and yet we nonetheless insist that there are knowable facts, and that our knowledge can serve us in tangible ways.

The difficulties of knowing, of identifying the truth, are compounded as we cross lines of culture, class, age, religion, ideology, and ethnicity. Images that one group finds compelling may be flatly rejected by others; and any or all parties to some "reality" may deliberately seek to distort or obfuscate representative images in order to further their own particular ends. The danger of caricature, most often resulting from the combination of ignorance and ethnocentrism, is ever present. Misrepresentation may be neither intentional nor obvious.

One way of approaching the entire conference theme centers on this struggle among images. How are they created, and in whose interest? How are they utilized? How do academics perceive, control for, create, and perpetuate particular visions? What are the systematic distortions, both deliberate and inadvertent, engendered by different disciplines' research agendas and paradigms? What are the biases introduced by documentary collections that only partly reflect different societies, and that unconsciously but inevitably overrepresent groups sharing the sensibilities particular to literate, Western culture? Image and reality: the tension is pervasive.

Awareness of such complexity can lead to a kind of over-particularization, to an insistence on the infinite uniqueness of humankind and a concomitant failure to address the patterns, values, and constructs that organize life and meaning for groups of people. On the other hand, simplifying ideologies all too easily lends itself to simplistic determinism. The reification of structure and construct can lead to the elimination--sometimes in the most literal sense--of the individual.

Our first part incorporates three sets of papers addressing the knotty, but essential, task of understanding image, reality, and some of the interactions. We begin with three presentations

on "Media and the Creation of Image." These focus respectively
on the contraposition of "official" realities and observers'
perceptions; on the structural dimensions of media and their
images, and how patterns of economic and technological power
systematically distort both our appreciation of the Third World
and the images available to the countries themselves; and on the
painstaking process of constructing a documentary series on
internal and international conflict involving Central America,
Cuba, and the United States.

The following set of four papers takes a step back, shifting
from the analysis of events and structures as filtered through
various media to the process by which individuals--you and I--
establish our own truths, and define our own values, aspirations,
and priorities. The focus here is the 1980 "boatlift" from Mariel,
Cuba; the commentators are artists and writers who participated
in the exodus. Their evocative, deeply personal accounts not
only illuminate the tangible realities of the boatlift and subsequent
exile/adjustment but also demonstrate--on a very self-conscious
level--the kind of tensions in values and perceptions that make
our individual impressions so slippery and divergent. Here we
have, in the most basic sense, the grist of the scholar's mill.

Finally, then, we turn to academics--to those whose vocation
is to interpret and understand--and to various instances of their
efforts to decipher reality. As each paper deliberately or
unwittingly reveals, the process itself produces new images or
"meta-images." Successive approximations to the truth may entail
the superposition of ever-more abstract molds and models, even
as they suggest new appreciations and understandings. Such
inquiries are essential elements in the academic endeavor of
refining research paradigms, honing research strategies and
techniques, and exploring new sources. The authors of these
papers share a common quest for information on groups overlooked in traditional scholarship. Their sensitivity to innovative
uses of traditional materials, new sorts of data, and new kinds of
images--and truths--is crucial to librarians and scholars alike.

D.C.H.

I. Media and the Creation of Image

1. LATIN AMERICA: MEDIA AND THE CREATION OF IMAGE

Danilo H. Figueredo

Cuba, 1970s

Novelist Reinaldo Arenas tells the story: "A well-known Spanish writer arrives in Cuba and goes to the Union of Cuban Writers and Artists and tells the officials there--Nicolás Guillén and others--that he wants to see the novelist Reinaldo Arenas, and the officials show a list of writers where the name is not listed. He then visits the cultural institution Casa de las Américas and interviews another functionary who tells him, 'You're wrong, in Cuba we do not have any novelist by the name of Reinaldo Arenas'"[1] (free translation by author).

Mexico, October 2d, 1968

From a poem by José Emilio Pacheco:

> Eran las seis y diez. Un helicóptero
> sobrevoló la plaza.
> Me dió miedo.
>
> Cuatro bengalas verdes.
>
> Los soldados
> cerraron las salidas.
>
> Vestidos de civil, los elementos
> del batallón Olimpia
> --mano cubierta por un guante blanco--
> iniciaron el fuego.
>
> En todas direcciones
> se abrió fuego a mansalva.
>
> Desde las azoteas
> dispararon los hombres de guante blanco.
> Y disparó también el helicóptero.
> Se veían las rayas grises.
>
> Como pinzas
> se desplegaron los soldados
> se inició el pánico.
>
> La multitud corrió hacia las salidas
> y encontró bayonetas.
> No había salida:
> la plaza entera se volvió una trampa.

--Aquí, aquí batallón Olimpia.
Aquí, aquí batallón Olimpia.

Comenzaron descargas aún más intensas.
Sesenta y dos minutos duró el fuego.

--¿Quién, quién ordenó todo esto?

Los tanques arrojaron sus proyectiles.
Comenzó a arder el edificio Chihuahua

. . . Los gritos, los aullidos, las plegarías
bajo el contínuo estruendo de las armas.

Los dedos pegados a los gatillos.
Le disparan a todo lo que se mueve.
Y muchas balas dan en el blanco.

--Quédate quieto.
Si nos movemos nos disparan.

--¿Por qué no me contestas?
¿Estás muerto?

--Voy a morir, voy a morir.
Me duele.
Me está saliendo mucha sangre.

. . . --¿Quién, quién ordenó todo esto?

--Hay muchos muertos.
Hay muchos muertos.

Los iban amontonando bajo la lluvia.
Los muertos bocarriba junto a la iglesia.
Les dispararon por la espalda.

Las mujeres cosidas por las balas.
Niños con la cabeza destrozada.
Transeúntes acribillados.

--¿Quién, quién ordenó todo esto![2]

The headline, the following day, in El Universal, el Gran Diario de México: "Tlatelolco, campo de batalla. Durante varias horas terroristas y soldados sostuvieron rudo combate."[3]

Argentina, 1956

David William Foster writes: "In June 1956, a year after Perón was deposed, Peronist military officers stationed at the Campamento de Mayo base made an abortive attempt to overthrow the [new] military government. Although this government had claimed that it would operate on the principle of 'neither victors nor vanquished', it enacted severe reprisals against Peronist sympathizers, and [novelist Rodolfo Walsh in his book Operación Masacre] reports the summary execution of a group of men taken from a private home where they had . . . gathered to listen to a fight on the radio. The police, claiming that these men were part of the plot to overthrow the government and that they had used the home to store arms, transported them to a field and shot them. . . ."[4] Foster proceeds to tell us: according to "official reality [the event] never took place. . . ."[5]

These three incidents illustrate the hall of mirrors that is Latin America: image and reality are nebulous substances which, vampirelike, might disappear before a mirror, might change their appearance, might become distorted ghosts that fog the mind of the beholder. Image and reality, a thing of clay to be molded by a "general," a surrealistic game played by "políticos" with a creativity that only contemporary writers might attempt to match. What the incidents above tell us is simple: When you look at political events in Latin America, remember that the author who claims to exist might not exist and therefore he does, that the massacre that happened did not happen and therefore it did! It is a game of knowing and not knowing what is real, what is image.

Latin America is an entity of many images: Yours and mine and theirs. From the beginning there was always an image. The image existed way before the wind filled La Niña's sails and thus, when the Europeans left their caravels and rowed to the American shore, they saw the country that was in their heads, not the land before them. Latin America was the Orient, Eden, the New World--never mind that there were ancient civilizations and empires there that equaled Egypt, Greece, Asia. What the Europeans saw in the New World was the image they had brought.

Four centuries later, those rowing to the shore were still bringing their images. So, when the Marines go into Haiti, it is only American know-how that can "clean up" the streets, that can bring hygiene and progress. When war breaks out between the islands of the New World and the Mother Country, it is only the American who can win the war (a favorite image: Alan Ladd in the film Santiago teaching Cuban mambises how to fight Spaniards). When a missionary goes into the jungles, it is only he/she who can bring civilization to the savages who dwell in treetops.

It is the image that reigns. Of course, this is a natural development. We can only see so much; to comprehend we need to break down the world: pigeonhole is the word. Juan Goytisolo, in a recent New York Times article, says: "Our perception of foreign cultures is usually based not on their complex reality, but on the simplified image they project."[6] We see the world through our eyes, we cannot help it. Therefore, the Mexico Malcolm Lowry sees is his Mexico, the Mexico D. H. Lawrence writes about is his Mexico.

But the image is also created by those being seen, sometimes creating an image based on what others have brought from the outside which is then reinforced, reshaped, and returned, not only to the world out there but also to the world at home. Essayist Carlos Monsivais talks of how Mexican films, like La Perla, with Pedro Armendariz, borrowed America's concept of what Mexico was--such as dirt poor farmers dressing in a style designed by Hollywood, folklore dancers performing a so-called local dance that in reality was not endemic to the region--in order to make the movies more American and more sellable,[7] selling what Goytisolo calls a "recognizable image" that is familiar and comfortable. He writes: "A large sector of Latin American literature owes its current popularity . . . to the fact that it works within a very limited field of images already familiar to the reader: those of an oppressed continent taking up arms in revolt."[8] He further suggests that a Latin American writer who wants to be successful need only pick up that image and ship it right back to the European and North American image makers to be guaranteed success. René Cifuentes, a short story writer and coeditor of the now defunct review Mariel, tells me that García Márquez gives the American audience exactly what they want: "You have pigs on the lawn and chickens clucking away in the study of the President's mansion. An American would not imagine that in Reagan's White House, but he would see it in Castro's home, in Duarte's residence."[9]

The image is there; many images: What the outsider sees, what the government sees and would like others to see, what the opposition sees and says. It is this last one, what the opposition sees and says, which completes the image the government manu-factures, which sometimes brings us closer to the truth, which on many occasions preserves and makes the world aware of a reality the government wants not to exist. Operación Masacre, the Rodolfo Walsh novel about the killing of innocent people by the Argentine authorities, and La Noche de Tlatelolco, Elena Poniatowska's narrative detailing the slaughter of Mexican stu-dents in La Plaza de las Tres Culturas in 1968, are examples of documents that make us all aware of bloody incidents that two governments, the Argentine and Mexican, wanted to cover up, to erase from history. And these images were captured by the pen of writers, of journalists.

Which is why this piece comes into existence and why we are here today. Journalists often capture an image that otherwise, if left to the official image makers, would not be recorded. But in capturing that image, they also create another, they give birth to other realities. It was the death of a journalist--to silence him, to erase his words--that unleashed the forces that toppled the Somoza dynasty. It was a journalist who first brought Castro to the eyes of the world. It was a journalist who pleaded for the "prisoners without a name" in Argentina. It is the words, the image that a journalist creates, which often bring about the genesis of a revolution, the freedom of a prisoner, the end of a political system.

But how much of the image is true? How much of the image given by the official image maker is innocently repeated by a journalist, and thus reinforces an image created by someone else? How often are journalists so in love with the image they have created that they cannot see beyond it? Herbert Matthews believed Castro when he said he was not a Communist. Herman Whitaker believed the dictatorship of Porfirio Díaz was the best thing that ever happened to Mexico.

It is a deceiving game, the political image-making game. Dictator Castro tells Dan Rather he did not place criminals and the insane on the boats that sailed from El Mariel in 1980, yet many who came on the very same boats would say otherwise. Managuan officials point to the result of the recent elections held there as evidence of the Revolution's popular support. But anti-Sandinista leaders disclaim the elections, stating that it was basically a one-party affair.

It is a game--and a dangerous one at that. The 1983 massacre of the journalists who had gone into the Peruvian Andes to dispel the images manufactured by the military and the guerrillas, and to learn firsthand of the activities of Sendero Luminoso, proves just how deadly the game is. A deadly, deceitful game.

So the question must be asked again: What is real? What is the truth? Is it all image?

In this Orwellian world of illusive realities, where officials from the Ministry of Culture define and redefine words--so much and so often that terms such as "liberty," "democracy," "dictatorship," "pluralistic society" have lost their meaning--poets like Octavio Paz must cry for silence so they may invent words that speak the truth. But we, those who do not have the gift of word-inventing, must choose from the myriad of images assaulting us. And I for one want the image given us by the poets, the novelists, the journalists.

Jefferson chose free press over government restriction. I, a bibliographer, a man attempting to preserve the events of today for tomorrow's readers, choose the writers, no matter how misinformed, how confused, how naive they may sometimes be. I choose their words, their images.

NOTES

1.   Nestor Almendros and Orlando Jiménez Leal, Conducta impropia (Madrid: Editorial Playor, 1984), p. 61.

2.   José Emilio Pacheco, Desde entonces (México, DF: Biblioteca Era, 1983), pp. 93-96.

3.   El Universal, Oct. 3, 1968.

4.   David William Foster, "Latin American Documentary Narrative," PMLA, Jan. 4, 1984, p. 43.

5.   Ibid.

6.   Juan Goytisolo, "Captives of 'Our Classics,'" New York Times Book Review, May 26, 1985, p. 1.

7.   Interview with Carlos Monsivais, Center for Inter-American Relations, March 1, 1985.

8.   Goytisolo, p. 24.

9.   Interview with René Cifuentes, New York Public Library, May 29, 1985.

2. ISSUES OF INTERNATIONAL COMMUNICATIONS

Mauricio Gerson

We are living in the most rapidly changing period of human history. In one century we have traveled from an agricultural society, through an industrial society, to today's information age. As the Western world develops, and depends more and more on technology, the Third World lags further and further behind. Advances in communications technology have substantially increased our ability to produce, store, and disseminate information at a very fast pace. Nevertheless, these advances have not been used equally by all countries in the world. The gap between the developed and less developed countries grows ever wider.

We are living in a world in which virtually all means of international communications rest in the hands of the industrialized West--a world in which what is said and written, included or excluded, emphasized or ignored, largely depends on decisions made in New York, London, or Paris. The fact is that four news and wire agencies determine what you do--and do not--read, hear, or see. The First World controls information, and the Third World lacks information. As a result, we all lose.

The imbalance among the nations of the world deeply concerns those of the Third World. These countries lack the broad economic base that would enable private media to develop and serve the social needs of their people. Since World War II, the number of nations in the world has increased from about 40 to 150. The Third World makes up two thirds of the world. It could therefore stand as a potentially decisive block in international forums. The nonaligned nations, with a membership of 85 countries, first discussed communications in 1973. Nonaligned spokesmen have since called for a new "world information order," and established a pool of Third World news agencies. Providing current technology to less developed nations has been proposed as one way to help these countries create a media of their own. But this process also helps perpetuate Western domination through the cultural imperialism resulting from dependence on foreign films, TV programs, and wire copy (software).

Another issue of concern for the Third World involves the international implications of satellite television broadcasting, remote earth sensing, and cross-border flows of computer data. Some critics believe that these pose threats to the national sovereignty of both less-developed and developed countries. Technology has created a world information system of interconnected data banks, all for the use of the most powerful countries.

15

Let us take the Grenada invasion as an example. According to Christopher Nascimiento, Guyana's ambassador to UNESCO, most Americans believed that no matter how unpopular the invasion was elsewhere in the world, it was warmly welcomed by Caribbean nations. But Trinidad and Tobago did not support it, nor did the Bahamas, Surinam, or Nascimiento's own country of Guyana. In fact, most countries in the Caribbean basin opposed the action. Yet, Americans are only dimly, if at all, aware of that. American-controlled wire services chose not to emphasize such discord. American reporters did not go to these countries to write about it, and American TV crews did not record it. Lacking their own international wire services, satellite systems, radio and TV networks, Nascimiento said, these tiny nations had no way to counterbalance the mistaken impression.

The Third World's dependence on the Western world for international news, the current flow of news, and the difference in the amount of coverage for different countries have provided the most controversial subjects in the debate on the "world information order." The issue of internal news reporting within Third World countries was also the focus of the McBride commission, a board established by UNESCO to study the world's imbalance of information. Elie Able, a Stanford University professor and a member of the McBride commission, stated during a recent international conference on World Communications, held at the University of Pennsylvania:

> One of the most moving moments of the McBride commission was when a fellow member from a country I do not wish to identify explained that journalism has become the most dangerous and therefore the least popular profession. He said that dozens of journalists are giving up their work. They have discovered that journalism can be injurious to their health. They have discovered that printing the truth is far more dangerous than printing lies. That honest reporting can lead to prison, and sometimes death.

The issues of international communications are many and complex. The degrees of "information sophistication" vary from one country to another. While some countries are fighting for a "free press," others are struggling to sustain any press at all. The industrialized nations feel that the Third World's drift is not toward more and better information sources but rather toward censorship. The focus on concepts such as a "code of ethics" for foreign journalists leads some countries to anticipate that "freedom of the press" in fact means the right of a state to free itself of foreign information domination.

Not only does the Western world control the news, but it greatly influences the style in which the world receives information. News programs in Mexico, for example, are very similar in style to U.S. newscasts. Mexico even has a show called "60 Minutes" with the same format as its North American namesake-- even to the clock ticking away. But, at least, Mexico produces its own programs, and recently it launched its own satellite.

This is not the case with the rest of Latin America. Producing television programs is far more expensive than purchasing existing programming. As a result, most countries fill their broadcast schedule with American programs. A nationally broadcast program in America can reach a potential audience of 85 million. Such large audiences attract the advertising dollars that give American TV producers a distinct advantage in both covering production costs and accruing additional revenue. The producers can subsequently offer their programs to outside countries at relatively low costs. And the smaller countries simply cannot compete. All over the world people watch programs like "Dallas" and "Dynasty," programs that perpetuate the myth that America is the land of the rich.

All societies have evolved ways of explaining the world to themselves and to future generations. Television drama presents a socially constructed reality which gives a coherent picture of what exists, what is important, what is related to what, and what is correct. Images in television relate to the power structure in society. There is a positive correlation between a particular group or country's upward social and economic mobility and its representation in the media. That is, as a country reaches a higher "status" in its social, political, and economic environment, its media coverage and the depictions of its people inevitably improve. Nevertheless, the interdependence of the political structure and the images portrayed in the media lead to a vicious circle. Therefore, our task not only relates to the struggle for fair and equitable access to the media, but is also a struggle to reaffirm our identity as Latin Americans, and to firmly establish our strength as a political grouping in the international arena.

It is my belief that the first objective in achieving this agenda is to make available the necessary tools and instruments. Social change will follow thereafter. We must continuously monitor the mass media and the power structure, even as we collect and distribute accurate and comprehensive information. This conference is a prime example of what I am talking about. This is a task for educators, researchers, bibliographers, and students, for people concerned about, but not directly involved in, the industry. We must all become media watchdogs, and strive to give every country a voice in world communications. This will lead to better understanding among nations, and a better world to live in.

3. IMAGE AND THE DOCUMENTARY'S REALITY:
CENTRAL AMERICA FOR TV

Austin Hoyt

In his paper, Danilo Figueredo raised the question of how one sorts out "what is real" and "what is true" about Latin America. For experts, these are indeed profound questions about Latin America. For me, a year and a half ago, the question was how does a gringo who speaks no Spanish, and whose major contact with Latin America had been misbehaving on a spring vacation in pre-Castro Cuba, sort out the truth about Central America, about countries that I had never visited? And sorting out the truth for television involves more than just the reporter's or scholar's task of analyzing what has happened over the years. Television is a medium that tends toward oversimplification, toward sensationalism. It also leads us to think that if someone's camera did not capture an important moment in history, that moment does not exist. So, it was with some humility and a lot of heartburn that I set out to do a four-hour television history of the background to the current troubles in Central America.

Here I describe how we approached the task, how we got our material, and how we treated it--the editorial process by which we handled controversy.

There were many questions for which I, as an interested but uninformed citizen, wanted answers. Who are the Sandinistas? Where did they come from? Where are they heading? What are the causes of the civil war in El Salvador? What is Cuba's role? Is the United States on the wrong side of history? How did Castro end up in the Soviet camp? Was he pushed or did he leap? Did the Sandinistas leap or have they been pushed?

We got a small development grant from the Starr Foundation in New York to prepare a proposal. That was a process of deciding what questions ought to be asked. We held seminars in Boston for three days with various experts, and one question emerged which struck me as perhaps the overriding one: How much of the history of Central America and the Caribbean has been conditioned by U.S. involvement, and how much is the result of the internal dynamics of the region, of the tensions within and between countries? It is a big question with many ideological ramifications. The left thinks the United States is the

---

Author's Note. All research material and 86 hours of interviews are on sale to libraries. For information: Sandra Forman, WGBH, 125 Western Ave., Boston, MA 02134. (617) 492-2777

18

cause of the region's problems; the right thinks it is the solution. (Incidentally, I think we concluded that the United States
is a major actor but hardly an omnipotent one, that we share the
stage with local actors--forces that we did not create and cannot
always control. And what this means is that we should neither
flagellate ourselves with blame as the cause of the problems,
nor be too despairing if our proposed solutions do not always
prevail.)

We decided that four TV programs were necessary. Three
of them would be separate studies of revolution in Cuba, Nicaragua, and El Salvador. The fourth, our first program, traced
the history of U.S. involvement in the region in the early part of
this century.

These were some of our early editorial concerns. The
other major question was: Is this producible? As in WGBH's
thirteen-hour history of the French and American Vietnam wars,
we wanted to rely on the testimony of eyewitnesses to history--
not scholars or reporters--and on archival film.

Immediately, in this first program, we faced the problem of
the limits of the medium. Robert Pastor, President Carter's
national security advisor for Latin America, had suggested that
our opening minutes be only of local actors to set the stage for
U.S. involvement; that we show the local squabbles between León
and Granada in Nicaragua, for example; the role of the Church,
of the large landowners, of the vestiges of Spanish influence.
This was a splendid idea. But there had been no filmmakers
there at the time. The cameras had followed the U.S. Marines.
So our treatment of the early history is necessarily through a
U.S. lens, and it probably gives the impression that the United
States is the determining actor on the Central American stage.

Nonetheless, we were pleased to find material and people
dating back as far as we did. One of my first phone calls was to
Shirley Christian, who had won a Pulitzer prize for her coverage
of Central America for the Miami Herald. She assured me that
yes, there were alive and well in the hills of Nicaragua some
old-timers who had fought with Sandino in the early 1930s. We
then found Christopher Dickey, on leave from the Washington
Post to write a book, and he spent two weeks in Central America
in January, 1984. With his help, we discovered a Nicaraguan
National Guardsman and a U.S. Marine who fought against
Sandino in the early '30s. We found in a small village in western
El Salvador an eighty-two-year-old woman whose family had been
slaughtered in the Matanza--the massacre that followed a peasant
uprising in El Salvador in 1932. The uprising was led by
Farabundo Martí, for whom the Salvadoran guerrillas today are
named. Martí was executed, but Dickey said he talked to Martí's
defense lawyer in San Salvador, an old man today, a young man
just out of law school in 1932. This gentleman said Martí had
asked for no clemency; that if he had won, the heads of those

judging him would be rolling on the ground. All agreed to tell their stories.

We discovered in the Harvard library the books of Dana Gardner Munro, the retired history professor from Princeton who had served in the U.S. legation in Managua in the late 1920s. He agreed to face the television cameras for the first time--at, I believe, age ninety.

We also compiled an inventory of archival footage at all the networks and news services in New York, at the National Archives and Library of Congress in Washington, and at the military archives at Norton Air Force Base in California. And we cornered a Cuban economist visiting at Harvard and asked his help in getting access to what we knew were wonderful archives in Havana.

All this gave me faith that the project was doable. In March, 1984, I hired four producers--one for each of the four programs--and six stock footage researchers--four based in New York for each of the production teams, one in Washington for the National Archives, and one in California for the military archives. I also signed up some editorial advisors: Dickey from the Post; James Nelson Goodsell from the Christian Science Monitor (he had been covering Central America since Balboa); and Jorge Domínguez, a professor of government at Harvard. We had a ten-week research period which began with one week of what we called Central America School--seminars in Boston with seventeen scholars, diplomats, and reporters.

In May and June we fanned out and collected our interviews and old footage. We logged 86 hours of interviews with people from 12 countries, and gathered 107 hours of stock footage from 67 different sources.

Castro was a no-show, which was disappointing; but we had access to splendid old film in the Cuban archives. We waited in El Salvador for three weeks for President Duarte. On our last day, instead of us, he granted an interview to two Playboy reporters who had been chortling at the Camino Real bar every night about how they were going to ambush Duarte as the maga-zine had Jimmy Carter, when he confessed to lusting after ladies other than his wife Rosalynn. We finally cornered President Duarte after a luncheon at the Plaza Hotel in New York, two months later.

One of the interviews that pleased me most was to find in Paris someone who in 1967 had fought with Che Guevara trying to lead a continental revolution in Bolivia. Régis Debray is now an official in President Mitterand's government.

One disappointment was not finding a Salvadoran oligarch. I viewed all the films made about El Salvador, each of which traced the roots of the country's problems to the so-called thirteen families who owned everything. But they never showed us what an oligarch looked like. The press has not been kind to them, and naturally they are suspicious. But in Miami we did talk to the son of a recently deceased oligarch. His mother lives in San Salvador, and he promised that he would meet us there from June 3 to June 7 and open up the family album, tell how his family had made the jungle bloom, and give us his old film of the family's coffee plantation. When we got to San Salvador, he refused to talk. So we, too, joined the ranks of those whose programs on El Salvador fail to produce an oligarch. I hope someday one of them talks. One part of the Salvadoran story which is never told is that of the creation of the most productive coffee economy in the world. It is the other side of the repression. Land reform today is the gospel. It is a political necessity. But, economically, it has not yet worked. The productive economy is gone.

There was some material we did get, but at some risk. Our team in Guatemala tells me that, as they viewed films of the 1954 CIA-supported coup, they noticed holes in the wall and splotches of red. They were told that the last people to view that film had been shot. Some sympathetic officials helped us smuggle the film out. We made a print and returned it to the Guatemalan archives.

Everyone else was cooperative. The U.S. archives are efficient but expensive. The Cuban archives are almost as efficient and equally as expensive. The Nicaraguans are inefficient and need elaborate courting. It helps if the researcher falls in love with a Sandinista, which, I am told, happened to ours. Whether it was a pleasure or beyond the call of duty, I do not know.

El Salvador has no archives except the military's--showing only guerrilla atrocities. One private production company in San Salvador has a roomful of old film cans, uncataloged. We helped them organize it. But the film history of El Salvador hardly exists until the networks began covering the civil war in 1979. The decade of the sixties is a fascinating one in El Salvador. The economy was booming. A middle class emerged. It was the decade of the Alliance for Progress and the Central American Common Market, the flowering of the Christian Democrats as a force to challenge military rule. The USIA has a dozen films, but they cannot be released domestically without an act of Congress. We persuaded Tip O'Neill to introduce legislation on our behalf. He was confident it would clear the House, but it died in the Senate Foreign Relations Committee.

In editing all our material, we obviously had to make some choices. Our interest was not to promote any theory of history or any public policy option that exists today. It was to ask what happened--in a spirit of understanding, not of indictment. It was to understand the key moments, themes, and patterns of recent history. How do you do this when much of the history is controversial and ideologically charged? We deliberately hired people of all ideological stripes, but we created an editorial review procedure that purged the programs of anyone's ideological predispositions. In the case of controversy, we let the best evidence prevail. In the end, a consensus usually emerged, sometimes begrudgingly.

There were some potentially controversial areas that ended up not being controversial to our staff. One involved the United Fruit Company and its role in the U.S. intervention in Guatemala to help overthrow a left-leaning government in 1954. Stephen Kinser and Stephen Schlesinger, authors of the recent popular book Bitter Fruit, developed a thesis that the United States intervened to bail out United Fruit, whose lands were being expropriated, and that John Foster Dulles was influential because he had been a lawyer for United Fruit. Some reviews thought the book was factually accurate except for this point, and that it was Eisenhower's concern about communism during the cold war, not an interest in helping an American company, which led to the U.S. intervention. The producer did her own research and came to that conclusion as well.

Talking to people who were eyewitnesses to history clarified another key issue: did the United States push Castro to the Soviet camp, or did he leap? We interviewed Felipe Pasos, one of Castro's chief economic advisors as head of the Cuban National Bank just after the revolution. Pasos, now head of a bank in Venezuela, told us that when he boarded the plane for the States in April, 1959, he was convinced that Fidel was going to ask for aid, that it was an economic mission. Castro never asked for aid, although the State Department was prepared to give it. We concluded that at that key moment Castro did not want business as usual with the United States. In less than two years he welcomed aid from the Soviet Union. He was not pushed; he leaped. We found no evidence, however, that Castro was a Marxist-Leninist while he was in the Sierra Maestra fighting Batista.

Cuban involvement in Nicaragua has been controversial. Professor Jorge I. Domínguez of Harvard University said that, in reviewing a doctoral thesis of a student at the Fletcher School of Law and Diplomacy, he would not let the doctoral candidate say how many Cuban advisors were in Nicaragua after the Sandinistas took over. He said it simply was not known. Well, Nicaraguan Interior Minister Tomás Borge said on camera there were two hundred. We believed it was more credible to let a Sandinista say there were two hundred than to have a State Department official give the same or a higher figure. Sometimes, going to the source, as Al Haig would say, clarifies controversy.

Another contested issue is that of Cuban or Nicaraguan arms shipments to the Salvadoran rebels. State Department White Papers insist that it continued after the rebels' big offensive in January, 1981. We could not find out anything independent of that; Cubans and Nicaraguans deny it. So we sidestepped that one. Ten years from now someone may get a convincing answer. I found in doing the Vietnam series film on Lyndon Johnson's decision-making in 1964 and 1965 that the State Department White Paper, criticized at the time, turned out to be correct. It asserted that North Vietnamese troops were then fighting in South Vietnam. All during the war, North Vietnam denied this. When we interviewed Vietnamese in Hanoi in 1981, they admitted it with pride. It is hard to play historian when dealing with current events.

In the few instances where there was disagreement, we deferred to Jorge Domínguez if he felt strongly about a point. He started out not as our one and only editorial guru but as one of three. He gained all our respect the old-fashioned way: he earned it. One example of deference to him involved a line of copy in our El Salvador program which I had written. It said that the rebel offensive in 1981 fizzled because the government's repression had worked and because the government reforms had undermined the appeal of the rebels' programs. Dickey, who was then reporting from San Salvador for the Post, believed that. So did Robert Pastor, Carter's National Security advisor who had done his doctoral thesis at Harvard under Domínguez. Domínguez wanted to scratch the idea that the reforms undercut the rebels' programs. They might have in the countryside, he thought, because land reform was aimed at the peasants, but not in the cities, and the offensive called for a popular uprising in the cities. The repression had been particularly brutal in the cities. So we are stuck with the idea of repression and not reform. Sometimes, in making decisions on controversial issues, you appeal to authority. We did in this case, and Domínguez was our authority.

We would sometimes argue these points until midnight. Reasonable people can disagree with our conclusions, but there was not one newspaper review that took us to task on the grounds of bias or fairness. We received some rave reviews, the most enthusiastic from Howard Rosenberg of the Los Angeles Times, who a few weeks later won the Pulitzer Prize for television criticism. A few thought the series was pedantic and plodding, that a U.S. audience simply will not care about Central America until the body bags come home.

What are the lasting images that we projected? I hope one is a sense of complexity, even though it might push the limits of the medium of television. I think we did succeed in showing that the history of the region is not simple, and that the relationship between the United States and the region is not simple. The policy choices the United States faces are not simple. I hope another is the image that the ideological dividing line is peopled on both sides with Yankee and Latin voices. Those who say the United States is a force for democracy and security in the region are both Yankees and Latins. Those who say the United States is imperialistic are both Yankees and Latins. It is not simply a case of Yankee versus Latin.

I hope that the image of Central Americans and Cubans which emerges is one of a variety of intelligent and committed people, who often disagree violently. But this is a far cry from the ridiculous Hollywood image of Carmen Miranda with her banana hat.

I hope the image of U.S. decision-making is one of honest dilemma: the dilemma presidents face when they undercut friendly regimes they have supported once those regimes have lost the support of their people, not knowing what will replace them; the dilemma of trying to harness a revolution so that it does not end up being hostile to U.S. interests; the dilemma of whether to intervene when a revolutionary regime allies itself with your enemy; the greater dilemma of whether to intervene when that regime has reached a certain threshold of military power.

As for the revolutionaries, I hope the image we leave is one of sympathy for people who fight back against regimes that are oppressive, be they left or right. For moderate revolutionaries, I hope we leave the image of the anguish they feel when, once victorious, they are purged by their more radical allies. As for the radical allies, I hope we sense the dilemma they face of losing their revolutionary identity if they turn to Washington for support, and yet of incurring Washington's wrath if they turn to her enemies.

And, Señor Figueredo, your image of this particular gringo ought to be one of someone who pretends to have no answers but whose vision is a little wider than when he played the roulette tables at the Tropicana in 1958.

II. Individuals and the Creation of Image:
Exodus from Mariel

4. MARIEL: ANTECEDENTES Y CONSECUENCIAS

Los antecedentes más lejanos del Mariel fueron miles de fusilados, un dictador en el poder por más de veinte años, miles de presos políticos, la crisis económica que se ha hecho crónica, el rompimiento de todas las promesas, más trabajos y demandas por parte de la Revolución y menos frutos, y cientos de otras razones que sería imposible enumerar. Los antecedentes del Mariel más recientes fueron las visitas de los familiares a Cuba, los Cuban-Americans, las expulsiones de todos los estudiantes universitarios que constituyeran un peligro en potencia, la crisis económica, las guerras en Africa, especialmente en Angola, y, claro está, la Embajada del Perú.

Recuerdo la llegada del primer amigo de la familia, más de 35 personas lo acosábamos a preguntas, tiene que haber pensado que estábamos locos. Una tía que se aventura a preguntar: ¿Tú me vas a decir a mí que puedes sacar tu pasaporte e irte a Francia cuando quieras? Los Cubanos están fuera de la historia, sin una noción clara de lo que realmente es una democracia, puesto que Batista dió un golpe de estado en 1952 y desde entonces hemos tenido tiranía. Supongamos que a los 15 años ya se tenga una concepción política clara; para que un cubano haya conocido, más o menos, una democracia, tiene que haber nacido antes de 1937, nadie en este panel conoció un régimen democrático antes de llegar a E.U. El propio Arenas, siendo muy joven, se fue a luchar contra Batista a las montañas. Yo tenía tres años cuando Castro tomó el poder, es decir, que para nosotros, los más jóvenes, los Hombres Nuevos de los que hablaba el Che, no hubo un Fidel mitológico que vivía, moría y resucitaba en las montañas, no hubo para mí un Fidel-Cristo barbudo con 12 discípulos que descendía de la cima del monte desde donde leía las bienaventuranzas por Radio Rebelde; para los más jóvenes hubo un dictador demagogo que nos impedía soñar, crear, viajar, vivir sin temores, una especie de Jehová colérico contra todo aquel que no lo siguiera, o un Zeus de policía olímpica que podía tronar a cualquiera.

Soy de Matanzas, la ciudad cubana más cercana a Key West, desde niño escucho cuentos de ahogados y fusilados, y por suerte, de otros que llegaban. Ya a los siete años la familia comenzó a desintegrarse, tíos y primos arribaron en lancha a estas costas. Siendo adolescente supe que a Soriano, hasta ayer mi amigo de la cuadra, lo habían matado mientras trataba de irse, sin embargo, la vida cotidiana en Cuba es tan desesperante que desde que tengo uso de razón estuve en todo tipo de planes para

abandonar la Isla. En 1979 uno de mis hermanos menores estaba
en el S.M.O. (Servico Militar Obligatorio), lo querían enviar a
Angola, tuvo suerte, llegó a E.U. en bote, a riesgo de perder la
vida o enfrentar 30 años de cárcel. ¿Por qué el extranjero que
aún duda sobre la materia espantosa de la cual está hecho el
castrismo no se pregunta qué ocurre en un sitio donde el 10% de
la población ha escapado en todas las formas imaginables e
inimaginables? ¿Por qué el visitante prefiere emitir juicios de
experto después de pasar 15 días en un hotel de primera clase,
que para regodearnos más en la ironía son casi siempre hoteles
construídos antes del castrismo? ¿Somos acaso nosotros burgueses, batistianos, agentes de la C.I.A., dueños de centrales o
prostíbulos, machadistas? Ya estos juicios tampoco pueden
esgrimirse, y no pueden usarlos por la sencilla razón que los más
jóvenes sólo conocimos la Cuba de Fidel; ello me hizo, como está
formando a otros miles; produce, con calidad sobresaliente y
sobrepasando las metas, al anticastrista.

Sería tonto que yo tratara de destacar los horrores del
presidio político cubano, ahí está Contra toda esperanza, las
magníficas memorias de Armando Valladares; o que venga a
discurrir sobre la crisis económica, o los odios entre los militares
de mi país. No, prefiero dar algunos testimonios que todavía no
he hecho públicos, modestos testimonios en relación al sufrimiento
del pueblo, pero que ilustran la dictadura en detalles que
padecemos.

En 1979 un agente de Seguridad del Estado que decía
llamarse Saúl y que me había visitado con frecuencia, porque debo
decirles que cada estudiante universitario problemático tiene su
Saúl bíblico que desea ayudarlo, me dijo que la Revolución había
sido demasiado bondadosa conmigo. Ahora o trabajaba para ellos
o iba a la cárcel, el cuento es largo y voy a abreviarlo, le
respondí que trabajaría para ellos puesto que yo no tenía sangre
de mártir. Eso sí, debía darme 24 horas para pensarlo porque
estaba muy nervioso, con angelical sonrisa me otorgó las horas
pedidas y yo entré a la embajada de Francia en La Habana y
denuncié lo que ocurría. Lo que deseo destacar es la actitud
maternal que tuvo conmigo la decana de la Escuela de Filología
una semana más tarde. Me citó a su oficina y con voz delica-
dísima me dijo que ella estaba al día respecto a mis problemas con
Seguridad, me pidió que le contara todos mis problemas porque yo
era muy joven, ella me aconsejaría como una madre. Demás está
decir que tengo predisposición de hijo retrasado mental, se lo
conté todo, estuvo de acuerdo conmigo, dados mis principios
religiosos y éticos yo tenía todo el derecho a mi favor para no
colaborar en casos de espionaje. A los pocos días recibí una
citación para un juicio con la U.J.C. y el P.C. de la escuela. La
decana me acusaba de calumniar al honroso cuerpo de Seguridad
del Estado. ¿A quién se le podía ocurrir que ellos acudieran a
un vil gusano como era yo? Me pidieron pruebas, apellido

y dirección de Saúl, etc. Ella misma, que me dejaba en su oficina conversando con Saúl, me negaba que existiera tal personaje, y así me vi de pronto reducido a un miserable personaje de Kafka. A ustedes mismos les puede surgir la duda, y la única prueba que tengo a mi favor soy yo mismo. Lo peor es que esto puede estar sucediéndole a otros estudiantes.

El tiempo que tengo es limitado y he escogido una anécdota del bestiario que archivo. Después vinieron detenciones, arresto domiciliario y la embajada del Perú, 17 días de horror; vi, por primera vez, matar a compatriotas, llorar a los niños de hambre, golpear a otros cubanos hasta la inconsciencia o la muerte. Por eso existió Mariel, el gobierno abrió una grieta para que la lava fluyera porque todo el volcán estaba en peligro. La embajada del Perú y Mariel son hechos únicos e insólitos en nuestra historia y a la vez no lo son. Cuba vive desde hace años en vísperas del Mariel. Si mañana abren la embajada de Camerún, Macao o Belice y anuncian que todo el que entre puede irse, ocurrirá lo mismo. Casi 11,000 cubanos entramos a la Sede peruana, pero fuera había cerca de 60,000 más que físicamente no cabían. El propio Correa y parte de mi familia estaban allí. Si mañana las condiciones se dieran de nuevo, miles de cubanos conquistarían las aguas otra vez, hacia donde sea, lo que cuenta es huir.

La consecuencia del Mariel es que los cubanos seguimos creciendo en esta orilla. Todo exilio es doloroso, pero también enriquecedor. Detrás de cada cubano se esconde una tragedia, pero son muchos los que se están creciendo en conocimientos, en el dominio de las lenguas, son bilingües o políglotas, se actualizan en ciencias, en economía, en historia, crece el poder monetario e intelectual de los cubanos. Tenemos, curiosamente, el único pueblo del mundo donde su primera ciudad (La Habana) está solo a 90 millas de la segunda (Miami), pero las distancias ideológicas parecen separarlas por continentes.

Considero que la distancia es salvable. La esperanza que guardo, con cierto cuidado, sobre Cuba, es que seguimos en muchos aspectos entre los países líderes de América Latina. No voy a defender, claro está, que Cuba sea una potencia mercenaria, u otros de los llamados logros del castrismo, pero lo que sí sabe muy bien el pueblo cubano es que el comunismo no es la solución. Es doloroso confesarlo, pero me temo que una nación, sus intelectuales, sus obreros, todos sus ciudadanos, sólo sabrán que el comunismo no es la puerta de salida cuando esa puerta se les cierre. América Latina padece en muchos sitios hambre, terror, explotación, . . . pero Cuba no es el modelo a seguir, y es en ese aspecto que sigue nuestra gigantesca islita a la cabeza. Pasarán los años, pasará la pesadilla castrista, y una ola de cubanos vigorosos se desbordará sobre el país, vendrán de Europa, de Norteamérica, de América Latina, de todos los horizontes a olvidarse del odio y a democratizar la nación en unión de los más sufridos, los cubanos de adentro.

Resumiendo, yo diría que las consecuencias del Mariel le fueron desastrosas al gobierno castrista. Perdieron mucho material valioso que ellos mismos obligaron a emigrar por su ortodoxia medieval, perdieron en sólo unos días gran parte de su cuidadoso maquillaje. Y el exilio se enriqueció; el futuro, de eso que a fuerza de repetirlo llamamos patria, también se enriqueció. Demos gracias al señor todopoderoso que se llama Fidel porque ha permitido que nos sacudamos la provincia, y que en cada uno de nosotros habite un demócrata verdadero y un juez que lo señala a el como el mayor tirano de nuestra historia.

Reinaldo García Ramos

Hace poco, una periodista norteamericana y gran amiga mía me fue a buscar a las nueve de la noche a la salida de mi trabajo en un estado de total alarma y nos sentamos en un café de Greenwich Village a conversar. Mi amiga, necesario es decirlo, ha visitado varias veces Cuba y es uno de los happy few (o quizás debería decir de los unhappy few) que viniendo de los Estados Unidos y siendo una intelectual, no han caído en la mojigatería tradicional de que son víctimas otros periodistas jóvenes que han estado en la isla de Fidel Castro. A mi amiga le gustaron las playas, el sol, los mulatos, la música, el fervor milenario del pueblo por sobrevivir, le gustaron la fuerza resistente y callada de las familias deshechas, pero no se tragó ni una palabra de la propaganda oficial del régimen. A partir de los datos obvios que le entregaba como en una avalancha la realidad visible en La Habana, mi amiga captó en pocas horas el trágico trasfondo que se extendía tras la cortina de humo con que el poder dictatorial pretende engatusar a cuanto crédulo extranjero pone pie en aquellas tierras. Mi amiga vio el terror, la corrupción, la miseria, la injusticia, la presencia ubícua de las estructuras autoritarias y de los agentes policiales. Y regresó a Nueva York espantada, con una serie de fotos que parecen cuadros de Chirico y que sin embargo fueron tomadas en las calles del Vedado, a media cuadra del hotel donde se alojaba.

La noche en que me fue a ver hace poco, mi amiga estaba, como dije, en un estado de total exaltación. Había leído dos artículos escandalosos del señor Joseph B. Treaster en la página 2 del New York Times: uno sobre la presunta reconciliación del gobierno cubano con los cultos religiosos, y otro que exponía críticas supuestamente espontáneas sobre Radio Martí recogidas en las calles de La Habana. Esa noche, mi amiga recurría a mí para compartir su alarma ante esta nueva andanada de desinformación acera de la situación en Cuba. Un artículo similar había aparecido por esos días en el Washington Post (también sobre Radio Martí) y semanas antes dos o tres de los ansiosos creyentes que recluta el Village Voice para redactar sus páginas habían también hecho su correspondiente peregrinación a la "Meca" habanera y habían por supuesto producido a la vuelta sus almibaradas versiones de la vida bajo la dominación de Castro. Mi amiga estaba desesperada por la escasez en la prensa norteamericana de artículos, reportajes y crónicas que pudieran ripostar esa incompleta versión de los "creyentes" con un panorama más completo, más sensato, más humano, menos vil.

31

Escucharla aquella noche me conmovió tremendamente. Aparte de la ayuda que siempre le he brindado para sus escritos con la información de primera mano que yo acumulé en mi país hasta el año 80 en que logré huir, se veía que aquella noche lo que mi amiga necesitaba era más bien apoyo moral, solidaridad, simpatía, y no sólo nuevos datos, nuevos recuentos de cosas vividas y vistas allá. Su tácita solicitud me volvía a plantear algo que constantemente se me había ido definiendo en los últimos meses, y que con su ayuda esa noche se me delineaba en términos inequívocos.

¿Qué hacer?, parecía pedirme a gritos mientras alrededor nuestro la fauna del Village parloteaba sobre el último concierto de Madonna, el nuevo defecto que le habían descubierto ese día al actual gobierno de Estados Unidos, las sospechosas virtudes que le creen ver a Daniel Ortega, el precio del tofú en los health food stores del Lower East Side, o quizás sobre el último amigo que murió de AIDS.

¿Qué hacer?, me repetía yo a mí mismo a lo largo de nuestro diálogo aquella noche. ¿Una nueva carta que no será publicada? ¿Una nueva infinita lista de presos políticos, de abusos de derechos humanos, de estupideces económicas, de inaceptables y abominables realidades que el gobierno de Cuba oculta a los turistas y que los peores entre los visitantes, si las entreven, llegan a minimizar con sus disquisiciones abstractas? Traté de explicarle a mi amiga cuán cansado me sentía de la tontería (o de la mala fe) en los medios de prensa norteamericanos, que corren a publicar cualquier embelesado "análisis" de un viajero que constantemente parece buscar en el espectáculo de la isla circunstancias atenuantes al crimen puro y simple de la dictadura. ¿Qué cosa se le puede decir a alguien que, al escribir sobre la religión en Cuba, omite aclarar que las Navidades están prohibidas? ¿Qué explicarle, a quien todavía no ha descubierto que Fidel Castro lleva 26 años y medio en el poder, y que ningún tipo de crítica política es permitida?

Le tuve que confesar a mi amiga mi convicción de que tienen que ser los propios norteamericanos los que tendrán que ir pasando poco a poco por una especie de "cura del castrismo," del mismo modo que ahora parecen irse curando del síndrome Vietnam y de los complejos de culpa que la guerra les dejó. Así les pasó a los intelectuales, periodistas y simples seres progresistas en Francia, que tuvieron su "luna de miel" con Castro en los 60 y ya se curaron muy bien de ella. Los refugiados cubanos en Estados Unidos machacaremos una y mil veces nuestra verdad, escribiremos decenas de artículos, crearemos una obra que directa o indirectamente será siempre una negación de las inmundicias echadas al mundo por Castro, pero nuestra voz será en el mejor de los casos un dato que el racionalismo de los liberales ingénuos en este país tratará por ahora de reducir, para colocarlo en un panorama teórico de concatenaciones rebuscadas donde el real sufrimiento y la real postración de los cubanos de la isla no aparecerá. A los oídos del lector medio de la prensa norteamericana, en esta etapa de disyuntivas y confusiones necesarias e innecesarias, seremos siempre "parte" en un proceso, y nuestra objetividad será puesta en duda. Lo mismo pasó con los primeros que denunciaron el Gulag.

Pero ¿qué hacer? Le recomendé a mi amiga que siguiera escribiendo su libro sobre Cuba, que continuara aliándose con otros norteamericanos a medida que estos vayan progresivamente descubriendo los entretelones monstruosos del régimen castrista, y que sobre todo no perdiera la esperanza. Ella me repetía anécdotas casi bufonescas de innumerables <u>tontos</u> <u>útiles</u> que a diario tenían, en las columnas de importantes periódicos, en las cátedras de famosas universidades, la actitud "piadosa" de tratar de comprender las insuficiencias de los poderes en el Tercer Mundo, como modo de dejar sentado su presunta identidad progresista, pero que sin embargo se negaban a ver los costados más infamantes de esos poderes. Me habló de una famosa crítica inglesa que va mucho a Cuba, pero que se niega a saber que los niños cubanos tienen derecho a una sola venta de tres juguetes al año, hecho que la propaganda cubana jamás menciona.

Todo esto me atormentaba los oídos aquella noche, y todo esto me desesperó, quizás más que a mi amiga. ¿Cómo era que yo, cinco años después de haber llegado a Estados Unidos, yo que no era sino un refugiado que se había echado al mar en un bote atestado y sin equipaje, le podía decir a una norteamericana que tuviera paciencia y esperanza ante la estupidez, obnubilación o desidia de sus compatriotas?

Y en ese punto era que nuestra charla esa noche se empataba con lo que he ido pensando en los últimos meses, complementándolo. Yo podía hablarle a ella en ese tono, creo, porque había vivido en su país cinco años y había logrado alimentarme de las mejores tradiciones intelectuales de diálogo y tolerancia que son la base misma del poder democrático en Estados Unidos.

Cuando el 3 de junio en 1980 llegué por primera vez a Nueva York, apenas dos semanas después de haber escapado al ojo cruel de la vigilancia habanera, a la pobreza y al racionamiento, yo todavía era una especie de marioneta de Fidel Castro. Conmigo traía la impaciencia y la energía para sobrevivir y comenzar a partir de cero en una ciudad desconocida y difícil, pero también el miedo y la desconfianza, los recuerdos obsesionantes, la amargura, el odio. Veinte años de autoritarismo e inmovilidad habían deformado mi capacidad de diálogo, habían multiplicado mis pasiones, deformándolas inevitablemente, y me habían convertido, sin que pudiera aún determinarlo con exactitud, en portavoz de un dogmatismo que era opuesto al dogmatismo de Castro pero que también era un producto de Castro, un engendro coherente dentro de la vivencia unívoca de la historia que él les ha impuesto a sus esclavos en la isla.

Yo era un producto típico de la sociedad castrista: un intolerante, un individuo condicionado por los reflejos y espejismos del poder, un resumen de agresividad ciega y de rencor. Si dentro de ese maremágnum de vectores negativos pude ir detectando otros elementos igualmente energéticos pero positivos (como la necesidad de expresión inmediata, la voluntad de conocer a toda prisa la mecánica de esta otra sociedad), eso se lo atribuyo exclusivamente a lo que he logrado aprender de Estados Unidos, y específicamente, a mis vivencias en la ciudad de Nueva York.

En Nueva York, que considero el compendio más completo y la proyección más arriesgada de los múltiples discursos que componen el presente espiritual de este país, lo primero que llegó a mí fue la diversidad, la disonancia, la impredicción, la arbitrariedad. Yo, que venía de un país en que se escucha incesantemente un solo discurso, una sola versión de los hechos, un único y categórico plan de futuro, me enfrenté a una gama de expresiones, opciones y vías que eran todo lo opuesto al mundo encasillado e hiperdefinido de la isla.

Al principio me costó mucho trabajo funcionar dentro de la nueva dinámica. Por ejemplo, me encontraba con un escritor boliviano que me hablaba de las condiciones infrahumanas en que vive el indio en su país, y para el cual lo que yo le contaba de Castro eran como sofisticaciones de un cielo anhelado. Jóvenes norteamericanos que me descartaban de antemano como fanático o demasiado individualista. Militantes gays que todavía no se habían enterado de que el Partido Comunista de Cuba niega expresamente el ingreso a los homosexuales, los cuales constituyen al menos entre el 10 y el 15 por ciento de la población. Un estudiante de Columbia University me llegó a decir, una fría noche de 1981 en una fiesta de pintores en Soho, que no importaba que Cuba fuera una dictadura, porque también los Estados Unidos serían pronto (imagino que se refería a Ronald Reagan) otra dictadura.

Era cruel y defraudante sentir que mi mensaje, producto de veinte años de dictadura innegable y de conocimientos recibidos en el propio pellejo, era descartado brutalmente desde los primeros momentos, como una cacofónica reiteración de lo que se esperaba que "alguien como yo" dijera. Ante una situación así, era humano reaccionar con soberbia, con desprecio, con extremismo. No hay peor sordo que el que no quiere oír, y el único modo de intercambiar revelaciones sensatas es el diálogo. Los ataques de cólera y de indignación que sufrí ante la sordera de muchos con quienes conversé de Cuba me dejaron sucesivas impresiones de frustración y de aislamiento. Era como arar en el mar.

Desde luego, incluso la ira y las imprecaciones pueden dejar huellas en los demás y a la larga ser efectivas de alguna modo. La energía y la convicción que se expresan a través de esos canales emocionales dejan el trazo calcinante de una descarga eléctrica, exaltan, y pueden provocar impresiones en algunos casos más profundas que un examen sensato de elementos objetivos. Por eso me interesa aclarar que considero útil y necesaria toda expresión intelectual de contenido político, porque siempre, aunque tenga defectos, contribuye a completar el testimonio histórico y es parte esencial de éste. Considero, por ejemplo, que todo lo que hemos dicho y hecho los intelectuales cubanos salidos por Mariel desde que estamos fuera de la isla ha ido acumulándose sin que lo organicemos en un compendio de reacciones positivas que indudablemente contribuirá a enfocar con mayor corrección la situación de Cuba. No voy a entrar a revisar los posibles componentes que han ido formando la mentalidad de vastas capas de los intelectuales progresistas norteamericanos y de los estudiantes universitarios y jóvenes sensibles en las urbes mejor informadas de este país. No soy un sociólogo, ni aspiro a serlo. Pero me atrevo a suponer que lo que hemos dicho y hecho los intelectuales cubanos salidos por el Mariel desde que estamos en Estados Unidos, será un elemento primordial que contribuya a dejar atrás los aspectos políticamente inmaduros de esa mentalidad.

Sin embargo, y para terminar, lo que más me interesa destacar aquí es algo que considero determinante para nosotros, como generación, dentro de las opciones vitales que nos ha puesto al alcance este país. No habremos dejado atrás la prisión insular, no habremos escapado a nuestro dictador, hasta que no nos impregnemos del espíritu profundamente democrático que rige la vida intelectual en Estados Unidos, porque mientras no hagamos eso seguiremos pensando como criaturas de Fidel Castro. Y esto es una modesta reflexión que saco de mi experiencia personal; puede que esté equivocado. Si no aprendemos a completar nuestra identidad subjetiva con la pluralidad de datos que ahora nos ofrece esta sociedad abierta y este paraíso de la información tecnificada, seguiremos viviendo en una provincia reducida del mundo contemporáneo, seguiremos apareciendo como caricaturas dogmáticas, y poniendo de hecho en peligro la efectividad de nuestro criterio histórico.

Y no se trata, que se me entienda bien, de renunciar a nuestra misión de denuncia. No se trata de olvidar o poner en un segundo plano la trágica situación de los que en la isla se ven día a día hostigados por la dictadura. Se trata, por el contrario, de atacar esa injustica de una manera más habilidosa. La disponibilidad para ejercer siempre nuestro derecho a condenar el régimen cubano es algo a lo que no quiero renunciar, a lo que estoy incapacitado para renunciar.

Se trata de decirle adiós al dictador en nuestros hábitos de pensar y vivir. De despedir de nuestro interior el modelo autoritario, de eliminar de nuestro panorama subjetivo la necesidad de imponer opiniones como postulados únicos, pero sin disminuir el contenido de nuestra expresión. Los que no piensan como yo son mis enemigos ideológicos; lo sé. Es muy probable que estén conspirando para apoderarse de mi libertad y degollarme. Pero hay otros individuos que sólo son peones en el juego de las ideas, gentes de buena fe, que yo tendré que convencer tras armarme con el instrumental del debate abierto, dejando atrás las perretas agresivas, si es que quiero evitar que los otros, los conspiradores, dominen la escena y me impidan hablar.

En mi caso personal, repito, creo que eso ha sido lo más importante de estos cinco años. Gracias al hecho de vivir en una sociedad democrática, he tenido acceso a realidades y puntos de vista que la mutilación totalitaria me había bloqueado mientras permanecí en Cuba. Y he aprendido a respetar con calma el mensaje de los demás, aunque las conclusiones que ellos saquen de ese mensaje sean totalmente opuestas a las mías y me luzcan ingénuas, estúpidas o incluso infamantes. Si se quiere, digamos que he aprendido a oír mejor lo que dice mi rival, para conocer a cabalidad las debilidades de su discurso. Y lo más productivo que puedo hacer contra esas conclusiones equivocadas que muchos sacan por ingenuidad o ignorancia, es exponer mi propio mensaje con la mayor coherencia y rigor posibles, y confiar en que mis palabras harán efecto tarde o temprano, porque se unirán a las de toda mi generación, para que todos podamos decirle a Fidel Castro, de una vez por todas, y quizás en correcto inglés: Good-Bye, Dictator.

Juan Abreu

Casi lo primero que vi al apearme del bote en Key West, el 5 de Mayo de 1980, fueron unos seres blancos, de pieles almidonadas, purísimos, con unas aletas a los costados de las cabezas que parecían (eran) ángeles. Y quedé extasiado un buen rato contemplándolos mientras mis compañeros de viaje y de penurias se precipitaban sobre los "sandwiches" y las Coca-Colas. Me dije en susurro: ángeles. Después supe que no eran más que monjas, pero cinco años después esta visión ha pasado definitivamente al campo de la imaginación, y para mi eran sencillamente ángeles, aguardando la tropa de esclavos desarrapados que fluían desde la isla como una avalancha. Angeles al borde del agua, me digo a cada rato, y entonces, súbitamente, vuelvo a ver frente a mí como en una corriente corroída por el sol las figuras aladas, limpísimas, imponiéndose, aniquilando la realidad. Todo rodeado por todas partes por el batir acompasado de las aguas. Esta alucinación, esta aspiración, este afianzarse a la imaginación frente a una realidad destructiva y repugnante, ante el inexcusable peso de la realidad, me sirvió para sobrevivir en la isla, y me sirve actualmente para sobrevivir acá. Y hoy puedo afirmar, afortunadamente, que para mí ese lugar de ángeles, en el que también, claro, suelen haber demonios, tiene más valor físico y real, que lo que los que comparten el aire y el escaso tiempo que les ha sido concedido conmigo llaman la realidad. La realidad es algo realmente bochornoso. Con todas sus causas y sus efectos.

Por eso voy a hablarles de lo que me interesa, de aquello a lo que trato de dedicar el mayor tiempo posible, el esfuerzo creativo. Y esta problemática, trascendental para el mundo moderno aquejado de un vacío espiritual pavoroso, que en Cuba es sinónimo de padecimiento para el artista, nos sitúa ya (gracias a Dios) dentro del tema de "causas y efectos del éxodo de 1980." Hablaré de mis causas y efectos, fundamentalmente, pues son los que conozco mejor. Entonces, empezaré diciendo que estas circunstancias propicias al éxodo, en mi caso, incluyen tres años de servicio militar obligatorio, trabajos forzados en campos de caña (por ejemplo, todo recluta próximo a desmobilizarse del ejército, tiene que trabajar seis u ocho meses "voluntario" en la zafra, sino no se desmobiliza). Trabajos como peón en lugares infernales como la caldera de una termoeléctrica, sin protección alguna contra la contaminación, la ley contra la vagancia, la de la peligrosidad, los comités de defensa de la revolución, y hasta la federación de mujeres cubanas. Todo esto dentro de un ambiente de miseria espiritual programada, y un patrioterismo humillante. Que yo recuerde, la mayor parte de mis 28 años transcurridos allí, me los pasé tratando de robar tiempo a las tareas priorizadas por el gobierno, para leer. Leer como pasión, como salida, leer como alimento. Para tratar de ver quién era yo. En una guagua atestada, en un hueco bajo la caldera, mientras el capataz trataba de localizarme, sobre el techo de una barraca en un campamento militar, y hasta recogiendo plátanos.

Así, con el transcurrir del tiempo fuí desarrollando un desprecio que ha ido en aumento por los tejeymadejes culturales. Porque la cultura allí no era más que hipocresía y muecas, simulación y miedo, y muchos farsantes y mucho egoísmo por un puesto en la burocracia cultural, por poder estudiar en una universidad, para publicar el librito, etc. El ambiente cultural cubano es el típico de estos países fascistas de izquierda (la definición no tiene nada que ver con los cubanos, aclaro, es de Hugh Thomas); represión sutil y abierta, planes de aniquilación de la iniciativa personal, prohibición de libros, desinformación programada, etc. Y llegué por estos caminos a la conclusión de que la llamada cultura es una actividad parasitaria de la creación. Y hoy sigo pensando lo mismo. Y como lo que me interesaba era el acto de crear, pues, cada vez fuí más anticultural y desarrollé una especie de furia en ese sentido. Esto debe ser producto, supongo, del totalitarismo, de la esclavitud. De las interminables jornadas bajo el sol, recogiendo pangola.

Allá, debe ser distinto, tiene que ser distinto, me decía, mientras marchaba marcando el paso embutido en un odioso uniforme verde olivo, el allá de mis sueños, era aquí, como ustedes supondrán. No puede ser que en todas partes sólo se viva para fingir, me argumentaba a mí mismo, que los hipócritas y los oportunistas sean los que trepen y dicten las pautas a seguir, que a nadie (y esto era lo peor, lo que me aterraba en mi ingenuidad) le interese realmente el arte, ese discurso misterioso en el que los hombres se obstinan hace milenios, sino el chismorreteo de salón, el cuchicheo, la anécdota pueril en torno al creador, lo intrascendente, la claudicación ante las exigencias de los comisarios de la cultural. Y siempre me decía, en la cola del pan, en la refriega para tomar el ómnibus, en el orgasmo apresurado en la posada pestilente en la que me habían dado dos botellas de agua al entrar para atender la higiene: allá . . . allá, será diferente, allá no existirá al menos el rencor, allá perdonarán al que trabaja, le perdonarán que trabaje, que no sea igual a los otros, que se esfuerce; y lo dejarán en paz (sobre todo eso) y no tratarán de neutralizarlo, de negar y minimizar su trabajo; los que no hacen nada, pero se pasan la vida hablando de hacer y escribiendo articulitos de ocasión, esa gente horrible. Es decir, pensaba que me dejarían reventar en paz, a ver si podía hacer mi obra, si es que era un elegido al fin y al cabo. Y todo esto era una ingenuidad. Allá, no era aquí. Allá no está en ninguna parte.

Y cuando se formó la locura de la embajada, cuando llegué tarde y pensé que había perdido el último tren, y Fidel Castro de una patada creó el Mariel y llegaron los barcos. Yo, que había pasado por casi todo, y no tenía ni la más mínima esperanza de escapar, me vi de pronto en un centro de tramitaciones de la policía, habilitado a la carrera, mostrando mi carta de libertad, la que me dieron después de pasarme seis meses recogiendo plátanos en Artemisa . . . la que me salvó. Me vi mintiendo como tantos, argumentando en mi propia contra, pues sólo quien demostrara que era lo peor podría recibir el precioso salvoconducto que lo autorizaba a largarse del paraíso. Y más tarde estaba apretujado en un ómnibus que se deslizaba por la madrugada, en dirección al campo de concentración llamado El Mosquito.

Luego, ya estaba en el sueño, en el deseo de casi todo cubano, en el bote, aturdido y sucio y temeroso de que aquellas cañoneras grises hundieran la embarcación o simplemente la hicieran regresar. Allí, rodeado por la gente más disímil, presos recién sacados de las celdas (contra su propia voluntad muchas veces), ingenieros, estudiantes, amas de casas y militantes del partido, todos rumbo a la Florida, rumbo a allá. Y allá resultó ser aquí.

Cinco años no son suficientes para comprender a fondo un fenómeno tan complejo como el de un país que goza de la democracia. Hace varios años, recién llegado, escribí un artículo en el que decía que estaba en el paraíso. Hoy sigo pensando lo mismo. Porque el paraíso no puede ser otro sitio que aquel en el que podemos ser nosotros mismos, no sin inconvenientes, claro está, no sin luchar, pero por lo menos sin que nos metan en una mazmorra por no cantar loas al tirano de turno. La libertad es un término vago, que, creo, tiene que ver fundamentalmente con nuestro mundo interior. Como dijera un joven poeta cubano que recientemente logró abandonar la isla: "la libertad consiste, no en ser libre, sino en sentirse libre."

Sin embargo, es abismal y absolutamente maravillosa, la diferencia entre países en los que podemos publicar y exponer nuestra opinión, y aquellos en los que te patean por pretender publicarla, o simplemente no renegar de ella. Pretendo ser un creador, teorizar es algo que entra en mi campo de interés en rarísimas ocasiones. No obstante, me parece pertinente decir aquí, que como ser humano que vive diariamente en una ciudad en la que el 43% de la población es hispana, me refiero a Miami, veo en ella uno de los fundamentales efectos del éxodo, que es el tema por el cual nos reunimos hoy. Es fundamental decir que son gentes que no muestran un gran interés por integrarse a la cultura norteamericana, que allí, en un futuro cercano los candidatos políticos anglos tendrán que tener esto muy en cuenta si quieren aspirar a un cargo público. Este es un tema interesante que ocupará, supongo, a especialistas y a gente más interesada en esos asuntos que el que les habla.

Yo por mi parte (y esto podría considerarse otro efecto) he llegado a la conclusión de que nunca seré norteamericano, en el sentido de asimilar su cultura y apropiármela, en el sentido de pretender ser uno de ellos. Sencillamente no me interesa. 28 años de comunismo me han convertido en un ser desasido y escéptico para el cual la vida es más que todo una calamidad. Encerrados en un círculo reducido, el de nuestra lengua (y esto no tiene nada que ver, por supuesto, con que se hable inglés o no) y el de nuestra latinidad, tenemos pocas oportunidades en el mundo norteamericano que conserva profundos sustratos racistas. Los pintores, como es mi caso, se ven reducidos a tratar de imitar las cartas de triunfo que vienen de las grandes galerías neuyorkinas, donde ya se sabe lo que piensan del arte latinoamericano; si es que quieren triunfar. De esta forma penetran en un círculo vicioso, sin salida, por lo menos personal, porque la mayoría de estos movimientos que inventan esos centros de poder, son pura fanfarria comercial. Estamos en peor situación aun que los artistas latinos que residen en sus países o en Europa. Somos hombres sin un país detrás, y esto es sumamente grave. Un Botero, o un Lam, son imposibles de concebir entre cubanoamericanos, por ejemplo, o entre colombiano-americanos. Ese "gran mundo" se niega a aceptarlos. A lo sumo los considera artistas de segunda. El caso de los escritores, es similar. A luchar por un puesto en las universidades para poder vivir. Y ya se sabe el interés del público por estos escritores para minorías, entre una mayoría que ignora no sólo a los clásicos de la lengua española, o cualquier otra lengua, sino hasta los suyos propios. Realmente no sé si hay una solución para estos problemas, pero no me preocupa demasiado. La fama, el reconocimiento, los considero ahora cosas tontas y estupidizantes. Y esto se me antoja, otro efecto del éxodo, así que espero poco a poco, haber ido contribuyendo en algo con la temática del evento que nos reune.

Este magnífico y generoso país que nos permite ser, es la última esperanza del mundo que agoniza sometido a la esclavitud de uno de los fanatismos mayores que ha sufrido la humanidad. A los norteamericanos pues, me gustaría pedirles desde mi insignificante posición de emigrante sin estatus, que presten atención a esas voces desesperadas, que les llegan de todas partes, que mediten las razones de los que huyen, que los escuchen; sobre todo aquellos que llevan sobre sus hombros la inmensa responsabilidad de la educación de los jóvenes. Para que los libren del riesgo de sufrir una esclavitud similar a la que nosotros hemos padecido. Una esclavitud que avanza, que ya padecen tantos.

7. UN LARGO VIAJE DE MARIEL A NUEVA YORK

Reinaldo Arenas

Cuando la pequeña embarcación (un bote de veinticinco pies) salió del Mariel, una sensación, no de alegría, pero sí de inmenso descanso invadió a los treinta viajeros que hambrientos y apelmazados partíamos. Atrás quedaban veinte años de nuestras no-vidas, vividos bajo una misma consigna, un mismo estado, una miseria y una represión siempre en aumento incesante. Veinte años de los cuales los últimos diez (cifra conservadora) podrían resumirse en un solo año, en un solo día, en un solo instante presente, incesante, reiterativo, fatigozo e ineludible. Instante que de un fogonazo se transformaba y abolía la mitad de nuestra vida . . . El tripulante y dueño de la ilusoria embarcación llamada "San Lázaro," a quien le habían llenado el bote de desconocidos--nosotros--, permitiéndole sólo traer una tía y dos primos de toda la familia reclamada por la que había hecho el viaje y se había arruinado, nos cuenta, aún alterado, cómo vio pasar a cuchillo a un miliciano de guardia quien en el momento en que salían las embarcaciones rumbo a Cayo Hueso tiró el rifle y se lanzó al agua, intentando también marcharse. Veloces los guarda-costas del litoral le dieron alcance y, para no alarmar con disparos a la inmensa población flotante (unas tres mil embarca-ciones ancladas en el puerto), lo calaron a ballonetazos sobre las aguas.

Aún escoltados, salimos ya al mar abierto. Por la mañana nos recibe y arrastra, en incesante torbellino, la Corriente del Golfo que atraviesa el Estrecho de la Florida. Corriente que no es corriente, sino torrente enfurecido; estrecho que no es tal, al menos para quien, como nosotros, lo atravesase en una pequeña y bamboleante embarcación que ahora (tres de la tarde), sin mayores trámites, se rompe (se le apaga) el motor . . . ¿Qué estadísticas-- ¿compiladas acaso por la UNESCO?-- podrán enumerar la cifra exacta de cadáveres que yacen (o mejor dicho fluyen y se deshacen) en el fondo de esta corriente? ¿Diez mil? ¿Treinta mil? La aleta de un tiburón, que rápida emerge y vuelve a desaparecer cerca de nosotros, no quiere--discreta--darnos el número exacto . . . La selva sigue fluyendo, arrastrándonos, no precisamente a la Florida, sino al océano Atlántico. Por fortuna, la radio de la embarcación funciona y nuestro improvisado y temerario capitán (primera vez que coge un timón) no cesa de enviar señales de SOS. Algunas embarcaciones repletas pasan cerca de nosotros, diciéndonos adiós. Nadie, en estos momentos, está para perder tiempo . . . Como no queda otra alternativa que esperar a que alguien nos rescate, nos dedicamos a vomitar la bilis (lo único que nos quedaba dentro), mientras nos balanceamos aferrados unos a los otros y nos dirigimos algunas palabras. El viajero que viene pegado a mí, se niega rotundamente a aceptar la teoría de que vamos hacia la Florida. "USA, USA," le gritan, pero él no admite no sólo que vayamos para USA, ni siquiera que exista un lugar llamado así. Emite extraños ronquidos, alza los brazos y mira, en otro mundo (¿el de la demencia?, el de la inocencia?), el mar que se nos abalanza. Así, desistimos de intentar hacerle entrar en razón comprendiendo que el pobre hombre desde hace mucho tiempo la ha perdido, y que, precisamente por eso, había ido a parar (lo habían llevado), del manicomio, a aquella tabla que se bamboleaba, junto con algún pícaro acribillado de tatuajes, y--la gran mayoría--gente, jóvenes, viejos, mujeres, que se las había agenciado, entre pedradas y golpes, para conseguir el salvo-conducto liberador. La inquietud mayor de uno de ellos (un muchacho) es que, aunque lo llevaron con toda su familia hasta el Mariel, sólo a él lo embarcaron, y ahora no sabía si su madre y demás parientes vendrían en otro bote, o dónde habían ido a parar.

Al oscurecer, agotada la bilis, solamente arqueamos. En el horizonte aparece un helicóptero; desciende. Nos tira unas cuantas fotos y se marcha. El viejo "que se hizo pasar por delincuente" se desmaya. Todos, aferrados a cualquier objeto, nos recluimos un poco en nuestras propias calamidades. Sólo el hombre que no sabe a dónde va, alza los brazos--en su mundo--y sostiene sus ininteligibles gemidos. A media noche, un enorme barco con el estimulante nombre de Vigorosus II se nos acerca, conducido por el helicóptero. Es un guardacostas norteamericano. Que ya tira sus botes-salvavidas al agua, que ya llegan hasta nosotros, que ya nos transportan, que ya, subidos por sogas, nos depositan en la cubierta. Los enfermos de cuidado son trans-portados por el helicóptero que aterriza y despega sobre el mismo guardacostas. Su tripulación, en su mayoría puertorriqueña, nos recibe con júbilo. Podemos secarnos, tomar algo caliente, comer . . . Así pasamos la madrugada, y al día siguiente (el tercero de nuestra travesía) estamos ya frente a Key West.

Amalgama de voces, cuerpos sudorosos y sucios, pies descalzos, bocas en su mayoría desdentadas, abrazos. Un pueblo entero que en oleadas desciende y atraviesa, harapiento, los primeros pasillos, las primeras improvisadas oficinas de inmigración. Raro, el que hable algo de inglés. El mismo español a veces sólo se balbucea: logros irrefutables de la educación en la Cuba actual . . . Ciento treinta mil personas lanzándose, como ganado en estampida, al mar; llegando los más afortunados al otro lado, para volver (intentar) de nuevo nacer, comenzar, tratar, urgentemente, desgarradoramente, de recuperar, veinte, quince, diez años perdidos.

¿Qué es lo más conmovedor? ¿Qué es lo que, sometido a un survey de la N.V.S., el New York Times, o Selecciones, señalaría usted, distinguidísimo ciudadano, como lo más patético?

Las manos. En Cayo Hueso, en las bases militares convertidas transitoriamente en campos de refugiados, en los estadios convertidos en albergues, en todos los sitios por los cuales multitudinariamente pasamos, por encima de los gritos de vivas y libertad, brazos y abrazos, lo más patético son esas manos, manos, por lo general enflaquecidas, afanadas en coleccionar hamburguesas, bocaditos, perros calientes, para irlos a guardar (de reserva) bajo las literas. Imposible hacerles comprender a los dueños de esas manos, que ya no es necesario tomar tales precauciones, que ya no es necesario almacenar, acaparar, guardar comida para cuando se acabe. Que los alimentos no son aquí artículos que se "sacan" eventualmente y que al instante desaparecen. Imposible hacerles ver (por ahora) que bastaría sencillamente con ir al mostrador y pedir otro "hamburger" cuando tengan hambre. Veinte años bajo la urgencia de la sobrevida, bajo la inseguridad de mantener esa sobrevida, bajo la desconfianza, el escepticismo o la mera burla, ante cualquier promesa que implique asegurarnos la sobrevida, no se olvidan así como así. Por eso, ellos siguen en otro tiempo--allá--ahora, llenando jabas de perros calientes y escondiéndolas debajo de la cama. No se trata de ambición o egoísmo, se trata, sencillamente, de un hambre y una desconfianza antiguas. De haber tenido--padecido--una racionalización rigurosa, una estricta libreta de racionamiento, donde aún lo racionado casi nunca podía obtenerse . . . Alguien da la voz de "alerta, la ropa." Y allá van, allá vamos, despotricados. Uno intenta colarse en la fila. Breve altercado en el tumulto . . . No es fácil, no es fácil adaptarse--comprender--la seguridad, el orden, cuando desde siempre se ha vivido en la inseguridad y el desorden. Resulta difícil hacerles ver a los que organizan las donaciones, los que desde hace años viven acá, no lo desagradable, sino lo patético, lo trágico de esos rostros, de esos jóvenes desesperados por acumular hamburgers o coger un pulover . . . Miro para mi alrededor y sólo el hombre que aún no sabe que ha llegado a los Estados Unidos--que quizás nunca lo sabrá--se mantiene abstraído, fuera del tumulto ("en Babia y nada menos que ahora," dicen algunos que pasan apresurados, rumbo al molote . . .). Sigue haciendo gestos desconcertantes y produciendo ese ruido como de gemido, apagado, lejano, bocarriba, tirado en la cama, sin preocuparse siquiera por comer, a pesar de mis insistencias . . .

La voz de Olga Guillot inunda ahora todo el stadium--u Orange Bowl--repleto, no de turistas, no de visitantes endomingados con sus autos parqueados en el gran parqueo, no de hispanos residentes; sino de un mar de gente averiada, esquilmada, magra--unos con piernas rotas, ya enyesadas, otros exhibiendo orondos una camisa nueva y desproporcionada a su talla--. Esa voz, y el mar de gente extasiado, cautivado, escuchando. Esa voz--allá, también, prohibida--ronca y desgarrada, en el recuerdo navegando, una vez más identificándonos. Nuevamente congregados para empezar.

Esa voz--y ya andamos por las calles--intentando reconstruir un tiempo, sosteniendo un tiempo, una época, una ciudad, unas noches, una ilusión, que ya sólo en el timbre que la emite y en los emocionados que escuchan existe. Esa voz y los que la escuchan, los que pueden escucharla, ya en la otra ciudad, en Miami, re-edificando un mundo que hace mucho tiempo se derrumbó . . . Un pueblo entero intentando reconstruir una ciudad que ya no existe, un pueblo entero fregando platos, conduciendo automóviles, manipulando cajas y ladrillos, limpiando escaleras, dirigiendo, ya, bancos, bibliotecas, escuelas, cines y librerías, mercados o supermercados, pero aun dedicados a la terca--minuciosa y heróica--tarea de reinventar un país, de materializar una sombra. Un pueblo entero reinventando un edificio, una fachada, una calle, un parque, un gesto, una voz, un nombre, un lenguaje, un ritmo, un mundo, cuyo patrón sólo en el recuerdo existe ya. Una ciudad heróicamente fantasmagórica, mágica, expandiéndose vertiginosa por la arenosa Península, queriendo hacer de la Península una Isla, de la Isla un mito, queriendo a toda costa resuscitar el cadáver putrefacto de un fantasma. Una ciudad patética e irreal, heróica e irreal, reinventando, reconstruyendo, remodelando (caricaturizando) lo que no existe. Una ciudad patéticamente empecinada, lanzándole al tiempo su heróico y triste desafío . . . Esa voz, esa voz. ¿Volver a lo que ya no existe? Difícil. ¿Olvidar lo que ya no existe? Imposible.

¿Imposible?

Nueva York no es realmente una ciudad heróica. Es una ciudad auténtica. Su autenticidad radica precisamente en su desinterés por esa palabra. Nueva York--y cuando se dice Nueva York, se dice, desde luego, Manhattan--no es una ciudad norteamericana; es, además de eso, china, suramericana, puertorriqueña, negra y alemana, judía, rusa, italiana, cubana . . . En su fluir incesante, ¿qué rostro puede sorprendernos? ¿qué idioma llamarnos la atención? La inmensa muchedumbre se abalanza de nuevo, y yo con ella--hay que aprovechar el WALK iluminado--yo, pleno, anónimo, auténtico, sólo integrándome a esa desintegración. El corazón de esta ciudad está en ese desconsuelo universalizador, gentil y febril, apresurado. Para esta muchedumbre desconocida, la amistad es algo más que una palabra; una simple mirada es algo ya digno de tomarse en consideración . . . Esos trenes que parten cruzando incesantes bajo nosotros, estos edificios que lanzan a las nubes el reto de sus empalmes, ese millón de luces que ahora convierten la Isla en una lámpara gigantesca, ese fluir que no se detiene, esos ríos sobre los cuales parece que incesantemente navegáramos, ese tumulto que se hace y se difumina hacia cines, subways, teatros, bares y bibliotecas, cuevas y torres, parques y avenidas, museos, iglesias, antros, puentes y cementerios, pistas, tiendas y universidades, taxis o quién sabe a dónde demonio, ese torrente que, en hormiguero multicolor y sin igual, se precipita, rápido, rápido, rápido, secretamente nos toca con su sabiduría desconocida, secretamente nos impregna, nos conmina, nos dice en qué consiste la verdadera, la única sabiduría: No te detengas.

New York, febrero 14 de 1981

III. *Academics and the Creation of Image:*
The Changing Structure of Research
Questions, Methodologies, and Sources

8. SOCIAL MOVEMENTS IN EARLY TWENTIETH-CENTURY LATIN AMERICA: A RECONSIDERATION

Michael F. Jiménez

I

Late July of 1929 was marked by a number of uprisings throughout Colombia against the Conservative government of Miguel Abadía Mendez. In isolated towns and villages from the Cauca Valley in the southwest, up through the Magdalena River Valley, and into the Santander region to the northeast, armed bands of provincial middle-class radicals, artisans, peasants, and workers assaulted police stations and attempted to occupy local administrative offices. The rebels attempted to take the important river port of La Dorada in the mid-Magdalena Valley, and railway workers attacked a train depot at San Vicente in southern Santander. The insurgents announced the beginning of a revolution in Colombia, which was supposed to coincide with a military campaign by Venezuelan Liberals against the dictatorship of Juan Vicente Gómez. But the national insurrection never materialized, fizzling by the middle of August into isolated guerrilla operations as the Conservative government moved rapidly to dismantle the national conspiracy and crush the regional rebellions.[1]

The abortive 1929 uprising occurred during a period of economic crisis and social unrest. Even before the great financial crash at the end of the year, Latin America was experiencing the effects of contractions in the North Atlantic economies.[2] Prices for coffee and other export commodities had already begun to plummet downward in 1928, and anxious foreign creditors were pulling out of the region. In Colombia, the crisis resulted in reduced government expenditures and massive unemployment.

From the middle of the decade, the country had witnessed an expanding and increasingly militant protest movement among artisans, students, white-collar workers, and urban proletarians. The most notable protests were among wage laborers in the nation's transportation network and export enclaves. The radicalization of an important segment of the Colombian working class was given shape and direction by the Partido Socialista Revolucionario (PSR). This indigenous collection of Marxists, socialists, anarchists, and Liberal leftists was founded in 1925 at the Third National Workers' Convention. Soon thereafter it became affiliated with the Communist International. The July insurrection had, in fact, been preceded by more than a year of fierce encounters between the government and militant unionists at the Tropical Oil complex at Barrancabermeja and in the banana districts controlled by the United Fruit Company, near the

49

Caribbean port of Santa Marta. The PSR organizers had played major roles in both places.

At the time, the failed insurrection was perceived as part of an international Communist conspiracy. The Colombian government spared no pains to identify the uprising with the radical left, and took the occasion to finish dismantling what had been one of the region's most militant proletarian movements. The New York Herald Tribune editorialized in early August of 1929 that, while the new labor policies of the Mexican government were leading to sovietism, there were other causes for concern as well: "Radical labor outbreaks are becoming increasingly common in Latin America. In Colombia which has shown remarkable progress during the last few years there were recent recurrences of the sanguinary demonstrations of a few months ago. The Bogotá government has placed the responsibility for the outbursts on imported Communist agitators who had received their cue from Moscow."[3] This view of the 1929 rebellion, as a failed proletarian uprising, has informed the predominant historical interpretations of this still virtually unresearched episode. The principal student of Colombian labor history, Miguel Urrutia, placed the incidents within the context of a brief stage of revolutionary syndicalism in the 1920s and described them as "mass uprisings organized by communists . . . [some of] which were particularly bloody, and were put down only at some cost to human life."[4]

But the 1929 Colombian insurrection was more than a mechanical response to worsening economic conditions by an emergent working class manipulated by a militant radical sect linked to international communism. As elsewhere in Latin America, the deepening of the export economy and the initial stages of industrialization in the first three decades of the twentieth century had spawned a small but strategically located proletariat in mines, plantations, oil fields, factories, and along the nation's transportation networks. The spread of capitalist social relations in urban areas and export enclaves, and to a lesser extent in the Colombian countryside, was accompanied by the adoption of European radical ideologies by an influential minority of workers as a way of understanding their condition and envisioning fundamental changes in their society. This led to the emergence of an oppositional culture among some proletarians, a culture emphasizing international working-class solidarity and fierce resistance to the owners and managers of capitalist enterprises, the large landowners and merchants who composed the core of the nation's oligarchy, and the Colombian state. Strikes, shutdowns, sabotage, and mass demonstrations became commonplace as the 1920s wore on, and the PSR became the focus of Colombia's class struggle.[5]

Nonetheless, other oppositions to the spread of capitalism and the growing power of the central government were also evolving. Displaced Indian villagers in southern Colombia fought

back against landowners and real estate speculators who had
struck deals with local officials to take away their ancient lands.
In frontier zones throughout the central part of the country,
where export agriculture had set down roots barely a half-
century before, tenants and peons battled large estate-owners for
higher wages, better working conditions, and access to land.
Squatters attempting to hold on to recently acquired plots in the
glens and vales of the eastern and central Andean <u>cordilleras</u>
were locked in fierce combat with encroaching landlords and the
authorities.[6] Throughout the countryside, excisemen and peasants engaged in ongoing guerrilla warfare over the collection of
liquor and tobacco taxes.[7] Finally, in the nation's cities, the
remnants of the nineteenth-century artisanry continued to defend
their ever more precarious position in the face of imported manu-
factures and a growing modern domestic industry.[8] A radical
critique of capitalism based on European ideologies easily became
interwoven with local demands for protection of old ways and some
glimpse of a different future.

As important as these growing connections between lower-
class movements and radical European ideologies was a native
strain of opposition to the upper classes, opposition rooted in the
intraelite civil wars of the previous century. In Colombia, as
elsewhere on the continent, one of the legacies of the nineteenth
century was a militant, popular liberalism which was provincial in
origin and concerned with local autonomy, civil liberties, and
social equality. At the turn of the century, the last of those
civil conflicts between the Conservative and Liberal parties--
the War of a Thousand Days--was followed by a rapprochement
between those competing oligarchical factions in which the latter
shed its traditional social and political radicalism. The Liberal
oligarchs allowed the Conservatives to manage the state and
utilize the Church to control the lower classes in exchange for
economic stability and continuing opportunities to connect the
nation firmly into the world economy, primarily through coffee
exports.[9]

But the Liberal establishment did not anticipate the survival
of radical liberalism, especially in the provinces. Small-town
merchants, professionals, artisans, and landowners marginally
connected to the export economy found themselves under pressure
from agrarian capitalist entrepreneurs, whether local or foreign
owners of plantations and marketing firms. Moreover, they were
in sustained conflict with the local representatives of the Conservative state for whom the bare semblance of a Liberal conspiracy
was reason enough for repression. This situation nourished a
strong nationalism among these dispossessed middle-class Liberals,
kept alive their social radicalism, and encouraged an insurrectionist mentality in key areas of the Colombian countryside,
especially Tolima, western Cundinamarca, and the Santander
region, all of which had been Liberal bastions in the nineteenth

century.   Further, the Liberal provincial middle classes found
support among the rural poor, for whom conditions were worsening owing to the changing nature of agrarian relations and a
repressive state allied to the large estate-owners and merchants.

Clearly, the economic project of Colombia's national upper
classes, based on a close connection to the world economy, had
not yet been fully accepted by some segments of its regional
elites.   Nor had it been effectively imposed on the mass of rural
poor in a large part of the country.   In short, early century
attempts to redesign the Colombian economy in terms of dependent
capitalism had raced far ahead of the export oligarchy's ability to
wield state power.   The oligarchy had not yet succeeded in
elaborating a national politics or a civic culture which would
ensure its unchallenged hegemony.

This dilemma became increasingly evident by the middle of
the 1920s.   Despairing of ever being able to return to power by
electoral means, a segment of the Liberal party began to question
the deal that the oligarchs had struck at the beginning of the
century.[10]   The loss of confidence in a moderate political
strategy, under conditions of persistent government repression,
resulted in a surge of insurrectionist sentiment among Liberals
after 1925.   This sentiment was further encouraged by young
urban middle-class intellectuals and publicists who were influenced
by European radical thought.   These ambitious Liberal youths
provided some important linkages, both ideological and strategic,
between the provincial Liberals and the proletarian radicals.
Major elements within the party struggled to contain the
enthusiasms for rebellion among the veterans of the War of a
Thousand Days and their provincial supporters.   But with a
weakening economy after 1927, and growing antiradical hysteria
among the Conservative authorities, the militant wing of the
Liberal party was positioned for an uprising by the middle of
1929.

Two years earlier, in September of 1927, at the PSR national
convention in the Magdalena port city of La Dorada, an alliance of
radical proletarians and Liberal leftists had laid the groundwork
for national insurrection.   Although certain proletarian militants
were purportedly uneasy about any attempt to seize power
militarily without mass organizing, those elements with links to
Liberal veterans and provincial party dissidents gained the upper
hand at the convention.   They established a national underground
network known as the Consejo Central Conspirativo (CCC), which
was charged with preparing for a general uprising.   Over the
course of the next two years, plans were laid for an insurrection
that would combine armed assaults on the government with a
shutdown of the national transportation system by organized
labor.   Underground bomb factories were established, secret
Liberal militias gathered arms, and the unions were urged to gird
themselves for a sharp struggle.   It was further hoped that a

military initiative by Venezuela's Liberal opposition against the dictatorship there might help throw the Colombian government off balance.

By June of 1929, the momentum for a national uprising had crested among the various opposition elements throughout Colombia. The leadership set July 28 as the date for rebellion. Escalating conflict in the countryside and in the cities seemed to hasten the confrontation. A deeply divided Conservative party, the presence of a large part of the army in the nation's capital for the July independence day celebrations, and the launching of an attack on the Venezuelan government from Colombia by that country's Liberals on the same day, all seemed to present a perfect opportunity to strike at the Conservative regime. By then, however, an important ingredient was missing. The Conservatives had moved swiftly in 1928 to quell unrest among workers in the export enclaves and the transportation system with a campaign of arrests and harrassment. The PSR's radical proletarian factions were effectively neutralized, and this appears to have precluded the nationwide labor strikes that were intended to coincide with an armed uprising.

Nonetheless, the CCC, by then fully under the control of Liberal leftists and the old insurrectionist wing of the party, persisted with its planning--despite some evidence that major party figures might not favor a rebellion. Just a few days before the appointed date, however, last-minute snags, largely tied to the timing of the Venezuelan invasion, caused the leadership to delay the uprising. The message reached through the CCC network to most parts of the country, but not everywhere. On July 28, ragged bands of veterans and armed workers, artisans, and peasants throughout Colombia attacked their preassigned targets, unaware that they were fighting a postponed revolution.

II

In the past two decades, studies of Latin America covering the first third of the twentieth century have shifted decisively from political to social and economic history. Two major aspects of the region's history during the high period of neocolonialism have received particular attention. First, historians and economists have undertaken a multifaceted reconstruction of the processes of economic change based on export capitalism. A wide range of studies has focused on accelerated urbanization, the extension of capitalist social relations into the countryside, and the creation of plantation, oil, and mining enclaves.[11] Closely following these studies of a crystallizing dependent capitalism in the late nineteenth and early twentieth centuries has been a host of works on lower-class reactions to the remaking of their worlds. Considerable attention has been paid to the repeated violent eruptions in the Latin American countrysides as well as to occasional sustained agrarian rebellions, all of which emerged in response to the continued dispossession of the rural poor beginning in the middle decades of the nineteenth century. The emergence of a wage-labor class, which was often explosively resistant to national and foreign businesses and to the governmental authorities who defended elite interests, has likewise commanded increasing attention. The result has been the reconstruction of the ideologies and organizational histories of agrarian insurrections and of working-class opposition to export oligarchies. The long silenced and dispossessed majority of Latin Americans has, at last, received its voice.[12]

How has this shift in the concerns of students of Latin America's recent past been marked among those who gather the basic research materials? The economic history of the period is well on its way to maturity. Ironically, the success of economic history may have upstaged the emergence of a labor or an agrarian history comparable with the increasingly rich literature on North America and Europe. Research questions have tended to be framed in terms of "developmentalist" or dependista models, each of which emphasizes the dilemmas of economic change at a national level. The consequent bibliographic focus on national-level statistical materials and governmental reports has undercut efforts to locate the materials needed to investigate this history from below. The traditional assemblage of official publications in most North American libraries has rarely included materials from the less-accessible or since-disbanded offices that dealt with agrarian or labor questions during the first decades of this century. Further, only recently have some researchers and bibliographers turned toward source materials heretofore generally ignored. These include radical pamphlets, the proletarian press, union archives, and oral and written testimonies. They also encompass a range of previously underutilized official documents including notarial records, prefectural reports, and relevant collections in the ministries of commerce, interior, and war. Finally, there are critical materials in the labor and social welfare offices which were often created in this era, but which suffered a rather haphazard early existence. In some measure, the reach of the researchers has far exceeded the grasp of the bibliographers.

A new generation of historians has struggled within these limits, and the story of the dispossessed and heretofore voiceless mass of Latin Americans is now being told. But there have been problems within a literature spawned by the study of the rise of dependent capitalism and its social consequences. In the first place, there is a tendency to flatten out the history of the various classes, and to make the actions of peasants, artisans, and proletarians in the three decades before the Great Depression little more than narrow, mechanical responses to the implantation of export economies throughout the region. Moreover, politics seems to have been emptied from the story. Political events have been explained almost solely in terms of economic and social structures, often to the exclusion of the ideological, organizational, and ethnic elements that helped shape the work and lives of the lower classes.[13]

A modified approach to the study of popular movements during the critical first decades of this century is likely to enrich our understanding of the history of that period, and also to pose new methodological and research challenges to historians and bibliographers alike. The current interest in the state's role in the formation of Latin America's dependent capitalist societies from the 1880s through the 1920s may help stimulate a fresh look at that era's great popular movements.[14] The 1929 uprising in Colombia clearly reveals the limitations of understanding the opposition to the neocolonialist order only in terms of the resistance of the working poor in town and country. The expansion of dependent capitalism and the accompanying growth of state power involved a complicated and often volatile mix of social classes. In Colombia, as elsewhere in the region, one of the central and heretofore neglected features of the resultant social movements was the ongoing struggle between the provincial middle classes and the national oligarchies, with the latter usually closely connected to foreign interests and served by a state seeking to deepen and extend its power. From the upheavals in Mexico during the second decade of this century to Peru's aprista movement of the 1920s, we can now see that our history from below can only be one part of a larger, more complicated picture of the ways in which a new design was set on the economic life, social relations, and political institutions of Latin America.

Recent research on the Mexican Revolution has contributed greatly to our understanding of the complexity of social movements in the first third of this century. It also may indicate the new directions that historians are likely to take in the coming years. The traditional emphasis on the "peasant" nature of that episode has yielded to a far more supple analysis of the interpenetration of agrarian uprisings, proletarian resistance, and the efforts of the rural middle classes to take advantage of the collapse of the porfiriato after decades of defending their interests against its centralizing tendencies.[15] The Sonoran provincial middle classes, exemplified by Alvaro Obregón, rose to the commanding heights of Mexican politics by the early 1920s, and were subsequently transformed into a national bourgeoisie. Research on this trajectory reveals the importance of similar groups in other parts of Latin America. The Sonoran local elites organized a successful rebellion, but were then unable to fulfill lower-class expectations for a genuine social revolution. Hector Aguilar Camín, writing of this "emergent semirural, semiurban lower middle class," notes that their

> traditions appear to have been more decisive for Mexican society than the backward looking dreams of zapatismo or the contradictory, lightning intervention of

villismo. If the participation of these two movements gave the revolution its facade of exotic populism, nevertheless it is clear that the Sonoran tradition affords the likeliest explanation of the fundamental direction and final resting place of that movement.[16]

While it was only in Mexico that the provincial petty bourgeoisie successfully dismantled the oligarchy's power, a similar drama was played out in other areas of Latin America from the 1880s onward.[17] There were several dimensions to this struggle. First, the petty bourgeoisie that then resisted the national oligarchs and the expanding state tended to hail from relatively new zones of settlement and economic change rather than the older and more densely populated regions of their countries. In Mexico, the northern states of Sonora, Coahuila, and Chihuahua formed a major area of rapid commercial growth in the years before the revolution.[18] Similarly, the declining rural petty bourgeoisie of the northern Peruvian coast provided the infrastructure for Haya de la Torre's nationalist and popular movement. This group resisted the alliance between sugar planters and the state which sought to redesign the region's economy and politics after the turn of the century.[19] Finally, that small segment of the provincial middle classes which was involved in the Colombian uprising was rooted in the internal frontiers of western Cundinamarca and Tolima, which had developed into major coffee zones from the 1870s onward.

Second, the regions where the provincial middle classes proved most resistant to oligarchical rule tended to have a much looser social fabric than in more traditional and more populated areas. The hegemony of the great estates remained relatively uneven: while the extension of export-oriented enterprises was proceeding apace, the upper-class monopoly of land, labor, and the marketing of essential commercial products was not entirely secure. They were often districts of relatively recent settlement, as in northern Mexico or central Colombia's inner frontier. The great estates had not sunk very deep roots, and there was a relatively fluid social order characterized by a mobile labor force, independent smallholders and semiautonomous tenants, and a vast array of modest entrepreneurs. Thus, the majority of their populations neither lay beneath the heel of a traditional manorial order nor was moored to tightly organized peasant communities.

Further, the relatively weak states of the mid-nineteenth century had not been able to establish the tight latticework of social control in these areas, in collaboration with clerics and local bosses, which characterized more settled areas. The expanding government apparatus of the late nineteenth and early twentieth centuries had little, in the way of compliant local elites, on which to build or with which to connect. The modernizing state of that period might thus encounter resistance from a broad range of social classes, all with a vested interest in preventing absorption into a national economy dominated by an export oligarchy and its foreign partners.

Third, the local middle classes in some of these areas had inherited the legacy of mid-nineteenth-century liberalism. The period of intense reformism, between the 1850s and the 1870s, was the heyday of Liberal politicians and publicists in places like Colombia and Mexico, and, to different degrees, elsewhere in the continent. These Liberals consciously sought to dismantle the centralist bureaucracy, ecclesiastical power, and traditional civic culture which Latin America had inherited from the colonial period. In its place, they hoped to implant a social order characterized by a politically independent, educated, and economically self-sufficient yeomanry: the liberal vision of the state was essentially minimalist. In Mexico, the broad social coalition that resisted the French intervention in the 1860s added a strongly nationalist component to the liberal tradition, bequeathing it a heroic quality which informed Mexican civic culture well into the twentieth century.

By the 1880s and 1890s, it was clear, however, that the liberal tradition in Latin America had become bifurcated. Upper-class liberals, fearful of the social unrest that accompanied the midcentury reform projects and hoping to connect their nations to the world economy, cut a deal with the more traditional conservative elites, the Catholic Church, and foreign interests. In doing so, they created an oligarchic variant of liberalism which celebrated free enterprise and utilized the Church and the growing state apparatus to control land and labor. This model provided the underpinnings for Latin America's emergent neocolonial order.

In the provinces, however, and especially in areas where the traditional latifundista elites were less powerful, the "heroic" and popular variants of nineteenth-century liberalism survived. The rural middle classes, with their Masonic lodges and theosophical clubs, nourished a social vision that was deeply antagonistic to the positivism of the national elites. Their Jacobinite liberalism was anticlerical and nationalistic, and emphasized libertarianism, social justice, and the popular will. Most provincial towns had their own printing presses which churned out pamphlets, newspapers, and broadsides. Small-town professionals, modest businessmen, and landowners--though dependent on more powerful regional bosses with national connections, and increasingly subordinated to representatives of the national government-- thus kept alive a volatile mixture of mysticism and egalitarianism. Caught between what they saw as a feudal past and the modernizing present, these provincial petty bourgeois were as much the social dynamite of the early twentieth century as the dispossessed peasantry or the exploited proletarians.[20]

The politics that emerged from this confluence of place and class were extremely complicated. In most cases, the provincial middle classes were inexorably woven into the neocolonial economic and political structure. Individuals may have nursed old grudges against the merchant-landowner elites, but they nonetheless served them well as administrators, magistrates, and publicists. But when the system slid into crisis, these members of the regional petit bourgeoisie often became the core for caudillista politics. They were the intellectuals and organizers in movements as varied as Alvaro Obregón's and Plutarco Elías Calles' warlord bands of northern Mexico; or the veterans of the Colombian War of a Thousand Days, who encouraged the uprising in the late 1920s; or the aprista militants who followed Haya de la Torre.

Inspired by the insurrectionist and military political models of the nineteenth century, most of these movements tended to replicate the very authoritarianism against which they purportedly struggled. The fragile combination of ardent nationalism, idealization of the general will, and personalism which sprang from Latin America's Jacobinite tradition could not go very far in its challenge to the neocolonial order. Nonetheless, there is little question that these ideals were immensely popular among the working poor in town and country; and, in the case of Mexico at least, that they provided much of the ideological underpinnings for the new revolutionary state that emerged in the 1920s.

But these remnants of the nineteenth century's militant, popular liberalism also provided fertile ground for the introduction of radical European ideologies by--and even before--the 1880s. The Flores Magón brothers, with their combination of Mexican liberalism and anarchism, exemplify the process by which European critiques of capitalism and imperialism entered Latin American political discourse.[21] The notion that anarchist, syndicalist, and revolutionary socialist ideas seeped into the region's civic culture primarily through the actions of trans-Atlantic radical journeymen is misleading. Such a view fails to consider the vital oppositional culture sustained among the provincial middle classes and their children in the university and café societies of the large cities. Here these models of social analysis and political change were adopted, and altered, in response to local needs and circumstances.

In the Colombian case, the Liberal towns of Tolima and western Cundinamarca, in the central part of the country, produced the men and women who led the nation's first revolutionary socialist movement in the 1920s. Raúl Eduardo Mahecha, a major organizer of the PSR, moved up and down the Magdalena River with his portable press. He established a proletarian newspaper, Voz Obrera, in the oil town of Barrancabermeja in the mid-1920s, and finally organized the unsuccessful and bloody strike of the banana workers in the Santa Marta region in 1928.[22] These sorts of people, hailing from the provincial middle class, constructed the Latin American solidarity network in the late 1920s and early 1930s which, for example, defended Augusto

César Sandino's contemporary struggle against North American intervention in Nicaragua. With the onset of Depression, some of these people drifted toward the populist coalition that the liberal oligarchs and the new bourgeoisie in Mexico and elsewhere were then creating. But many, including José Carlos Mariátegui in Peru, remained committed to an anticapitalist revolution. They provided the initial foundations for modern Latin American communism.[23] Latin America's revolutionary movements of the second third of the twentieth century should be seen, in large measure, as outgrowths of the militant, Jacobinite liberalism which had been reshaped by new circumstances within the region, as well as by new ideas from abroad.

III

This reconsideration of social movements in the early twentieth century is intended to illuminate some of the new directions in historical inquiry. It also suggests a research agenda that should, in turn, focus on three general areas of investigation and of research resources. The first requirement is a concerted effort to site regional economic and social histories within the broader national framework in Latin America. The impact of the neocolonial order clearly varied within the Latin American countries themselves; and there is a growing realization that the broader analytical frameworks of dependent capitalism must now be tested by solid regional and local histories.[24] This process will require us to rethink the dependency paradigms, and will also enrich our understanding of the ecological, economic, and social complexity of Latin America's encounter with the world economy from the end of the nineteenth century onward.

In this regard, we need a number of sources in order to extend the regional economic and social studies that are already beginning to form the core of a new history. The provincial press should lie at the center of this new effort. The weekly and monthly publications of provincial capitals and smaller towns throughout Latin America are an extraordinarily rich source for historical investigation. Local price quotations for foodstuffs and other commodities can assist economic historians in compiling series to add depth to the otherwise relatively flat, national statistical profiles currently available. These newspapers also afford a much richer sense of the degree to which machinery, fertilizer, and new forms of animal breeding were making their way into the countryside, and of what sort of people played important roles in agricultural improvement.[25] Second, we must reassess our strategies for collecting government documents. We may have reached the point, in our historical inquiries, of exhausting the predominantly national-level materials that are available in the United States. We need a general plan to collect the official publications of regional and perhaps even subregional entities: gubernatorial and prefectural communications to the national authorities, the deliberations of provincial assemblies, and the reports of state and departmental offices charged with such widely varying functions as education, law enforcement, and commerce.[26]

A second issue involves the expansion of state power in the neocolonial period. These were the years in which the modern Latin American armies were created, often under the aegis of foreign advisers. Forces of urban police and rural gendarmes were likewise streamlined and consolidated in order to control increasingly restive populations.[27] Many Latin American governments began to extend their bureaucratic presence into their hinterlands, hoping to intersect with or--if necessary--eliminate local networks of power and authority, many of which had provided the political arena for the provincial middle classes. The encounter between the state governments and their populations has been told largely from the top down. Even those who have written history from below have relied heavily on official sources to reconstruct the lives and social movements of the lower orders. Official documents are indispensable and, sometimes, the only available materials. Nonetheless, our histories of the expanding state will inevitably suffer from imbalance if we depend so heavily on documentation offered up by the state itself. The story will likely be skewed toward a view of state-building as an inexorable historical process, much to the detriment of any understanding of how lower- and middle-class opposition to the central governments altered their new impositions of power and authority from region to region.

Once again, the regional press can provide historians with a local view of the process of state expansion. Used carefully, they should help us understand the nature of local elites, their relations to the state, and their interactions with the middle and lower classes within their districts. Such a portrait will, in turn, facilitate an examination of provincial reactions to national regulations and policies, the linkages between local feuds and conflicts and broader national questions, and the role of national authorities in the small towns of Latin America. A shift in documents collections toward regional materials will allow historians a much more intimate look at these questions. Moreover, official and commercial press materials should be complemented by published and unpublished materials from local political figures and institutions. A systematic effort to gather the biographies, autobiographies, and reminiscences of regional bosses, for instance, would help historians to flesh out the story of caudillismo--a story crucial to this period's transition from weak to strong states.

Finally, the cultural history of the provinces has yet to be written. We have glimpses of a universe frozen in time, a mid-nineteenth-century moment where traditional paternalist social relations stood cheek by jowl with radical freethinking, where local caudillos preached the Rights of Man to their retainers, where townsfolk in dusty little towns around the continent traded in manufactured goods from Manchester and learned their lessons in Lancastrian schools.   Yet these were also places where new ideas, from theosophy to anarchism, found resonance among both the literate and the illiterate, and catalyzed new syntheses in the realms of knowledge, belief, and politics.   In fundamental ways, we have yet to begin to understand the prism through which the rural middle classes experienced the modern world, the context that shaped their responses and their attempts to alter its shape and direction.

Analysis of the regional press can allow students of provincial cultural and political history to reconstruct the intellectual ethos of the small-town middle classes.   These publications will illuminate the kinds of solidarities formed outside of the capital cities: the clubs people joined, the meetings they attended, their diversions and entertainments.   The ubiquitous local printing press also provided a forum for local fiction, poetry, and drama. These works in their aggregate, because of their generally costumbrista content, can help us draw a truer and more complex portrait of early twentieth-century life in the Latin American provinces.   The literary sensibility that was nourished in these places might also give historians deeper insights into the psychological landscape of these small-town universes.   The provinces produced not only military strongmen and radical agitators, both in great numbers, but also such luminaries as Peru's poet laureate César Vallejo, who came from the northern coastal town of Trujillo, and Rubén Darío, whose experiences in the Nicaraguan city of León shaped a verse that dramatically transformed Latin American intellectual life and culture at the turn of the century.

IV

The Sandinista commander Omar Cabezas has written a recently published memoir about growing up to adulthood in small-town Nicaragua in the 1940s and 1950s.[28]   His portrait of petty struggles, exalted visions of a better world, and heroism and banality in the face of dictatorship is in all probability similar to what Latin America's provincial middle classes were experiencing at the turn of the century.   Indeed, much of what is suggested in this essay about research on early twentieth-century social movements, and strategies for collection development, is applicable to current work on contemporary Nicaragua.

The diligent efforts to chronicle and analyze the Nicaraguan Revolution are likely to make it one of the more exhaustively studied social transformations of the late twentieth century.   The wealth of materials on political mobilization and state management, agrarian reform, economic planning and income redistribution, the literacy campaign and revolutionary culture, and the nature and

effects of Nicaragua's militarization in response to outside intervention and internal crisis will surely provide future historians
with a wide array of information.

Yet, bibliographers and students of contemporary Nicaragua
need to extend the boundaries of current research strategies, to
go beyond the shifts and turns of the revolutionary process
today. More concretely, they should also be attempting to ensure
that it will be possible to study the political economy and culture
of Nicaragua in the decades before 1979. The insurrection was
focused in the provincial towns, places like Granada, Masaya,
León, and Estelí. Since many of the revolutionary leaders were
born and raised in those places, the character of those communities over the last half century would seem an important starting
point in studying the origins of modern Nicaragua. The preservation of the revolutionary record is important. But it is also
necessary to reach back and examine the social origins of the men
and women now in command, the children of provincial Liberal
families long opposed to dictatorial rule. Once we understand the
small-town universes in which these people grew up, were educated, and reached adulthood, we may begin to see more clearly
the limits and the possibilities of Latin America's most recent
uprising of the provincial middle classes.[29]

NOTES

1.   For materials on this uprising and the events leading
up to it, see Ignacio Torres Giraldo, Los Inconformes, Vol. III
and IV (Bogotá, 1973-1974), part memoir and part history by a
major Colombian radical organizer and intellectual active in those
years. Also see Julio Cuadros Caldas, Comunismo criollo y
liberalismo autóctono, 2 vols. (Bucaramanga, 1938). A fine
recent history of the uprising in one coffee town in central
Colombia is Gonzalo Sánchez G., Los 'bolcheviques' del Libano
(Tolima) (Bogotá, 1976).
2.   For a succinct analysis of the economic history of this
period, see Jesús A. Bejarano, El regimén agrario de la economía
exportadora a la economía industrial (Bogotá, 1979), Parts 1
and 2.
3.   Aug. 4, 1929, p. 4.
4.   Miguel Urrutía, The Development of the Colombian Labor
Movement (New Haven, CT, 1969), p. 106.
5.   Urrutía (ibid.) has some material on the oil fields and
Caribbean plantations where there was continuing organization
among the lower classes in these years, but there have been few
studies of these export enclaves outside of the various works on
the banana plantation districts on the Caribbean coast. An
original analysis and a good review of the materials on that
region, long dominated by the United Fruit Company, is Catherine

LeGrand, "Colombian Transformations: Peasants, Wage Laborers, and the Santa Marta Banana Zone," Journal of Peasant Studies, 11:4 (July 1984), 178-200. For other materials on the rise of the Colombian wage-labor force and the labor movement in this period, see Daniel Pecaut, Política y sindicalismo en Colombia (Bogotá, 1973), Víctor Manuel Moncayo and Fernando Rojas, Luchas obreras y política laboral en Colombia (Bogotá, 1978), and Edgar Caicedo, Historia de las luchas sindicales en Colombia (Bogotá, 1971).

6. For a sketch of agrarian conflicts in early twentieth-century Colombia, see Pierre Gilholdes, "Agrarian Struggles in Colombia," in Rodolfo Stavenhagen, ed., Agrarian Struggles and Peasant Movements in Latin America (Garden City, NJ, 1970). For an interesting portrait of one Indian leader, in the south-eastern part of the country, who led invasions of great estates in order to recover native lands, see Gustavo Castrillón Arboleda, El Indio Quintim Lamé (Bogotá, 1937). For a provocative and well-documented analysis of the relations among squatters, landlords, and the state in this period, see Catherine LeGrand, "Labor Acquisition and Social Conflict on the Colombian Frontier, 1850-1936," Journal of Latin American Studies, 16 (1984), 27-49.

7. E.g., in both the coffee districts of western Cundina-marca and the altiplano, the departmental authorities waged ongoing warfare with contrabandists in liquor and tobacco closely tied to smallholder communities. For documentation of these state-peasant conflicts before the Great Depression, see the annual reports of the following departmental offices: the Informe del Secretario de gobierno al señor gobernador del departamento and the Informe del Secretario de hacienda al señor gobernador de Cundinamarca.

8. Urrutía, Colombian Labor Movement (chap. 4), has interesting materials on the rise of craft unionism in these years.

9. Charles W. Bergquist, Coffee and Conflict in Colombia, 1886-1910 (Durham, NC, 1978), chaps. 9 and 10.

10. Gerardo Molina, Las idea liberales en Colombia, 1915-1934 (Bogotá, 1974).

11. For an excellent review of the emergence of economic history, see the introduction in Robert Cortés Condes and Stanley J. Stein, eds., Latin America: A Guide to Economic History, 1830-1930 (Berkeley, CA, 1977) and bibliographical essays on selected countries by major scholars in the field. Fine examples of the thrust of this approach are the various papers collected in Kenneth Duncan and Ian Rutledge, eds., Land and Labour in Latin America: Essays on the Development of Agrarian Capitalism in the Nineteenth and Twentieth Centuries (Cambridge, 1977).

12. There is, of course, John Womack, Jr.'s classic study of the agrarian rebellions in Morelos, Zapata and the Mexican Revolution (New York, NY, 1968). This landmark work was followed, particularly for Mexico, by a vast number of studies of

rural movements in the first three decades of this century, including Heather Fowler Salamini, Agrarian Radicalism in Veracruz, 1920- 1938 (Lincoln, NE, 1978). There is no general survey of agrarian movements on the order of Hobart Spalding's sweeping, if flawed, study of the urban working classes in the region from the late nineteenth century onward, Organized Labor in Latin America (New York, NY, 1977). There is an emerging labor history, exemplified by John M. Hart's excellent study of Mexican anarchists, Anarchism and the Mexican Working Class, 1860-1931 (Austin, TX, 1978), and, more recently, Peter DeShazo, Urban Workers and Labor Unions in Chile, 1902-1927 (Madison, WI, 1983).

13. For a sense of the major issues evolving in the field of Latin American labor history, see Thomas E. Skidmore, "Workers and Soldiers: Urban Labor Movements and Elite Responses in Twentieth Century Latin America," in Virginia Bernhard, ed., Elites, Masses, and Modernization in Latin America, 1850-1950 (Austin, TX, 1979), pp. 79-126; a review of the recent litera-ture, including the Spalding book, by Eugene Sofer, "Recent Trends in Latin American Labor Historiography," Latin American Research Review, 15:1 (1980), 167-176, followed with a rejoinder by Spalding, Kenneth Paul Erickson, and Patrick V. Peppe in the same issue, "Dependency versus Working Class History: A False Contradiction," pp. 177-181. Charles Bergquist makes a valiant effort to pull together the various approaches to labor history in his essay "What Is Being Done? Some Recent Studies on the Urban Working Class and Organized Labor in Latin America," Latin American Research Review, 16:2 (1981), 203-223.

14. For some interesting theorizing on this question, see Oscar Oszlack, "The Historical Formation of the State in Latin America: Some Theoretical and Methodological Guidelines for Its Study," Latin American Research Review, 16:2 (1981), 3-32. For a more historical approach, see Lorenzo Meyer, "Historical Roots of the Authoritarian State in Mexico," in José Luis Reyna and Richard S. Weinert, eds., Authoritarian Mexico (Philadelphia, PA, 1977).

15. Some of the best examples of these new approaches are in Thomas Benjamin and William McNellie, eds., Other Mexicos: Essays on Mexican Regional History, 1876-1911 (Albuquerque, NM, 1984), D. A. Brading, ed., Caudillo and Peasant in the Mexican Revolution (Cambridge, 1980), and an excellent, full-length study by Gil Joseph, Revolution from Without: Yucatan, Mexico, and the United States, 1880-1924 (Cambridge, 1982).

16. "The Relevant Tradition: Sonoran Leaders in the Revolution," in Brading, Caudillo and Peasant . . ., p. 123.

17. It should be noted that these observations, focused on Mexico, Colombia, and Peru, are applicable to greater or lesser degrees in other countries in the region. Obviously, the economic structures, social relations, and political traditions

varied from country to country; for example, in Argentina, Brazil, and to lesser extent Chile, the large-scale immigration of southern Europeans at the turn of the century provided different ingredients for the emergence of working-class culture and politics than in other parts of Latin America where the numbers of foreign laborers were fewer and their contributions to the institutions of laboring people less important.

18. See Friedrich Katz, The Secret War in Mexico: Europe, the United States, and the Mexican Revolution (Chicago, IL, 1981), chap. 1, "Origins, Outbreak, and Initial Phase of the Mexican Revolution."

19. See Peter Klaren, Modernization, Dislocation, and Aprismo: Origins of the Peruvian Aprista Party, 1870-1932 (Austin, TX, 1973).

20. For a compelling portrait of the social and intellectual life of the small-town urban middle classes in Colombia, where the radical temperament of the teens and 1920s germinated, see Ignacio Torres Giraldo's powerful biography of the feminist, labor union organizer, and socialist agitator, María Cano. Mujer rebelde (Bogotá, 1972).

21. See Hart, Anarchism and the Mexican Working Class, and James D. Cockcroft, The Intellectual Precursors of the Mexican Revolution, 1900-1913 (Austin, TX, 1968).

22. Torres Giraldo, Los inconformes, Vol. III, chap. 3, and Vol. IV, chap. 1.

23. See Jesus Chavarría, José Carlos Mariáteguí and the Rise of Modern Peru, 1890-1930 (Albuquerque, NM, 1979).

24. For some important formulations on the problems of regional history in Latin America, see Joseph L. Love, "An Approach to Regionalism," in Richard Graham and Peter H. Smith, eds., New Approaches to Latin American History (Austin, TX, 1974), pp. 137-155.

25. For the Colombian case, a cursory comparison of Antonio Cacua Prada, Historia del periodismo colombiano (Bogotá, 1968) and Steven M. Charno, Latin American Newspapers in United States Libraries: A Union List (Austin, TX, 1968), and a later update by Laura Gutíerrez, "Newspaper Titles from Colombia, Ecuador, and Venezuela Unavailable in United States Libararies," XVIII SALALM Working Papers (April, 1973), indicates that the collections of mid-nineteenth-century provincial papers are quite good, but that from the 1880s onward the publications in the capital and in a handful of each country's larger cities tend to dominate. There are virtually no sources in the United States for researchers seeking to examine periodicals from the score of larger towns in the central Colombian region, such as Girardot and Ibague, where there was an active rural middle class.

26. In the first decades of the century, before the contemporary governmental apparatus was set in place throughout much of the region, there were various efforts to establish offices and subministries dealing with the so-called social question. Since these entities were not long lived, it would be important to undertake a study of government publications in this transitional period in order to discover the lacunae in current holdings. One such entity, in the Colombian case, was the National Labor Office, which existed between the mid-1920s and early 1930s as an agency of the Ministry of Industries and which published extensive reports on labor conditions in its Boletín de la Oficina Nacional del Trabajo.

27. For an example, see Paul J. Vanderwood, Disorder and Progress: Bandits, Police, and Mexican Development (Lincoln, NE, 1981).

28. Omar Cabezas, La montaña es algo más que una inmensa estepa verde (Managua, 1982), translated into English by Kathleen Weaver, and introduced by Carlos Fuentes, as Fire from the Mountain (Avenel, NJ, 1985).

29. The two principal studies of contemporary Nicaragua which have any pretense at historical background neglect to analyze the social origins and background of the middle-class leadership of the Nicaraguan Revolution: Richard Millet, Guardians of the Dynasty (Maryknoll, NY, 1977), and George Black, Triumph of the People: The Sandinista Revolution in Nicaragua (London, 1981).

9. RECONSTRUCTING THE JEWISH PAST IN LATIN AMERICA

Judith Laikin Elkin

The threshold problem in reconstructing the Jewish past in Latin America is that of defining who is a Jew. A clear enough definition exists in Jewish law, but in practice the matter is far more complicated. Some persons who fall outside the legal definition identify as Jews, while others who meet the technical requirements of Jewish law choose not to so identify themselves. This is particularly true in Latin America, where historically there has been tremendous pressure on Jews to abandon their religious and ethnic identity.

The high rate of assimilation prevailing among Latin American Jews further impedes the process of identifying the subject population, since those who are blending into the majority society have no desire to preserve records of their past as members of a deprecated minority. Depreciated status springs from the antique Spanish concept of limpieza de sangre, according to which only those of verifiable Christian descent can meet the standard of purity set for holding office in government, the church, and the military. Far from being a dead letter, limpieza de sangre continues to function today in many Latin American countries as a form of triage, barring entry of persons of Jewish descent into central institutions of society. The Argentine officer corps may be cited as the outstanding example. The question then arises: if Brazil and Chile have the only armed forces that commission Jews as officers, is this fact relevant to Jewish history, to Latin American history, or to both?

From the point of view of individual Jews, most actions of daily life are taken without regard to the circumstance of having been born a Jew. Thus, there is no certain method of determining the role of "the Jews" in any particular sector of national life. For example, it would appear from preliminary research that individual Jews, and enterprises founded by Jews, played a substantial role in the development of import substitution industries. But there is no way of breaking out of national statistics the precise amount of capital or entrepreneurial initiative that was contributed by Jews, since they made this effort as businessmen and as Brazilians (or Mexicans or Bolivians), not as Jews. Furthermore, when a person engages in business, or any other daily activity, without reference to her/his origins, is it ethical for the historian to attempt to trace those origins, possibly against the desire of this individual to be so identified?

There have been a handful of individuals in public life in Latin America of known Jewish origin: Perön's minister of finance, for example, and the chair of Mexico's development corporation. It would be possible to write a sort of contribution history based on their several careers but, to my knowledge, this has not been attempted. Perhaps the peripheral Jewish involvement of these individuals has failed to bring them to the attention of Jewish historians, while their exceptionality within their national contexts has limited the interest of Latin Americanists. Perhaps this interest should be aroused: is there not a fecund field of research on the question of why Latin American societies do not make fuller use of the energies, experience, and talent of their Jewish citizens, who are, literally, the cousins of those Jews who contribute so much to public life in the United States?

The problematic nature of these topics and the difficulty of documenting their study have led to the concentration of almost all efforts at writing the history of Latin America's Jews on the organized communities. This approach entails some immediate advantages. In the first place, the communities group identifiable individuals together; and communities are more likely than individuals to keep records of their activities. The disadvantages to such studies are that they may concentrate on structure to the neglect of human interaction, resulting in the creation of peculiarly flat chronicles that are tedious in the extreme. That the record can be brought to life by a skilled historian has been demonstrated by Eugene Sofer's excellent study of the Ashkenazic Jews of Buenos Aires, a study based on records of the Asociaciön Mutual Israelita Argentina.[1]

On the one hand, the clearly identifiable nature of Jewish institutions renders them more accessible to research, and also provides the opportunity to explore the marginalization of this minority group. On the other, study of the unaffiliated affords the opportunity to assess the degree to which societal demands for assimilation have been reinforced or rebuffed by social barriers to persons of Jewish descent.

Another problematic area in the study of Latin American Jewry is periodization. There was, for all intents and purposes, no colonial period, since Jews and their descendants were prohibited by both Spain and Portugal from emigrating to their Americas. This has not prevented a considerable number of historians, philo-Semites, and anti-Semites from writing about them. An unknown number of secret Jews or Jewish converts did migrate to the Indies, settling into the same occupations they had followed in the mother country. What we know of their presence is derived from records of the Inquisition, a situation that might be likened to studying Communism through the records of the Moscow trials.

The necessarily covert nature of the Jewish presence in the New World, combined with the diabolic nature attributed to Jews by sixteenth- and seventeenth-century missionaries, led to the creation of a substantial number of myths concerning their mysterious powers. These were allegedly employed in engendering treasonous plots and causing crucifixes to bleed. Demythologizing the Jewish presence in colonial Ibero-America would seem a political necessity before the present-day Jewish communities can be accepted on a level of equality. This is particularly true for Indo-America, but the task has scarcely begun. Anita Novinsky has done yeoman work on the early history of Jews in Brazil,[2] as has Gunter Bohm for Chile and Peru.[3] Seymour Liebman's approach to Mexican history is a good deal more problematic.[4] No comprehensive bibliography of works for this period has been compiled, but attention may be drawn to Jacob Rader Marcus's effort, which was peripheral to his study of Jews in the North American colonies.[5]

The national period, though it finds more actual Jews in Latin America, attracted far less scholarly attention until recently. The reasons for this no doubt include the small size of the population (possibly three-quarters of a million scattered from the Rio Grande to Tierra del Fuego) and its fragmentation among so great a number of national sovereignties. At the same time, the Jewish communities themselves, made wary by the suppression of Judaism and Jews in the past, tend to keep a low profile. They are not always hospitable to researchers, fearing (with some grounds) that any information derived from the community could be turned against them. The saga of the Argentine Jewish agricultural colonies provides one instructive example. Founded in the nineteenth century and subsequently the pride of Argentine Jews, who believed they were rooting themselves in the country at the most basic level, Jewish-owned farms became the basis in the 1960s for the charge that "the Jews" were conspiring to detach a part of the country and hand it over to the State of Israel. Self-defense has had to be the primary concern for Jews in Latin America; consequently, there is a fear of divulging information, however harmless it may appear. Researchers need to approach the communities with tact and with substantial credentials as personas de confianza.

Language offers another barrier to the study of these communities. Many early records were kept in Yiddish or Judezmo (both in Hebrew script), not languages widely disseminated among Latin Americanists. Second- and third-generation immigrants converted quite rapidly to Spanish or Portuguese, so that language is now less a barrier than before. But an additional linguistic complication was introduced after 1948, when Israeli researchers who turned their attention to Latin America began publishing their findings in Hebrew.

What are the primary sources for studying Latin American Jewry? In most cases, the national census has not been a useful tool. Reflecting the ideal of religious toleration, and also reflecting to a considerable extent the invisibility of non-Catholics generally, most censuses, most of the time, do not record the respondent's religion. Where this question has been asked, it has been subject to much distortion. For example, while the 1950 Mexican national census recorded 17,574 Jews in that country, the 1960 census recorded 100,750 (this, without any interim Jewish immigration). Demographers analyzing the results encountered returns listed as Jewish in which the family was engaged in agriculture, had ten or more children, and was descalzado-- parameters not hitherto known to define Jews. The same demographers, U. O. Schmelz and Sergio della Pergola of Hebrew University, had greater success in breaking out presumed Jewish responses from the Argentine national census of 1960. As a result of their work, they have become the only reliable source of demographic information on Latin American Jews.[6] Several partial community censuses have been carried out, but these are rendered problematic by the variety of methodologies employed; by the resistance of many individuals to being identified officially as Jews; and by political conditions in society at large, which are not always conducive to surveys.

Communal records remain the principal sources of data. Synagogues, benevolent associations, cemeteries, libraries, sports clubs, schools, credit cooperatives, and commercial associations all generate records. Some maintain archives. However, since these are not always kept under optimal conditions, the history of the Latin American Jewish communities is disappearing at a faster rate than the communities themselves. This neglect of history can be accounted for by a concatenation of mutually reinforcing factors: the commercial nature of the communities, with their concomitant disinterest in scholarship; the resort to secrecy in the face of frequent changes in government, any one of which might prove hostile to Jews or to entrepreneurship; and the high rate of assimilation among Jewish intellectuals, which leaves the organized communities without strong motivation to preserve their history. The problems here may be summarized as disinterest, dispersal, defensiveness, and disintegration.

Faculty and graduate students of the Institute of Contempo- rary Jewry of Hebrew University, in the spirit of the ingathering of the exiles, have taken on themselves the task of collecting the archives of Latin America's Jewish communities and transferring them to Jerusalem. The scholar should therefore be aware that research into any of these communities may require stays on more than one continent.

The American Jewish Archives in Cincinnati has a program to microfilm archives, leaving the original documents in place. But the holdings of the major repositories in this country (the American Jewish Appeal, American Jewish Historical Society, and Harvard University), may by now be outweighed by the largely uncataloged holdings at Hebrew University. The best solution would be an educational program in archival preservation aimed at the communities themselves, but here the attitudes already discussed would no doubt intervene.

Oral interviews are coming more and more to supplement the written record. Here, the lead has been taken by the Center for Oral Documentation at the Hebrew University. Extensive records of interviews taken in Israel and abroad are available on microfilm through the New York Times. Oral history projects have also been undertaken by Robert Levine of the University of Miami at Coral Gables and by Samuel Proctor of the University of Florida at Gainesville.

Only partial collections of Latin American Jewish periodicals are available in this country. A preliminary survey of U.S. collections of periodical, monograph, and archival material undertaken by Richard Woods found the most extensive collections of periodicals at YIVO Institute for Jewish Research, the New York Public Library, American Jewish Historical Society, and Harvard University.[7]

Martin Sable undertook to compile a universal polyglot bibliography in his Latin American Jewry: A Research Guide.[8] Although some of these periodicals were published for sixty years or more, none was ever indexed by the Pan-American Union. Most perished before they could be picked up by HAPI. A union list of serial publications in Latin American Jewish Studies (SPLAJS!) is a project presently being designed by members of the Latin American Jewish Studies Association.

Until the mid-1930s, almost all Latin American Jewish periodicals were published in Yiddish, Judezmo, or the language of the immigrants' country of origin, particularly German. Today, almost all are published in Spanish or Portuguese. Perhaps the most interesting aspect here is that, in accurate reflection of the circumscribed influence of Jews in Latin American life, no Jewish-oriented periodical of the salience of Commentary has yet emerged on that continent.

Only one comprehensive history of the national period has been published.[9] A recent article of mine summarizes the state of current research and provides citations to relevant works, many of which were published after the completion of Sable's Guide.[10] There are excellent studies of some few contemporary communities (the City of São Paulo,[11] Costa Rica,[12] Paraguay[13]), but research on other communities is either partial, in progress, or filiopietistic. Certain subjects have generated a great deal of literature of varying quality: immigration, education, and the agricultural colonies. Acquisition and retrieval of the finished works present special problems. With the exception of a few monographs published by known commercial or university presses, most research results are available only as articles in periodicals that might not be regularly consulted by Latin Americanists, such as Jewish Social Studies (United States), Forum (Israel), and

Controversía de ideas sionistas (Argentina). The most reliable
access to these is through the annual bibliographic publication of
the Jewish National and University Library in Jerusalem.[14]

Resources for Latin American Jewish Studies (Latin American
Jewish Studies Association Publication 1) offers four useful essays
geared to the American scholar new to the field. In addition, the
Latin American Jewish Studies Newsletter publishes current
bibliography twice yearly.[15]

There are problems and challenges associated with research
into the Latin American Jewish experience, but the results are
rewarding. Increasing our knowledge of the Jewish diaspora
enhances our understanding of Latin American societies. In
addition to the intrinsic interest of these communities, their
marginalized status reveals a great deal about the host
societies.[16]

A literature sufficient to integrate the Jewish experience into
Latin American studies now exists, and it may be argued that a
course that omits this ethnic group is not complete. Problems of
bibliographic control, including proper indexing for ease of
retrieval, remain--but these are subjects for another day.
Meanwhile, the bibliographic tools are available to enrich Latin
American studies and to open new avenues of exploration.

NOTES

1. Eugene Sofer, From Pale to Pampa: The Jewish
Immigrant Experience in Buenos Aires (New York, NY: Holmes
and Meier, 1982).

2. Anita Novinsky, Cristãos novos na Bahia (São Paulo:
Editora Perspectiva, 1972).

3. Gunter Bohm, "Judíos en Chile durante el siglo XIX,"
in Comité Judío Americano, Comunidades judías de Latinoamérica,
(Buenos Aires, 1966) pp. 196-208; idem, Judíos en el Perú
durante el siglo XIX (Santiago: Editorial Universitaria, 1984).

4. See, inter alia, Seymour B. Liebman, The Jews in New
Spain: Faith, Flame, and the Inquisition (Coral Gables, FL:
University of Miami Press, 1970).

5. Jacob Rader Marcus, The Colonial American Jews,
1492-1776 (Detroit, MI: Wayne State University Press, 1970).

6. U. O. Schmelz and Sergio della Pergola, "The
Demography of Latin American Jewry," in American Jewish Year
Book 1985 (New York, NY: American Jewish Committee, 1985).

7. Richard D. Woods and Arnona Rudavsky, "United States
Library Collections on Latin American Jews," in Resources for
Latin American Jewish Studies, LAJSA Publications 1 (Ann Arbor,
MI, 1984).

8. Cincinnati: Hebrew Union College Press, 1978.

9. Judith Laikin Elkin, Jews of the Latin American Republics (Chapel Hill, NC: University of North Carolina Press, 1980).

10. "Latin America's Jews: A Review of Sources," LARR, 20:2 (May, 1985), 124-141.

11. Henrique Rattner, Tradição e mundança: A comunidade judaica em São Paulo (São Paulo: Atica, 1970).

12. Jacobo Schifter Sikora, Lowell Gudmundson, and Mario Solera Castro, El judío en Costa Rica (San José: Editorial Universidad Estatal a Distancia, 1979).

13. Alfredo M. Seiferheld, Inmigración y presencia judías en el Paraguay, vol. 1 (Asunción: Revista de la Universidad Católica, 1981).

14. Reshimaat Maamarim indexes, in the language of publication, articles about Jews appearing worldwide.

15. Judith Laikin Elkin, ed., Resources for Latin American Jewish Studies, LAJSA Publication 1 (Ann Arbor, MI, 1984). In addition to Woods and Rudavshy, in n. 7, above, essays include Arnona Rudavsky, "Using Jewish Reference Sources for the Study of Latin American Jewry"; Thomas Niehaus and María Hernández-Lehmann, "United States Archival Resources for the Study of Jews in Latin America"; and Robert M. Levine, "Disappearing Memories: The Loss of Jewish Records in Latin America." The LAJS Newsletter is published twice annually from 2104 Georgetown Blvd., Ann Arbor, MI 48105.

16. In recognition of the relevance of the Jewish dimension to Latin American studies generally, in March, 1984, the Latin American Institute of the University of New Mexico cosponsored, together with LAJSA, a research conference on the Jewish experience in Latin America. Proceedings of this conference are being edited for publication by Gilbert Merkx and Judith Elkin.

10. CUBA: REALITIES OF A HIDDEN SEGMENT--
"PLANTADO" POLITICAL PRISONERS
IN BONIATO PRISON

Luisa Pérez and Lesbia Orta Varona

Introduction

On Saturday, June 30, 1984, The Miami Herald dedicated a three-page report to the arrival in Miami of twenty prisoners who were brought out of Cuba by Democratic presidential candidate Jesse Jackson.

Some Cuban plantado political prisoners included in that group told the story of their release:

> At 4 p.m. Wednesday, four Cuban police officials in plainclothes stood at a narrow hall in Boniatico, a windowless jailhouse within the high security Boniato Prison. They called out eleven names. . . . At a state security facility in the city of Santiago de Cuba, two were returned to Boniato without an explanation, including Orlando Santos Mirabal, a 30-year-old who has reportedly been in jail since he was about 10 years old.

This study has determined that there are still at least sixty-eight plantados being held in Boniato Prison. Deprived of all visitors since March 1981, no one from the world outside Cuban jails, not even their closest relatives, has seen them. Since they are kept in punishment cells, with just a small opening for food, they hardly see each other. Starting in October 1984, a few official letters written by them have reached relatives outside.

These long-term political prisoners, most of them now incarcerated for more than twenty years, represent the entire spectrum of political trends: from Batista supporters to a commander of the revolutionary army and member of a traditionally socialist family in Spain. They all have been mistreated, regardless of religious or political beliefs, race, or social origin.

Ten previously resentenced prisoners from this group, freed in 1983 and 1984 (for different reasons but including international pressure on their behalf), have served as primary sources of information for this study. Their testimonies were obtained through personal interviews carried out by means of a written

Author's Note. The Project Staff: Luisa Pérez, Project Director; Lesbia O. Varona, Assistant Project Director; Online Researchers, Phyllis Levy, Lyn McCorkle; Assistant Researchers, Rosa Abella, Rosa Mesa, Elena V. Peraza, Sara M. Sánchez.

questionnaire (Appendix A). The interviews were conducted in January, February, and March 1985. Relatives of the remaining plantados still in Boniato have provided additional information and helped to collect and document the data.

All findings in this report are corroborated by at least two witnesses who are identified and quoted verbatim.

Appended to this report is a bibliography (Appendix C) listing books that contain poems, short stories, narratives, and letters smuggled out of Cuban prisons and published abroad with the author-prisoner still in a maximum-security jail in Cuba.

This report acquaints individuals and organizations interested in defending the dignity of the human being and ending the practice of torture with some background on the state of human rights in Cuban prisons. These are fundamental issues that affect the lives of all human beings and, as such, are not inappropriate for presentation and discussion at a meeting of librarians who have a tradition of concern for freedom of expression. Censorship and other curbs on freedom of expression, including imprisonment, are diametrically opposed to the goals and ideals of professional librarians and free persons throughout the world.

Part I. Boniato Prison

Chronology of Major Events Since 1979

1979   July 26: From 100 to 115 political prisoners were transferred from Habana del Este Prison or Combinado del Este to Boniato Prison.

1980   November: (1) Search with violence; (2) metal plates welded to doors of cells; (3) imposed hunger strike for 33 days.

1981   March to present: Plantado political prisoners deprived of visitors.

1982   October 10: Hunger strike in protest against continued detention of prisoners after their sentences had expired.

1984   January 9: Use of loudspeakers for mental torture.

January 10: Search with violence; as a result, for 72 days prisoners had to eat with their fingers and were left without shoes.

June 27: Nine resentenced prisoners were released and left Cuba with the Democratic presidential candidate Jesse Jackson.

Witnesses: Identification

Ten plantado political prisoners, released from Boniato Prison during 1983 and 1984, were interviewed by means of a

Ten Former Cuban Plantado Political Prisoners Interviewed

Names	Age	Civil status	Children	Trial #	Education	Occupation/Profession	Length of sentence	Sentence served	Released from	Date of release	Reason for release	Place of birth
Defana, Angel	46	Married	1	458-1962	Secondary 3 years	Manager-shoe store	20 years	20 years 7 months	Boniato	4/6/83	Hunger strike	La Habana/La Habana
Gonzalez Rodriguez, Pedro A.	43	Divorced	no	293-1962	Secondary 2 years	Photographer	20 years	21 years	Boniato	3/14/83	Hunger strike	La Habana/La Habana
Infante Jiménez, Servando	44	Married	1	46-1965	5th grade	Milkman	12 years	18 years 5 months	Boniato	5/11/83	Hunger strike	Madruga/La Habana (Rural)
Martinez Pérez, Gerardo	59	Married	no	429-1963	8th grade	Photographer/Waiter	20 years	22 years	Boniato	6/28/84	Jackson's visit	La Habana/La Habana
Martinez Roque, Wilfredo	38	Single	no	470-1968		Military service	15 years	17 years	Boniato	6/27/84	Jackson's visit	Mantua/Pinar del Río
Mesa Schuman, Esturnio	52			53-1964	4th grade	Farmer	20 years	20 years 5 months 10 days	Boniato	6/28/84	Jackson's visit	Guantánamo/Oriente (Rural)
Ramos González Justino R.	48	Married	no	87-1963	4th grade	Farmer	20 years	21 years 3 months	Boniato	6/28/84	Jackson's visit	San Cristóbal Pinar del Río (Rural)
Rodriguez Pérez, Nelson Eduardo	52	Divorced	5	395-1964	8th grade	Construction worker	18 years	18 years 9 months	Boniato	2/83	Hunger strike	Jatibonico/Camagüey
Valls Arango, Jorge Manuel	52	Married	no	259-1964	University 3 years	Student/Writer	20 years	20 years 40 days	Boniato	6/21/84	International pressure	Marianao/La Habana
Yong Martinez, Armando	43	Married	no	21-1962	5th grade		20 years	22 years 7 months	Boniato	6/27/84	Jackson's visit	Guines/La Habana

questionnaire (see Appendix A). As shown in the table, all of them were kept in prison after the completion of their sentences. Their names are well established in the literature issued by human rights organizations, and in newspaper and magazine articles reporting their release (see Note on Sources). As of this writing, they are the latest witnesses to the situation of the group of plantado political prisoners in Boniato, a group deprived of visitors since March 1981.

Cuban Plantado Political Prisoners: Identification

According to the statements of ten former political prisoners interviewed for this report, there are 136 long-term plantado political prisoners in Cuba. They are located as follows: 61 in Combinado del Este Prison, in Havana Province; 7 in Kilo Siete Prison, in Camagüey Province; and 68 in Boniato Prison, in Oriente Province (see Appendix B).

Boniato Prison: Location and Description

Location--Boniato Prison is located in the eastern province of Cuba, on the outskirts of Santiago de Cuba City. The prison is in a valley called Puerto Boniato, surrounded by the Sierra Maestra Mountain range. Santiago de Cuba City is 1,000 kilometers from Havana.

Description--Boniato Prison is a complex of buildings connected by corridors and surrounded by walls and barbed-wire fences with watchtowers. The buildings include: headquarters, hospital, kitchen, five two-story buildings for prisoners, some small auxiliary structures, workshops for forced labor (for common prisoners and rehabilitated political prisoners), and the firing-squad wall. Each of the five buildings for prisoners has two wings with two floors named A-C and B-D. Plantado political prisoners are in building 2, wing A-C, called Boniatico by prison authorities. Trained dogs are kept between two barbed-wire fences surrounding Boniato Prison.

On the outside, wing 2A-C has been isolated from the rest of the edifices by a wall surrounding its small patio. The wall is as high as the roof of the building, 8 or 9 meters high. A wire netting extends from the top of the wall to the roof.

On the inside of wing 2A-C (Boniatico) there are 40 cells on each floor. They are 1.5 meters wide by 2.5 meters long. All the cells are tapiadas--cells with metal plates (tolas) on the doors and windows, which allow no light to come through. Sanitary facilities consist of a hole in the floor. There is a faucet on the wall above the hole in the floor. The water is monitored by prison authorities and is turned on three times a day; five minutes in the morning, five minutes at noon, and five minutes in the evening.

Part II.   Statements of Witnesses

Boniato Prison

Mi nombre es Gerardo Martínez Pérez, ex-prisionero político cubano. El 28 de junio de 1984, fui sacado de un calabozo tapiado en la Prisión de Boniato, en calzoncillos y sin zapatos; conducido al Departamento de Seguridad del Estado de Santiago de Cuba, donde se me suministró un pantalón, una camisa y un par de zapatos, a mí y a ocho compañeros más que sacaron junto conmigo. Nos montaron en un avión militar y nos trasladaron para La Habana, donde a las cinco y media de la mañana junto con otros 15 compañeros del Combinado del Este y 2 del Kilo Siete en Camagüey, nos informaron que nos íbamos para los Estados Unidos. Al protestar y alegar que hacía 5 años que no veíamos a nuestros familiares por el estado de incomunicación en que se nos mantenía, ellos nos respondieron que no podíamos quedarnos en Cuba, que teníamos que salir del país. Despueś de 5 años incomunicados, sin asistencia médica, sin visita, sin paquetes, sin recibir el sol y el aire que a todo ser humano pertenece, y encerrado durante las 24 horas del día en calabozos tapiados con olor a excremento y a orines de uno mismo, nos sacaron de la prisión y nos mandaron para los Estados Unidos.

Esta Prisión de Boniato es la más siniestra que existe en Cuba. Allí nosotros oíamos con frecuencia descargas cerradas de fusilamiento, gritos y otras cosas. Nos encontrábamos en un pabellón completamente aislado del resto de la población penal y todo contacto con ser humano. Rodeados por muros que alcanzan 8 metros de altura, y atendidos única y exclusivamente por miembros de la seguridad cubana y la contra-inteligencia de Cuba. Esa es la situación de los presos políticos de Boniato que hasta la fecha, que yo tenga conocimiento, no ha mejorado absolutamente en nada.

Gerardo Martínez Pérez
Interview: January 10, 1985

Mi nombre es Armando Yong, soy un ex-preso político cubano que fuí puesto en libertad con la visita de Jesse Jackson a Cuba. Mi situación fue que yo había cumplido mi condena de 20 años y tuve que estar 3 años más. La situación allí en Boniato es difícil, tapiado, prácticamente hacinado pudiéramos decir, sin visión exterior y la presión psicológica y de maltrato por parte de la dirección penal allí hacia nosotros es diaria, es contínua. Es impresionante estar allí entre rejas, y más que entre rejas entre paredes, y más que entre paredes entre muros, sin ventanas, sin luz, sin ningún tipo de contacto con la civilización exterior. Allí la asistencia médica es bastante, qué pudiéramos decir, no aceptable para un ser humano. Los compañeros que dejé detrás, llevan veintipico de años presos. Algunos veintipico, otros un poquito menos, pero casi todos están en una medida superior de veinte años.

Armando Yong Martínez
Interview: March 7, 1985

Search: November, 1980

Mi nombre es Servando Infante. Estuve preso en las cárceles de Cuba durante 18 años y 5 meses. Salí el 11 de mayo de 1983 de la Prisión de Boniato. En noviembre de 1980, hicieron una requisa muy fuerte y además de llevarse las cuchillas, se llevaron las tijeras. Nos tenían aparte en un saloncito del ala del pabellón en que estábamos, empezaron a sacar a los presos que allí nos encontrábamos al salón del centro del pasillo, donde habían barberos de los presos comunes. Cuando sacaron a los primeros 5, lleno de guarnición todo aquello, armados de cabillas y tubos, estos presos que salieron allí, se negaron a pelarse con los comunes, dado que siempre nosotros habíamos puesto como condición de que nosotros nos pelábamos nosotros mismos y que no queríamos estar ligados a los comunes, por ciertas normas que teníamos nosotros de diferenciar el presidio político. Esta negación tuvo como resultado de que le fue dada una paliza tremenda a estos presos que se negaron a pelarse con los comunes.

Cuando esto ocurría, de que le estaban dando golpes a estos presos, uno de ellos que fue brutalmente golpeado fue Luis Zúñiga, Roger Reyes y otro más. Los compañeros que quedaban encerrados en el salón, que era un antiguo comedorcito que había allí, empezaron a gritar y a tratar de romper la reja para ir a defender a sus compañeros que estaban brutalmente golpeados por más de 50 o 60 guardias con cabillas y tubos de metal. Se formó un escándalo grande allí y alteración de los ánimos de todos los compañeros que allí estaban y el director del penal vino y entonces acordó que estaba bien, que si estábamos en disposición de afeitarnos y pelarnos, pero pelarnos todos y afeitarnos, pues que se entregaban las tijeras y las cuchillas y

seguía la cosa como antes había sucedido, que nosotros
siempre nos habíamos afeitado y nos habíamos pelado.
Entonces así fue, y comenzamos de nuevo a pelarnos
nosotros mismos entre nosotros mismos.

Y esto fue ya la antesala de la huelga de los
33 días que fue impuesta por ellos mismos hacia
nosotros, que ya sería otro relato.

Servando Infante Jiménez
Interview: February 6, 1985

Imposed Hunger Strike: November, 1980

Se nos practicó una requisa violenta en que se
nos destruyeron pertenencias y se usó violencia.
Rechazamos los alimentos unas horas para atraer la
atención de autoridad superior y buscar conversación.
Vinieron y declararon que estábamos en huelga de
hambre. Así se nos tuvo por 32 días. Al fin de este
tiempo las autoridades prometieron reponernos en las
condiciones originales (celdas abiertas, patio, visita).
Pocos días después se nos practicó otra requisa más
violenta aún y se nos encerró en las tapiadas. Cuando
se les hizo saber la contradicción con lo prometido y
acordado y la falta de justificación de tal actitud la
respuesta fue: "Lo prometemos pero no lo cumplimos.
Te lo damos y te lo quitamos."

Jorge Valls Arango
Interview: March 10, 1985

Search and Imposed Hunger Strike: November, 1980

Mi nombre es Nelson Eduardo Rodríguez Pérez.
Estuve en las prisiones de Cuba 18 años y 9 meses.
Salí en libertad en 21 de febrero de 1983. En
noviembre del año 80 nos sacaron de las celdas donde
estábamos y nos hicieron una requisa donde nos botaron
todas las pocas pertenencias que teníamos, ya que lo
único que vestíamos eran calzoncillos, porque estábamos
sin ropa. Después, frente a nuestras celdas en un
mismo pabellón, había como especie de otra galera donde
tenían los homosexuales y los locos. Allí se nos fue
llevando uno por uno, y encerrándosenos en las mismas
celdas en que habían estado los homosexuales y los
locos como antes dije. Esas celdas estaban llenas de
excremento, llenas de infinidades de cosas, que es
hasta bochornoso decirlo. Según nos iban encerrando
en las celdas, le ponían una plancha de acero a la reja,

e iban encerrando al personal uno por uno hasta que nos encerraron a todos allí.

Se nos llevó allí para someternos a una prueba más. Fue una huelga de hambre que fue impuesta por el Penal de Boniato, por los dirigentes de ese penal. Allí estuvimos en huelga 27 días unos, otros estuvieron 31. Los enfermos fueron llevados al hospital, cuando ya no podían más y allí los amarraban, les ponían un suero y los rechazaban otra vez hasta que a los 31 días, un sargento que era jefe de orden interior, un buen sargento, que después estaba preso por robar, fue y prometió al jefe de la galera resolver todos los problemas por los que ellos nos habían sometido a la huelga, porque ellos fueron los que nos sometieron a la huelga.

Allí los hombres ya estaban que no podían más. Sin embargo con la fé esa en Dios, querían continuar. Se le ofrecieron visitas, mejores alimentos, asistencia médica, y en definitiva la huelga terminó pensando en que ellos iban a cumplir lo prometido y no cumplieron nada. Sólo dijo un día que llegó allí ese señor sargento: hoy les doy una cosa y mañana se la quito, nosotros somos los que mandamos. Infinidades de hechos sucedidos en esa Prisión de Boniato, en la prisión más represiva que hay en Cuba, donde llevan a los hombres para tratar de someterlos a la voluntad que ellos desean. Aun así, allí todavía los hay que no se someten a nada.

Nelson Eduardo Rodríguez Pérez
Interview: February 4, 1985

Hunger Strike: October 10, 1982

(In protest against the continued detention of prisoners after their sentences had expired)

La Prisión de Boniato, cada vez que fui allí siempre presentaba o había problemas grandes: las huelgas de hambre, las tapiadas . . . Fui recondenado, cuando terminé mi condena de 20 años, le hice una carta a Castro, donde le decía en la carta, haciéndole un parangón con su prisión comparándola con la mía, que era una jaula de oro y que si no se conformaba con la barbarie que había utilizado durante 20 años conmigo y me iba a recondenar, que yo prefería que me fusilaran. Salí de la celda cuando fueron a llevar agua y pude llegar hasta el edificio, hasta el útlimo edificio pegado al orden interior del edificio No. 1, llevaba esa carta y se la entregué personalmente al jefe de orden interior. La guarnición entera fue para allí para verme. Ese día había un cambio de director, cosa que yo no sabía y pude hablar con más de 100 miembros del Ministerio del Interior. Pedí que se me permitiera un habeas corpus, cosa que me dijeron rotundamente, que para los contra-revolucionarios no existían habeas corpus. Me cargaron, me llevaron hasta la celda tapiada cargado, no me dieron, no me tocaron, sólo fue a base de llaves (judo). Les causó impacto lo que yo les dije y además la prisión completa estaba cantando el himno nacional y pidiendo mi libertad. Esto duró 3 días y tuvieron acuartelada la guardia. Después de esto, mis com- pañeros me llamaron y me dijeron que no tomara una actitud individual, que regresara al grupo de los demás. Tenían una idea un grupito de compañeros, que éramos 24 los que estábamos recondenados, habíamos planeado una huelga de hambre para exigir nuestra libertad y así lo hicimos. El día 10 de octubre de 1982, nos lanzamos a la huelga de hambre un grupo de 11. Había un compañero que llevaba ya un año en huelga de hambre, en el hospital recluído y lo incorporaron a nuestra huelga. A los 10 o 12 días de estar en huelga, el propio director del penal con los miembros del Ministerio del Interior y el delegado de Ministerio, o sea el jefe de la provincia, llamado Roberto Valdés, nos quitaron el agua oficialmente y nos dijeron que ahora era sin agua y había que morirse. A los 26 días de huelga, llegaron y nos plantearon que la huelga cesaba si nosotros aceptábamos le deportación del país, cosa que todos al unísono aceptamos, porque era lo que queríamos que nos soltaran bajo cualquier condición, pero que nos soltaran.

Pedro González Rodríguez
Interview: January 10, 1985

Veintiséis prisioneros recondenados de la Prisión de Boniato, 14 de la Prisión de La Habana del Este y uno de Kilo Siete (Camagüey) fuimos puestos en libertad como resulto de una huelga de hambre llevada a cabo por 11 de los prisioneros recondenados en la Prisión de Boniato, más uno que se estaba recuperando de una huelga anterior y se nos sumó y otros, que no eran recondenados de la Prisión de Boniato, también se nos sumaron.

La huelga de hambre comenzó en la fecha patriótica del 10 de octubre de 1982. Duró 25 días. En los últimos 13 días de la huelga de hambre no se nos permitió, por las autoridades de la prisión, beber agua.

Fuimos puestos en libertad paulatinamente, 2 todos los lunes en Boniato y uno en La Habana del Este, a partir de febrero de 1983.

Servando Infante Jiménez
Interview: February 6, 1985

Resentencing Procedures

Fui condenado a 12 años de prisión. Al cumplir esos 12 años, recondenado a 2 años más. Acusación: peligrosidad preventiva. Siete meses después: nuevo juicio y condena a 5 años. Delito: quema de bandera soviética en el comedor y botar la comida en protesta por haber suspendido la visita sin previo aviso a los familiares, que acudieron a la misma. También, por difamación del llamado primer ministro de Cuba y de Lenín.

Con esta condena quedó sin efecto la recondena anterior de 2 años. Comencé a cumplir esta nueva sentencia de 5 años a partir de los 12 años y 7 meses que ya había cumplido en prisión. Al cumplir los 5 años, de nuevo fui recondenado a 2 años por peligrosidad preventiva.

Aunque inicialmente había sido condenado a 12 años de prisión, cumplí en total: 18 años y 5 meses.

Servando Infante Jiménez
Interview: February 6, 1985

Loudspeakers: January 9, 1984

El 9 de enero de 1984, pusieron una bocina electrónica a las once y media de la noche en la puerta del rastrillo y elevaron el volumen. El ruido golpeaba contra las paredes del pasillo y penetraba en las celdas tapiadas a través de las aspilleras y de las hendijas. Nosotros empezamos a golpear las tolas, o sea, las planchas de hierro para evitar enloquecer. Esto duró hora y media. Esta operación fue practicada por el siniestro capitán Alvis Matos. Dirigida y orientada por el director de la prisión Israel Cobas, mayor de la contra-inteligencia cubana.

Gerardo Martínez Pérez
Interview: January 10, 1985

Search: January 10, 1984

Uno de los hechos que recuerdo con más vivencia fue exactamente el 10 de enero de 1984, cuando el pabellón 2-C y 2-A alto y bajo, se llenó de guardias con palos, cabillas, cadenas, escopetas de gases, AK [Russian rifles with drawn bayonets], rifles, perros de presa y emplazaron unas 30 en la puerta del rastrillo apuntando para el pabellón. Allí nos sacaron uno a uno de las celdas y nos hicieron una requisa, donde nos llevaron los zapatos, las chancletas, los espejos, las medias, las cucharas, los jarros y los platos. Después nos mantuvimos 72 días comiendo con los dedos y tomando agua con las manos; y en algunas oportuni-dades nos veíamos obligados a rechazar los alimentos porque éstos no podían comerse con los dedos y entonces nos sosteníamos con un pedazo de pan y un poco de agua.

Un día se aparecieron dos hombres vestidos de civil al pabellón alegando que eran los fiscales de la provincia. Estos representantes del gobierno, fueron celda por celda informándose de lo que había sucedido y dando la respuesta. Cuando llegaron a mi celda, yo desconocía la respuesta que estaban dando. El fiscal, el llamado fiscal me preguntó . . . Buenas, cómo se siente, a lo cual le respondí . . . adaptándome a mi nueva condición de bestia.

Gerardo Martínez Pérez
Interview: January 10, 1985

Yo soy de los que viajé a Boniato, de La Habana hasta el Combinado en el 79, julio 26, vi lo que nunca había visto: la requisa más bárbara de la historia la hicieron allí. El 10 de enero del 84, por la mañana, sobre las 10 de la manaña, hubo una requisa sencilla, habitual en ellos, requisa que es sólo para molestar, para no dejarnos ubicar, cosa que nosotros nos imponemos. A la requisa le prestamos el mínimo interés, todo lo que nos quiten nunca lamentamos nada, ya estamos habituados a que se nos quite todo y a que se nos bote todo, estamos acostumbrados a vivir sin nada. Ellos, los rojos, nos han enseñado. Bueno, se fueron como a las 12 del día y a las 2 de la tarde, invadieron el pabellón aquél con más de 70 u 80 militares, arma larga, bombas lacrimógenas, etc., etc. Rodearon el edificio y coparon todo el pasillo con más de 40 o 60 guardias. Todos con un tolete de granadillo en la mano y una balloneta, en la otra. Después que tomaron el pasillo de punta a punta, se situó el Capitán Alvis Matos Durán, un sujeto que acababa de pasar un curso en Rusia de 5 años, para llevarlo a la práctica en su propia patria. El director de penal Israel Cobas Reyes, y el jefe de orden interior al pie de nuestro pabellón, Félix Zamora Blanco, se situaron entre la celda 17 y la celda 18. Quien vivía en la celda 17, pero no pensaba que la cosa fuese primero para mí. La primera puerta que abrieron fue la mía. Cuando el Teniente Zamora me dijo, Mesa, hacia fuera, de inmediato salí, cogí como es costumbre la pared. No había yo salido de la puerta, cuando ya estaban todos los militares dentro de la celda. Sacaron los jarros, las cucharas, y los platos, zapatos, de todo lo que había. Yo mantenía mis botas puestas. Cuando ya terminaron aquello, me dijo el Teniente Félix Zamora Blanco, quítese los zapatos, Mesa. Me quité los zapatos y se los zumbé para el cajón donde tenía los otros, me quité las medias y se las zumbé y me dice, las medias no. Le respondí, para qué quiero medias si no hay zapatos. A las 40 celdas del pabellón de arriba, que es el C, y de la A que es en los bajos, idénticamente para todos, nos dejaron sin nada para consumir el alimento, sin nada para ponernos en los pies. Esa es la situación de los presos políticos cubanos en la tapiada de Boniato.

Pero tal parece que en la requisa, ya sea en los bajos, en el A, del mismo pabellón 2, hubo un detalle que se les fuese a ellos. Miguel Cantón, preso político también, histórico, logró ese día quedarse con las chancletas, no se percataron quienes entraron a su celda y dejaron las chancletas. Como a los 6 o 7 días entra el Capitán Alvis Matos y ve a Miguelito con las chancletas. Inmediatamente ordenó al otro día al Teniente Zamora que fuese a recoger las chancletas de Miguel Cantón. Querían verlo descalzo como a todos los demás y allá fue Félix Zamora Blanco y le recogió las chancletas a Miguelito Cantón. Así en esa situación, transcurrió o transcurrimos durante 75 días. Quizás ellos nos hicieron eso para provocar una huelga general, ya que cada vez que vamos a una huelga, aunque la ganemos, la pérdida es nuestra.

¿Qué actitud tomamos para no ir a una huelga? Se lo voy a explicar. Los comunistas nos sirven la comida todos los días entre macarrón, huevo y alguna vez más que otra un poquito de carne rusa de lata y algunos plátanos, yuca, vianda. Adoptamos coger todo lo que podíamos comer con la mano, rechazar todo lo que no podíamos coger con la mano, y para no hacerlo muy largo, con la mano nada más que podíamos coger el huevo salcochado, el plátano o el boniato y de desayuno que mandan un poquito de leche clara, nunca más la tomamos, pues no teníamos con qué tomarla, nos comíamos el pan. Esa situación duró 75 días.

Esturnio Mesa Schuman
Interview: February 18, 1985

Psychological Mistreatment

Lo más peligroso en el tratamiento a los presos políticos cubanos es el proceso de desestabilización de la personalidad. ¿Cómo se trabaja esto? Aprovechando la situación psicológica funcional del preso y el sistema de valoraciones que se desarrolla en toda comunidad. ¿Cómo trabaja la autoridad? Tratando de impedir que se desarrollen vínculos comunitarios profundos y dialécticamente ricos. De ahí que cualquier grupo es siempre dividido, trasladado, impedida la comunicación entre unos y otros, o movidos de forma tal de que la composición psico-social nueva resulte contradictoria con lo que se había desarrollado. De ahí los presos en unas condiciones de un tratamiento benévolo con respecto a otros con un tratamiento muy cruel, sin que haya una explicación lógica de por qué se escogen a unos personajes y por qué a otros. Esto es para que dentro del preso haya una escala diferente en cuanto al tratamiento y que no puede explicarse nunca si los que son peor tratados son porque valen más o valen menos.

La pérdida de los puntos de referencia, tanto objetivos y materiales como intelectuales. De ahí que una fotografía sea autorizada hoy y mañana sea quitada, que hoy haya agua y mañana haya un conflicto con el agua, de que hoy se autorice un cordel y mañana se quite un cordel, de que no se permitan libros, u hoy permitan el libro y mañana lo quiten, que estén atrás de los papeles escritos, de la correspondencia, para que no haya la posibilidad de un desarrollo intelectual. No es posible realizar una obra larga y constructiva de formación intelectual en presidio.

En cuanto al aprovechamiento de situación es presentarle al preso una medida que implica una ambigüedad de interpretación. De acuerdo con la explicación del guardia, la medida que se aplica tiene una lógica perfecta, pero esconde un sofisma en su abstracción. El caso de pretender que los presos plantados vistan el uniforme de los presos rehabilitados o de los presos comunes. No se le dice que se va a convertir en un preso común, pero se le propone una conducta en que la imagen que él debe tener de sí ya entra en contradicción con la noción que tiene de sí mismo. Esto permite sobre un pretexto prácticamente baladí, el de un uniforme u otro uniforme, una escalada de violencia y una superestructura de coacción y de perturbación. Y acaba alienando al grupo; unos porque aceptan o porque no pueden comprender de que haya una cosa tan importante en vestir un uniforme u otro, y otros que llegan al extremo de resistencia, porque consideran de que el vestir un uniforme u otro puede hacer la cosa más desdichada. Y el grado de crueldad extraordinaria durante muchos meses para que vista un tipo de uniforme, llega un momento en que eso se convierte en un símbolo de una carga afectiva extrema y durante un período largo, alienante, es lo único en que se puede pensar.

La relación con la familia es aprovechada extra-ordinariamente. La relación con los hijos, con la esposa, con los padres o hermanos. Esta relación afectiva es aprovechada con mucha frecuencia. Todos los conflictos que puedan estimularse desde la calle o desde presidio con los familiares se buscan. El caso de la hija de un preso que tiene dificultades en la escuela, más tarde o más temprano es porque el padre es preso y el padre no quiere aceptar algo que le proponen. El caso del preso que espera que lo lleven a ver a su madre que está agonizante y se ha pasado tantos días en una tensión extraordinaria porque su madre agoniza y espera en cualquier momento, y le están diciendo que sí, que lo van a llevar a ver a su madre agonizante. Por fin, después de tantos días se entera que su madre murió y que no lo han llevado. La autoridad que promete dar una cosa y después no la cumple, hace todo lo contrario.

Todo esto va estimulando una conducta a la defensiva. El preso siempre está esperando una agresión o una situación extraña. Una situación que no puede comprender por qué se produce. Así tiene que vivir como un adolescente, sin patrones de conducta, sin hábitos valiosos, sino cada día improvisando la situación del agua, la comida o la guarnición.

Jorge Valls Arango
Interview: March 10, 1985

Death Penalty

. . . Otro hecho fue el del fusilamiento del joven Periche (su apellido). Otro de los hechos que me impresionaron fue el de seis jóvenes que fusilaron unos días antes de salir de Cuba, ellos eran políticos y según tengo entendido el promedio de edad era de 22 años. Estos jóvenes fueron fusilados detrás de la Prisión de Boniato, bajo las matas de mango. Desde nuestras celdas oímos las descargas de los fusiles y el tiro de gracia.

> Wilfredo Martínez Roque
> Interview: January 14, 1985

El paredón de fusilamiento lo pusieron desde mediados del 84 en una frondosa mata de mango a menos de 100 metros del ala A-C del pabellón 2.

Diego Lorenzo Roche Periche de 21 años de edad, de raza negra, natural de Banes, Oriente, fue fusilado allí por un delito político el 19 de marzo de 1984.

> Esturnio Mesa Schuman
> Interview: February 18, 1985

Un drama difícil y pudiéramos decir hasta horrendo fue el que sucedió en febrero del 84, es decir el mismo año en que tuve la suerte de salir de allí. Dos muchachos, políticos, fueron dicen que fusilados, pero yo diría más bien masacrados. Ese día fueron sacados como a las ocho y pico o las nueve de la noche, los pusieron cerca de la prisión, cerca de allí donde nosotros podíamos oir y a los dos los pusieron debajo de una mata de mango y los masacraron. Es decir, supimos que los masacraron porque eran dos, hicieron una descarga grande, después dos tiros de gracia. Uno de ellos, por lo menos lo recuerdo yo que se llamaba Rafael; el otro como un apodo o algo así por el estilo, que le decían Calunga, no recuerdo bien. Pero bueno, ellos eran prisioneros políticos, que los tenían con los comunes para resquebrajar su moral, y tratar de que no siguieran en la lucha y de que no se unieran a nosotros. Eso es una parte difícil; quizás muchos no sepan eso, pero allí se sigue fusilando, se sigue matando, se sigue maltratando a todos los que en una forma u otra se oponen al régimen actual.

> Armando Yong Martínez
> Interview: March 7, 1985.

Individual Cases

Osvaldo Baró Miranda

En una oportunidad, un compañero, Osvaldo Baró Miranda, que necesitaba asistencia médica con urgencia decretó una huelga de hambre en reclamo de esa asistencia. A lo cual el director, lo sacó del pabellón y lo metió en un calabozo completamente aislado fuera del penal y le cortó el agua. A este compañero lo llevaron al estado de coma. Cuando perdió el conocimiento, lo amarraron, le pusieron un suero y le vistieron la ropa del preso común. Cuando el compañero Baró Miranda recobró el conocimiento, se quitó la ropa y le quitaron el suero: volvieron a llevarlo al estado de coma a tal extremo que los médicos de la prisión tuvieron que correr mucho para salvarle la vida.

A este compañero, después de terminada la huelga, se lo llevaron de Boniato y en la fecha en que yo salí de allí aún no se sabía de él.

Gerardo Martínez Pérez
Interview: January 10, 1985

Justino René Ramos González

Mi nombre, Justino René Ramos González. Cumplí 21 años y 3 meses en la prisión. Hoy quiero dar un testimonio de los casos que más me conmovieron. El recluso Osvaldo Baró Miranda, preso desde septiembre del año 1981, condenado a 30 años de prisión, después de reclamar desde meses antes asistencia médica por un problema del conducto urinario, le daban evasivas, pero no asistencia médica, se vió obligado a declararse en huelga de hambre el 10 de enero del año 1983. El 18 del mismo mes lo llevaron para una celda especialmente preparada para castigo, que está situada dentro del llamado hospital de la Prisión de Boniato. Esta celda está totalmente tapiada, sin agua ni servicio sanitario. Allí le dijeron que tenía que rehabilitarse o morirse, no había regreso. Contestó, --reclamo asistencia médica, derecho que tiene todo ser humano. Le quitaron el agua, y al cabo de 12 días lo sacaron de dicha celda de castigo, muy grave, y le pusieron un suero. Cuando volvió en él, después de 2 días, se encontró a un psiquiátra sentado a la cabecera de su cama; le dijo que era muy joven, que él no había vivido, que tenía que deponer o morir, etc., etc. Ya lo habían vestido inconsciente con el uniforme de los comunes. Le afectó mucho un golpe en la cabeza, durante la desesperación por la falta de agua y ventilación. Pasaron 4 días;

cuando volvió en sí completo, se volvió a declarar en huelga y le volvieron a quitar el agua 11 días más. Después que el Dr. Stalin certificó que ya no había casi posibilidad de vida, lo sacaron de la celda de castigo y le dijeron que por problemas humanos le iban a dar la asistencia médica y el 2 de mayo del año 1983 lo llevaron para la prisión de la Habana del Este. El 29 de junio del año 1984, ese mismo hermano de cautiverio se encontraba desde hacía 40 días, en los calabozos "tostadoras" de dicha prisión sin darle la asistencia médica. El pedía que en vista del engaño, después de todo lo sucedido, que lo trasladaran a las tapiadas de Boniato otra vez. Y hoy en día no he sabido más desde esa fecha de la suerte de ese hermano de cautiverio.

Justino René Ramos González
Interview: January 13, 1985

Luis González Llorente

En esa misma Prisión de Boniato cuando nosotros llegamos, había más de 200 presos políticos históricos plantados, como ocurre en Pinar del Río, en Las Villas, en Camagüey, y en donde quiera, que nos tienen regados por todas las provincias y por cada rincón de Cuba. De aquellos presos plantados, hay un preso que se llama Luis González Llorente. Está preso desde el 1º de enero de 1959. Nunca lo han presentado ante un tribunal de justicia, nunca ha concurrido a juicio, no tiene tarjetero en el penal, pues como no ha sido condenado, no tiene tarjetero. Cada vez que hay una requisa, como lo hacen por el tarjetero, tienen que dejarlo para último para después pasarlo, pues ese señor no aparece como preso. El teniente Banderas, jefe de re-educación de nuestro pabellón, un negrito santiaguero él, alto, palunchín, cuando el censo de la población cubana en el 84, se acercó a Llorente y le dijo, --tú sabes que no se te pudo censar Luisito, y Llorente le dice, ¿cómo que no se me ha censado? Tu no estás censado, porque tú no apareces como preso aquí. Y cómo puede entenderse eso, que un hombre que ya lleva 26 años en la prisión no aparezca como preso? Pues Luis González Llorente no aparece como preso, pues no fue censado por eso. Y ésta no es palabra ni opiniones de uno de la calle, es palabra del teniente Banderas, que fue el que hizo el censo allí de la porción penal, y es uno de los instructores, jefe de la Prisión de Boniato de re-educación.

Esturnio Mesa Schuman
Interview: February 18, 1985

Part III. Official Position of the Cuban Government on
the Status of Human Rights in Cuba

On February 25, 1985, the United States Mission to the
United Nations held a press conference using United Nations
facilities. At the conference three Cuban former political
prisoners were introduced to the members of the press by
American Ambassador Dr. Jeane Kirkpatrick. In addition, a
United States Information Agency (USIA) publication, In a Place
without a Soul, which describes firsthand experiences of political
prisoners in Cuba, was distributed to the press. In reference to
that conference, the Permanent Representative of Cuba to the
United Nations stated:

> With regard to the incident itself, the distinguished
> representatives of the international community to the
> United Nations know all too well that for the past
> 26 years Cuba has been victoriously resisting the
> attacks of every kind, the economic blockade, the
> threats of military aggression and the propaganda
> campaigns directed against it by the United States and
> that it has been able to do so, among other reasons, by
> virtue of its morality, its dignity and its unshakable
> principles, which do not allow Cuba to resort to
> torture, physical mistreatment or humiliation of its
> adversaries. Such procedures have no place in our
> country, for they are precisely the ones which the
> revolution eliminated from Cuba for ever.

(For the full text of this letter, see Appendix D.)

Appendix A

Questionnaire

1.   Nombre

2.   Dirección

3.   Teléfono

4.   Número de causa

5.   Fecha de nacimiento

6.   Lugar de nacimiento

7.   Estado civil

8.   Hijos

9.   Grado de escolaridad

10. Ocupación/Profesión

11. Fecha de encarcelamiento

12. Fecha de juicio

13. Lugar de juicio

14. Número de años de condena

15. Número de años de prisión

16. Prisiones donde estuvo

17. Nombre de la última prisión donde estuvo

18. Fecha de excarcelamiento

19. Fecha en que salió de Cuba

20. País al que viajó

21. Fecha de entrada en los Estados Unidos

22. ¿Dónde está situada la Prisión de Boniato?

23. Describa brevemente, en términos generales, la Prisión de Boniato

24. Describa una celda tapiada

25. ¿Cuántos presos políticos cubanos fueron trasladados para la Prisión de Boniato en julio de 1979?

26. ¿Cuántos presos políticos cubanos pertenecientes a ese grupo quedaban en la Prisión de Boniato cuando Ud. salió de la misma?

27. Escriba en papel adjunto los nombres de los prisioneros políticos de ese grupo que quedaban en la Prisión de Boniato cuando Ud. salió de la misma.

28. ¿Además del grupo antes mencionado, había otros presos políticos en la Prisión de Boniato cuando Ud. salió de la misma?

29. ¿Sabe Ud. cuántos eran en total?

30. ¿Llegaban personas recién detenidas por causas políticas a la Prisión de Boniato?

31. ¿Puede Ud. ofrecer alguna información sobre las características de los prisioneros políticos recién detenidos, como: edad promedia, tipo de acusación, etc.?

32. Fecha de llegada a la Prisión de Boniato

33. Fecha de salida de la Prisión de Boniato

34. Tiempo que estuvo en la Prisión de Boniato

35. Número de visitas que recibió en la Prisión de Boniato durante ese tiempo

36. Explique su relación de parentesco o amistad con las personas que lo visitaron

37. ¿Recibía Ud. correspondencia de amigos y familiares?

38. ¿Cada qué tiempo recibía Ud. correspondencia?

39. ¿Podía Ud. escribir a amigos y familiares?

40. ¿Cada qué tiempo podía Ud. escribir a amigos y familiares?

41. ¿Recibían atención médica los prisioneros políticos en la Prisión de Boniato durante el tiempo que Ud. permaneció allí?

42. ¿Recibían atención dental?

43. ¿Con qué frecuencia los sacaban al patio para que pudieran recibir la luz de sol y ejercitarse?

44. ¿Podían relacionarse los prisioneros políticos entre sí?

45. Describa el tipo de celda en que Ud. estuvo en la Prisión de Boniato

46. Escriba los nombres de otras prisiones o lugares de detención para presos políticos que Ud. sabe existían en Cuba cuando Ud. salió del país. Primero escriba la fecha exacta en que Ud. salió del país.

47. ¿Ha recibido Ud. información sobre algún cambio en el trato o las condiciones de vida de los prisioneros políticos que permanecen en la Prisión de Boniato?

48. Si su respuesta es SI, explique en qué consiste el cambio

49. ¿Podría Ud. relatar algún hecho que tuvo lugar en la Prisión de Boniato que Ud. considere ilustrativo de la situación de los prisioneros políticos en ese lugar?

50. Escriba los nombres de los presos políticos, pertenecientes al grupo trasladado para la Prisión de Boniato en julio de 1979, que tenían problemas de salud cuando Ud. salió de la misma. Identifique la enfermedad o el tipo de trastorno que padecían, si le es posible.

Appendix B
Plantado Political Prisoners in Cuba

Boniato Prison

1. Alonso Valdés, Juan Miguel
2. Alvarez Cardentey, Miguel Angel
3. Argüelles Garrido, Angel Luis
4. Arroyo Ramos, Luis L.
5. Cabrera Adorna, Carlos M.
6. Cantón Gómez, Victor Manuel
7. Capote Bernal, Benito
8. Casasus Toledo, Guillermo
9. Castillo Pérez, Dominador
10. Cuesta Valle, Ignacio
11. Díaz Millo, Plácido
12. Díaz Rodríguez, Ernesto
13. Echevarría Granda, Francisco
14. Escalada Montalvo, Guillermo
15. Fernández Guerra, Isnaldo
16. Feros Gambara, Pitagoras
17. Fibla González, Alberto, Dr.
18. Figueroa Gálvez, Osvaldo
19. Figueroa Gálvez, Reinaldo
20. Flores Franqui, Julio
21. García Palomino, Enrique L.
22. García Rojas, Francisco
23. González Alvarado, Teodoro
24. González Llorente, Luis
25. Grau Alsina, Ramón
26. Grau Sierra, Alberto
27. Gutiérrez Menoyo, Eloy
28. Hernández Hernández, Celestino
29. Hernández Ramírez, Juan Evelio
30. Hernández Verdecia, Jesús
31. Jane Padrón, Alberto
32. López Lima Rodríguez, Reinaldo
33. López Muñoz, Antonio
34. Macuran González, Pastor
35. Mariscal Legorburo, Carlos
36. Márquez Batista, Tomás
37. Márquez Trillo, Manuel
38. Martínez Hechevarría, Armando
39. Méndez Pimentel, Ramón
40. Mendoza Rojas, Miguel
41. Mirabal Rodríguez, Santos O.
42. Molina Contreras, Orlando
43. Mora Rosales, Elieser
44. Mustelier Nuevo, Alfredo
45. Oviedo Alvarez, Eleno
46. Pardo Mazorra, Angel
47. Parra Nieves, Liberato
48. Perdomo Díaz, Roberto
49. Pérez Guerra, Ladislao
50. Pérez Hernández, Onofre
51. Pérez Rodríguez, Reinaldo
52. Pérez Rodríguez, Roberto Martín
53. Pérez Soa, Emilio Rafael
54. Peñalver Mazorra, Eusebio
55. Piña Proto, Félix R.
56. Pons Walter, Carlos
57. Prats Rodríguez, Gilberto
58. Prieto Castillo, Pablo
59. Pujals Mederos, José L.
60. Reyes Hernández, Roger
61. Rivas Porta, Guillermo
62. Rodríguez Barrientos, Silvino
63. Rodríguez Esquía, Juan
64. Ruiz Pitaluga, Julio
65. Soto Guevara, Juan
66. Vázquez Robles, Félix R.
67. Vinent Bonis, Adolfo
68. Zúñiga Rey, Luis Manuel

Combinado del Este

1. Alzamora Alvarez, Rafael
2. Arroyo Morgado, Arnaldo
3. Baro Miranda, Osvaldo
4. Benítez Hernández, Felipe
5. Casanova Balbuena, Silvio Cruz
6. Castrillejo Laburi, Francisco
7. Chanes de Armas, Mario
8. Chiang Pérez, José
9. Crespo González, Pablo
10. Delgado Alvarez, Juan Humberto
11. Díaz Espinosa, Antolín
12. Díaz Garriga, Francisco
13. Díaz Silva, Ruperto
14. Falcón Rodríguez, Pablo
15. Faraminan Fernández, Guido Rafael
16. Fe Mirabal, Emiliano de la
17. Gala Mederos, Anselmo
18. García Arrieta, Isidro
19. García Placencia, Orlando
20. Gómez Blanco, Juan
21. González Migollo, Vicente de Paul
22. González Ramírez, Víctor
23. Guin Díaz, Ramón
24. Hernández García, Felipe
25. Lamela, Víctor
26. López Castellanos, Francisco
27. López Fernández, Pablo Ramón
28. Marcel Soa, Manuel Antolín
29. Martia de la Cova, Carlos
30. Martínez Martínez, Jesús
31. Montenegro Sánchez, Roberto
32. Nuñez Trujillo, Domingo
33. Oliva Soa, Plutarco
34. Peguero Ceballos, Arcadio
35. Pérez Benítez, Urbano Gregorio
36. Peña Valdés, Pedro
37. Prado Fernández, Alejandro
38. Rivera Barrios, Raimundo
39. Rodríguez Barrios, Elio
40. Rodríguez Delgado, José
41. Rodríguez Rodríguez, Luis
42. Rodríguez Vega, José Fernando
43. Ruidíaz Marichal, Nestor
44. Ruiz Hernández, Sergio
45. Salabarria Valdés, Juan
46. Salas Ledo, Bruno
47. Salazar López, Vicente
48. San Román Novo, Ramón
49. Sanabria Morales, Osvaldo
50. Sánchez Otero, José
51. Silva Gil, Eugenio
52. Soca Domínguez, José M.
53. Sol Díaz, Juan G. del
54. Suárez Cruz, Raúl
55. Suárez Fernández, Antonio
56. Tamayo, Francisco
57. Torres Martínez, Juan V.
58. Uria Ramos, Martín
59. Valdés Cancio, Ricardo
60. Valdés Terán, Juan
61. Viera Izquierdo, Julio

Kilo Siete

1. García Rodríguez, Félix
2. Gómez Orosco, Osvaldo
3. Hernández Camejo, Nemesio
4. Rivera Milián, Agapito
5. Rochevalle, Santiago de Jesús
6. Rosa Ruíz, Alejandro la
7. Urra, Ramón

Appendix C

*Annotated Bibliography of Works
Smuggled Out of Cuban Prisons*

Introduction

The works listed in this bibliography were written inside and smuggled out of Cuban prisons. All the books were published abroad while the author was or is still incarcerated in Cuba. Three of the author-prisoners were freed after the publication of their books: Armando Valladares, Jorge Valls Arango, and Angel Cuadra Landrove. The rest of them are at present in Boniato Prison, in Cuba. The entries are arranged alphabetically by author. A brief biographical sketch of each author is included. Different works by a given author are listed in alphabetical order by title. Different editions of a given work are also recorded. Two works that could not be viewed are included, to establish the fact that they exist. They are marked with an asterisk.

Casasus Toledo, Guillermo

Born in Regla, Havana Province, in 1951. The son of a broken home, he spent his childhood moving from one place to another, staying with different relatives. At an early age, he was earning his living at many kinds of odd jobs, and had very little schooling. In the 32 times he traveled to Mexico, as a worker with the Gulf Cuban Fishing Flotilla since 1964, he had many opportunities to flee from Cuba. He was accused of conspiracy at the age of 17, and again at 19, and sentenced to 20 years. At present he is a plantado in Boniato Prison.

1. Casasus Toledo, Guillermo, Hapai, y otros poemas; [arte y portada por el artista Siro del Castillo]. [Miami, FL]: CIELO, [1984?] [45] pp.; ill.; 18 cm.

    A collection of poems with a two-page presentation signed by Comité de Intelectuales y Escritores Libres de Oposición (CIELO) explaining how this committee was organized in 1982 by Fernando Arrabal, Spanish playwright. Other members of the committee are Eugene Ionesco, Bernard Henry-Levy, Eduardo Manet, and Carlos Alberto Montaner. He was awarded the Premio Anual José Martí de Poesía by CIELO. The prologue is a poem written by Jorge Valls. Some of the poems are dated 1980.

Cuadra Landrove, Angel

Born in 1931, in Havana. One of the most celebrated poets of Cuba is a lawyer who once worked as a legal counselor for

UNEAC (Unión de Escritores y Artistas de Cuba, created as a cultural institute by the Castro regime). In 1967 he was sentenced to 15 years in prison, accused of "conspiring against the powers of state." Cuadra's second book, Impromptus, was published abroad in 1977, weeks after his first release from prison. He was immediately reincarcerated until 1982. International human rights organizations, intellectuals, and government officials from all over the world lobbied for the poet's exit from Cuba. Finally, in March 1985, Cuadra and his wife arrived in Frankfurt, Germany. Cuadra has been chosen as an honorary member of the Swedish PEN Club.

2.   Cuadra Landrove, Angel, Impromptus. Washington, DC: Solar, 1977. 62 pp.; 21 cm.

A compilation of poems written in prison, and published abroad by the poet's longtime friend Juana Rosa Pita. In the presentation of the book, Juana Rosa compares Cuadra with two other poet-prisoners: César Vallejo and Miguel Hernández. Cuadra wrote a letter acknowledging her plans to publish the book, and it is also included here.

*3.   _____. Korrespondenz in Gedichten aus dem Gefangnis. 1. Aufl. [S.1.]: AI Amnesty International, 1981. [76] pp.; 21 cm.

4.   _____. Poemas en correspondencia desde prisión--A Correspondence of Poems from Jail; Trans. Donald D. Walsh. Ediciones de poesía 15. Washington, DC: Solar, 1979. 69 pp.; 21 cm.

A compilation of poems written in response to the ones the poet received from his longtime friend Juana Rosa Pita. "Bring forth each poem of mine from one of yours, as if it were bred in it like cause and effect. . . ." All were written between April 9 and June 5, 1979. Almost all have epigraphs from the poems or the letters of Juana Rosa. A prefatory letter, written by Cuadra to Juana Rosa, explaining this work, is included.

5.   _____. Tiempo del hombre. Poetas de América. Madrid; Miami, [FL]: Hispanova de Ediciones, 1977. 103 pp.; 21 cm.

A collection of poems, most of them written in prison and full of remembrances of his life as a student at the Universidad de La Habana. The prologue is by Pura del Prado.

Díaz Rodríguez, Ernesto

Born to a fisherman's family in Cojímar, Havana, on November 11, 1939, he did not have much schooling when he himself went to work as a fisherman and, later, as a bus driver. He fled from Cuba by boat in 1961, and lived exiled in the United States. In 1968 he was captured in Cuba's Pinar del Río Province and sentenced to 15 years. He was resentenced in 1974 to 25 additional years in prison, accused of conspiring against the government from inside the prison. At present, he is a plantado in Boniato Prison.

6.   Díaz Rodríguez, Ernesto. La campana del alba. Madrid: Playor, [1984?]. [123] pp.; port.; 18 mm.

A compilation of poems for children, dedicated: "A mi hermano Rodolfo, como un recuerdo intransferible en estos tiempos de óxido y olvido." Signed by the author at Prisión de Boniato, Noviembre de 1981. The book is a facsimile edition of the manuscript papers smuggled out of prison, 2.5 by 3 inches.

7.   _____. Un testimonio urgente : escrito en las cárceles de Cuba. Miami, FL: Réplica, 1977. 95 pp.; 21 cm.

A collection of poems with a prologue written by Guillermo Rivas Porta at Presidio Político Cubano, La Cabaña (Prison), 1976. The author includes a 14-page narrative of his activities during the first three years of his exile in the United States, from 1961 to 1964. The narrative was not finished, because of the great difficulty in mailing letters or smuggling them out of Cuban prisons. Dr. Diego Medina wrote a summary of Ernesto's activities until the day he was captured in Cuba, in 1968, and it is also included here.

Fibla, Alberto

Born June 23, 1928. He graduated as a physician from the School of Medicine, Universidad de La Habana, in 1954. A Navy official, he was accused of conspiracy in 1962 and sentenced to 30 years in prison. At present, he is a plantado in Boniato Prison.

8.   Fibla, Alberto. Cuentos. Biblioteca cubana contemporánea. Madrid: Playor, 1984. 129 pp.; 21 cm.

A compilation of short stories mainly on a fixed theme: imprisonment of men by men. All are dated, and some are dedicated to the memory of prisoners who died in prison. The prologue "Para Presentar al Médico" is by Jorge Valls.

Gutiérrez Menoyo, Eloy

Born in Madrid, to a traditionally socialist family which sided with the Republicans, on December 8, 1934. In 1948, after losing a son in the Spanish Civil War, the family moved to Cuba. The first years were very difficult, since his father, a physician, could not practice and had to work at odd jobs. In 1957, a second brother, Carlos, was killed in Cuba, in the so-called Ataque a Palacio, where a group of young men tried to overthrow the Batista regime. Eloy's reaction was to join the rebels and to combat the regime. He fought alongside Castro during the revolution, but later became disillusioned and led guerrilla attacks against the Castro regime. He was captured in 1965 entering Cuba clandestinely, and sentenced to 60 years in prison. At present, he is a plantado in Boniato Prison.

9.   Gutiérrez Monoyo, Eloy. El radarista. Prólogo, Elena
     Patricia Gutiérrez Sala; epílogo, Pedro Páramo. Biblioteca
     cubana contemporánea. Madrid: Playor, 1985. 117 pp.;
     17 cm.

     A short story full of symbolism, dedicated in a letter
     (Prologue I) to his daughter Elena Patricia on her
     fifteenth birthday. Prologue II is a letter from Elena
     Patricia requesting from Fidel Castro the freedom of her
     father. Eloy's daughter reminds Fidel Castro how he
     himself was pardoned by Batista after two years in prison
     for attacking a military garrison, and authorized to leave
     the country. An article titled "La saga de los Menoyo"
     published in Cambio 16, October 15, 1978, in Spain, is
     the epilogue of this book. The short story is printed on
     one side of each page, across from the facsimile of the
     original text.

Pérez Rodríguez, Roberto Martín

Born in Santa Clara, Cuba, on August 11, 1934. Incarcerated since August 12, 1959, and sentenced to 30 years, he is the Latin American political prisoner who has served the longest term in prison. He was seriously hurt in a testicle in the so-called Massacre of Boniato on September 5, 1975. For more than 9 years he suffered severe infections and acute abdominal pains, and finally, on January 18, 1984, he underwent surgery. The operation was a failure for lack of proper care. The prisoner was returned to his tapiada cell, walking from the hospital only four days after surgery was performed. He is one of the founders of APELCU (Asociación de Poetas y Escritores Libres de Cuba) in prison. In 1984 he was awarded the Premio de Poesía José Martí by CIELO. At present, he is a plantado in Boniato Prison.

10. Pérez Rodríguez, Roberto Martín. De la sangre de otras
    venas. Biblioteca cubana contemporánea. Madrid:
    Playor, 1984. 63 pp.; 21 cm.

    Collection of poems about faith, eternity, love to mankind
    and joie de vivre entirely written in prison. Includes a
    prologue signed by Ninoska Pérez Castellón, with some
    biographical information on the author-prisoner.

Valladares, Armando

    Born in Pinar del Río, Cuba, on May 30, 1937. He was
jailed on December 27, 1960, and sentenced to 30 years for
"offenses against state authorities." During his confinement,
Valladares wrote and smuggled out of Cuban prisons letters,
poems, and narratives. A volume of his poems entitled From My
Wheelchair was published in 1977. The Heart with Which I Live,
a compilation of poems, was published in 1980. A collection of
those same poems, together with many of the prisoner's letters,
was published in France, under the title Castro's Prisoner, in
1979. In 1980 he was awarded the Freedom Prize by the French
Chapter of PEN, the international writers' organization. On
October 22, 1982, thanks to the efforts of French President
François Mitterand and the Spanish writer Fernando Arrabal,
Valladares was freed and at the Paris airport was greeted by his
wife Martha and by Regis Debray, Mitterand's special counselor
for cultural affairs and an associate of Ernesto Che Guevara, the
Argentine-born guerrilla leader.

11. Valladares, Armando. El corazón con que vivo: (nuevos
    poemas y relatos "desde mi silla de ruedas") Colección
    Espejo de paciencia. Miami, FL: Ediciones Universal,
    1980. 140 pp.; facsims.; 21 cm.

12. _____. El corazón con que vivo. 3rd ed. Madrid:
    Playor, 1983. 132 pp.; 21 cm.

    The narrative "Boniato: Anatomía de una prisión" is
    included in the two editions.

13. _____. Desde mi silla de ruedas. Colección Lesa:
    Poesía. Coral Gables, FL: Interbooks Corp., 1976.
    136 pp.; 18 cm.

14. _____. Prisonero de Castro. Anotado y presentado
    por Pierre Golendorf; epílogo de Leonid Pliouchtch;
    [traducción del francés por Beatriz Podesta]. Colección
    Tablero. 2d ed. Barcelona: Planeta: Instituto de
    Estudios Económicos, 1982. 174 pp.; facsims., map,
    plan; 24 cm.

*15. _____. Prisonnier de Castro. Traduit, annoté et
presenté par Pierre Golendorf; postface de Leonid
Pliouchtch. Paris: B. Grasset, 1979. 222 pp.; ill., map;
21 cm.

The poem that describes the massacre at Boniato in
September, 1975, entitled "Cárcel de Boniato: Relato de
una masacre," is included in works 13, 14, and 15.

Valls Arango, Jorge

Born in Havana, Cuba, on February 2, 1933. When Batista
took power in 1952, he was studying Liberal Arts at the Universidad de La Habana. He was persecuted, and went into exile.
In 1959, he returned to Cuba. He was sentenced to 20 years
imprisonment in 1964, after he testified against the Castro regime
in a political trial. In prison he wrote poems and prose. Some
of his works were smuggled out of the Cuban jail and published
in two volumes in the United States and Europe. His best-known
work is entitled Where I Am There Is No Light and It Is Barred.
He was released after 20 years and 40 days in prison, due to
international appeals on his behalf. He was awarded the 1984
Freedom Award of the French Chapter of the International PEN
Club of authors, poets, and playwrights. A week after being
released, he received the Grand Prix de Poésie de Rotterdam,
which had been awarded to him in 1983.

16. Valls Arango, Jorge. Donde estoy no hay luz y está
enrejado: el libro de Jorge Valls Arango. Prólogo de
Carlos Alberto Montaner. Biblioteca cubana contemporánea. Madrid: Playor, 1981. 125 pp.; ill.; 21 cm.

A collection of poems with an introductory poem entitled
"Jorge Valls Arango," by Pura del Prado.

17. _____. Donde estoy no hay luz y está
enrejado = Where I am there is no light and it is barred =
Ou je suis il n'y a pas de lumière mais un grillage.
Biblioteca cubana contemporánea. Madrid: Playor, 1984.
46 pp.; 20 x 27 cm.

A trilingual selection of 24 poems with two forewords,
one by Stephen Spender, from the English Centre of
International PEN Club, the other by René Tavernier,
president of the PEN Club Français.

18. _____. A la paloma nocturna, desde mis soledades,
Hojarasca y otros poems. Miami, FL: SIBI, 1984.
109 pp.; 20 cm.

One volume with two collections of poems: "A la paloma nocturna," a profound meditation on the Virgin Mary dedicated to the memory of his dead father, and "Hojarasca y otros poemas," more than twenty poems written in 1981.

Appendix D

**UNITED
NATIONS**

A

General Assembly

Distr.
GENERAL

A/40/152
27 February 1985
ENGLISH
ORIGINAL: SPANISH

Fortieth session
Item 140 of the preliminary list*

REPORT OF THE COMMITTEE ON RELATIONS WITH THE HOST COUNTRY

Letter dated 26 February 1985 from the Permanent Representative of
Cuba to the United Nations addressed to the Secretary-General

I have the honour to write to you in connection with the press conference held yesterday morning by Mrs. Jeane Kirkpatrick in room 226 at United Nations Headquarters, with the participation of some stateless individuals of Cuban origin, which turned into a disgraceful political show concerning alleged violations of human rights by my country.

While it is true that every diplomat has the right to express freely his opinions concerning other States and to accept the relevant responses or consequences, it is absolutely intolerable that the machinery of the United Nations should be used, as Mrs. Kirkpatrick has used them, to promote this slanderous attack against Cuba, taking advantage of the fact that there would not be an immediate reply to the mendacious statements made there.

The practice of using the United Nations for such actions may have grave implications for the normal functioning of our Organization. I therefore consider it appropriate to request that the Secretariat should inform Ambassador Kirkpatrick that her action violates the established rules and should take suitable measures to prevent such reprehensible actions from being repeated in future.

With regard to the incident itself, the distinguished representatives of the international community to the United Nations know all too well that for the past 26 years Cuba has been victoriously resisting the attacks of every kind, the economic blockade, the threats of military aggression and the propaganda campaigns

A/40/50.

85-05880 1972a (E)

/...

A/40/152
English
Page 2

directed against it by the United States and that it has been able to do so, among
other reasons, by virtue of its morality, its dignity and its unshakable
principles, which do not allow Cuba to resort to torture, physical mistreatment or
humiliation of its adversaries. Such procedures have no place in our country, for
they are precisely the ones which the revolution eliminated from Cuba for ever.
Brutal and repressive methods of this kind are what the United States, through the
CIA and other subversive agencies, is promoting and disseminating among the régimes
that serve as its allies, régimes which are dictatorial and which violate human
rights. It is not surprising that Mrs. Kirkpatrick has arranged this grotesque
exhibition in a suspicious attempt to silence the voices in the United Nations
which on that very day were condemning the bloody tyranny now suffered by Chile and
condemning United States policy in Central America.

It also comes as no surprise that the aforementioned individuals, who are
traitors to their country and some of whom have been known in the past to be agents
of the CIA, in the service of a foreign Power, are willing to appear as extras in
the show staged by Mrs. Kirkpatrick. It is precisely the revolution's policy of
respect for human life and for the application of legal principles that enables
those individuals to take the stage today as living evidence of the failure of the
United States in its actions against the Cuban revolution, to accompany
Mrs. Kirkpatrick on the path of her personal failure in the effort to turn
reactionary thinking and hatred of Cuba into stepping stones of her own political
career.

I request you, Sir, to have this note circulated as an official document of
the General Assembly under item 140 of the preliminary list.

(Signed) Oscar ORAMAS OLIVA
Ambassador
Permanent Representative

Glossary

BONIATICO: Wing A–C of building number 2 of Boniato Prison. This wing holds 68 long-term political prisoners, totally incommunicado since March 1981.

BONIATO: A maximum-security prison located in the eastern province of Cuba, Santiago de Cuba.

COMBINADO DEL ESTE: A maximum-security prison on the outskirts of Havana City, built in the '70s. Also known as Habana del Este.

KILO SIETE: A maximum-security prison in Camagüey Province, Cuba.

PAREDON: Firing-squad wall.

PLANTADOS: Political prisoners planted firmly in opposition to the Cuban regime.

RASTRILLO: Hall between the first and second barred doorways to a dungeon or wing of a prison.

TAPIADA: Hermetically sealed cells with welded doors with a small opening to pass through food.

TOLA: Metal plate welded to the door of a punishment cell.

TOSTADORAS: Punishment cells on the ground floor of Combinado del Este Prison, extremely hot inside. While in these cells, the prisoner is fed once a day.

TURCO: The only sanitary facility of a punishment cell, consisting of a hole in the floor with a water faucet high above on the wall.

Note on Sources

The following list of reports and articles, from magazines and newspapers, is highly selective. The references cited are intended mainly to document the identity of the author-prisoners, included in the Annotated Bibliography (Appendix C), and the ten witnesses interviewed for this study (see table). The names of resource persons are also registered.

Resource Persons

Rosa Cosío.   Comité   de   Intelectuales   Libres   de   Oposición (CIELO).
Guillermo Estévez.   Director,   International   Rescue   Committee, Inc., New Jersey.
Ada   Pérez.   Organization   of   Relatives   of   Cuban   Political Prisoners.
Enrique   Trueba.   Presidente   del   Centro   Cubano   de   Madrid, Madrid, Spain.

Articles

"Cuba Frees Valls after 20-year Term." Miami Herald, June 23, 1984, p. 1A.
"Cuba Refuses LULAC's Bid to See Prisoners." Miami Herald, Sept. 9, 1984, p. 24A.
"Cuban and American Released Prisoners List." Miami Herald, June 29, 1984, p. 15A.
"Cuban Poet Is Set Free after 20-year Imprisonment." New York Times, June 25, 1984, p. B8.
"Cuban Poet, Jailed 22 Years, Arrives in Paris." New York Times, Oct. 23, 1982, p. 3.
"A Cuban Poet Uncaged." Editorial. New York Times, Oct. 24, 1982, Sec. 4, p. E22.
"Cuban Poet Valladares Finally Free." Miami Herald, Oct. 22, 1982, p. 1A.
"Deliverance." Time, 120:18 (Nov. 1, 1982), 57.
"Dr. Jekyll and Fidel Castro." Editorial. Wall Street Journal, Dec. 16, 1980, p. 32.
"Freed Cubans Savor Dreams, Make Plans." Miami Herald, July 1, 1984, p. 1A.
"Inside Castro's Prisons." Time, 122:7 (Aug. 15, 1983), 20.
"Jailed Poet's Tiny Book Sees Light." Miami News, Sept. 1, 1984, p. 1A.
Kelly, Sheldon. "The Prisoner Castro Couldn't Break." Reader's Digest, 123:738 (Oct., 1983), 157-162.
"Poet Jorge Valls Pledges to Free 'Brothers.'" Miami Herald, June 25, 1984, p. 5A.
"Prisoners Embrace Freedom." Miami Herald, June 30, 1984, pp. 1A, 17-19A.

"Pujal Smuggles Letter to Son from Cuban Jail." Miami News, Nov. 12, 1982, p. 1A.

"Recent and Renowned Prisoners on Jackson's List." Miami Herald, June 25, 1984, p. 5A.

Remos, Ariel. "Realizarán este sábado 26 diversos actos en favor de un preso en Cuba: Alberto Fibla." Diario Las Américas (Miami, FL), Jan. 26, 1985, p. 2B.

Ripoll, Carlos. "The Poet and the Jailor: Cuadra's Case." Miami Herald, July 19, 1981, p. 6E.

Santiago, Fabiola. "Cuba Allows Famous Dissident Poet to Leave." Miami Herald, March 15, 1985, p. 4C.

"26 Cuban Prisoners OK'd for Flight to Washington." Miami News, June 28, 1984, p. 1A.

Valladares, Armando. "Los presos más antiguos." El Miami Herald, Oct. 22, 1984, p. 5.

Reports

Americas Watch Report. The Treatment of Political Prisoners in Cuba and the American Response. New York, NY: Sept., 1983. 51 pp.

Amnesty International Report 1984. London: Amnesty International Publications, [1984]. Covers the period January to December 1983.

Amnesty International USA. Prepared Statement of Amnesty International USA on the Human Rights Situation in Cuba; before the Subcommittees on Human Rights and International Organizations and Western Hemispheric Affairs of the U.S. House of Representatives. [Washington, DC?] June 27, 1984. 7 pp.

Of Human Rights. A Report on the Human Condition in Cuba. vol. 4, 1, Winter 1981. Washington, DC: Of Human Rights, Inc. 31 pp.

_____. _____. 1982-1983. Washington, DC: Of Human Rights, Inc. 24 pp.

_____. _____. 1983-1984. Washington, DC: Of Human Rights, Inc. 31 pp.

Organization of American States. Inter-American Commission on Human Rights. Seventh Report on the Situation of Human Rights in Cuba. Washington, DC: Organization of American States, General Secretariat, 1983. 183 pp. (Organization of American States. Official Records. OEA/Ser. L/V/11.61, doc. 29 rev. 1)

11. SHIFTING APPROACHES AND RESEARCH PROBLEMS IN THE EXAMINATION OF URBAN SQUATTERS IN LATIN AMERICA

Richard J. Moore

This paper explores some of the difficulties in conducting research on urban squatters in Latin America. Inseparable from this research agenda, however, is a brief examination of the issues surrounding rural-to-urban migration and the relationships among migration, urban poverty, and the residential circumstances of urban squatters. Thus, while the principal context of this discussion of research problems and perspectives focuses on urban squatters, some introductory remarks on the study of internal migration in Latin America are also in order.

My own research has focused principally on political participation and urban poverty in one context: Ecuador. Many of the observations draw on my work in Guayaquil, which began in 1968. Principal organized field research was conducted from 1974 to 1976. During that two-year period I conducted intensive participant observation in one community (El Cisne), carried out a number of lengthy visits to several additional communities, and conducted a survey in six communities in the area known as "suburbio." That initial study relied on close interaction with a number of officials of the municipal government, particularly within the Office of Urban Planning. In addition, two subsequent research visits of several months each were conducted in 1981 and 1984.

This paper is organized in several sections. I begin with a discussion of the migration process and its links to urbanization and the growth of irregular residential settlements. A second section traces research on urban squatters and the urban poor. In both sections I argue that there have been important shifts in the kinds of research questions posed, and in the research agenda itself, over the past two decades. These shifts in both ideological and methodological focus have encouraged concomitant shifts in the perception of the urban poor. Such changes have been important not only because of their implications for academic research but also because at several junctures research findings have been translated into policy. Finally, I examine some of the pitfalls and shortcomings of various perspectives and methodologies employed in the study of urban "masses" in Latin America. I do not seek to provide the reader with definitive answers about urban squatters or migrants. Rather, I hope to fill in some gaps and to provide a review of important trends.

Urbanization and Migration in Latin America

A substantial body of literature on the rural-to-urban migration process in Latin America has accumulated over the past two decades. The reason for this intellectual curiosity is in many ways obvious: the rapid postwar growth of Latin America's major cities has, to considerable degree, resulted from in-migration. In conjunction with birth (fertility and natality) and death, migration accounts for the manner in which population grows or declines. While fertility, natality, and declining urban death rates have accounted for increasing proportions of recent population growth, migration remains its principal engine.

An important opening caveat is the now classic observation by William Mangin (1967): that squatters, the urban poor, and migrants do not form some undifferentiated mass; they are theoretically and empirically distinct. Not all squatters are migrants; not all of the urban poor are squatters; not all migrants are poor. The converse of each of these statements also holds true. In defining a research agenda, the first problem is to decide which population, or which research universe, is of interest. The theoretical dilemma is compounded by the empirical difficulty in identifying any of these populations in a meaningful, consistent, scientific way. I return to these two difficulties at several points in this discussion.

For many residents of squatter settlements, arrival at a site where urban residence becomes relatively permanent is merely the latest stage in a continuing process of migration. In this respect, the city of Guayaquil and its "suburbio" (squatter settlements) share the common experience of most major urban centers in Latin America. The overall distribution of migrants in the urban stratification system responds to a number of factors, not least among which are the conditions that first prompted a move from the place of origin. The presence of migrants in other geographic areas than squatter settlements, and among other status groups than the urban poor, is clearly evident. However, the mix of migrants and natives in the city as a whole is rarely the focus of study in Latin America.[1] The squatter settlements nonetheless represent a final step for many of the urban poor, and most particularly the migrant poor.[2]

The list of research questions raised by the migration process is virtually endless. One way to cut into the research agenda is to distinguish between studies that have approached the issue from a macroscopic perspective and those addressing the microscopic issues of individual behavioral responses. Each of these approaches generates different research questions, and different research problems.

In the broadest sense, migration can be thought of as the "cumulation of individual acts made in response to perceived opportunity differentials" (Simmons et al., 1977:83). Nice, but not necessarily useful! That basic statement of the determinant of migrant decisions belies the process's analytical complexity. From a macroscopic perspective, the structural relationship between migration and urbanization requires the analyst to first step back. As Morrison notes, many studies of the internal migration process in the aggregate do little more than describe net patterns which, for analytical purposes, may be "little more than statistical fictions" (1977:61). Studies of this nature rely heavily on national census reports, and they ordinarily address only a limited set of questions focusing on such patterns of aggregate movement as migrant origins, major routes and destinations, and distances traveled. The difficulties are compounded by the lack of reliable census data until quite recently. In the case of Ecuador, for example, the first reasonably accurate and reasonably comprehensive national population census took place in 1950. Between the first and the second census (1962) a number of definitional changes occurred which rendered comparison difficult at best. The 1974 census, while much more sophisticated and accurate, has also proved problematic for longitudinal analyses.

The questions noted above are important. However, one must move beyond purely descriptive approaches and statistics. As Friedmann and Wulff note, the preoccupation with descriptions of net movements, based on aggregate statistical data, can lead demographers and others to treat migration as the major policy variable. In fact, migration is "dependent upon the major structural features of the economy" (1976:34). By focusing only on the aggregate, researchers may overlook that "migration to cities reflects merely a demographic adjustment in the spatial structure of economic and social opportunities that result from the major urbanization processes [of] . . . the exercise of power, capital movements, and innovation diffusion. Migration is a derived phenomenon, a symptom of urbanization and not the thing itself" (ibid., p. 33). Similar concerns have been raised with regard to the international movements of people. These larger structural questions and their relationship to the migration of individuals are equally important in their policy implications for population distribution.

In the past two decades, studies of internal migration in Latin America have increasingly focused on migration to a particular urban center, usually the national capital or some other major city (Elizaga, 1970; Cardona Gutiërrez, 1971; Herrick, 1971; Balan, Browning, and Jelin, 1973). The usual methodological approach is the survey, which may focus on both macroscopic issues (e.g., routes, origins, time frames, stages in the migration process) and more microscopic concerns (migrant characteristics, selectivity, individual mobility, adaptation, behavioral responses). In either case, the degree to which findings may be generalized--and the utility of any such generalizations--are major concerns. For example, studies at all levels suggest that migrants move for economic reasons (Shaw, 1975; Lowder, 1978). Whether one examines individual decision-making processes, life histories, or broader theoretical rationales for the push and pull of migration forces, the evidence is quite conclusive. Yet even here, the role of such other factors as information about oppor-tunities (Harris and Todaro, 1970; Sovani, 1964; Gugler, 1982); the broader structural forces that produce areas of stagnation and growth (Singer, 1973; Amin, 1974); or alternative poles of attraction (Rondinelli, 1983; Gilbert, 1976) all mediate migration's economic rationale.

Surveys of migration to individual cities have tended to focus on more microscopic questions, probing migrant char-acteristics, migrant-native differences, migration and labor employment, and, most especially, migrant adaptation. This last focus in particular--how migrants adapt to their new urban surroundings and the impact of this adjustment process--has provided much of the linkage between studies of migrants, studies of the urban poor more generally, and studies of urban squatters. As early as the 1940s, the linkages between migra-tion, social-psychological adaptation, and urbanization became a guiding focus for much of what was to follow in the exploration of urbanization and urban poverty. The early question became: What is the impact of "uprooting" the migrant from his rural environment, and imposing him on the terra incognita of the urban milieu.

Migration, Urban Poverty, and the Urban Squatter: Shifting Perceptions

Research on and the image of the urban squatter and his environment have taken a number of major turns in the past quarter century. These shifts have been evident not only in terms of methodology and perspective (ideology) but also in terms of the likely policy implications.

Early perspectives on squatters drew heavily on American urban sociology. Urbanization, development, and the growth of democratic institutions were linked together; or, alternatively and in a more pronounced way, the consequences of urbanization, urban poverty, and rural-to-urban migration were phrased in terms of the radicalization of the poor. Studies from the 1960s drew on pioneering early work by Robert Park (1928), Louis Wirth (1938), and the Chicago School of Sociology. The result was a barrage of pejorative images of the disruptive migrant, of urban sojourners, of unintegrated urban masses.[3] From a macro perspective, urbanization was seen as an agent exacerbating intergroup tensions and creating the conditions for mass involvement in radical political activity.   One proponent of this perspective identified the threat of "teeming urban populations . . . so highly politicized that they have become in a sense, loaded revolvers pointed at the responsible governments and on the verge of being triggered off by the slightest provocation" (Pye, 1962:87).   The images provided by Pye and others (Lerner, 1958; Yalour de Tobar et al., 1967; Germani, 1964; Johnson, 1964) did not, however, focus on any particular population or universe.   The discussions intermingled migrants, the urban poor, the urbanization process, and--the most troubling manifestation of rapid urbanization--the squatter settlements.

Psychosocial analyses complemented these broad and sweeping studies of the consequences of rapid urbanization.   As Nelson (1979:110-112) notes, microlevel analyses characterized the recent migrant (read urban poor) as having been torn from a tightly structured rural environment and thrust into an urban milieu without personal or social cues to orient his life.   Loss of security, disillusionment, and poverty combined to create the mobilizable mass, swaying with every radical breeze.   This interpretation of the urban poor and their community as pathological and disorganized found support in early versions of "marginality theory" (Vekemans, 1969) as well as Oscar Lewis's popular work on the "culture of poverty" (1966).[4]

These images found further complements in policy.   Urbanization was generally seen as carrying positive overall consequences for development, yet also incorporating significant negative "externalities" through the psychosocial maladjustment of the poor and their communities.   The goals of policy, therefore, should be to eliminate (eradicate) the communities perpetuating this negative syndrome, to substitute positive community environments, and/or to reeducate individuals.   The community development movement, the Alliance for Progress, and many national governments incorporated these policies in their actions.

This first phase of perception of the urban squatter had thus found a "theoretical" base, a popular translation of that base, and a set of governmental policies with which to implement change.   Many of these policies and perceptions survive today throughout Latin America.   In part, one might argue, this image survives because it serves to separate the "we" and the "they" in urban contexts, and because it is easier to impose policies on those who are "different."   Deep-seated fears of the communist menace also provided elites with a justification for containing unwanted populations and physical eyesores.

Scholars had begun to test, and challenge, the early paradigm by the late 1960s.   Portes (1971:700) notes, "No single empirical study of lower-class urban settlements in Latin America has uncovered significant amounts of leftist extremism among these groups." The assumption of social disorganization among migrants, lower-class groups, and squatters was challenged by a generation of scholars involved in empirical field research, and conjectural shibboleths began to fail the tests of reality. A new image began to emerge on the basis of research by anthropologists (Mangin, 1967; Peattie, 1968; Roberts, 1973), urban planners (Turner, 1967), and other empirically oriented social scientists (Cornelius, 1975; Goldrich, 1970; Portes, 1971; Perlman, 1976).

The new paradigm suggested a much more positive role of the urban poor: (1) social disruption does not necessarily occur in the city; (2) in-migrants may be politically conservative or moderate, either because of negative sanctions by existing political authorities or because of small-scale improvements; (3) structures of support do exist in the urban milieu in the form of kinship, regional associations, mutual aid associations, and so on; (4) residents of settlement areas make positive contributions to the urban economy in housing and land improvements, labor markets, small-scale contributions to the markets for goods and services, and the more intangible social capital invested in creating the communities (Moore, 1977). The urban poor, migrants, and urban squatters were essentially positive contributors to society, meriting encouragement to improve their lot and increase the national welfare.

Just as the earlier paradigm had led to policy options, so too the participatory image of squatters stimulated new government programs. Latin American and U.S. government programs, together with segments of the international lending community, took up the cry of "freedom to build" and self-help as means of individual improvement and societal transformations. Conservatives applauded these efforts because they would: (1) help overcome resource deficiencies; (2) increase the individual's independence; and (3) reduce the need for and dependence on state action. Liberals saw these new efforts as a means for encouraging local decision-making and the expansion of the democratic ideal (Gilbert and Ward, 1984a:769).

Some neo-Marxists anticipated issues of collective consumption such as housing and social services as rallying points for organizing squatters, and the poor more generally. The contemporary crisis of the capitalist state, centered on issues of collective consumption (provided by the state), would lead to mobilization and conflict. However, this model assumed that effective leadership could translate consumption issues into class issues (Castells, 1977; Harloe, 1977; Evers, 1981).[5] "Autonomous, grassroots" urban social movements would thus provide the opportunity to create social transformation (Castells, 1983). One of the leading proponents of this view, Manuel Castells, asserted that: (1) social movements originate in and reflect the contradictions of prevailing social structural arrangements; (2) the role of the state has increased and is fundamental; and (3) urban social movements and conflicts can be significant forces in fostering interclass coalitions. "Urban movements are those which most unify the interests of various classes and groups against the dominant structural logic, and which leads them to confront a state apparatus which has become the principal manager of collective goods" (Castells, 1977:151).

The intensity of the challenge to earlier images of urban pathology may have led scholars to an unwarranted optimism, in which squatter settlements became "communities of hope" with broad capabilities for collective action. As they searched for normalcy in individual behavior, scholars underplayed the broader institutional context that established the parameters of individual response. Research "discovered" problem-solving capabilities, demands on governments, organized mutual aid, associations for gradual improvement, and more generalized social, political, and economic participation. However, it failed to take into account the roles of those larger institutions that consciously manipulated the symbols and actions of participation. The sometimes unbridled optimism of a second generation of scholars began to be challenged.

These latest challenges have become manifest in several forms, but they ultimately rest on the rather grim premise that the existing social order, the state, and its attendant institutional structures are much more resilient than first believed. Recent studies point to the manipulation of the urban poor by institutional support structures. Cooptation, rather than shared decision-making or local autonomous grass-roots organizations, is the emergent image. Studies of SINAMOS and the National Office of Pueblos Jóvenes (ONDEPJOV) in Peru point to the emergence of supralocal institutions that coopted both local leadership and local efforts at self-improvement (Collier, 1976; Dietz, 1980; Skinner, 1983). Chile's Promoción Popular provides another example of the incorporation of local self-improvement into institutionalized supralocal organizations, in this case the PDC (Moore, 1974; Nelson, 1979). And Mexican studies reveal the ability of the PRI, as well as social service agencies, to contain local demands (Connolly, 1982; Cornelius, 1975; Eckstein, 1977; Moore, 1984; Ward, 1975). Cornelius (1975) and others further note the persistence of clientelist relations as forms of cooptation in Mexico. Similar containment, cooptation, and clientelist policies by the state have been documented for Brazil (Portes, 1979), Ecuador (Moore, 1983), and Colombia (Murillo C. and Ungar, 1978).

Various studies have documented the sequence of events by which independent local decision-making among squatter communities has been minimized. Collier describes the manipulation of

Lima's squatters by President Odria. The urban poor were "allowed" and in some cases encouraged to occupy state-owned peripheral urban lands as a means of consolidating support and popularity. In many cases, these lands lacked any alternative use (Collier, 1976:72-73; Gilbert and Ward, 1984a:772). Similarly, Asaad Bucaram actively promoted land seizures in marshland areas of Guayaquil's suburbio as a means for generating mass support for his own candidacy and for his Concentración de Fuerzas Populares (CFP) (Moore, 1983). What at times appear organized, independent, and autonomous invasions in Guayaquil have proven to be efforts orchestrated by "invasion entrepreneurs," who reap great profits at little cost or risk (Moore, 1984).

A classic case of this manipulation of the urban poor by extralocal authorities and entrepreneurs occurred in Guayaquil just before the municipal and national elections of 1979. The outgoing mayor (who was seeking reelection) issued Municipal Decree 2740, which fixed the sale price of municipal land in suburbio at 10 sucres per square meter. He argued that his policy was in keeping with earlier decrees and ordinances, and merely extended the area of eligible land to include newly invaded areas (El Guasmo). The private, and illegal, sale value of those plots then approximated 300 sucres per square meter. The mayor's move was blatantly political. The ensuing conflicts, debates, and actions by residents, administrators, and politicians eliminated any chance of orderly development in the new sectors of suburbio. Confusion led to new invasions while the conflicting interests of political groups led to administrative stalemate. By 1983, the "occupation" of El Guasmo involved several hundred thousand people--up from an original invasion by less than one thousand. Between 1978 and 1982, four major parties, the municipal administration, the Supreme Court, the national housing bank, and, finally, the President of Ecuador, became involved in this attempt to manipulate land invasions in El Guasmo (ibid., 1984)! Similar situations in Colombia, Venezuela, Mexico, and Brazil, most particularly in the province of social-interest housing, have been cited by Gilbert and Ward (1984a:772).

Recent research, thus, projects a less optimistic image of the urban squatters' capacity to gain access to power or to alter significantly the structural circumstances of his life. Even the sanguine vision of Castells's earlier work on urban social movements has become somewhat muted:

All social movements are unable to fully accomplish their project, since they lose their identity as they become institutionalized, the inevitable outcome of bargaining for social reform within the political system. . . . They are not agents of structural social change, but symptoms of resistance to the social domination even if,

in their effort to resist, they do have major effects on
cities and societies (1983:329).

Those on the left are becoming increasingly aware of the
limits on autonomous action by the urban squatter, in a trend
reminiscent of the cautions of the 1970s (Nelson, 1979). Autonomous social actions, and movements built around issues of
collective consumption issues, alike face a great hurdle. For
their demands must be mediated through the political system:
there are few avenues of protest outside the framework afforded
by established political forces, and the squatters' vulnerability
permits their manipulation by these forces. Castells, referring to
Lima's urban poor, provides a succinct--albeit somewhat ironic--
image of this capacity for action:

> The picture of Lima squatters' movements appears as
> one of a manipulated mob, changing from one political
> ideology to another in exchange for the delivery (or
> promise) of land, housing, and services. And this
> was, to a large extent, the case. . . . But their
> attitude [the squatters'] is quite understandable if we
> remember that all politically progressive alternatives
> were always defeated and ferociously repressed. . . .
> The behavior of these squatters was not cynical or
> apolitical, but realistic (1983:196).

Social movements thus become instruments of subordination, not
mechanisms of social transformation.

Recent studies of urban squatters and "self-help" communities have revealed the increasing importance of the state as the
mediator of political action, as well as the manager of production
and of collective consumption. The squatters' organized social
actions elicit governmental response. Such actions are thereby
diminished as a form of democratic involvement, and rather
provide a channel for the state to legitimate itself, maintain social
control, and contain social unrest. In the words of Gilbert and
Ward, "community participation has been used by government as a
means of legitimating the political system, either as a structure
for garnering votes, or as a means of ensuring compliance with
urban political decision-making" (1984a:780).

The despair explicit in this statement suggests that state
action in capitalist society is incapable of ever serving the
subjective interests of the urban poor. I find myself somewhat
uncomfortable with so drastic a scenario, perhaps because of its
implications. This image also rules out actions by the urban
squatter that can actually achieve "growing control by poor
people over the resources and institutions that determine their
quality of life" (Gilbert and Ward, 1984b:921). Castells carries
this despair to an extreme in the following, apocalyptic summation

of social movements and, by inference, of squatters' rights and capabilities:

> So, faced with an overpowered labor movement, an omnipresent, one-way communication system indifferent to cultural identities, an all-powerful centralized state, loosely governed by unreliable political parties, a structural economic crisis, cultural uncertainty, and the likelihood of nuclear war, people go home. Most withdraw individually, but the crucial, active minority . . . organize themselves on their local turf. . . . Urban movements do address the real issues of our time, although neither on the scale nor terms that are adequate to the task. And yet, they do not have any choice since they are the last reaction to the domination and renewed exploitation that submerge our world (1983:370).

Studying Urban Squatters: A Brief Caution

How does one sift through these varying visions of the relationship between the urban poor and their larger social, economic, and political environment? So many issues, so many seeming contradictions. As a result, so many choices for the researcher. In less than a quarter of a century, we have seen no fewer than three major shifts in the way we examine (and conclude about) urban squatters. Each changing vision has very different policy implications. From a rather patronizing and pessimistic vision of the urban squatter as pathological and in need of reeducation, we moved to a more optimistic image of squatters who were in charge of their destinies--albeit in a world of gradualistic change. The more recent scenario retains a positive image of the individual squatter, but suggests that the structural circumstances of his world make his actions tantamount to spitting into the wind. The last image, I fear, is the most realistic of the three.

In the next few paragraphs, I do not intend to offer "the" answers about who the urban poor are and what they want. I offer instead some cautionary notes on how to evaluate both prevailing and earlier visions of urban squatters. I also point to some of the limitations of and possibilities for source material in studying this group.

1.   The danger of the unyielding universality.--Our studies of migrants and urban squatters have not reached the level of paradigmatic unity. Researchers too often advance conclusions and generalizations on the basis of limited case studies. Even when limited generalizations are in order, the sample and the context must be borne in mind.

2.   Identifying the population under study.--The problem of identifying the population is pervasive for a number of

reasons. First, merely identifying the members of these groups is difficult. Where does one "community" leave off, and another begin? Since there are few "legal" markers for these divisions, how should the limits be defined? This problem is particularly intransigent in survey research. In order to establish a sampling frame, one must first identify or estimate the population from which the sample will be drawn. Let us suppose for a moment that a researcher seeks to investigate the impact of an overall community context on the community's individual members. (Oscar Lewis's "culture of poverty" presumes precisely this kind of contextual impact.) During survey research, or even participant observation, what happens if the community of residence is misidentified? Squatter settlements, unlike the township or borough of Princeton, are not neatly demarcated. External definition may not correspond to subjective definition of residence.

If the problem of identifying a universe is difficult for a residential population, it becomes even more taxing with migrant groups. The complexities peak in the case of minority and/or illegal migrant populations.

Survey research presents other sampling problems as well. Not only are the lines of sampling demarcation somewhat ephemeral, but establishing the sampling frame can require exceptional and innovative techniques. In advanced countries, we often rely on census counts to establish a sample frame. Even here, we know about problems of systematic underreporting and overreporting. In the case of squatters, the difficulties are once again compounded. During my research in 1975, I discovered whole blocks that had been left out of the national census count. In one case I discovered that the census taker had charged families to be included, maintaining that they would benefit by being counted. Inability to pay could mean exclusion from the count! Such cases forced me to recount "my" population. I hired a helicopter and a photographer, and took density photographs of suburbio. With photographs in hand, my photographer and I walked off each block to count separate residences (especially important in multifamily structures). We photographed each block from the corner, and reenumerated the families. Only then could we develop some reasonable estimate of the population. The photographs formed the basis for the initial count, and also helped our interviewer find preselected sample units in an environment where consecutive street numbers, streets, and permanent abodes were often absent.

3. Assessing comparability between studies limited by space and time.--It is often difficult to make comparisons between even well-conducted field research efforts. Changing contexts, different sampling frames, new methodologies, the peculiarities of questionnaire construction, selection criteria may all limit

comparability. Very few studies have been replicated. In my own fieldwork, I consciously attempted to follow the techniques, guidelines, and even survey questions of two previous studies (Cornelius, 1975; Dietz, 1980). But even with this conscious effort, the specific context forced me to make choices that affected the comparability of my findings.

4. <u>Monitoring the level of analysis</u>.--As previously noted, the choice between "macro" and "micro" perspectives often affects a study's conclusions. Researchers are often warned of the "ecological fallacy"--attributing characteristics of the aggregate to the individuals within it. Studies that are process oriented or structurally oriented may not reveal much about individual behaviors, just as aggregates of individual characteristics may not illuminate structural phenomena.

5. <u>The role of anecdotal data</u>.--Life histories are an increasingly important part of field research on minority populations. This is equally true for studies of urban squatters. In the relative absence of structured data, we necessarily rely to some extent on these informal appraisals. However, there are limits to the utility of such inquiries, and the researcher should beware.

Other cautions might be noted. However, I would like to offer some brief suggestions on sources of data that may be available to researchers studying squatters. Such traditional sources of information as censuses, newspaper accounts, and surveys may not provide a clear picture. Life history data, even with their limits, are a useful supplement. Many somewhat informal organizational structures within squatter settlements-- women's groups, regional associations, sports clubs--can also provide valuable information. Such groups often keep records of memberships, meetings, actions taken, and confrontations within the community or with the larger institutional structure. Local parishes are a particularly valuable information source. They often serve as the only official register, so their records can reveal exciting nuances of community life. Insofar as the local church often serves as the organizing mechanism for political and social action, parish priests and parish records can provide invaluable information.

Finally, squatter studies too often limit their sources to formalized points of contact between the community and the larger social structure. One must consider these institutional nexuses, to be sure. Data from social service agencies, planning departments, and standing municipal committees often yield essential insights. But focusing exclusively on these institutions, on the recognized local leadership, on formal periodicals and news sources, can cause the researcher to miss much of importance. In Guayaquil, a suburbio-wide, irregular magazine entitled <u>La Voz del Suburbio</u> has served me well in following many local events, actions, and personalities. Unfortunately, acquiring copies is a hit and miss proposition. Informal pamphlets about organizations, meetings, celebrations, and the like similarly serve as a useful-- albeit haphazard--source of information.

These brief remarks ultimately suggest one overarching reality: to examine minority, often "invisible," populations requires us to break with some of the traditional rules of social science research. Unusually innovative methods are essential if we want to gain a clear picture of much of "what's happening" in Latin America.

NOTES

1.   Of course, the numerous studies by the Centro Latino- americano de Demografía (CELADE) have focused on these questions for more than two decades. See, e.g., Elizaga (1970 and 1971).

2.   In my sample of six settlement areas, migrants represented the vast majority of residents, ranging from 62.8 percent to 100 percent in the various sites. Indeed, the most comprehensive study of Ecuador's "popular sector" reports that 77.2 percent of all members are migrants by birth, and fully 60 percent resided outside of Guayaquil prior to age 12 (Junta Nacional de Planificación, 1975:95-96).

3.   Perhaps the best single review of the literature on urban poverty and political participation in Latin America of this early time period is Nelson (1969). This brief volume is incorpo- rated in her later comprehensive volume (Nelson, 1979). See also the early work done by Cornelius (1969).

4.   Many studies have pointed to the methodological and theoretical weaknesses of these perspectives. See Leacock (1971), Portes (1972), Moore (1974), and Perlman (1976). Ironically, the culture of poverty argument has reared its head more recently in the popular U.S. media in the guise of a permanent "Underclass." See, e.g., Auletta (1982).

5.   Although this is not the appropriate place to analyze the contributions of this recent literature at length, the argument of the crisis of the capitalist state has a broader theoretical base than the focus on urban squatters here suggests. Much of the literature of the French structuralists focuses on advanced capitalist nations. More recently still, the focus has shifted to retrenchment policies, particularly in the United States and Great Britain (Fainstein and Fainstein, 1982; Harloe and Lebas, 1982).

BIBLIOGRAPHY

Amin, Samir. 1974. Accumulation on a World Scale. New York, NY: Monthly Review Press.

Auletta, Kenneth. 1982. The Underclass. New York, NY: Random House.

Balan, Jorge, Harley Browning, and Elizabeth Jelin. 1973. Men in a Developing Society: Geographic and Social Mobility in Monterrey, Mexico. Austin, TX: University of Texas Press.

Butterworth, Douglas. 1975. "Rural-Urban Migration and Micro-demography: A Case Study from Mexico," Urban Anthropology, 4(3):265-283.

Butterworth, Douglas, and John Chance. 1981. Latin American Urbanization. Cambridge: Cambridge University Press.

Cardona Gutiérrez, Ramiro, ed. 1971. Las migraciones internas. Bogotá: Asociación Colombiana de Facultades de Medicina, División de Estudios de Población.

Castells, Manuel. 1977. The Urban Question: A Marxist Approach. London: Edward Arnold.

_____. 1983. The City and the Grassroots: A Cross-Cultural Theory of Urban Social Movements. London: Edward Arnold.

Collier, David. 1976. Squatters and Oligarchs: Authoritarian Rule and Policy Change in Peru. Baltimore, MD: Johns Hopkins University Press.

Connolly, Patricia. 1982. "Uncontrolled Settlement and Self-Build: What Kind of Solution?" In Peter Ward, ed., Self-Help Housing: A Critique. London: Mansell. Pp. 141-174.

Cornelius, Wayne A. 1969. "Urbanization as an Agent in Latin American Political Instability: The Case of Mexico," American Political Science Review, 63(3):833-857.

_____. 1975. Politics and the Migrant Poor in Mexico City. Stanford, CA: Stanford University Press.

Dietz, Henry. 1980. Poverty and Problem-Solving under Military Rule: The Urban Poor in Lima, Peru. Austin, TX: University of Texas Press.

DuToit, Brian M. 1975. "A Decision-Making Model for the Study of Migration." In Brian M. DuToit and Helen I. Safa, eds., Migration and Urbanization: Models and Adaptive Strategies. 9th International Congress of Anthropological Sciences, Chicago, 1973. The Hague: Mouton. Pp. 212-235.

Eckstein, Susan. 1977. The Poverty of Revolution: The State and the Urban Poor in Mexico. Princeton, NJ: Princeton University Press.

Elizaga, Juan. 1970. Migraciones a los áreas metropolitanas de América Latina. Santiago: CELADE.

_____. 1971. "Migraciones interiores: Evolución y estado actual de los estudios." In Ramiro Cardona Gutiérrez, ed., Las migraciones internas. Bogotá: Asociación Colombiana de Facultades de Medicina, División de Estudios de Población. Pp. 25-47.

Evers, Adalbert. 1981. "Social Movements and Political Power: A Survey of a Theoretical and Political Controversy," Comparative Urban Research, 8(2):29-47.

Fainstein, Norman, and Susan Fainstein, eds. 1982. Urban Policy under Capitalism. Beverly Hills, CA: Sage.

Friedmann, John, and Robert Wulff. 1976. The Urban Transition: Comparative Studies of Newly Industrializing Societies. London: Edward Arnold.

Germani, Gino. 1964. "Social Change and Intergroup Conflict." In Irving L. Horowitz, ed., The New Sociology: Essays in Social Science and Social Theory, in Honor of C. Wright Mills. Oxford: Oxford University Press. Pp. 69-83.

Gilbert, Alan. 1976. "The Arguments for Very Large Cities Reconsidered," Urban Studies, 13(1):27-34.

Gilbert, Alan, and Josef Gugler. 1982. Cities, Poverty and Development: Urbanization in the Third World. New York, NY: Oxford University Press.

Gilbert, Alan, and Peter Ward. 1984a. "Community Action by the Urban Poor: Democratic Involvement, Community Self-Help, or a Means of Social Control?" World Development, 12(8):769-782.

_____. 1984b. "Community Participation in Upgrading Irregular Settlements: The Community Response," World Development, 12(9):913-922.

_____. 1985. Housing, the State, and the Poor: Policy and Practice in Three Latin American Cities. London: Cambridge University Press.

Goldrich, Daniel. 1970. "The Political Integration of Lower Class Urban Settlements in Chile and Peru." In Irving L. Horowitz, ed., Masses in Latin America. New York, NY: Oxford University Press. Pp. 175-214.

Gugler, Josef. 1982. "Overurbanization Reconsidered," Economic Development and Cultural Change, 31(1):173-189.

Guillet, David, and Douglas Uzzell, eds. 1976. New Approaches to the Study of Migration. Houston, TX: William Marsh Rice University Press.

Harloe, Michael, ed. 1977. Captive Cities: Studies in the Political Economy of Cities and Regions. London: John Wiley and Sons.

Harloe, Michael, and Elizabeth Lebas, eds. 1982. City, Class, and Capital: New Developments in the Political Economy of Cities and Regions. New York, NY: Holmes and Meier.

Harris, John R., and Michael P. Todaro. 1970. "Migration, Unemployment, and Development: A Two-Sector Analysis," American Economic Review, 60(1):126-142.

Herrick, Bruce. 1971. "Urbanization and Urban Migration in Latin America: An Economist's View." In Francine F. Rabinovitz and Felicity M. Trueblood, eds., Latin American Urban Research. Beverly Hills, CA: Sage. I:71-81.

Johnson, Kenneth F. 1964. "Causal Factors in Latin American Political Instability," Western Political Quarterly. 17(3): 432-446.

Junta Nacional de Planificación y Coordinación Económica. 1975. El desarrollo urbano en el Ecuador. Guayaquil (?): JUNAPLA.

Kemper, Robert V. 1977. Migration and Adaptation: Tzintzuntzan Peasants in Mexico City. Beverly Hills, CA: Sage.

Leacock, Eleanor, ed. 1971. The Culture of Poverty: A Critique. New York, NY: Simon and Schuster.

Lerner, Daniel. 1958. The Passing of Traditional Society: Modernizing the Middle East. Glencoe, IL: Free Press.

Lewis, Oscar. 1966. La Vida: A Puerto Rican Family in the Culture of Poverty, San Juan and New York. New York, NY: Random House.

Lowder, Stella. 1978. "The Context of Latin American Labour Migration: A Review of the Literature Post-1970," Sage Race Relations Abstracts, 3(3):1-49.

Mangin, William. 1967. "Latin American Squatter Settlements: A Problem and a Solution," Latin American Research Review. 2(3):65-98.

Molina S., Juan. 1965. Las migraciones internas en el Ecuador. Quito: Editorial Universitaria.

Moore, Richard. 1974. "Urbanization, Marginality and Promoción Popular in Chile." Unpublished doctoral essay, University of Texas at Austin.

_____. 1977. "Assimilation and Political Participation among the Urban Poor in Guayaquil, Ecuador." Ph.D. diss., University of Texas at Austin.

_____. 1978. "Urban Problems and Policy Responses for Metropolitan Guayaquil." In Wayne A. Cornelius and Robert V. Kemper, eds., Metropolitan Latin America: The Challenge and the Response. Latin American Urban Research, v. 6. Beverly Hills, CA: Sage.

_____. 1983. "Urban Development and the Politics of Land Use in Guayaquil, Ecuador." Paper presented at the meetings of the International Studies Association, Mexico City.

_____. 1984. "Urbanization and Housing Policy in Mexico." In Pedro Aspe and Paul E. Sigmund, eds., The Political Economy of Income Distribution in Mexico. New York, NY: Holmes and Meier.

Morrison, Peter A. 1977. "The Functions and Dynamics of the Migration Process." In Alan A. Brown and Egon Neuberger, eds., Internal Migration: A Comparative Perspective. New York, NY: Academic Press. Pp. 61-72.

Muñoz, Humberto, et al. 1974. Las migraciones internas en América Latina: Consideraciones teóricas. Buenos Aires: Ediciones Nueva Visión.

Muñoz, Humberto, Orlandina de Oliveira, and Claudio Stern. 1977. Migración y desigualdad social en la Ciudad de México. México, DF: Instituto de Investigaciones Sociales, Universidad Nacional Autónoma de México.

Murillo C., Gabriel, and Elizabeth B. Ungar. 1978. Política, vivienda popular y el proceso de toma de decisiones en Colombia: Análisis de la coyuntura actual y viabilidad de las soluciones propuestas durante el Frente Nacional. Bogotá: Universidad de los Andes.

Nelson, Joan. 1969. Migrants, Urban Poverty, and Instability in Developing Nations. Cambridge, MA: Center for International Studies, Harvard University.

_____. 1979. Access to Power: Politics and the Urban Poor in Developing Countries. Princeton, NJ: Princeton University Press.

Park, Robert E. 1928. "Human Migration and the Marginal Man," American Journal of Sociology, 33(6):881-893.

Peattie, Lisa R. 1968. The View from the Barrio. Ann Arbor, MI: University of Michigan Press.

_____. 1979. "Housing Policy in Developing Countries: Two Puzzles," World Development, 17(11/12):1017-1022.

_____. 1980. "Anthropological Perspectives on the Concepts of Dualism, the Informal Sector, and Marginality in Developing Urban Economies," International Regional Science Review, 5(2):1-31.

Perlman, Janice. 1976. The Myth of Marginality: Urban Poverty and Politics in Rio de Janeiro. Berkeley, CA: University of California Press.

Portes, Alejandro. 1971. "Urbanization and Politics in Latin America," Social Science Quarterly, 52(3):697-720.

_____. 1972. "Rationality in the Slum: An Essay on Interpretive Sociology," Comparative Studies in Society and History, 14(3):268-286.

_____. 1978. "Migration and Underdevelopment," Politics and Society, 8(1):1-48.

_____. 1979. "Housing Policy, Urban Poverty, and the State: The Favelas of Rio de Janeiro, 1972-1976," Latin American Research Review, 14(2):3-24.

Pye, Lucian W. 1962. "The Political Implications of Urbanization and the Development Process." In Science, Technology, and

Development: United States Papers Prepared for the United Nations Conference on the Application of Science and Technology for the Benefit of the Less Developed Areas, v. 7. Washington, DC: U.S. Government Printing Office. Pp. 84-89.

Richmond, Anthony, and Daniel Kubat, eds. 1976. Internal Migration: The New World and the Third World. Beverly Hills, CA: Sage.

Roberts, Bryan. 1973. Organizing Strangers: Poor Families in Guatemala City. Austin, TX: University of Texas Press.

Rondinelli, Dennis. 1983. Secondary Cities in Developing Countries: Policies for Diffusing Urbanization. Beverly Hills, CA: Sage.

Shaw, R. Paul. 1975. Migration Theory and Fact: A Review and Bibliography of Current Literature. Bibliography Series, 5. Philadelphia, PA: Regional Science Research Institute.

Simmons, Alan, Sergio Díaz-Briquets, and Aprodicio Lacquian. 1977. Social Change and Internal Migration: A Review of Research Findings from Africa, Asia, and Latin America. Ottawa: IDRC.

Singer, Paul. 1973. "Migraciones internas en América Latina: Consideraciones teóricas para su estudio." In Manuel Castells, ed., Imperialismo y urbanización en América Latina. Barcelona: Editorial Gustavo Gili.

Skinner, R. 1983. "Community Participation: Its Scope and Organization." In R. J. Skinner and M. J. Rodell, eds., People, Poverty, and Shelter: Problems of Self-Help Housing in the Third World. New York, NY: Methuen. Pp. 125-150.

Sovani, N. V. 1964. "The Analysis of Overurbanization," Economic Development and Cultural Change, 12(2):113-122.

Todaro, Michael. 1976. Internal Migration in Developing Countries: A Review of Theory, Evidence, Methodology, and Research Priorities. Geneva: International Labour Office.

Turner, John C. 1967. "Barriers and Channels for Housing Development in Modernizing Countries," Journal of the American Institute of Planners, 33(3):167-181.

_____. 1976. Housing By People: Towards Autonomy in Building Environments. London: Marion Boyars.

Vekemans, Roger. 1969. La marginalidad en América Latina: Un ensayo de conceptualización. Santiago: Centro para el Desarrollo Económico y Social de América Latina.

Ward, Peter M. 1975. "The Squatter Settlement as Slum or Housing Solution: Evidence from Mexico City," Land Economics, 52(3):330-346.

_____. 1981. "Financing Land Acquisition for Self-Build Housing Schemes," Third World Planning Review, 3(1):7-20.

Wirth, Louis. 1938. "Urbanism as a Way of Life," American Journal of Sociology, 44(1):1-24.

Yalour de Tobar, Margot R.   1967.   "Marginalidad y alienación en
    la clase obrera."   In Margot R. Yalour de Tobar, María
    Magdalena Chirico, and Edith Soubie, Clase obrera, economía y
    cambio   social.   El   proceso   de   socialización   urbana.
    Marginalidad y alienación en la clase obrera.   Centro de
    Estudios Urbanos y Regionales, CEUR, 9.   Buenos Aires:
    Instituto Torcuato di Tella.

12. NEW IMMIGRANTS IN THE UNITED STATES: SOME PERSPECTIVES ON THE CARIBBEAN COMMUNITY IN NEW YORK CITY

Marco Antonio Mason

Introduction

Current data indicate a dramatic increase in immigration to the United States, yet this phenomenon has been largely overlooked in the contemporary literature. I therefore give a brief overview of how new immigrants are transforming the ethnic composition of America. The Caribbean community is among the fastest-growing immigrant groups. I thus present a contextual perspective on its long migratory tradition as it relates to the development of the Americas, particularly focusing on current demographic data that indicate that this population is becoming more visible as it enters the mainstream of American life.

The lack of emphasis on migration research has resulted in a dearth of information on expatriation, migration, and population movements of ethnic groups from Third World countries. I append a list of some resource agencies involved in compiling and disseminating such data.

Finally, since this seminar seeks to improve library documentation and to formulate strategies for acquiring and disseminating information about the cultures and peoples of the Caribbean and Latin America, I offer some observations specifically directed to professionals in the field.

New Immigrants Are Transforming the Nation's Ethnic Composition

Current immigration represents a significant historical shift. Beginning early in the nineteenth century, U.S. immigration policies overwhelmingly favored immigrants from Northern and Western Europe in an effort to preserve the nation's European character. The United States Immigration Reform Law of 1965 has dramatically reversed this trend. The current bulk of immigrants hail from the Third World, namely from the Caribbean, Latin America, and Asia.

During the peak immigration years from 1900 to 1920, 85.2 percent of all immigrants came from Europe, with 3.9 percent from Asia (the 1917 Immigration Act excluded Asians), and only 10.4 percent from the Western Hemisphere. By contrast, during the period between 1960 and 1984, only 22 percent of new immigrants hailed from Europe. More than 30 percent came from Asia, mostly from the Philippines, Korea, China, and India. The largest contingent of today's new immigrants, 45.2 percent, comes from the Western Hemisphere. Within this group, immigrants from the West Indies lead (15 percent), followed by those from Mexico (13.7 percent). (The appendixes, with figures emphasizing New York City, provide statistics to further illustrate these changing trends.)

Demographic projections anticipate worldwide population growth from 4 billion to 6.35 billion over the next fifteen years. Ninety-two percent of this increase will occur in developing countries. Two thirds of the world's migration is to America, and migration from developing countries to the United States will increase tremendously by the year 2000. The new immigration is dramatically and irreversibly transforming the nation's demographic patterns, cultural mix, and ethnic fabric.

The current level of immigration also poses a challenge to American foreign policy toward the Third World. This foreign policy currently contributes to social and economic distortions within the sending countries, and thus intensifies the "push factors" for continued migration between them and the United States. In light of the emerging interdependence between the United States and the strategic Caribbean, Latin American, and Pacific markets, the United States must initiate bold new policies.

The impact of the new immigration to the United States has been reflected in a devastating brain drain, and corresponding economic and social distortions in the Third World's sending countries. However, the new immigrants have radically and permanently changed the face of America. They are enriching the nation's cultural diversity and invigorating its economic growth. These immigrants come with a solid purpose--to seek a better life. A generalized immigrant profile would embody traits of hope, courage, determination, and hard work.

Cheap immigrant labor tends to create new jobs and to increase productivity, and thus has a positive impact on the economy. Since the low U.S. birth rate of the 1960s has slowed the growth of America's native labor force, the country will need more immigrants to propel its future economic growth.

The Context of Caribbean Migration in the Americas

The African diaspora has left a dramatic and hemisphere-wide legacy of extreme human sacrifice and notable achievement. It nonetheless remains largely obscure. Blacks, for example, played a significant role in Spain's conquest of the Americas. The Maroon movement later facilitated England's penetration and eventual control of the insular territories in the Caribbean, and provided a backdrop for the exploits of privateers like Henry Morgan and Francis Drake. The Black insurrection in Haiti forced the French to relinquish their claim to the Louisiana Territory, thereby fostering the western expansion of the United States. And Blacks played a strategic military role in the hemisphere's struggles for independence.

The legacy of the African diaspora continues with the sustained movement of Caribbean people throughout the world. Before our era, the heaviest migration within the Americas occurred during the 1880s. Large-scale migratory movements were subsequently directed toward Panama, the United States, Canada, and Britain.

The earliest Black migrations were involuntary, and occurred as slaves were forcibly transported to the New World. However the Blacks' rebellions resulted in the abolition of slavery in the English Antilles in 1833, in the French Antilles in 1848, and in the Spanish colonies as follows: Argentina, 1813; Central America, 1824; Mexico, 1829; Peru, 1854; Puerto Rico, 1872. In the United States, President Lincoln signed the Emancipation Proclamation in 1863.

Migration is an integral component of the Caribbean experience. Ten to fifteen years after emancipation, former slaves from the English-speaking Caribbean became the first wave of a migrant labor force. Their disciplined working style, learned on the islands' plantations, suited them well for work gangs on the Panama railroad. This crucial link facilitated interoceanic transit following the California Gold Rush of 1848-1850.

With Panama as a base, West Indians emigrated as a crucial cheap labor force to build railroads in Cartagena, Barranquilla, and Santa Marta in Colombia; the Cuban Railroad; the Guayaquil railroad in Ecuador; and the Caracas and La Guaira railroad in Venezuela. They also left Panama to build plantation railroads throughout Central America (Costa Rica, Honduras, Nicaragua), and the Central Pacific and Union Pacific railroads in the United States. Some also migrated from Panama to work on large-scale agricultural enterprises in Peru, Brazil, and the United States.

During the ten years between 1856 and 1866, a wave of Caribbean migrants left Panama for the United States. Most traveled via the Pacific Mail Steamship Company of New York, following its routes between Panama and New York, and Panama and San Francisco. The company assumed the costs of transporting these West Indian workers to help meet the demand for cheap labor created by industrial expansion. In 1860, Blacks in the U.S. South were still slaves: that year, West Indians on one northern steamship touching at Charlestown and Savannah were impounded. (See U.S. Federal Case No. 4366.)

High labor demand, in conjunction with union organizing campaigns, led to 1885 legislation blocking the use of cheap, imported laborers as strikebreakers. Immigrants from the Caribbean region--including Mexico, Cuba, Haiti, and the Dominican Republic--were exempted from the restrictions.

A second wave of mostly Jamaican immigrants arrived in Panama in the 1870s. Most came to work with the French Canal Company, whose 1889 collapse left many stranded. Construction of the American Canal, at the turn of the century, sparked a third wave of labor migration. Thousands of canal diggers died from explosives and tropical disease. These West Indian workers lived and toiled under a segregated Jim Crow system, extending even to pay: white workers received gold, Blacks were paid in silver.

Caribbean migration to New York City increased around the 1900s, when the introduction of European beet sugar caused a depression in the Caribbean sugar industry. By the 1930s, more than half of the Caribbean people in the United States lived in New York. More than 70 percent of subsequent arrivals also settled in New York. Migration slowed following the 1952 Immigration Law. However, the 1965 Immigration Act again increased Caribbean migration to the United States. Britain's 1962 decision to close its doors to immigrants from Black commonwealth nations, then emerging as independent states, also contributed to the flow toward the United States.

The Impact of Caribbean Migration on New York City

New immigrants cluster in the major cities of six states: California, New York, Florida, Illinois, and New Jersey. This settlement pattern has a special significance for New York City. No other city contains so many diverse ethnic groups, in such large numbers, as this traditional city of immigrants.

New York remains the major port of entry to immigrants from around the world, and new immigrants constitute almost one third (2.1 of 7.1 million) of its residents. The current influx of immigrants is the greatest since the 1940s, and the flow is expected to increase sharply over the next decade. A large portion of this fast-growing immigrant population hails from the circum-Caribbean region.

The new wave of immigrants from the more than two dozen Caribbean nations has most obviously resulted from the relatively favorable provisions of the 1965 Immigration Act. Also significant are labor-related push-and-pull factors, affordable air fares, and the Caribbean region's geographic proximity to the United States. The following example affords one glimpse of this influx: during the ten-year period from 1967 to 1976, more than 180,000 Jamaican and Haitian immigrants were admitted to the United States. The vast majority of both these groups, approximately 68 percent, came to New York City.

This rapid growth highlights the need to develop mutually beneficial relationships between the immigrant community and mainstream American society. The Caribbean population's increasing visibility has altered both the demographic patterns and the ethnic fabric of New York City. Current census data reveal that this population is a defined and vibrant constituency. In 1984, the Caribbean population was estimated as more than half of Brooklyn's 800,000 Blacks--a number also making Brooklyn the country's largest Black community.

The impact of the Caribbean population can already be seen in the shifting ethnic compositions of specific neighborhoods. The Crown Heights-East Flatbush section of Brooklyn, for example, has become the heart of the city's Caribbean community: immigrants set the flavor of this area just as they do in Chinatown or Little Italy. Other major clusters include Central Harlem, the North East Bronx, and the Cambria Heights-Laurelton section of Queens.

The Caribbean immigrant community has substantial economic and political significance. Its political capabilities were dramatically revealed in its large vote for the Reverend Jesse Jackson during the Democratic primaries. Caribbean-American consumers are estimated to comprise a lucrative $6 billion market.

Migration studies suggest that immigrant groups take about twenty years to adjust to and enter into the mainstream of their host countries. It is now twenty years since the influx of new immigrants began. Having settled and adjusted, these groups are rapidly entering the mainstream of American life. Caribbean immigrants are beginning to flex their political muscle as a voting bloc, conducting large-scale voter registration drives and making sizable campaign contributions.

Dual citizenship provisions mean that they are becoming U.S. citizens, and exercising their suffrage, at an impressive rate. Immigration and Naturalization Service records show an extremely high naturalization rate among these new immigrants. One major incentive to American citizenship is the ability to sponsor the migration of relatives from back home. Three generations of West Indians now live in New York City, and solid sociocultural linkages have formed within the Caribbean-American communities. Brooklyn has the largest number of first- and second-generation West Indians in the United States.

Caribbean immigration has contributed substantially to New York's cultural diversity. According to Police Department statistics, the West Indians' Labor Day Parade--in Brooklyn--is the largest public event in the United States, attracting more than a million participants. Recent Caribbean immigrants are younger than average, and concentrate in the young adult ages of 15 to 44 years. The immigrants are disproportionately female, live in larger than average households, and tend to have a larger than average share of households maintained by females. Caribbean immigrants, during the 1970s, possessed less education than native Americans. The immigrants also boasted fewer persons employed as managers and professionals. As a result, the immigrants' median family income was below average.

Immigration from the Caribbean into New York has continued into the 1980s, and it will continue to affect the City's social and economic fabric. This immigration (detailed further in the appendixes) has serious implications for information professionals. Ironically, however, the immigrant communities remain basically untapped and underserved. This reality highlights the need for new programs.

Comments and Recommendations

We need better quantitative data, as well as specific research, on America's fast-growing immigrant population. Professionals in the fields of information collection and dissemination need to expand their grasp to incorporate technical and professional resource agencies dealing with migration studies.

Libraries tend to direct their services to mainstream communications networks, overlooking the information outlets of community-based and ethnic groups. Libraries should strive to be more transcultural in their acquisitions. Ethnic newspapers, magazines, and the like should be pursued. Similarly, libraries should obtain more Caribbean and Latin American materials in their original languages, as well as works in translation.

Materials dealing with immigrant and ethnic groups should be made more widely accessible to the mainstream society. But the new communities themselves also need education in library services, to enhance their own capabilities. Finally, computer-based technology should be made available to developing countries. More effective collection, retrieval, and dissemination of information should all result.

Appendix A

Immigrants Admitted by Country of Birth
1971 to 1978 (Caribbean Region)

Country of birth	1971	1973	1975	1977	1978
Caribbean	72,348	69,963	72,856	123,131	103,936
Barbados	1,731	1,448	1,618	2,763	2,995
Cuba	21,611	24,147	25,955	69,708	29,801
Dominican Republic	12,624	13,921	14,066	11,655	19,510
Haiti	7,444	4,785	5,145	5,441	6,503
Jamaica	14,571	9,963	11,076	11,501	19,299
Trinidad	7,130	7,035	5,982	6,106	6,006
Panama	1,457	1,612	1,694	2,389	3,100
Guyana	2,115	2,969	3,169	5,718	7,615
West Indies	3,665	4,082	4,151	7,850	9,107

Source: U.S. Immigration and Naturalization Service.

Appendix B

Registered Aliens in New York City – January, 1980

1. Dominican Republic	88,350	41. Chile	2,413
2. China	44,443	42. Grenada	2,285
3. Italy	42,953	43. Hungary	2,219
4. Jamaica	38,025	44. Brazil	2,144
5. U.S.S.R.	31,803	45. Egypt	2,022
6. Ecuador	27,475	46. Nicaragua	1,777
7. Colombia	26,112	47. Belize	1,626
8. Cuba	21,569	48. Austria	1,586
9. Trinidad/Tobago	17,234	49. Scotland	1,521
10. Guyana	14,947	50. Thailand	1,421
11. Korea	14,843	51. Czechoslovakia	1,364
12. India	14,487	52. St. Vincent	1,289
13. Greece	14,148	53. Lebanon	1,285
14. Haiti	12,283	54. Uruguay	1,235
15. United Kingdom	11,409	55. Venezuela	1,172
16. Philippine Islands	9,305	56. Antigua	1,094
17. Barbados	9,268	57. Norway	1,024
18. Poland	9,180	58. Cyprus	1,020
19. England	8,128	59. Burma	982
20. Germany	7,836	60. Malta	928
21. Japan	7,373	61. Bangladesh	906
22. Yugoslavia	5,868	62. Switzerland	892
23. Panama	5,670	63. Sweden	844
24. Ireland	5,589	64. Netherlands	828
25. Peru	5,525	65. Antilles	802
26. Argentina	5,471	66. Australia	757
27. Canada	5,236	67. Ghana	729
28. Honduras	4,892	68. Bolivia	709
29. Israel	4,817	69. West Indies	684
30. Spain	4,362	70. Nigeria	642
31. Romania	4,142	71. Syria	636
32. France	4,136	72. Belgium	603
33. El Salvador	3,789	73. South Africa	574
34. Turkey	3,323	74. Morocco	550
35. Mexico	3,136	75. Finland	546
36. Vietnam	3,105	76. Iraq	527
37. Iran	2,929		
38. Portugal	2,693	Total These Nations	592,824
39. Costa Rica	2,673		
40. Pakistan	2,661	Total All Nations	607,534
41. Chile	2,413		

Prepared by: Population Research & Analysis, New York City
                Department of City Planning.

Appendix C

Total Foreign-Born in New York City, 1980

Italy	156,280	England	22,720
Dominican Republic	120,600	Hungary	22,660
China	95,100	Yugoslavia	22,300
Jamaica	93,100	India	21,500
U.S.S.R.	78,340	Philippines	21,260
Poland	77,160	Panama	20,840
Germany	60,760	Barbados	19,680
Haiti	50,160	Korea	18,480
Cuba	49,720	Romania	17,560
Ireland	42,360	Czechoslovakia	16,320
Greece	41,760	Israel	15,780
Colombia	41,200	Canada	15,320
Trinidad/Tobago	39,160	France	11,860
Ecuador	39,000	Argentina	11,000
Guyana	31,960	Peru	10,620
Austria	26,160		

Source: 1980 U.S. Census.

From: New York City Department of City Planning Population Division.

Appendix D

**Foreign-Born Population from Selected Caribbean Countries for
the United States, New York State, and the New York City
Standard Metropolitan Statistical Area (SMSA)**

Country of birth	United States	New York State	New York City SMSA	New York City SMSA as a Percentage of	
				United States	New York State
All countries	14,079,906	2,388,938	1,946,800	13.8	81.5
Caribbean	1,258,363	463,759	439,969	35.0	94.9
Cuba	607,814	56,895	54,267	8.9	95.4
Dominican Republic	169,147	131,313	127,692	75.5	97.2
Haiti	92,395	55,363	52,586	56.9	95.0
Jamaica	196,811	107,130	98,834	50.2	92.3
Trinidad & Tobago	65,907	41,524	39,565	60.0	95.3
Other West Indies	126,289	71,534	67,025	53.1	93.7

Source: 1980 U.S. Census.

Appendix E

Non-Hispanic Caribbeans in New York City by Borough, 1980

Country of birth	Total N.Y.C.	Bronx	Brooklyn	Man-hattan	Queens	Staten Island
Total Non-Hispanic	299,600	45,320	164,300	22,140	66,280	1,560
Jamaica	93,100	24,460	42,660	5,460	20,140	380
Haiti	50,160	1,680	30,260	3,620	14,340	260
Trinidad/Tobago	39,160	2,120	27,080	2,120	7,640	200
Guyana	31,960	4,920	15,840	2,540	8,620	40
Panama	20,840	1,900	13,280	1,740	3,760	160
Barbados	19,680	2,020	13,000	1,600	3,040	20
Grenada	5,660	160	4,860	180	460	--
St. Vincent	2,700	160	2,140	40	360	--
Antigua-Barbuda	2,380	1,380	320	180	500	--
Dominica	1,660	360	500	420	380	--
Bahamas	1,540	380	400	400	340	20
Aruba	1,140	100	680	140	180	40
St. Kitts-Nevis	1,000	160	280	180	380	--
All Other	28,620	5,520	13,000	6,140	6,140	440

Source: 1980 U.S. Census.

Appendix F

Non-Hispanic Caribbeans in New York City
by Period of Immigration, 1980

Birthplace	Total	Period of Immigration to the United States		
		Pre-1965	1965-1974	1975-1980
Total	299,600	58,580	156,920	84,100
Jamaica	93,100	16,820	52,620	23,660
Haiti	50,160	6,380	29,940	13,840
Trinidad/ Tobago	39,160	4,860	23,660	10,640
Guyana	31,960	2,540	13,700	15,720
Panama*	20,840	8,720	7,580	4,540
Barbados	19,680	5,160	9,040	5,480
Grenada	5,660	720	2,960	1,980
St. Vincent	2,700	480	1,340	880
Antigua- Barbuda	2,380	560	1,220	600
Dominica	1,660	460	660	540
Bahamas	1,540	780	340	420
Aruba	1,140	480	500	160
St. Kitts- Nevis	1,000	520	380	100
St. Lucia	960	300	520	140
Curacao	500	120	300	80
All Other	27,160	9,680	12,160	5,320

Source: 1980 U.S. Census Microdata Sample.

Prepared by: Department of City Planning New York City.

*Panamanians in New York tend to be of British West Indian, not Hispanic ancestry.

Appendix G

*Rank Order of Top Ten Sending Nations to New York City
by Period of Immigration, 1980*

Total 1980	Pre-1965	1965-1974	1975-1980
1. Italy	1. Italy	1. Dominican Republic	1. Dominican Republic
2. Dominican Republic	2. Poland	2. Jamaica	2. U.S.S.R.
3. China	3. Germany	3. China	3. China
4. Jamaica	4. U.S.S.R.	4. Italy	4. Jamaica
5. U.S.S.R.	5. Ireland	5. Haiti	5. Guyana
6. Poland	6. Cuba	6. Trinidad/ Tobago	6. Haiti
7. Germany	7. Austria	7. Ecuador	7. Korea
8. Haiti	8. China	8. Colombia	8. Colombia
9. Cuba	9. Dominican Republic	9. Cuba	9. Trinidad/ Tobago
10. Ireland	10. Hungary	10. Greece	10. India

Source: 1980 U.S. Census Microdata Sample.

Prepared by: Department of City Planning New York City.

Appendix H

Resource Agencies Collecting Data on Migration

The major sources on migration include a select list of research centers, professional associations, foundations, academic centers, and governmental and international agencies. The following is a partial listing of some of these sources.

OMNI Resources Corporation
Research Specialists in
  Caribbean-American Affairs
94 South Oxford Street
Brooklyn, NY 11217
(718) 625-0470

New York Migration Forum
2 Lafayette, Suite 2107
New York, NY 10017

Community Council of
  Greater New York
Research and Program Planning
  Information Department
275 Seventh Avenue
New York, NY 10001

The Center for Migration
  Studies of New York, Inc.
209 Flagg Place
Staten Island, NY 10304
(718) 351-8800

The Caribbean Cultural Center
408 West 58th Street
New York, NY 10019

The Caribbean Women's Health
  Association, Inc.
314 West 53d Street
New York, NY 10019
(212) 621-9177

New York City Dept. of Health
Bureau of Health Statistics
  and Analysis
125 Worth Street
New York, NY 10013
(212) 566-8200

New York City Health and
  Hospitals Corporation
Reimbursement Reporting
125 Worth Street
New York, NY 10013
(212) 566-6675

New York State Department
  of Health
Bureau of Biostatistics
Vital Statistics Unit
Nelson Rockefeller Empire
  State Plaza, Room 308
Albany, NY 12237
(518) 474-3069

United Hospital Fund
Division of Research Analysis
  and Planning
3 East 54th Street
New York, NY 10022
(212) 754-1080

The Population Council
One Dag Hammarskjold Plaza
New York, NY 10017
(212) 644-1300

New York University Center
  for Latin American and
  Caribbean Studies
New York Research Program on
  Inter-American Affairs
19 University Place, Room 310
New York, NY 10003
(212) 598-3395

New York City Department
of Employment
Office of Review, Evaluation
and Planning
220 Church Street
New York, NY   10013
(212) 433-2130

New York State Department
of Commerce
Division of Policy Development
and Research
One Commerce Plaza
Albany, NY   12245
(518) 474-8602

New York State Department
of Labor
Labor Market Information
2 World Trade Center
New York, NY   10047
(212) 488-6772

U.S. Department of Commerce
Business Library
26 Federal Plaza, Room 3710
New York, NY   10007
(212) 264-0603

U.S. Department of Labor
Bureau of Labor Statistics
Regional Office
1515 Broadway
New York, NY   10036

New York City Department
of City Planning
Population Division
2 Lafayette Street
New York, NY   10007
(212) 566-8467

New York State Department
of Commerce
State Data Center
99 Washington Avenue
Albany, NY   12245
(518) 474-5944

U.S. Department of Commerce
Bureau of Census
Regional Office Library
26 Federal Plaza, 37th Floor
New York, NY   10007
(212) 264-4730

New York City Department
of City Planning
Office of Immigrant Services
2 Lafayette Street, Room 2220
New York, NY   10007
(212) 566-2944

U.S. Department of Justice
Immigration and Naturalization
Service
26 Federal Plaza
New York, NY   10007
(212) 957-9008

Part Two

Sample Inquiries into Latin American
Masses and Minorities

INTRODUCTION

Part One of these Papers considered the complex processes through which images and realities are described, analyzed, and compared. Its presentations particularly considered the role of the media, the mind of the individual, and the inquiries of the academic. We now turn to more limited topics and questions. This specificity allows our authors to more directly address the bibliographic dimensions of the research conundrum.

This part's first group of papers discusses the recent history of the Southern Cone, and more specifically how the publishing industry has been affected first by repressive regimes and then (and albeit not in all cases) by a return to nominal democracy. Censorship and repression attempted to enforce grossly distorted images within these countries, although a broader spectrum of opinion and interpretation persisted throughout. As the papers suggest, the factors shaping the volume and nature of publication are social and economic, as well as narrowly political. The conjunction of perceptive participants and persuasive scholars--of individual clairvoyance and academic ingenuity--does not, alone, set the limits for what we can know of a particular situation.

The focus then shifts to Latin American women, who are addressed through four essays. Two papers on Puerto Rico, stressing the problems of historical resources on this perpetually peripheral, perpetually colonized island outpost, come next. And we conclude with a range of papers exploring different aspects of social and political change, and the resultant documentation.

All of our authors seek to identify, confront, and overcome the bibliographic limitations upon their research. Our image of masses and minorities too often remains either empty, or grossly removed from reality. The nature of sources currently at hand has helped perpetuate this situation.

D.C.H.

145

*I.   The Printed Word through Democracy and
Repression: The Southern Cone*

13. LA LITERATURA ARGENTINA EN LA
POLITICA DE TRANSICION, 1982-1985

María Cristina Capel

Durante los años de 1976-1983, época del gobierno militar argentino, la producción literaria se vió seriamente afectada. La severa censura coartó a escritores de envergadura en las letras argentinas de continuar una fructífera labor creativa. La censura no sólo actuó sobre el contenido literario de una obra, sino también sobre el escritor mismo, como individuo. Muchos de ellos figuraban en las famosas "listas negras." Aunque sus libros no fueran de carácter político, el solo hecho de describir la realidad social significaba para la dictadura un serio peligro. A partir de entonces, se trató a todo nivel de evitar que el hombre de la calle viera la realidad tal cual era y reflexionara sobre la misma. Pensar era peligroso.

Se produce una despolitización de la cultura en general. Una importante cantidad de argentinos se ven obligados a exiliarse, ya sea por ser perseguidos, amenazados o simplemente porque deseaban vivir un clima de libertad, que les permitiese desarrollar sus tareas intelectuales.

La literatura argentina, dice Noé Jitrik: "derivó hacia un rumbo en el cual el escritor podía sentirse autorizado a no sentirse concernido por el asesinato de un diputado, de un abogado, de un gremialista o simplemente por la brutalidad de una represión cuya exhibición velada pudo llegar a horrorizar hasta pacíficos pequeños burgueses barriales. Los más sensibles en términos profesionales crearon una buena caparazón y se tornaron menos sensibles a una vinculación corporal . . .".

Por un lado tenemos una literatura cada vez más aséptica y más inmaculada, entre los escritores que permanecieron en el país, pero no por ello en algunos casos menos valiosa y fecunda; y por el otro, la literatura de aquellos escritores exiliados, la que era prácticamente desconocida para el público argentino.

Es un doble exilio que sufre la literatura argentina, el exterior y el interior. En el primero, el intelectual cuenta con la libertad para trabajar aún en circunstancias más difíciles. En el interior, en cambio, la censura y la amenaza de los poderes opresores impiden la libre expresión de las ideas y las obligan a un trabajo sigiloso, a una comunicación difícil y azarosa. Sin embargo, casi siempre terminan por abrirse camino y llegar al lector.

Con la decadencia del "Proceso," que se da justamente después de la derrota de Puerto Argentino, comienza una nueva etapa en las publicaciones y libros argentinos. Sin embargo esa guerra innecesaria tuvo un saldo positivo, hizo que el país creciera en su conciencia nacional. El pueblo demostró casi de inmediato la ansiedad y el deseo de absorber, de todos las formas posibles, el material cultural del que había sido privado durante años. Se manifiesta así, en los lectores argentinos, sed de conocimiento y participación. Basta con leer un libro o una revista para darse cuenta de la diferencia con la etapa anterior.

La literatura del período de transición se inicia en 1982 y a medida que el poder de la censura se debilita, adquiere nuevos matices, propios de la realidad en la cual está inmersa. En esta compleja etapa influyen tres tipos de factores: sociales, políticos y económicos, los cuales actúan como incentivos o frenos de la creación literaria y de la producción editorial en la Argentina.

Los factores sociales y políticos, actuando como inputs positivos, llevan a un cambio notable en la temática literaria. Es así que en el primer año, los temas principales fueron las declaraciones de los ex-combatientes de Malvinas y todo lo relacionado con la guerra, sus causas, la actitud de los altos oficiales, la fundamentación de la soberanía de las islas, las acusaciones sobre los culpables de la derrota.

En 1983, con la perspectiva de las futuras elecciones democráticas, se agregan a los temas anteriores: las declaraciones de funcionarios sobre la llamada "guerra sucia," críticas al gobierno militar e infinidad de libros desarrollando las plataformas políticas de los partidos. Aparecen también en este momento, libros que denuncian las torturas y desapariciones de personas. Es claro, en toda esta problemática, el gran peso que ejercieron los factores sociales y políticos. Literariamente, se manifestó en sus diversos géneros: poesía, novela y ensayo, como una necesidad de la sociedad y de sus individuos por decir y hacer conocer todo lo que hasta entonces había estado reprimido y oculto.

Se reeditan libros de autores argentinos exiliados, obras que habían sido escritas y editadas en el extranjero durante 1976-1982, desconocidas en nuestro país por problemas de censura. Se publican centenares de obras antes prohibidas y las ediciones se agotan en pocas semanas.

Dice Cortázar: ". . . No, no hemos perdido el tiempo quienes contra viento y marea, dentro y fuera del país, hemos continuado nuestro trabajo; como los antiguos veleros, el viaje hacia esa Itaca que es la Argentina ha encontrado vientos y tempestades, pero al igual que Ulises nuestra barca llega a puerto y es recibida con la alegría de todo reencuentro entre hermanos."

En esta nueva etapa del país, los partidos políticos han influído indirectamente en la literatura, a través de la posición ideológica de los escritores, los cuales en muchos casos al pertenecer a determinado grupo político, volcaban en su obra la línea de pensamiento del mismo. Si comparamos las obras impresas en estos años y las de otro período de transición, que se dió antes de 1973, notamos que la producción literaria 1982-1985, si bien es una literatura comprometida social y políticamente, no presenta la clara propaganda partidaria que tuvo la literatura de 1973, en la cual el papel de los grupos políticos tuvo mayor influencia.

Las publicaciones de los partidos políticos propiamente dichos son en general folletos, volantes, discursos o breves ensayos sobre determinados problemas. Este tipo de material, en general, se distribuye en forma gratuita; ya sea al concurrir a un mítin político o a una conferencia, o porque es repartido por militantes del mismo en las calles.

No podemos diferenciar las publicaciones que editan los partidos políticos de las de los grupos estudiantiles, puesto que tienen igual finalidad, forma y distribución. No debemos olvidar que estos grupos estudiantiles, no son más que la representación de los partidos dentro de las universidades o escuelas secundarias.

El material que editan los grupos universitarios es vendido dentro de las universidades, en mesas de exhibiciones, que los alumnos instalan en los corredores del edificio. El material que ellos venden incluye gacetas, folletos y algunos pocos libros. Los volantes o circulares son distribuidos en forma gratuita; su finalidad es informar al alumnado de la posición política del grupo que representan, con respecto a un determinado hecho de la realidad social, política o económica.

En cuanto a las publicaciones periódicas, generalmente los partidos políticos editan una o dos publicaciones, como máximo. Según la importancia del grupo político, tendrá una difusión a nivel más ámplio, como por ejemplo la revista "Línea" del Partido Justicialista, o la revista "Propuesta" del Partido Radical. Estas revistas pueden adquirirse en los puestos de diarios y revistas de las calles. Es decir que tiene acceso a ellas cualquier individuo, no importa su ideología. Los partidos políticos más pequeños distribuyen gacetas o periódicos en forma gratuita entre sus afiliados.

Este material editado por los partidos políticos y los grupos estudiantiles debería ser tenido en cuenta como una fuente de información muy importante para los investigadores y bibliotecarios. Si bien estas publicaciones no tienen la forma tradicional del libro o la revista, sino que son volantes, folletos de pocas páginas, afiches, etc., su contenido nos brinda datos que muchas veces son imposibles de conseguir por otros medios. Constituyen documentos que se encuentran por lo tanto más cercanos a la realidad, y son imprescindibles para aquel que desee conocer la problemática de nuestro país.

Pero quizás el punto crítico de esta literatura de transición sea el factor económico, que está actuando como freno. La grave situación económica imposibilita el aumento de la producción bibliográfica, la cual ha ido decayendo año a año. Según la Dirección Nacional del Autor, en 1976 se registraron 6,674 títulos;

en 1981: 4,249; en 1982: 4,946. Podemos observar que en 1982, al levantarse la censura, aumenta notablemente la producción literaria. Pero en 1983 vuelve a caer, con 4,198 títulos; y en 1984, 3,298 títulos.

Las cifras nos muestran la reducción cada vez más marcada de la edición de nuevos libros argentinos. Si durante la dictadura militar el libro es víctima de la brutalidad represiva, el problema económico es ahora una nueva traba que la cultura argentina trata de superar desesperadamente.

La literatura argentina del período de transición no surgió de la expresión de un proceso democrático bien cimentado, sino de la retirada de un proceso autoritario. La inconsistencia del sistema democrático argentino tuvo un efecto disolvente para la formación de una literatura nacional.

La creación literaria se encuentra así, influída por esa realidad pendular que va de la opresión a la libertad, de la dictadura a la democracia, del silencio forzado al exilio. Es de esperar que la consolidación del sistema republicano permita a nuestra literatura alcanzar una identidad fundada en analizar e interpretar la realidad en la sinceridad, la creatividad y la libertad.

BIBLIOGRAFIA

"La censura, un fantasma infinito; Charla con Ernesto Sábato sobre la libertad de expresión." In Clarín (Buenos Aires), 4 de abril de 1985.

Cortázar, Julio. Argentina; Años de alambradas culturales. Buenos Aires: Muchnik, 1984.

"Crisis de la industria editorial." In El Periodista de Buenos Aires, 1:30 (abril 5-11, 1985).

Del Colapso militar al triunfo de Alfonsín; Claves de dieciocho meses de transición política. Buenos Aires: Cuadernos del Bimestre, 1984.

Jitrik, Noé. Las armas y las razones; Ensayo sobre el peronismo, el exilio, la literatura, 1975-1980. Buenos Aires: Sudamericana, 1984.

Kovadloff, Santiago. Argentina, oscuro país; Ensayos sobre un tiempo de quebranto. Buenos Aires: Torres Agüero, 1983.

14. LA CREACION DE LA LITERATURA DE TRANSICION A TRAVES DE LOS PARTIDOS POLITICOS: ENFOQUE EN LOS TIPOS Y FUENTES DE PRODUCCION

Nicolás Rossi

Comenzando con el tema que nos ocupa, vamos a intentar hacer una definición de la literatura de transición que pueda desarrollarse a través de los partidos políticos en Argentina. Podríamos definirla como toda forma de expresión escrita, con contenido político, que se produce en épocas de relativa falta de libertad de prensa y/o persecución a los respectivos autores y editores, y que parta de cualquier partido, agrupación política o línea partidaria desarrollada dentro de un mismo partido.

Esta literatura se caracteriza, muy especialmente, por poseer un contenido coyuntural, adecuado a momentos políticos críticos en los cuales los partidos políticos no pueden funcionar en la plenitud de sus estructuras organizativas. Por esta razón, y sumado al peligro que entrañaba su posesión debido a la represión política, es un material de difícil obtención y vida efímera.

Los tipos de esta literatura los dividimos según el medio en: revistas, libros, folletos, circulares, volantes, mariposas, afiches e incluso las tradicionales pintadas o graffitis. Según el contenido, se dividen en ensayo, crítica, manifiesto, proclama, estudio, resolución, plenario, congreso, plan, plataforma, etc. Estos tipos de literatura se hacen llegar, en la medida de las posibilidades, a la mayor cantidad posible de receptores, para lograr un fin ideológico como atacar al adversario, tratar de captar adherentes o un objetivo de comunicación en general.

La importancia de este tipo de literatura está dada, en primer lugar, por su carácter de difusora del pensamiento y acción política. Pero, además, sirve a fines de organización y discusión dentro de los mismos partidos. Cuando el gobierno militar prohibió las reuniones y actos políticos, y suspendió los partidos políticos, fueron los volantes, folletos, libros, documentos, etc., muchos de ellos publicados clandestinamente, los que se constituyeron en el vehículo de comunicación entre la dirigencia partidaria y las bases. Es así como esta literatura se convierte en fuente directa para el investigador interesado, tanto en la evolución ideológica de un partido político, como en su accionar directo dentro de una coyuntura determinada--en este caso, lo que fue el "proceso militar" en Argentina y el subsiguiente retorno a la democracia.

Para poder hablar de literatura de transición a través de los partidos políticos, tenemos que enmarcar esta propuesta entre los años 1976-1982, de 1982 a 1983 y, finalmente, de 1983 en adelante, con la esperanza que se abre en nuestra sociedad con la asunción de un gobierno democrático que ha abolido toda clase de censura.

La primera etapa, 1976-1982, abarca el período en el cual los partidos políticos fueron suspendidos por la dictadura militar que derrocó el gobierno constitucional de Isabel Perón. La literatura política de esta época bien puede llamarse clandestina y se circunscribe a esporádicas volunteadas; edición de revistas de escasa periodicidad que circulaban, en algunos casos, de mano en mano; folletos de algunos partidos con una organización muy estructurada que pudo resistir el embate de la represión. También los impresos que producían grupos de estudio, en general universitarios, que se formaban independientemente de la estructura de un partido y que se reunían para discutir cuestiones ideológicas. Este material era de muy difícil acceso por las medidas de precaución tomadas por los responsables de elaborarlo, y su difusión limitada a quienes se hallaban comprometidos en una acción política.

La segunda etapa, 1982-1983, comienza a partir del fin de la guerra de Las Malvinas. La dictadura debe enfrentarse a una derrota militar que termina por resquebrajar el débil frente interno y que agrava otros problemas como una situación económica cada día más deteriorada, el pago de la deuda externa, el aislamiento en política exterior, el cuestionamiento del método con que se encaró la lucha antisubversiva y, sobre todo, el aumento de la presión social que hace temer por un estallido social. Todos estos factores que conspiran contra la permanencia de la dictadura militar los podemos rastrear en la literatura política de la época. Es así que los militares empiezan a hablar de una salida electoral como posible solución a la crisis por la que atraviesa el país. En 1983, el gobierno militar crea el Estatuto de los Partidos Políticos, legalizando su actividad y propiciando su organización. En este momento, la actividad editorial de los partidos políticos crece rápidamente. La propaganda política para las futuras elecciones es el centro de la producción: propuestas, plataformas electorales, volantes, folletos, congresos, etc. son impresos en cantidad. Estas fuentes son diversas debido a la complejidad con que se presenta el panorama político y su organización en la Argentina.

La tercera y última etapa se inicia con la restauración del sistema democrático y el triunfo inesperado del Partido Radical en las elecciones del 30 de Octubre de 1983. El Dr. Raúl Alfonsín asume la presidencia de la Nación el 10 de Diciembre de 1983, pero si bien el restablecimiento de las instituciones democráticas está dado, las condiciones no son las más propicias para que se dé el libre y natural juego democrático que permita un real debate ideológico. Confluyen varios factores para que así sea: la pesada herencia recibida del gobierno militar, la crisis del Partido Peronista, el peligro de desestabilización, entre otros.

Las fuentes de producción de esta literatura incluyen, en primer lugar, los partidos políticos. Aún estando suspendidos en sus actividades los partidos políticos, se han dado casos en que ciertos partidos, en una política de enfrentamiento contra la dictadura militar, editaron o presentaron trabajos como directamente avalados por el partido. Es el caso concreto del Partido Radical, del Partido Peronista y del Partido Comunista. Durante el período 1976-1982 editaban material bajo la sigla del partido, y a la vez tenían publicaciones bajo otros sellos editoriales.

En segundo lugar, la fuente de producción puede ser un ente con vinculación y dependencia hacia determinado partido político, pero sin que el mismo sea mencionado. El grado de vinculación o dependencia varía si el mismo es de simpatizantes o miembros del partido. En el primer caso las publicaciones pueden contener material no directamente partidario. En el segundo caso, la publicación es de total exposición partidaria. Los entes pueden ser Centros de Estudios, Fundaciones, Círculos de Profesionales, Bibliotecas y/o Agrupaciones.

En tercer lugar, la fuente de producción puede estar originada por los medios habituales de prensa que presentan alianzas con ciertos sectores políticos. Por ejemplo, algunos de los suplementos económicos de diarios de gran influencia en la sociedad argentina están redactados y supervisados por miembros destacados de ciertos partidos políticos, quienes, con sus análisis y comentarios, ejercen presión sobre medidas y políticas de gobierno.

Es importante destacar, en cuanto a las fuentes de producción, la rigidez o libertad que existe dentro de cada partido para la publicación de material. Por un lado está la absoluta prohibición para sus miembros de presentar o editar material como partido, sin la intervención del departamento de prensa del mismo. Me refiero al Partido Comunista. Por otro lado, el Partido Peronista permite que sus líneas internas, sus distintas fracciones ideológicas, puedan usar indistintamente la denominación partidaria, aún cuando el partido en pleno no avale el texto en cuestión. Lo beneficioso de tal libertad estriba en que, por lo general, los autores de un determinado trabajo no desean perder su individualidad como línea partidaria y se identifican como línea o bloque para, a continuación, indicar el partido, permitiendo así expresar una mayor riqueza ideológica en el material publicado.

A continuación voy a hacer una breve síntesis de la trayectoria de los partidos políticos en Argentina y sus líneas internas, para después referirme específicamente a un muestreo de las publicaciones que éstos produjeron en las épocas anteriormente citadas.

Pero antes quiero destacar que la Argentina posee un régimen político pluripartidista, pese a que la polarización electoral generalmente lo convierte en un sistema bipartidista. La importancia de los partidos pequeños reside en que suelen participar de frentes electorales o tácticos y en que presionan sobre medidas o políticas gubernamentales, participando en la discusión de los problemas nacionales con una trascendencia que no es para nada proporcional con el caudal de votantes que poseen. Sus dirigentes son, casi la mayoría de las veces, políticos que se han destacado, convirtiéndose en figuras notables de la política argentina y que, abandonando un partido en el que desarrollaron una labor notoria pero secundaria, fundaron su propio partido que existe, más que nada, debido a su prestigio.

Los Partidos Peronista y Radical, que son los que poseen mayor caudal electoral, tienen como característica una variedad de líneas internas que van desde la izquierda a la derecha. Los partidos de centro-derecha que, en general, apoyaron al gobierno militar, tienden, en la actualidad, a aglutinarse en un solo partido. La centro-izquierda está representada por el Partido Intransigente. El espectro de la izquierda se completa con el Partido Comunista y variedad de agrupaciones minoritarias.

Unión Cívica Radical

Es el partido político más antiguo de la Argentina, habiéndose fundado en 1891. Se constituyó en un partido con fuerte raigambre en las clases medias para convertirse, con el advenimiento del peronismo al escenario político, en 1945, en el polo de la oposición antiperonista. Durante el gobierno de la Revolución Libertadora, se divide en dos ramas: la Unión Cívica Radical del Pueblo, liderada por Ricardo Balbín y la Unión Cívica Radical Intransigente, por Arturo Frondizi. Perdió, de esta manera, parte de su fuerza política.

En el año 1962, la U.C.R. accede al gobierno con Humberto Illía como presidente, en elecciones que tuvieron carácter proscriptivo, pues el peronista que era el partido más popular, fue excluído. El Dr. Illía es derrocado por la Revolución Argentina liderada por el Gral. Onganía, en el año 1966.

El Partido Radical contaba con dos líneas internas, la mayoritaria Línea Nacional, de extracción balbinista, y la minoritaria Renovación y Cambio. Esta última tiene un crecimiento inusitado durante los últimos años del "proceso militar" bajo el liderazgo del Dr. Raúl Alfonsín, derrotando por amplia mayoría a Línea Nacional en las elecciones internas del año 1983.

Tenemos que destacar que la Junta Coordinadora Nacional, si bien forma parte del Movimiento de Renovación y Cambio, congrega a la Juventud Radical y tiene influencia sobre las decisiones del actual gobierno del Dr. Alfonsín. La Coordinadora Nacional genera amplia adhesión en los sectores juveniles por sus propuestas participativas y de movilización popular, ocupando lo que podríamos definir como la izquierda del Partido Radical. Se ha ido destacando dentro del Movimiento de Renovación y Cambio como una línea independiente con propuestas y peso político propio.

El Partido Radical oficialmente imprimía sólo documentos internos y comunicaciones mimeografiadas. En el año 1980, se publica en forma no oficial el libro fundamental del Dr. Raúl Alfonsín "La cuestión Argentina." En ese mismo año también se publica un Congreso bajo el título "La U.C.R. propone." Un año después se edita "Apuntes para la historia del radicalismo," también en forma no oficial. Línea Nacional, a cargo del Comité Nacional, publica los "Discursos de Ricardo Balbín" en 1982. El Movimiento de Renovación y Cambio, habiendo ya triunfado en las elecciones internas del Partido, edita en 1983 dos libros sobre cultura y educación.

En el año 1976 se publican seis números del periódico "Propuesta y control," dirigido por Raúl Alfonsín. En 1977, y dirigido por Ricardo Balbín, se edita la Segunda Epoca del periódico "Adelante." En 1982, la Junta Coordinadora inaugura su periódico "Respuesta," del que se publican sólo pocos números. Actualmente "Propuesta Radical para la Unión Nacional, el Periódico de la Juventud" es el Organo de la Coordinadora. Una característica de esta agrupación es que cada comité partidario que le pertenece imprime periódicamente boletines de muy pocas páginas que contienen material elaborado por sus militantes, que distribuyen a los afiliados partidarios.

Partido Justicialista

Debemos destacar que el peronismo no es un partido más dentro del espectro político de la Argentina, sino que su rasgo distintivo es el de constituírse en un movimiento. Es decir, un gran ente unificador de corrientes opuestas entre sí, pero que obedecen a una jefatura central y que comparten consignas políticas fundamentales. El Movimiento Peronista se divide en Ramas. Hasta Febrero de 1985, eran la Rama Sindical, la Rama Femenina, y la Rama Política. En Febrero de 1985, el Congreso de Río Hondo, que expresa al peronismo renovador, incorporó la Cuarta Rama, la de la Juventud.

Independientemente del Partido, cada una de esas Ramas está dividida en función de objetivos políticos. Se agrupan de acuerdo a líderes y consignas propias, que van desde la izquierda a la derecha. En lo que respecta al Partido, las Ramas se organizan en Unidades Básicas y Seccionales.

Las fuentes de producción editorial son, en primer lugar, la oficial, constituída por las resoluciones y posiciones emanadas del Consejo Nacional Justicialista, la máxima autoridad partidaria.

También emite comunicados de prensa y declaraciones sobre problemas de política nacional o internacional como, por ejemplo, el Tratado del Beagle.

La otra fuente de producción es la no oficial. El carácter movimientista del peronismo le otorga un dinamismo interno que produce la creación espontánea, en ciertos casos, de Grupos de Estudios, Ateneos, Agrupaciones Universitarias, etc., que expresan su interpretación de la doctrina justicialista o de los problemas nacionales a través de publicaciones varias. Así mismo, algunas de las líneas internas del peronismo, tanto zonales como nacionales, han editado sus propios trabajos. Podemos citar las Ediciones del Bloque, las Ediciones del Fuerte Peronista, Frente Valle, Centro de Estudios Nacionales y Populares, Centro de Liberación Popular y Nacional. El Centro de Estudios Comunitarios y Planificación edita, en 1982, el libro "Reflexiones sobre la Nación Argentina," de Francisco de Figuerola. La Mesa Nacional de Centros de Estudio, que se constituyó en 1981, publicó en 1982: "Argentina, Propuestas para un programa nacional." En 1983, Convocatoria Peronista--una línea interna dirigida, entre otros, por Carlos Grosso--publica un volumen de 300 páginas con las "Bases para una política programática justicialista." También en 1983 el Centro de Doctrina, Investigación y Estudios, perteneciente al sector gremial del peronismo, publica "Desarrollo urbano y vivienda," un plan nacional de viviendas populares.

Otro tipo de publicación que producen los Centros de Estudios y las diferentes líneas partidarias es reediciones de obras clásicas del General Perón o de Eva Perón, con fines de actualización de la doctrina o de discusión ideológica, como por ejemplo: "Actualización política doctrinaria para la toma del poder" de Juan Domingo Perón, editada por la Juventud Peronista a principios de 1983. También con fines de divulgación y propaganda se han editado mensajes clásicos de Perón y Eva, o simplemente fragmentos de dichos mensajes.

El peronismo, a nivel del Consejo Nacional del Partido, se opuso al proyecto de editar un diario o algún tipo de publicación oficial. También se negó apoyos financieros a los diarios que nacieron con el propósito de representar al justicialismo, como fue el caso del diario "Mayoría," y las publicaciones "Las 62," "Patria Une" y "Cuadernos Sindicales." Hay sectores del peronismo que tienen su diario, caso de "La Voz," pero sólo representan una parte del movimiento.

Durante el período 1976-1983 el peronismo publicó, en el país, a través de los Centros de Estudio ya citados. Por lo general, estos Centros sólo tenían una vida efímera. Otra práctica común fue la grabación de mensajes o conferencias de dirigentes destacados, y su posterior impresión y difusión de mano en mano.

En cuanto a las revistas, un caso de notable continuidad es "Línea," que comenzó a publicarse en 1979. Otras revistas que aparecen en la época son "Temática 2000," que apareció en 1977, "Pensamiento y Nación" (1981-1982), "Movimiento" (1983), "Hechos e Ideas" (Tercera Epoca, 1983).

Partido Intransigente

El Partido Intransigente, o PI, es un partido de centro izquierda. Su líder es el otrora dirigente radical Oscar Alende, ex-gobernador de la Provincia de Buenos Aires durante la presidencia del Dr. Arturo Frondizi (1958-1962). En las elecciones del 30 de octubre de 1983 resultó con tres diputados electos, y en estos momentos es el partido político de mayor crecimiento. Ha logrado captar a la juventud y a algunos sectores descontentos tanto con la política del gobierno radical como con la evolución de la lucha interna dentro del Partido Justicialista.

El PI editaba su periódico "Primera Línea" clandestinamente durante dos años desde 1976 hasta 1978. Fue dirigido por Mariano Lorenzes, en la actualidad uno de sus más destacados dirigentes. También distribuía el PI, de mano en mano, un Boletín Interno de pocas páginas y algunas otras publicaciones impresas a mimeógrafo.

Posteriormente editó un folleto titulado "Propuesta intransigente," que ha sido reeditado recientemente con un agregado. Este año la Juventud Intransigente ha presentado el librito "Apuntes para la liberación."

Actualmente este Partido se manifiesta a través del periódico "Alternativa Intransigente."

Movimiento de Integración y Desarrollo

El líder del MID es el Dr. Arturo Frondizi. Es un partido que no ha logrado penetrar en el electorado argentino. Sin embargo, el pensamiento de sus principales dirigentes, el Dr. Frondizi y Rogelio Frigerio, tiene influencia en parte del empresariado argentino y en algunos sectores del Ejército por sus propuestas económicas.

El MID no tiene líneas internas importantes. Durante el período militar, podemos notar que la dirigencia midista se expresaba normalmente a través de libros editados por editoriales no partidarias. Editorial Crisol publicó un homenaje a Isidro Odena, un libro de Frigerio, "Opulencia y desarrollo" y "16 Conferencias sobre Cultura Nacional," y un libro de Odena sobre política exterior desarrollista. Posteriormente, el MID publica, en 1981, el libro "La crisis argentina," que es una crítica a la política económica del gobierno militar. También publica un folleto titulado: "Qué es y qué piensa el MID," los discursos de Arturo Frondizi y las polémicas de Frigerio con Alsogaray y con Martínez de Hoz.

El periódico oficial del MID es "El Nacional," que se editó normalmente durante el gobierno militar.

Partido Demócrata Cristiano

Su ideología está basada en la Doctrina Social de la Iglesia Católica. En el espectro político argentino, ocupa una amplia franja de la centro-izquierda. Es un partido frentista, es decir, favorable a establecer alianzas programáticas con sectores políticos afines.

Concurre a las elecciones del año 1973 dividido en el Partido Revolucionario Cristiano y el Partido Popular Cristiano, el primero aliado con los Partidos Intransigente y Comunista, el segundo aliado con el peronismo e integrante del FREJULI. En el año 1980, estos dos sectores de la democracia cristiana se unen nuevamente. En su debate interno se destacan cuatro líneas: Humanismo y Liberación, que en política externa apoya al Sandinismo; Convocatoria, línea cercana ideológicamente a la ya citada; y las más tradicionales Línea Nacional y Línea Federal.

Durante el "proceso militar" editaron "Síntesis Social Cristiana" una revista de pequeño formato de circulación interna, dirigida por Néstor Vicente que actualmente milita en el Partido Intransigente.

En 1980, comienzan a publicar la revista "Proyecto Social Cristiano," que se distribuía en forma comercial y cuyo director era Juan Manuel Ramos.

En otro orden de cosas, el Partido Demócrata Cristiano mantiene un destacado centro de estudios, la Fundación Argentina para la Promoción del Desarrollo Económico Social (FAPES) que publicó folletos como "Aportes para una definición de la identidad de la democracia cristiana argentina," Congresos realizados por la Democracia Cristiana y otros trabajos varios.

En este año, ha aparecido a la venta el periódico "La Unión. Una Voz Social Cristiana."

Partido Demócrata Progresista

Es un partido que se destaca por el prestigio de su fundador, el Dr. Lisandro de la Torre, y que se ha ido trans-formando en un pequeño partido que solamente tiene alguna influencia en la provincia litoraleña de Santa Fé.

Su principal medio de comunicación fueron los comunicados de prensa o gacetillas que el mismo Partido enviaba a los periódicos. Recientemente ha publicado un folleto conmemorativo de los 70 años de su fundación que es, prácticamente, su plataforma política.

El órgano oficial de este Partido es el mensuario "El Progresista," que se halla en su Tercer Epoca.

Partido Demócrata

Es la denominación del antiguo Partido Conservador que tuvo gran influencia en la política argentina durante la primera mitad del presente siglo y representó los intereses de la clase alta. En la actualidad su influencia se ha reducido notoriamente, convirtiéndose en una agrupación minoritaria. No tiene, ni ha tenido publicaciones partidarias en los últimos tiempos. En la época que nos ocupa se manifestó ideológicamente a través de los influyentes diarios "La Nación" y "La Prensa."

Unión de Centro Democrática

Dirigida por el Ing. Alvaro Alsogaray, es el partido que en este momento está aglutinando a las fuerzas políticas de centro-derecha. Su plataforma se basa, principalmente, en propuestas económicas: la defensa de la libre empresa y la no ingerencia del Estado en las actividades económico-sociales.

El Ing. Alsogaray se ha expresado a través del diario "La Prensa" como comentarista económico. Tuvo una postura crítica de la política económica de Martínez de Hoz, el Ministro de Economía del Gral. Videla.

Partido Socialista

Uno de los partidos más antiguos de Latinoamérica. Ha sufrido un gran desgaste a través del tiempo y, sobre todo, a partir de la pérdida de sus banderas políticas, las que fueron captadas por el peronismo. De esta manera se convirtió en un partido sin predicamento entre la clase trabajadora. Esto ha hecho que se fuese atomizando y dividiendo en varias agrupaciones minoritarias.

Partido Socialista Democrático

El socialismo de Ghioldi y Repetto está en posición más cercana a la derecha y es fuertemente antiperonista.

La obra cultural de este partido, a lo largo de su historia, se desarrolla y presenta principalmente a través de la prensa escrita. Gran cantidad de folletos y libros fueron distribuídos por estos medios.

Durante los años posteriores a 1976, se publicaron algunos pocos folletos como "La reseña histórica del Partido Socialista Democrático" y "La génesis de la crisis," ambos escritos por Emilio Gianonni; cuatro números de su clásica colección "El pequeño libro socialista"; y algunos Congresos del Partido.

Tienen, también, varios libros publicados, entre ellos los "Idearios" de Repetto y de Solari, dos antiguos y prestigiosos dirigentes.

El tradicional periódico "La Vanguardia," ya en su tercera época, se siguió editando durante el "proceso militar" y continúa en publicación. A fines del año 1983, se publica "La Revista Socialista," también en su tercera época. La Juventud del Partido Socialista Democrática comenzó, así mismo, a publicar a fines de 1983 su Organo Oficial con el nombre de "Venceremos."

Partido Socialista Popular

Dirigido por Guillermo Estévez Boero, es un partido minoritario con cierta importancia en la Provincia de Santa Fé. Trabaja conjuntamente con el Partido Socialista del Chaco y apoya tácticamente al peronismo.

Ha editado varios folletos con propuestas partidarias tal como "Argentinicemos nuestra Argentina" en 1977 y reeditado en 1983; "Sin pan y sin trabajo," un corto trabajo sobre la desocupación; "La propuesta del Partido," un trabajo de 50 páginas que es la plataforma desarrollada; una declaración del Comité Nacional con el título "Para cambiar al país"; y un libro con la presentación de un proyecto de Constitución nacional titulado "Una Constitución para la liberación nacional." A través de la Mesa de Unidad Socialista publicó "Las II Jornadas Nacionales de Abogados Socialistas."

Durante el período militar se editó "La Vanguardia Popular y Socialista," que sigue en publicación como "La Vanguardia Popular," y que es el Organo de Prensa del Partido Socialista Popular.

Partido Socialista Auténtico

Es una pequeña agrupación política que todavía no está reconocida como partido político. Es una rama del desaparecido Partido Socialista de Alfredo Palacios y Alicia Moreau de Justo.

Ha publicado una serie de folletos sobre problemas políticos latinoamericanos, uno sobre la posición de esta agrupación sobre el Tratado del Beagle y su periódico "La Vanguardia Auténtica" que curiosamente está numerado siguiendo el orden del viejo y desaparecido periódico fundado por Juan B. Justo.

Partido Comunista

Cuenta con una de las estructuras partidarias más organizadas de la realidad política argentina. Esto le ha permitido, por un lado, mantener una importante imprenta propia muy bien montada y una librería o departamento de publicaciones que canaliza la venta del material impreso a sus afiliados. Por otro lado, mantiene una prolífica producción editorial. Por estas razones, fue uno de los partidos que editó mayor cantidad de material durante la dictadura militar.

En el Partido Comunista, no existen las líneas internas que podemos observar en otros partidos políticos argentinos. Sin embargo, y pese a su férrea conformación ideológica, ha mantenido cambiantes posturas tácticas dentro de la evolución política argentina, que ha expresado en numerosas publicaciones.

El tipo de material publicado consta de libros sobre obras clásicas del marxismo internacional; obras de destacados dirigentes comunistas argentinos, por ejemplo "Los escritos de Ghioldi," editado por Anteo (la editorial oficial del Partido Comunista); un libro de Fernando Nadra, "Democracia y partidos políticos," editado por Fundamentos (otro de los nombres editoriales usados por este partido); y una obra en cuatro volúmenes de Jerónimo Arnedo Alvarez. Pero el mayor volumen de material impreso está constituído por folletos de distintos tipos: Congresos del Partido; discursos, proclamas, informes y conferencias de dirigentes comunistas argentinos; discursos y proclamas de dirigentes comunistas latinoamericanos; propuestas económicas, ideológicas y políticas; temas sobre los problemas de la mujer en su inserción a la sociedad, etc. Podemos citar discursos de Fidel Castro, de dirigentes sandinistas y comunistas paraguayos en el exilio. También "El Gran Octubre y su influencia en la Argentina," por Rodolfo Ghioldi, editado en 1977. En el año 1979 varios autores presentan un "Plan alternativo para salir de la crisis." En 1980, una conferencia de Gerónimo Arnedo Alvarez, "Diálogo amplio y acción concertada para abrir caminos a la democracia"; y, sobre la política económica de Martínez de Hoz, el folleto "10 preguntas a Fernando Nadra." Del año 1981 es una conferencia de Athos Fava, "Una solución democrática estable para el progreso del país y la paz." Ya en el año 1982, y refiriéndose a la guerra de Las Malvinas, un trabajo de Athos Fava publicado por Editorial Fundamentos: "Malvinas. Batalla por una nueva Argentina" y, de la misma editorial, "El país que empezó en Las Malvinas." En 1982, el Partido Comunista, por intermedio de sus apoderados, también presenta un folleto sobre los comunistas argentinos desaparecidos.

Entre el material publicado con fines didácticos y de formación ideológica para los afiliados, citaremos la Escuela del Primer y Segundo Nivel, que contiene los fundamentos de la teoría marxista.

Los periódicos oficiales son "Qué Pasa," publicado a partir del año 1980 y que sigue en publicación; "Aquí y Ahora la Juventud," publicado por la Federación Juvenil Comunista y que va por su segunda época.

"'Nueva Era,' La Revista Teórico-Política del Partido Comunista de la Argentina," continuó publicándose durante el "proceso militar" y sigue en publicación, igual como la revista "Problemas de Economía."

Frente de Izquierda Popular

Liderado por el intelectual de izquierda Jorge Abelardo Ramos, es uno de los exponentes de la llamada izquierda nacional que, desde bases marxistas, reivindica al peronismo por su alto contenido nacionalista.

Este partido logró muy pocos votos en las últimas elecciones, pero sus propuestas son apreciadas por intelectuales y algunos sectores del peronismo, sobre todo por su análisis histórico de nuestro país.

El F.I.P. editó de sus "Cuadernos de Política, Economía e Historia" un sólo número. De la revista "Política," publicó dos números.

También editó algunos folletos con propuestas partidarias, uno de ellos dirigido a la mujer con propuestas de un feminismo criollo y latinoamericano. Otro folleto se tituló "Ejército, clase obrera y revolución nacional," por Guillermo Maldonado.

La obra ya clásica de Abelardo Ramos, "Revolución y contrarevolución en Argentina," fue prohibida durante la dictadura militar y reeditada por la Editorial Mar Dulce (propiedad de Abelardo Ramos) en 1983. Esta editorial publicó también "Sabattini y la decadencia del Yrigoyenismo" de Roberto Ferro, "Condición obrera y despilfarro oligárquico" de Rodolfo Balmaceda y "Fuerzas Armadas y nacionalismo económico" de Blas Alberti.

Un desprendimiento del F.I.P. es el Partido de la Izquierda Nacional (PIN), una agrupación política de muy reciente conformación dirigida por Jorge Enea Spilimbergo, cuya separación se debió a pequeñas diferencias ideológicas con Jorge Abelardo Ramos, a quien le criticaba su creciente autoritarismo.

El PIN publicó un folleto explicativo de la creación del Partido y otro folleto acerca de las elecciones del 30 de Octubre de 1983. Actualmente edita el periódico "Izquierda Nacional," que va por su número 10.

Partido Obrero

Anteriormente se denominaba Política Obrera. Es un partido muy pequeño de tendencia trotskista. Durante el "proceso militar" publicaba clandestinamente el periódico "Política Obrera" (Sección de la Tendencia Cuarta Internacionalista). En el año 1981 editaba "Libertades Democráticas," del que se publicaron alrededor de catorce números. También aparecen seis números de la revista "Internacionalismo," en la que se incluía una historia del trotskismo argentino.

En el año 1983, edita "El Informe político al Tercer Congreso." Un año después, un folleto sobre el fracaso de un intento de frente electoral con el MAS y, por último, dos libros: "Qué es el P.O." y "El P.O. y el peronismo."

Recientemente se comienza a publicar la nueva época de "Política Obrera" en forma de revista, continuando con la numeración anterior.

Destacamos que el MAS (Moviemiento al Socialismo) es un partido afín con el Partido Obrero y con alguna influencia en sectores gremiales. Tiene en publicación el periódico "Solidaridad Socialista."

15. LA CREACION LITERARIA EN LA TRANSICION POLITICA: URUGUAY

Alvaro Risso and Rosa M. Feria

Para poder hablar de la creación literaria en la transición política uruguaya, y comprenderla, es necesario hacer un poco de historia, ubicándonos en la problemática del Uruguay de esos años.

Hasta 1973, nuestro país tuvo una larga tradición democrática, que se cortó con el golpe militar del 27 de junio de ese año.

Los años que van de 1973 a 1979, los más duros de la dictadura, fueron también los más difíciles para la cultura nacional. Innumerables fueron los problemas que debieron soportar autores, editores y libreros. Es necesario extenderse en esta problemática para poder comprender los años posteriores a 1979, cuando podemos considerar que comienza la transición política.

A partir de 1973, conjuntamente con la prohibición de toda actividad política y sindical, comienza la persecución a los creadores nacionales. Muchos de ellos debieron exiliarse, eligiendo principalmente los países de habla hispana como España, Argentina, Venezuela y México. Entre ellos podemos nombrar a Juan Carlos Onetti, Mario Benedetti, Eduardo Galeano, Lucía Sala de Tourón, Angel Rama, Daniel Vidart, Blanca Paris de Oddone, Carlos Quijano, Juan Antonio Oddone, Carlos Martínez Moreno y Arturo Ardao. Otros fueron encarcelados, otros desaparecieron, y todos fueron silenciados. Debe destacarse que a la censura gubernamental no sólo le interesaba el contenido de las obras: eran prohibidos los autores por su ideología, aunque ésta no estuviera manifestada en la obra. Un ejemplo claro de esto es el caso de la novela La Tregua, de Mario Benedetti, a la cual no se le puede adjudicar contenido político, y que igualmente fue prohibida. La censura gubernamental tuvo como un ensañamiento con la cultura en sí misma.

Los autores, para poder publicar, debieron autocensurarse, cambiando el contenido de sus textos para así evitar la censura. Esta misma autocensura existió también en los editores, que debieron escoger con sumo cuidado las obras a publicar. Tanto los creadores como los editores debieron mantener un difícil equilibrio para evitar no sólo el riesgo de la confiscación de los libros, sino la clausura de las editoriales o el encarcelamiento. El Profesor Heber Raviolo, director de la Editorial Banda Oriental, sin duda la más importante de las sobrevivientes, ante una pregunta periodística sobre los efectos de la censura en los años de dictadura, respondió: ". . . estrictamente censura clásica, la previa, no hubo. Por supuesto hubo autocensura, cada uno sabía hasta qué límites podía llegar. En ese sentido, hay una parte que puedo conocer y otra que no, acerca de los efectos reales que tuvo la autocensura . . ." y concluye ". . . El asunto era saber hasta dónde se podía llegar y eso significaba una situación muy incómoda muchas veces, como estar en el filo de la navaja . . ."

Es en este período que desaparecen varias editoriales, algunas de larga trayectoria, como Ediciones Pueblos Unidos, Sandino, Aquí Poesía, Ayuí, Grito de Asencio, Marcha, Nuestra Tierra, Comunidad del Sur, entre otras.

Las librerías también sufrieron un fuerte control gubernamental, con periódicas revisaciones, donde los censores señalaban las obras que no se podían tener a la venta, y requisaban los títulos que les parecían dudosos. Los encargados de estas revisaciones dejaban en evidencia que no eran expertos en la materia. Como demostración de ello citaremos el ejemplo siguiente: en nuestra librería fueron requisados ejemplares de la obra titulada Izquierdismo en la Iglesia, compañero de ruta del comunismo. Este libro fue realizado por la Sociedad Uruguaya de Defensa de la Tradición, Familia y Propiedad. Como es notorio, esta Sociedad T.F.P. es totalmente antimarxista. Fueron requisados, es de suponer, porque su título incluía la palabra "comunismo."

Viendo la censura existente tanto para autores, editores y libreros, es fácil suponer el aislamiento cultural en que se vivía. Pero ese aislamiento no fue sólo dentro del Uruguay, sino también con respecto a la cultura internacional. En las oficinas de correo, existían controles policiales para impedir el ingreso al país de toda publicación que, según su criterio, no debía conocerse. El criterio utilizado por estos controladores era muy peculiar. Llegó a sucedernos que en los paquetes de libros que llegaban para nuestra librería fueron requisados obras sobre Cuba, siendo el motivo de la requisa que uno de los libros se titulaba La Revolución Cubana. Pero este libro era publicado bajo el gobierno de Batista, y se refería a la revolución de José Martí. Es obvio que todo lo publicado por los uruguayos en el exilio no lograba pasar los controles, creando esto un desconocimiento, sobre todo en las nuevas generaciones, de los creadores uruguayos ya consagrados.

Este fue el panorama hasta 1979, cuando consideramos el inicio de la transición. A partir de ese año, todas las características del período anterior se mantienen, pero se ven levemente atenuadas, en un proceso muy lento y lleno de dificultades.

En enero de 1979, aparece el suplemento La Semana del diario El Día, el periódico más antiguo de nuestro país. Es en él que vuelven a escribir autores que no tenían dónde publicar. Contiene artículos sobre política, economía, cultura, donde levemente y leyendo entrelíneas, podemos saber algo de la realidad nacional, de la cual estábamos bastante desconectados ya que en estos años de dictadura, lo que mejor funcionó como medio de información fue el rumor. La importancia de este suplemento semanal es que fue el primero y marcó el rumbo, que luego sería continuado por muchos otros. El periodista uruguayo Angel Ruocco, director de la Agencia Prensa Latina, declaró a la prensa recientemente: ". . . aunque doce años de dictadura fueron un golpe muy bravo, no sirvieron para liquidar a un periodismo que tenía antecedentes tan valiosos. Si bien la falta de libertad y la censura le quitó fuentes y medios para conocer la verdad y le negó la posibilidad de decirlas, los periodistas uruguayos supieron desarrollar un estilo de periodismo inteligente, donde las entrelíneas eran la sustancia de lo escrito, como lo advertían quienes leían en el extranjero . . .."

A fines de noviembre de 1980, se realizó el plebiscito constitucional, donde el gobierno militar propugnaba una reforma de la Constitución de la República. Esto promovió cierta libertad de discusión política, lo que animó a un sector opositor a lanzar el semanario Opinar. Es en él donde más fuertemente se sostuvo la posición de rechazo al proyecto propuesto por los militares. Con respecto al plebiscito, citaremos lo escrito por Gabriel García Márquez en el diario El País de Madrid, días después del resultado negativo de éste: ". . . Es la trampa del poder absoluto. Absortos en su propio perfume, los gorilas uruguayos, debieron pensar que la parálisis del terror era la paz, que los editoriales de la prensa vendida eran la voz del pueblo y, por consiguiente, la voz de Dios, que las declaraciones públicas, que ellos mismos hacían eran la verdad revelada, y que todo eso, reunido y amarrado con un lazo de seda, era de veras, la democracia. Lo único que les faltaba entonces, por supuesto, era la consagración popular y, para conseguirla se metieron como mansos conejos en la trampa diabólica del sistema electoral uruguayo . . .." Este rechazo masivo a la reforma constitucional, también fue un rechazo al gobierno dictatorial.

Es a partir del plebiscito que renace el movimiento cultural. Es la inquietud popular la que logra, paso a paso, caminos y medios de expresión. Uno de los medios de expresión, usado por la poesía, fue el canto, conocido como "Canto Popular." Es a través de él que tenemos la presencia de Benedetti, Líber Falco, Saúl Ibargoyen Islas, Washington Benavides, etc.

En este período tomaron mucha importancia los Centros privados de investigación, que lentamente fueron logrando editar estudios sobre el pasado nacional, relacionándolo con la situación actual. Estas investigaciones abarcaron las áreas de sociología, agricultura, vivienda, salud, economía, estadística, historia, industrias, literatura y, poco a poco, algunos trabajos sobre política. Destacamos como los principales centros de investigatión y edición a CIESU, CLAEH, CINVE, CIEDUR, CIEP. Estos centros posibilitaron que la nueva generación de investigadores tuviera contacto con la vieja generación. Es así que circulan nuevamente trabajos de investigadores ya conocidos antes del golpe militar de 1973 como Danilo Astori, Raúl Jacob, César Aguiar, Juan Rial, Horacio Martorelli, etc. Pero estas investigaciones, ya editadas, no eran conocidas a nivel masivo, por la escasa distribución que tenían.

Paralelamente, en este período, la creación en prosa y poesía estuvo representada por autores como Mario Arregui, Enrique Estrázulas, Alejandro Paternain, Idea Vilariño, José Pedro Díaz, Amanda Berenguer, y Miguel Angel Campodónico.

Para noviembre de 1982, el gobierno militar convocó a elecciones internas de los partidos políticos. Otra vez, como en el plebiscito, estos hechos políticos posibilitaron una mayor apertura en la creación literaria, a pesar de las restricciones que aún permanecían vigentes. Meses antes de estas elecciones, donde algunos partidos políticos fueron imposibilitados de participar, comienzan a aparecer nuevas revistas y semanarios, como el caso de Opción, La Democracia, Correo de los Viernes, El Dedo. El semanario La Democracia responde al Partido Nacional (o Blanco), y se convirtió en la voz oficial de ese Partido. Correo de los Viernes respondió al Partido Colorado. La revista Opción representaba a un sector del Frente Amplio y fue clausurada definitivamente meses antes de las elecciones internas. Es importante señalar que todas estas publicaciones, conjuntamente con Opinar y La Semana de El Día, lograron un gran espacio público para los creadores. La revista El Dedo dio lugar a dibujantes y escritores humorísticos, convirtiéndose en un boom editorial. Es a través del humor, que esta revista logró una crítica sostenida contra el régimen militar. Estas críticas y los altos niveles de venta, fueron lo que provocaron que el gobierno militar la clausurara en el número siete, definitivamente. En este período, casi todos los semanarios sufren clausuras temporarias.

Dos hechos culturales, que reunían en estos años a los escritores, editores y libreros con el público, fueron la Feria Nacional de Libros y Grabados y la Feria Internacional del Libro. Estas dos exposiciones lograban mostrar, en forma reunida, la producción literaria nacional de los últimos años.

Al realizarse en noviembre de 1982 las elecciones internas de los partidos políticos autorizados, el pueblo uruguayo demostró nuevamente su rechazo al gobierno dictatorial. Los resultados de estas elecciones dieron el triunfo a los sectores más opositores al gobierno militar. Los grupos conservadores de cada partido, que eran los más comprometidos con la dictadura, tuvieron escasa votación.

En estos dos años, que van de 1980 a 1982, en el campo literario se editaron libros de Marosa Di Giorgio, Ariel Méndez, Washington Benavides, Selva Márquez, Germán D'Elía, Alfonso Fernández Cabrelli, Mario Levrero, Armonía Somers, etc.

En las elecciones internas de noviembre de 1982, se eligieron autoridades de los partidos políticos y éstos comenzaron a funcionar legalmente. Pero en agosto de 1983, el gobierno, mediante un Decreto, limitó la actividad de dichos partidos y la posibilidad de los medios de comunicación de informar sobre actividades políticas. Esto produjo un retroceso en la lenta apertura que se había logrado, creando asimismo muchos inconvenientes para la creación literaria. A partir de ese Decreto, la censura fue más dura aún que en años anteriores. Se establecieron métodos nunca utilizados, tales como permitir la venta de un semanario, pero exigirle a sus editores que un artículo fuera quitado. El semanario Aquí, en su número 18, ya impreso y pronto para su venta, debió retrasar su distribución dos días para que los responsables pudieran recortar en cada ejemplar el artículo censurado.

Uno de los métodos más graves de censura que se aplicó en este año '83, y comienzos del '84, fue lo que mal se llamó "censura previa." En realidad no era previa. El método utilizado era el siguiente: exigían que la edición completa de las publicaciones estuviera terminada de imprimir, retiraban el último ejemplar salido de las prensas, dejaban una guardia policial, y ese ejemplar era llevado a los censores. Si éstos consideraban que algún artículo no se debía conocer, impedían la circulación de la publicación. Eso hacía que si el número era censurado, se perdía todo lo ya impreso, con la consiguiente pérdida económica para los editores.

Se produjeron censuras nuevas en la historia uruguaya: se clausuraron, por determinada cantidad de días, una radio, un canal de televisión y el periódico más antiguo.

Dentro de este panorama de censuras y clausuras, aparece un semanario que viene a llenar un vacío, sobre todo en la parte cultural, Jaque. Publicación impulsada por un sector joven del Batllismo, es donde comienzan a aparecer artículos de las más importantes figures de la intelectualidad uruguaya. Es así que se publican por primera vez, desde el comienzo de la dictadura, autores como Juan Carlos Onetti, Angel Rama, Carlos Maggi, Ida Vitale, Manuel Flores Mora, y colaboraciones de autores extranjeros, principalmente latinoamericanos, que no habían tenido lugar en otras publicaciones. También abrió un importante espacio a los nuevos creadores. Jaque se convirtió en un boom editorial, haciendo recordar a la desaparecida Marcha.

Los autores que publicaron en 1983, fueron Mario Delgado Aparain, Selva Casal, Saúl Ibargoyen Isias, Tomás de Mattos, Nancy Bacelo, Gley Eyherabide, Héctor Galmés, etc. A fines de este año se nota una apertura de la censura, al editarse libros de autores exiliados, o prohibidos en años anteriores. Pero continuaron algunos problemas de censura hasta junio de 1984.

En los meses que van de julio a noviembre de 1984, mes en que se realizarían las elecciones nacionales, se notó una casi total libertad de expresión, tanto literaria como política. Es así que se editaron tanto autores como títulos absolutamente prohibidos en años anteriores. Asimismo, comenzaron a circular nuevas publicaciones periódicas.

Entre los creadores jóvenes que surgieron o se afirmaron en estos años, citaremos a Tatiana Oroño, Marcelo Pareja, Teresa Porzecanski, Roberto Viola, Ruben Loza Aguerrebere, Alicia Migdal, Hugo Giovanetti Viola, Víctor Cunha, Alfredo Fressia, Hugo Burel, Eduardo Espina, Roberto Mascaró, Alejandro Michelena, Alvaro Miranda, Juan Carlos Mondragón, en prosa y poesía. En sociología, economía, historia, política, citaremos a Rafael Bayce, Suzana Prates, Nelly Niedworok, Luis E. González, Graciela Taglioretti, Walter Cancela, Miguel Angel Vasallo, Jorge Notaro, Gerardo Caetano.

El pueblo uruguayo, luego de once años de dictadura, en noviembre de 1984 tuvo la posibilidad de eligir nuevamente un gobierno democrático. Aunque el gobierno militar entrega el poder el 1º de marzo de 1985, fue a partir de las elecciones de noviembre que hubo libertad total en la creación literaria uruguaya.

Para nuestra satisfacción, a pesar de todas las limitaciones a la libertad de expresión que hemos relatado, hoy las voces vuelven a ser libres y se expresan sin limitación ni temor.

16. LITERATURE IN PRESENT-DAY CHILE

Pedro Hernán Henríquez

Contemporary Chilean literature encompasses a broad range of titles and types, and is therefore difficult to classify. In this brief outline, we suggest five categories and explain each one. We particularly emphasize clandestine forms, since these provide some of our best insights into the "real country"--the country that exists and endures despite the government's censorship and repression.

1. Governmental literature.--This includes books, newspapers, and magazines, many of which can be obtained by subscription. Governmental literature projects the official position of the dictatorship, and it may be found or bought anywhere in the country. The category includes books authored by the government's partisans, magazines like Ercilla, Qué pasa, or Gestión, and publications from such official agencies as ODEPLAN, the Ministry of Finance, and DINACOS.

2. Classic literature.--This category includes world-famous writers, published for the most part by houses in Spain, Argentina, and Chile.

3. Political opposition literature.--This category includes two major strands:

Publications of the Roman Catholic Church. These can be difficult to acquire. The most effective contact point is the Archdiocese of Santiago's Vicariate of Solidarity, which serves as a limited clearinghouse. Church literature includes essays, political studies, and scientific and technological publications. Mensaje is a good example.

Publications of the political parties. Each of these groups used to have its own research center to investigate social and political issues. The leftist organizations were closed following the "state of siege." By now, nonetheless, publications from the rightist, center right, and moderate opposition may be found in any bookstore. Leftist publications may be obtained from the political parties, although a good contact is essential.

4. Shantytown literature (Literatura poblacional).--The most common forms within this category are poetry and testimony. The writers of "shantytown literature" usually meet in cultural centers, or organize their own literary workshops. They are not trained in the history of literature, nor in literary theories or techniques. They are self-motivated.

Both poetry and personal testimony are grounded in each writer's historic circumstances. Only a few of these authors write "pure poetry." Instead, their principal point of reference

is the current political situation.   Others write against the
backdrop of their own ideological experience within political
parties.

Testimonial literature is based on real situations and
conditions within the shantytowns.   Like poetry, testimonial
literature is not concerned with "translating" reality.   Rather, it
denounces it.   The literature takes its main themes from the twin
realities of torture and hope.   These works are printed in small
numbers, and they are difficult to acquire.   They only circulate
among the group's members, and rarely go beyond the cultural
center.

Designing and producing these books and brochures are
collective jobs.   There is no record of the documents, so many
are lost.   Only careful, on-site research would allow a full listing
of titles.   While a few are mentioned in alternate "boletines," such
inclusion does not ensure their survival.   Indeed, the "state of
siege" led many people to destroy such publications, rather than
face the consequences of their discovery.

5.   <u>Consignment literature</u> (Literatura de consignación).--
This material is created by writers and publishers who leave their
books, articles, or essays with bookstores to sell.   Such publications will not reach a broad audience, and can only be secured if
collectors or bibliographers specifically ferret them out.

II. Women

17. SOURCES FOR THE STUDY OF
WOMEN IN LATIN AMERICA

Asunción Lavrín

Ten years ago, the field of women's history in Latin America was practically unexplored and remained terra incognita for most historians. With the exception of a few essays in still-rare interdisciplinary volumes dedicated to women's issues, only a few bold spirits had attempted to include a chapter on women in their works, or had advanced beyond the usual references to famous women such as Sor Juana Inés de la Cruz, the heroines of the wars of independence, or the mistresses of famous men.

Fortunately, the situation has changed considerably. Social scientists and historians, in Latin America as well as the United States, increasingly view women as an essential part of the social, economic, and political processes in both past and present. This has become possible through the growing interest in socioeconomic history, the study of development and change, and the realization that the apparent absence of women from social processes was attributable more to male academicians' lack of sensitivity and perception than to women's own inertia or lack of importance in their many roles.

Before considering the problems involved in studying women, and the materials that should be in U.S. libraries but are not—the agenda I received for writing this paper—I discuss briefly the issue of whether women should be considered as part of the masses or as minorities in either research or library acquisitions. A contemporary political cliché lumps women and minorities together as sharing similar problems in gaining representation and power in local and national political affairs. This assumption has the pragmatic objective of highlighting the limited channels through which women and minorities have been able to gain either voice or influence in local governments, corporation and business directorates, labor unions, academics, or any other leadership or decision-making position. Restricted access to influential or record-making positions has limited the number of historical "tracks" left by women, and has complicated the effort of finding their traces.

But to consider women as a minority obscures the issues that are specific to women—or gender related—and for which feminist scholars claim a research priority. It also makes it difficult to

Author's Note. I wish to thank Professor Edith Couturier for a critical reading of this paper.

177

understand the argument of the nonfeminists; that is, that the issues that divide women among themselves--ideological differences, economic cleavages, educational advantages or disadvantages, ethnocultural heritages--are more important than a common gender. Both positions have their critics, and they will probably be the subject of more debate. Since women form a slight demographic majority, and since a society in which the two sexes do not interact is inconceivable, my own position in this paper is that, from the point of view of research, all efforts should be made to treat women as essential members of society. While their past and present alike bear specific nuances of gender, they must always be taken into consideration when examining social and historical processes.

The increased interest in women's history and women's participation in Latin American social change has resulted from the growth of women's studies in the United States. As such, existing approaches in studying Latin American women bear the imprint of North American academic interests. Research has focused on the social sciences, since many academics, politicians, and economists are, above all, interested in present conditions and contemporary problems. I take this orientation into consideration but, as a historian, I must also consider the sources that will eventually allow us a more complete knowledge of both past and present.

Immersion in the family and community have generally predominated over women's individual activities throughout both the colonial and the contemporary periods. Individuality has not been totally lost, but research must first address women's strong ties to others within community activities. The use of personal sources to study the daily activities and cycles of women's lives is difficult when dealing with Latin America. Until recently, Latin women wrote few letters, diaries, or autobiographies. In conducting research in archives and libraries in Mexico, Peru, Chile, Argentina, and Uruguay, I have only exceptionally found personal papers.[1] Nor do Latin American universities serve as repositories of private papers. Women's organizations have likewise neglected to preserve their own files; even those still functioning today, such as the National Councils for Women, are unlikely to have any materials available to the researcher. One has to look into more "public" sources to find other sociobiographical background for their history.

Some such public sources remain nearly barren of women's tracks for a considerable time through the colonial period and much of the nineteenth century. The lack of female participation in activities like wholesale trade, municipal government, or judiciary processes rules out administrative sources in the search for women's history until relatively recent times. Even then, women are more likely to appear as employees than as leaders.

Women's history thus depends far more on sources that record the daily personal activities of people of both sexes: documents tracing the purchase and sale of houses and personal effects, litigation over properties and inheritance, membership records for charitable and educational activities, lists of donations of properties to religious institutions, and the like. In my own research on nunneries and ecclesiastical institutions, I was not only able to pursue the activities of the institutions themselves, but also to find less-known material on women as lenders of money, small business partners, and patrons of charity. I could follow these paths not simply because I was studying feminine institutions, but rather because the institutions reflected women's deep involvement in the everyday activities of their communities. A study of male ecclesiastical institutions would have rendered similarly important information about women, for the same reasons. Notarial records, which are rich in inventories, dowries, and wills, record a myriad of day-to-day operations among a large cross-section of society. They reveal important data on personal and familial strategies to preserve properties, on the colonies' material culture, and on feminine involvement with both.

Several historians of Spanish and Portuguese America are now preparing papers on male-female relationships from betrothal through divorce, on the Church's social control of marriage, and on the sexual behavior of the upper and lower classes. Inquisition and matrimonial records handled by the Church (permissions for relatives to contract marriage or involving persons who had committed transgressions of a moral character) form the base for such studies. Such research demonstrates how traditional materials may illuminate women's behavior if the appropriate questions are raised.

Archival sources such as those mentioned above allow us to study women's life cycles, as well as their familial and social roles. Thus far they have been used most profitably by colonial historians. With few exceptions, such as Florencia Mallon and Silvia Arrom, historians of the nineteenth and twentieth centuries have yet to employ these materials.[2] To be fair, we must add that the archival sources that support this type of research on women are difficult to reach and to use. Were they on microfilm and thereby more accessible to researchers, we would have at hand the tools for a more meaningful social and economic history, and we would enjoy a firmer basis for studies of the role of women in contemporary issues.

Several small collections of notarial, civil, and judiciary records have been microfilmed. The Parral Archives and the notarial records of Guadalajara and Puebla in Mexico (filmed by the Church of the Latter Day Saints in the early 1960s) are prime examples. However, the Mormons are not now filming notarial records. The University of Massachusetts at Amherst recently published two guides for the notarial records of Mexico City for the years 1829 and 1847. A separate women's index of 1,210 names has proven extremely useful to researchers.[3]

Legislative and legal sources for both colonial and independent periods are also important sources for the study of women. The parameters of women's lives in their relations with men, and as members of the family and of society at large, were defined by law. The contours of women's juridical personalities are essential elements in understanding them through time. We still lack definitive studies of the laws regulating women's lives in the colonial period, and the same holds true for the twentieth century. The acquisition, preservation, and dissemination of legal texts and of collections of legislative materials would substantially strengthen the base for women's studies. Congressional debates are equally important. Although legislation on women is dispersed throughout these volumes, the appropriate debates are essential to gauge the consensus--or lack of it--on such matters of social change as the regulation of women's and children's work, divorce, and suffrage.[4]

Other important records for women's history include the baptismal, matrimonial, and death records which, up to the late nineteenth or early twentieth century, generally remained under ecclesiastical control. These sources have been made available in the United States by the Mormon Church. To date, no other microfilm project affords greater potential for the study of colonial demography. The Mormon records extend well into the twentieth century, allowing long-term studies of relevance to sociologists as well as to historians. The largest national collection within the Mormon holdings pertains to Mexico. Records become less numerous, and the gaps more frequent, for the nations further south. The Mormon microfilm project continues to grow, and it encompasses both a long time span and broad geographic areas. Libraries interested in microfilm projects should consequently focus on documents that the Mormons will not record. These include notarial records, Inquisition documents, matrimonial dispensations, divorce records, family property claims, liens and loans processes, and the like. Such sources offer a historically rich view of women as individuals, and also as part of a broad spectrum of social and ethnic groups engaged in the activities that form the very basis of socioeconomic history.[5]

National censuses, annual statistics, and civil records started to appear in the second half of the nineteenth century. These sources provide additional demographic profiles of women. Some problems of interest to contemporary sociologists, such as female-headed households and illegitimacy rates, could be better analyzed and understood as a continuous historical experience of women, and not just a contemporary phenomenon. This perspective requires us to use annual modern statistics in combination with colonial and nineteenth-century parish records. The latter would testify to the existence of a variety of types of family groupings, including consensual union, for several centuries in all Latin American countries.[6]

Statistical materials, however, must distinguish between the genders to be useful. I have been personally frustrated a number of times trying to trace, for example, the growth of women in the educational force, or in the overall labor force because the national, municipal, or institutional sources did not provide usable information. The researcher may not always be able to use these sources to draw general profiles of women engaged in particular activities. When gender breakdowns are available, these sources can illuminate the development of female participation in such social activities as the labor force, educational and electoral activities, and vulnerability to health problems. The lack of historical studies on most women's issues requires that researchers addressing basic questions of female participation in social change must first consult statistical sources: their chronological, factual data are indispensable. Boletines de Estadística, usually issued by National Offices of Statistics, are available for most Latin American nations since the late nineteenth century. Any library poorly endowed with such materials should strengthen its holdings as a first-aid measure to encourage and support research on women.[7]

Another important aspect of women's studies involves education. Two particularly important types of documents concerning female education are available from the eighteenth century onward. Educational institutions have generated their own records; and official entities have issued such materials as governmental budgets for women's schools, and special curricula for women. The adoption of national programs for women's primary, secondary, and higher education triggered important social changes in the nineteenth and early twentieth centuries. At the urging of educators and statesmen, most Latin nations accepted the concept that women's education could be a tool for development. As a result of an increasingly more varied and technical education, new white-collar and professional occupations became acceptable for a growing number of women. These individuals thus left the boundaries of the home, and incorporated themselves within the labor force. Education also trained women for the service sector--bureaucratic positions and the like--where they today exercise some of their most significant activities.

The educational institutions most likely to have preserved their records are religious private schools. One recent study on the teaching Order of Mary, by Pilar Foz y Foz, relied on the Order's records in Mexico and Spain.[8] Research into women's education, however, should go beyond the history of private institutions and tackle such topics as educational methodology, the philosophy and practice of women's education, and its place in national public policy. Appropriate sources include advisory manuals on women's education, which have appeared since the sixteenth century; educational journals; the national budgets for education; and even guidelines on women's mobilization issued by contemporary governments, which aim at setting behavioral models for women.

Women's education is an issue that stretches beyond institutional boundaries, and reflects the image that a society sets for its female population. The models presented in school texts are complemented by those transmitted through radio, television, and even fotonovelas, comics, and cartoons.[9] Many educators have employed the latter to explore male-female interaction, the status of women, and the expectations of middle- and lower-class females. A carefully chosen collection of such material might be considered by some libraries.

Closely associated with the development of education as a tool for social and role change, and as a vehicle for gender expression, are the numerous literary magazines published especially for women since the mid-nineteenth century. These are important sources for sensing women's own world, their aspirations, and their concerns.[10] Although some U.S. libraries have samples of such magazines, most remain in Latin America, ignored and unknown. The literary expressions of such nineteenth-century women as Clorinda Matto de Turner, Mercedes Cabello de Carbonera, and Juana Manso were recorded in these journals.[11]

The number of women's magazines increased in the twentieth century, forcing a distinction among literary journals in general, those produced for women, and those produced by women. While those by women are scarcer than those for women, they have existed and continue to be published. As such, they are perhaps just as interesting as expressions of women's entrepreneurial activities as for their literary content. Their availability in North American libraries is, generally, very limited. This gap precludes scholarly studies of the full range of women's writings, and of women's transition toward full maturity in self-expression.

Feminine journalism, however, goes beyond the literary field. Since the second decade of this century, women of diverse backgrounds have founded hundreds (considering the whole continent and a span of sixty years) of magazines and newspapers. To draw from my own research experiences in southern South America, without such magazines and newspapers I would have been unable to follow the activities of the feminist organizations, or to track the ideas of the women and men who rallied around causes like the regulation of women's work in factories, sex education in the schools, or female suffrage. Thus, for example, both Vida Femenina and Acción Femenina were indispensable in following the activities of the main nucleus of socialist women in Argentina during the 1920s and the 1930s. As feminism became an important concern for urban middle-class men and women through the same period, feminist organizations founded newspapers and magazines to acquaint the general public with the feminist ideology and to generate support. Feminist magazines and newspapers such as Nosotras (Valparaíso), La Mujer Nueva (Santiago), and Ideas y Acción (Montevideo), which are not available in the United States, are the only source to study these activities and their objectives.

The newspapers published by working women are equally important. So are labor newspapers which took an interest in women's issues; for instance, Chile's La Alborada and La Palanca, or Anima Vita, founded in Brazil in 1910 to demand the regulation of women's work. These examples represent activist or ideologically committed newspapers and magazines. Some lasted for a few issues, others for a few years. Their duration and commitment are in themselves significant as mirrors of public acceptance and of the economic capabilities of the groups that published them. Their ideological stands on social issues afford us invaluable resources with which to examine the nuances of specific social causes. Because these publications focus on particular issues, they also compress news and save the researcher a tedious and sometimes fruitless search in the daily press.

Publications of special women's groups, such as those cited above, are meagerly represented in most U.S. libraries. The scarcity of these sources greatly impairs U.S. scholarly contributions to Latin American women's history. Stronger collections of women's magazines, past and present, should be an important objective of U.S. libraries.[12]

The daily press and more home-oriented and nonideological magazines have their own uses. The large dailies of capital cities such as Caracas or Montevideo record factual events essential in following the political as well as social activities of women's groups and female personalities. They also chronicle legislative changes affecting women and the family. While U.S. holdings of Latin American newspapers on microfilm have increased significantly, we still fall far short of access to a representative sample from all historical periods. Holdings of special-interest newspapers are likewise weak. This deficiency not only is limited to women's magazines but also includes working-class dailies and publications of the right wing and of Catholic organizations. Finally, there are enormous gaps in the chronological coverage of many major newspapers. The weakest period for U.S. collections of Latin American newspapers is the first four decades of this century. Some important national dailies are available only from the 1940s onward, leaving researchers in the dark about the first decades of the century. For example, Michael Jiménez has noted that El Tiempo of Bogotá is not available until the early 1930s.

Labor newspapers are particularly important for women's history. Early century anarchist and socialist newspapers devoted considerable space to women's issues ranging from labor legislation to their role in society. Examples include La Reforma

(Santiago, 1906-1908) and El Despertar de los Trabajadores (Iquique, 1912-1926), both founded by Emilio Recabarren, a socialist activist who associated himself with the labor movement early in the century and who eventually founded Chile's Communist party. In these two dailies, Recabarren and others discussed the issues affecting working women and women in general. Likewise seeking to recruit working women to their cause were the anarchists and socialists of the other two countries in the Southern Cone, Argentina and Uruguay. Dailies such as La Batalla in Buenos Aires are well known to labor historians. Now we can add this and other anarchist and socialist newspapers to the list of sources for women's history.[13] A concerted effort to microfilm more workers' newspapers would serve the dual purpose of informing us about both men and women workers and helping us reconstruct the history of mass movements. Furthermore, these sources will allow us to delineate the ideological differences among women of different social strata.

Two other points need to be stressed about newspapers and magazines: their importance to still-pending studies of women journalists, and their value in mirroring the more mundane concerns of what may be termed popular feminine material culture. Each Latin American nation can boast scores of women journalists who have written on social and political issues. Some of our best writers and women activists have contributed both articles and short stories to newspapers and magazines.[14] Studies of this form of female literary and social activity would be highly desirable. As for the nonideological women's magazines, their home orientation could serve sociologists as well as historians in delineating the main contours of female and home images, material culture, methods of infant care, food consumption, and even cooking techniques and eating habits. All these subjects contribute to the current research agenda in history, anthropology, and sociology.[15]

Because the public activities of women have increased so dramatically over the last five decades, several other important sources should be mentioned. The publications of a number of women's organizations remain both essential for understanding the nature and activities of such organizations and elusive in their acquisition, given their lack of advertising apparatus and sometimes irregular publication patterns.[16] The early 1920s journal of the Uruguayan National Council of Women, for example, was an important source for my own research. It never reached foreign libraries, so I had to travel to Montevideo to consult it. For the future, we must collect the publications of contemporary centers for the study of women, as well as those of the activist groups which are appearing in significant numbers in most Latin American capitals. The first category includes the publications of already established centers like GRECMU (Grupo de Estudios sobre la Condición de la Mujer en Uruguay). This center has started to publish La Cacerola, which could become a major source of information on the activities and concerns of Uruguayan women in the 1980s. Other women's centers, such as the Centro Flora Tristán in Lima, and the Centros da Mulher Brasileira in São Paulo and Rio de Janeiro (both founded in the mid-1970s), must also be tapped for their materials.[17]

Many Latin American cities contain less well endowed centers oriented toward social action among women. Their activities suggest a new process of self-awareness among urban women which should be documented for future historical research. Some of these groups publish their own bulletins. These fragile traces of their activities could be made available to U.S. libraries if requested. One specific example is the Boletín del Centro de Promoción y Acción de la Mujer (CEPAM), in Quito and Guayaquil, Ecuador. This Boletín serves as the mouthpiece of the new Casa de la Mujer.

Another important source for both the early decades of the century and the present are the various publications issued through official Labor Departments or Offices and Offices for the Study of Women and the Family. Irrespective of their ultimate political objectives, or even their inability to enforce their rulings, the agencies' activities and publications constitute key records of government policies. Some of the most informative reports on the condition of working women in the early twentieth century were issued by the Labor Offices of Argentina and Chile. A complete set of these reports, for all other countries, would provide information on both male and female workers and thereby serve a double purpose for socioeconomic history.[18]

The Decade of Women, inaugurated in 1975, moved many Latin American nations to issue data on several aspects of women's lives, especially education and labor. Other nations have convened special conferences on women. The data emanating from this surge of activity, and from an increased sensitivity among women themselves to their own condition, will be extremely helpful to future researchers.[19]

The political activities of Latin American women are among the topics that have aroused the most interest among political scientists and sociologists since the mid-1970s. Most nations granted voting rights to women (and thereby adopted truly universal suffrage) after World War II. Social scientists have since been intent on discovering whether the fears and hopes of specific ideological groups have been fulfilled. Deteriorating political circumstances in many countries throughout the 1960s and 1970s meant that only a few nations can boast a continuous history of formal female electoral participation as both candidates and voters. Researchers who have ventured into this field seem to have used vote analysis and oral history as their main tools of investigation. Most studies focus on one country, generally during a short period of time. To date, such sources as election returns broken down by gender, opinion polls, and newspapers chronicling campaign activities remain the pillars of this research. In this context, any political material with gender information acquires special significance.

The efforts of various leftist governments to transform the character and activities of women, and the activities of the few outstanding female political leaders in Latin America, are of special relevance to the study of women. Eva Perón remains the continent's most popular female political figure, and the various studies of her activities have used the standard sources mentioned above. It appears, however, that we may be moving away from these stellar figures and starting to look into the organizations at the base of their power. For example, Silvia Bianchi, in Argentina, is carrying out a general prosopographic portrait of peronista women, on the basis of records from several ministries.[20]

In the case of revolutionary regimes, important documentary sources emanate from the government itself. These include data from women's associations, newspapers, and magazines. Oral history constitutes a necessary supplement. These sources must continue to be collected and preserved for solid and objective studies of women in the revolutionary movements.[21]

Rural women are one of the most difficult groups to research, owing to the anonymity usually surrounding their activities: many censuses do not even record them as economically active individuals. This is a problem that colonial historians are trying to resolve by analyzing notarial records, lawsuits, and the other sources mentioned above, because only these materials convey the faint traces of these women. For more recent periods, researchers rely on statistical data, provincial and labor newspapers, and the bulletins and data issued by governments and international agencies. Even so, the task is difficult because most of the research work must be carried out in the field.[22] Indigenous women have started to receive some attention from ethnohistorians, while sociologists such as Mexico's Lourdes Arizpe have investigated migration and working conditions through oral history and analyses of statistical data.[23] Similar tools could and should be used for black women, who remain barely studied either historically or in the contemporary societies of Spanish and Portuguese America. However, since writings from Latin American scholars generally categorize women by social class rather than race, it is unlikely that we will find sources specifically geared to North Americans' interest in interethnic relations.

The aforementioned problems of accessibility of sources, and the enormous gaps in the available published studies, suggest that other kinds of materials might prove fruitful. Visual resources might be employed to explore a number of themes about which little has been written. For example, many prints and photographs show women engaged in a variety of economic activities. If deftly used, these could illuminate topics such as women's economic role, or women and development. Visual sources do not answer all academic questions, but they are excellent tools to generate empathy for a subject, and their value as reliable sources of evidence has been recognized by most historians. One of their important assets is that they capture women of all social classes, not just the elites.

Visual sources must thus be identified in the numerous nineteenth-century travel books and the less-numerous but still-available illustrated books of the colonial period. Reproductions of paintings, up to the advent of abstractionism, are also important sources. Photographs of more recent vintage abound in newspapers, as well as in such magazines as Zig-Zag, Mundo Uruguayo, and Caras y Caretas. Constructing a viable set of slides for women's history is a time-consuming project demanding both patience and technical know-how, but it is not unfeasible. I particularly suggest it because of its pedagogical flexibility and general appeal.[24]

My final remarks underscore the importance of keeping track of that basic tool of knowledge, the published monograph. Many of us conducting research on women have discovered that the pamphlets and books on women from any given period are invaluable sources of basic data, as well as indicators of public and personal opinion. For example, a great deal of information on health, prostitution, and child and family care is found in pamphlets issued by governmental agencies and by campaigners for better national health or for legal reform. Books and debates by contemporary authors on such topics as women's suffrage, divorce, or women's political activities are necessary complements to statistical sources. Studies on the ideological content of social movements involving women are impossible without the contemporary literature, much of which appeared as inexpensive publications. Unfortunately, in the past some libraries neglected to acquire those publications, as well as books on women or by women. In trying to locate a book on women written by a noted essayist, for instance, I have discovered cases where all of the writer's works were available in the library except that particular one on women.

Whether we can improve this situation depends very much on the willingness of librarians and archivists to exchange information among themselves on their holdings on women's sources, and to enter into agreements to microfilm copies of unusual but important books by or about women.[25] General attention to improving the women's holdings in university libraries is a beginning step. Perhaps, given the difficulties of rapid collection development, libraries could consider creating a "special collection" or "topic," thereby generating a focus for future research on a given subject within women's history. They might,

for instance, focus on women writers, or female musical interpreters, or women's journals.   An approach based on theme
rather than country may be best, given the difficulties of
collecting all existing materials for any one country.   By building
such a collection, librarians and archivists would be doing a great
service to the new generation of researchers now emerging from
our academic institutions.   Women, for these researchers, are
indispensable actors in the narrative of human activities.

NOTES

1.   In Uruguay, National Archives, see Papers of Paulina
Luisi.   Her collection of pamphlets and iconographic materials is
at the National Library.   Her family is supposed to hold a substantial number of additional documents.   In Peru, the papers of
Zoila Aurora Cáceres, daughter of President Avelino Cáceres and
organizer of a feminist organization in Lima, are deposited in the
National Library.

2.   For works illustrating the use of these sources see,
Asunción Lavrín, ed., Latin American Women: Historical Perspec-
tives (Westport, CT: Greenwood Press, 1978).   This volume
gathered eleven essays on women in Latin America, from the
sixteenth through the twentieth century; Asunción Lavrín and
Edith Couturier, "Dowries and Wills; A View of Women's Socio-
economic Role in Colonial Guadalajara and Puebla, 1640-1790,"
Hispanic American Historical Review, 59:2 (May, 1976), 280-304;
Susan Socolow, "Women and Crime: Buenos Aires, 1757-97,"
Journal of Latin American Studies, 12:1 (May, 1980), 387-406;
Robert McCaa, "'Calidad,' 'Clase' and Marriage in Colonial Mexico:
The Case of Parral, 1788-1790," HAHR, 64:3 (Aug., 1984),
477-501; Silvia M. Arrom, The Women of Mexico City, 1790-1857
(Stanford, CA: Stanford University Press, 1985); Silvia Arrom
and Anne Gibson, "Mexico City's Tribunales and Penitencia
Archives: New Sources for Mexican History," The Americas, 35:3
(Oct., 1978), 249-252; Florencia E. Mallon, The Defense of
Community in Peru's Central Highland: Peasant Struggle and
Capitalist Transition, 1860-1940 (Princeton, NJ: Princeton
University Press, 1984).

3.   Guide to the Notarial Records of the Archivo General de
Notarias, Mexico City, for the Year 1829.   The same title is used
for the guide corresponding to 1847.

4.   The Library of Congress has started to replace its
collection of Latin American nations' congressional debates,
putting this material on microfilm.   This means that it may be
borrowed by other libraries in the United States.

5.   A recent study of marriage in colonial São Paulo is
based on ecclesiastical records of dispensations, divorces, and
suits against spouses.   See Maria Beatriz Nizza da Silva, Sistema

do Casamento no Brasil Colonial (São Paulo: Universidad de São Paulo, 1983).

6. See Elizabeth Kusnesof, "Household Composition and Headship as Related to Changes in Mode of Production: São Paulo, 1765 to 1836," Comparative Studies in Society and History, 22:1 (Jan., 1980), 78–108. As examples of statistical data collections, see República Argentina, Enseñanza Primaria. Suplemento Estadístico. Años 1940-1964 (Buenos Aires: Departamento de Estadística Educativa, 1966); República Argentina, Boletín del Departamento Nacional del Trabajo, 1907--; Brasil, Anuário Estatístico do Distrito Federal, VI-1938 (Rio de Janeiro: I.B.G.E., 1939); República de Colombia, Boletín Mensual de Estadística (Bogotá: Departamento Administrativo Nacional de Estadística).

7. See, for example, Samuel L. Baily, "Marriage Patterns and Immigrant Assimilation in Buenos Aires, 1882-1923," HAHR, 60:1 (Feb., 1980); Glaura Vasques de Miranda, "Women's Labor Force Participation in a Developing Society: The Case of Brazil," in Women and National Development: The Complexities of Change (Chicago, IL: Wellesley Editorial Committee, 1977).

8. Pilar Foz y Foz, La revolución pedagógica en la Nueva España (Madrid: Instituto Gonzalo Fernández de Oviedo, 1981). Gertrude Yeager, of Tulane University, is preparing a study of the secondary school teachers of the Order of the Sacred Heart in Chile and Peru.

9. As an interesting experiment in the fusion of mass media and education, see Episodios Mexicanos, published in Mexico by the Consejo de Fomento Educativo (1981). This cartoon series on Mexican history was devised by a team of historians. They made a concerted effort to incorporate women into the narrative in a natural manner that reflected their many roles in society.

10. June Hahner has successfully explored Brazilian nineteeth-century women's magazines to uncover a variety of feminine expressions, literary as well as social. See June Hahner, "The Nineteenth Century Feminist Press and Women's Rights in Brazil," in Lavrín, Latin American Women, pp. 254-285. See also Jane Herrick, "Periodicals for Women in Mexico City during the Nineteenth Century," The Americas, 14:2 (Oct., 1955).

11. See, e.g., El Búcaro Americano, directed by Clorinda Matto de Turner, and published in Buenos Aires from 1896 through 1907.

12. An example of an early twentieth-century Mexican women's journal is La Mujer Mexicana (1904-1908) cited by Anna Macías in Against All Odds: The Feminist Movement in Mexico to 1940 (Westport, CT: Greenwood Press, 1982). Closer to our times, Fem, published in Mexico City, speaks to the educated middle-class woman.

13. See La mujer y el movimiento obrero mexicano en el Siglo XIX. Antología de la prensa obrera (México, DF: Centro de Estudios Históricos del Movimiento Obrero Mexicano, 1975).

14. See, e.g., Bertha A. de Ospina's column in La República in the 1970s and Amanda Labarca's contributions to El Mercurio (Santiago) throughout the 1950s. The Argentine novelist Silvina Bullrich often contributes articles on contemporary issues to a number of magazines and newspapers in Buenos Aires. Influential women journalists remain unknown for lack of available sources for their study. As examples of widely read journalists in Argentina and Cuba, respectively, we have Herminia Brumana, Celinda Arregui, and Mariblanca Sabas Alomá.

15. In Mexico City, Carmen Ramos is engaged in the study of the image of the señorita in Porfirian times as mirrored in Mexican journals and writings of the period.

16. Northwestern University, in Evanston, IL, collects this type of material.

17. La cacerola, 1:1 (April, 1984). See also Vamos Mujer, a publication of Casa de la Mujer, Bogotá, Colombia. The Centro Flora Tristán, in Lima, has published a number of feminist publications. See, e.g., De niña a mujer: dos historias (1984); Las mujeres en el Perú (1985). See also Mujeres organizándonos, published by the Instituto de la Mujer Peruana since February, 1983.

18. See, e.g., Chile, Boletín de la Oficina del Trabajo, published in the 1910s and 1920s. Donna Guy has investigated female labor in provincial Buenos Aires using governmental records. See Donna Guy, "Women, Peonage and Industrialization: Argentina, 1810-1914," Latin American Research Review, 16:3 (1981), 65-89; Peter de Shazo, Urban Workers and Labor Unions in Chile, 1902-1927 (Madison, WI: University of Wisconsin Press, 1983); Peter Blanchard, The Origins of the Peruvian Labor Movement, 1883-1919 (Pittsburgh, PA: University of Pittsburgh Press, 1982). De Shazo and Blanchard include data on women, but monographic studies are possible and necessary.

19. See, e.g. Panorama Estadístico sobre la mujer (Panamá: Dirección de Estadística y Censo, 1975); Temática y Conclusiones del Foro Nacional de Líderes Femeninos (Asunción: Centro Paraguayo de Estudios de Población, 1976); Estadística sobre la mujer (México, DF: Secretaría de Programación y Presupuesto, 1980).

20. Personal communication.

21. See Margaret Randall, Todas estamos despiertas (México, DF: Siglo Veintiuno, 1980); Laurette Sejourné, La mujer cubana en el quehacer de la historia (México, DF: Siglo Veintiuno, 1980). Both these works illustrate the use of oral history techniques.

22. See, e.g., Magdalena León, ed., Las trabajadoras del agro (Colombia: Asociación Colombiana para el Estudio de la Población, 1982).

23. Lourdes Arizpe, "Mujeres migrantes y economía campesina: análisis de una cohorte migratoria a la ciudad de México, 1940-1970," América Indígena, 38:2 (April-June, 1978), 303-326.

24. See, e.g., Edward W. Mark, Acuarelas de Nueva Granada, 1843-56 (Bogotá, 1963); Las mujeres españolas, portuguesas y americanas, 3 vols. (Madrid, 1872); Bishop Baltasar Jaime Martínez Compañón, Trujillo del Perú en el Siglo XVIII, 9 vols. (Madrid: Biblioteca del Palacio Real); Patricia Londoño, "Imagen e Imágenes de la mujer en Colombia de 1830 a 1930," paper presented at the 45th International Congress of Americanistas, Bogotá, Colombia, 1985.

25. E.g., Raquel Camaña, a noted early twentieth century Argentine socialist, wrote a number of newspaper articles which were eventually collected in a book entitled Pedogogía social (Buenos Aires: "La cultural Argentina," 1916). The Library of Congress does not own a copy, and I doubt that many other major U.S. libraries do either. A copy was located at the library of the State University of New York, at Stony Brook. When accession of unusual but important books like these is impossible, microfilming could remedy the situation.

18. WOMEN IN THE MAQUILADORAS: A GUIDE TO
LITERATURE ON FEMALE LABOR FORCE PARTI-
CIPATION IN MEXICO'S BORDER INDUSTRIES

Karen J. Lindvall

A recent study of the participation of women in Mexico's work force concludes that the percentage of women employed is much lower than that of men and that the majority of women work in the service sectors of the labor market.[1] While these conclusions are clearly valid for the country as a whole, the situation for women is strikingly different in the industries of the northern border region of Mexico. This paper traces the economic and historical developments that have led to this situation, discusses the role of women in Mexico's border industries, reviews the current state of research, and concludes with a guide to research on women in the border industries.

The Border Industrialization Program

Mexico's decision to open its northern border region to industrialization was largely influenced by the termination of the United States' Mexican Labor Program (commonly known as the Bracero Program) in 1965, after nearly twenty years of operation. Approximately two hundred thousand agricultural workers were suddenly faced with unemployment. They returned to the border region, where they supplemented a continuing influx of landless peasants from the interior. Unemployment rates reached 40 to 50 percent in some Mexican border towns.[2] After several unsuccessful attempts to deal with the situation, the Mexican Minister of Industry and Commerce announced the Border Industrialization Program in 1965. This effort had the following objectives: (1) to create new jobs, larger incomes, and better standards of living for workers in the border area; (2) to improve labor skills through the acquisition of technology and through the training supplied by assembly plants; and (3) to reduce Mexico's trade deficit through the increased consumption of Mexican components in maquiladora operations.[3]

The proliferation of the maquiladora (the Spanish term for "off-shore assembly plant") has been the most visible outcome of the Program. Its operations for the most part entail the assembly of consumer products destined for export but exempt from Mexican export duties. Multinational industries were encouraged to set up assembly plants in Mexico not only by the very attractive wage differentials but also by revisions of the U.S. Tariff Code allowing for reduced tariff duties and by extremely favorable concessions on the part of the Mexican government.[4]

Only in 1971 did Mexican legislation address the operation of multinational companies in the border region. This delay has been explained by one author as a result of the Mexican government's vision of the Border Industrialization Program as a temporary, emergency measure to deal with the sharp rise in border unemployment.[5] Not only has the Program not been temporary, but its results have been very different from those anticipated by the Mexican government. The maquiladora, because of its characteristics--fragmentary processes, the import of primary materials, the export of completed articles, and its consequent disassociation from Mexico's national economy--forms part of a closed circuit beginning and ending in the United States. As a part of this larger system, the maquiladora's operation and production are controlled by the dynamics of the industrial process itself and by the North American economy, not by the Mexican economy.[6] The impact of this foreign control is easy to perceive: with the United States' economic crisis of 1974-75, 32,000 maquiladora workers along the Mexican border were dismissed in just ten months.[7] Rather than promoting the economic independence of the border region, the Border Industrialization Program appears to have increased its dependence on the United States. There has been little incorporation of Mexican components into the goods produced; in the apparel industry, in fact, the use of foreign fabric or materials is strictly forbidden.[8]

Probably the "most striking, although vastly neglected feature of this development, is its gender-specific nature. Although the majority of undocumented aliens working in the fields of the U.S. Southwest continue to be male, 85 percent of those working in the export manufacturing plants along the Mexican border are female."[9] So, although a major goal of the Border Industrialization Program was to provide employment for the pre-existing and largely male unemployed population, maquiladora industry has done little to alleviate the problems of the agricultural population, the workers expelled from the United States, the migrants from the Mexican interior, or the residents of the border regions who also lost their jobs with the decline of the cotton market.[10] Statistics published by the Banco de México in August, 1984 indicate that, despite efforts to reverse the trend, in a total of 678 maquiladoras (including 79 in the interior) employing 175,388 workers, 72 percent of the workers were women.[11] These statistics are even more significant when one considers that, in Mexico's entire manufacturing sector, 79.4 percent of the workers are men, and only 20.6 percent are women.[12]

Women in the Maquiladoras

Two major findings on women employed in the maquiladora industry are (1) that the Border Industrialization Program has in fact introduced an entirely new element into the labor market--the young woman who was not previously employed and who would probably not have entered the work force except for the maquiladora and (2) that the industry, in creating this new sector and in rotating workers every two to three years, has ensured for itself its own pool of laborers. The unemployment problem has been aggravated, and maquiladora workers are paid lower wages.[13] The maquiladora industry can avail itself of the least expensive and most productive sector of the population for its use without competition for the workers: women will work for less than men; young women are the most productive workers; workers who are still largely economically dependent on their fathers are the most docile.[14]

The reasons given by maquiladora management for the preference for women workers usually include their small hands, attention to detail, capacity for repetitive work, and physical characteristics that allow them to sit for longer periods of time than men. More realistic reasons also obtain: their lack of education and work experience makes them inexpensive and easy to control.[15]

Studies of women in the assembly plants in Mexican border cities have demonstrated the homogeneity of the worker population. Fernández-Kelly's findings for maquiladora women in Ciudad Juárez are representative: the predominant age was between 17 and 25; 57 percent of those interviewed were single; most had at least 6 years of schooling, in comparison with the national average of 3.8 years; 60 percent had no previous work experience; 79 percent lived with their parents; and, although 64 percent of the women were born outside of Ciudad Juárez, most of them had lived in the city for an extended length of time.[16]

A major characteristic of employment in the maquiladora is that "strangely, the work force never ages, nor accumulates seniority."[17] The average length of employment rarely exceeds four years, attributable not only to the availability of new labor but also to the health problems resulting from the difficult working conditions and the management's awareness that the longer women are employed, the more likely they are to become involved in union activities. The attitudes of the multinational corporations toward labor in the maquiladora industry are readily apparent. Health requirements are easy to circumvent.[18] Furthermore, the corporations are well aware of the constraints upon union activities: "It is possible that labor unions along the U.S.-Mexican border may take a more moderate approach toward wage increases in view of recent developments. They are painfully aware that their increases in wages hurt the maquiladora movement."[19]

The maquiladora industry, by providing short-term employment for women who were previously unemployable, allowing them to experience social and economic independence previously unthought of, and then dismissing them into an economy where they are unemployable, has "in spite of creating more jobs, only led to greater unemployment."[20]

The social/cultural factors involved in the employment of this particular group are many. Because traditional employment opportunities for women in the border cities had destroyed workers' reputations, many young women who wanted to work in the maquiladoras did so against the wills of their parents. By choosing to demonstrate their new independence by not getting married, these women often only further damaged their reputations.[21] In a section on "Maquila Mythologies," Fernández-Kelly discusses how "Impressionistic judgments and lack of empirical information have joined to generate a particular mystique, a nascent folklore, around maquiladora work and workers."[22] Profound ambivalence toward female employment and its consequences was a particularly noteworthy aspect of these perceptions. Ironically, considering that the multinationals' only investments in Mexico are the cost of foreign labor and the costs of administering the maquiladoras,[23] a large portion of the maquiladora employee's wages are spent across the border in the United States.

Norma Iglesias, in her recent book La flor más bella de la maquiladora (SEP/CEFNOMEX, 1985), sees the February, 1982, devaluation of the peso as a turning point in the history of maquiladoras in Mexico, and foresees a new era of expansion that will bring major changes to the industry.[24] A new era of expansion is also predicted in a United Press International report that appeared in June of 1985. It discusses a bill to be introduced in the U.S. House of Representatives that would transform the U.S.-Mexican border region into a tariff-free trade zone similar to that of the European Common Market. The zone would encompass major Mexican and U.S. border cities and allow any product grown, produced, or manufactured within it--whether in Mexico or the United States--to move throughout it duty free. Components manufactured within the zone in one country could be assembled in the other with no duties levied.

State of Research

The importance of the maquiladora industry in Mexico, including the economic, political, and social impact of this form of industrialization, has attracted the attention of scholars, students, government officials, economists, and businessmen. The severe economic crisis that shook the very foundations of the maquiladora industry in 1975 led to greatly increased research activity. Between 1965 and 1980, approximately 200 papers and studies and 210 articles were written on the subject, in addition to the many conferences held both by government agencies and by research institutions on each side of the border.[25] Carrillo and Hernández's guide to research on the maquiladora industry in

Mexico includes a list of institutions associated with the industry.[26] Many of these are conducting research studies. New studies constantly appear, as can be seen by the items annotated in the following section, which includes only a small selection of recent research. The Servicio de Alerta Biblioteca CEFNOMEX, an index to current Mexican newspapers since 1984, prepared weekly by the library of the Centro de Estudios Fronterizos del Norte de México, Tijuana, provides information on the variety of articles published on all aspects of the maquiladora industry.

A recent book by a research fellow at Centro de Estudios Fronterizos del Norte de México (CEFNOMEX) exemplifies the high-quality research being conducted on women in the maquiladora.[27] The author discusses some of the major research issues confronting those who study these women, including work routines, working conditions, employment policies, characteristics of women workers, the political-ideological controls used by plant managers, and the problems of unionization.[28] These issues, in conjunction with such concerns as the controversies surrounding the collection and interpretation of data on the maquiladoras, the differences between the industry in various cities, and the development of organizations such as the Centro de Orientación de la Mujer Obrera in Ciudad Juárez, suggest the amount of research yet to be done.

Research Guide

The purpose of this research guide is to provide a starting point for research on women workers in Mexican border assembly plants. As noted in the accompanying essay, the study of the maquiladoras and their impact on Mexican development and U.S.-Mexican relations is an increasingly important area of investigation, generating thousands of pages of research and a wide variety of conferences and workshops. This guide has been divided into sections: bibliographies, subject headings, periodical indexes, selected books, selected articles, selected periodicals, selected dissertations, and selected unpublished papers. It concludes with an index by author, or by title if no author is indicated.

Bibliographies

1.   Bustamante, Jorge A., and Francisco Malagamba A. México--
     Estados Unidos: bibliografía general sobre estudios
     fronterizos. México, DF: El Colegio de México, 1980.
     251 pp.

     A very complete bibliography on border studies which not
     only includes a great deal of information on maquiladoras
     (much of it included in Carrillo and Hernández, below)
     and on the Border Industrialization Program but also

provides a broader context of border issues within which to place the more specific areas addressed in this paper. It is divided by subject and includes a particularly useful section on socioeconomic aspects and industrialization. It includes books, periodical articles, theses, and unpublished papers.

2.   Carrillo V., Jorge, and Alberto Hernández H. La industria maquiladora en México: bibliografía, directorio e investigaciones recientes. La Jolla, CA: Program in United States-Mexican Studies, University of California, San Diego, 1981. 130 pp.

The key reference work for studying the maquiladora, and the result of four years of research. It is divided into five sections: an introductory essay; a bibliography listing most of the studies completed through 1981; a section on research currently in progress and including topic, investigator, project description, and state of research; a directory of private and public institutions in Mexico and the United States involved in research on the maquiladora; and a list of names and addresses of persons doing research in the field. The bibliography itself is divided into four areas: the Border Industrialization Program; workers in the maquiladoras; assembly plants at the global level; and reference sources, including sections on the border region, studies on women in the work force, legislation, and directories of maquiladoras. Included are books, periodical articles, newspaper articles, government and agency reports, proceedings, theses, and unpublished papers.

3.   Peña, Devon Gerardo. Maquiladoras: A Select Annotated Bibliography and Critical Commentary on the United States-Mexico Border Industry Program. Austin, TX: Center for the Study of Human Resources, University of Texas, 1981. iii leaves, 29, 121 pp.

Begins with an introductory essay which presents an overview of border studies research and then focuses on the impact of the maquiladoras on this research. The extensively annotated bibliography is divided into sections covering general overviews; survey research studies; evaluation, impact, and policy studies; government reports and decrees; and socioeconomic and demographic profiles.

4. Relaciones   México – Estados   Unidos,   bibliografía   anual.
    México,   DF: El   Colegio   de   México,   1982--.   (Volume 1
    covers   July   1980–June   1981,   with   subsequent   volumes
    following the same pattern.)

    Annual bibliography including books, articles in period-
    icals   and   newspapers,   working   papers,   unpublished
    papers, and government publications. The section "Rela-
    ciones   fronterizas--Desarrollo   económico   y   maquiladoras"
    serves   as   an   excellent   update   to   previously   published
    bibliographies.

Subject Headings

     The following headings may be used to locate books, but can
also   be   used   for   periodical   articles.   When   using   periodical
indexes, "Mexico" is another subject heading to employ.
           Electronic industries – Mexico
           Industry and state – Mexico
           International business enterprises – Mexico
           Mexican-American Border Region – Industries
           Mexico – Boundaries – United States – Industries
           Women and industry in Mexico's frontier
           Women electronic industry workers – Mexico
           Women in trade unions – Mexico
           Women textile workers – Mexico

Indexes and Abstracts

5. BorderLine. 1980--. (Updated on a continuing basis.)

    An online database available only to institutional members.
    (These now include University of California, Los Angeles;
    Stanford   University;   San   Diego   State   University;   the
    University of Arizona;   Arizona State University;   the
    University of Texas, Austin;   the University of Texas,
    El Paso; the University of New Mexico; New Mexico State
    University,   Las   Cruces;   El   Colegio   de   México;   and   the
    Centro de Estudios Fronterizos del Norte de México.)
    Focuses   on   the   border   region   between   Mexico   and
    the United States and now includes more than 9,000
    references   to   books,   pamphlets,   periodical   articles,
    unpublished papers, and theses published since 1960 in
    all disciplines.

6. Handbook of Latin American Studies. 1936--. (Covering
    works published 1935--.) (Annual.)

    The Social Sciences volume, published in alternate years,
    indexes more than 500 periodicals as well as books and
    conference proceedings published worldwide with a Latin
    American focus.

7.   HAPI: Hispanic American Periodical Index. 1977--. (Cover-
     ing works published 1970--.) (Annual.)

     Provides subject and author access to articles, docu-
     ments, reviews, bibliographies, and other items in
     approximately 250 journals published throughout the world
     which regularly contain information on Latin America.

8.   Public Affairs Information Service Bulletin (PAIS). 1915--.
     (Issued twice a month.)

9.   Public Affairs Information Service Foreign Language Index.
     1972--. (Covering works published 1968--.) (Quarterly.)

     Provides subject indexing for books, pamphlets, govern-
     ment publications, reports of public and private agencies,
     and selected articles in more than 1,000 periodicals
     published worldwide in English. The foreign language
     counterpart indexes the same types of publications in
     French, German, Italian, Portuguese, and Spanish. Both
     indexes can be searched online.

10. Social Sciences Citation Index (SSCI). 1973--. (Covering
     articles published 1969--.) (Issued three times a year.)

     Indexes periodical articles in more than 1,400 social
     science journals published worldwide. Especially useful
     are its key word index which allows one to look under
     maquiladora and other specific terms, and its citation
     index which allows one to look for references to earlier
     works in new publications. This index can be searched
     online.

11. Sociological Abstracts. 1952--. (Issued six times a year.)

     Publishes more than 7,000 abstracts each year from more
     than a thousand scholarly journals in sociology and
     related fields published worldwide. This index can be
     searched online.

12. Women Studies Abstracts. 1972--. (Quarterly.)

     Contains about 4,000 references per year to articles in
     more than 500 periodicals and to reports and papers read
     at professional meetings.

Selected Books

13. Arriola Woog, Mario. El programa mexicano de maquiladoras:
     una respuesta a las necesidades de la industria norte-
     americana. Guadalajara: Instituto de Estudios Sociales,
     Universidad de Guadalajara, 1980. 134 pp.

     Argues that the concessions granted to the foreign-owned
     maquiladoras through the legal framework of the Border
     Industrialization Program have operated to the almost
     exclusive benefit of those companies, and have not
     contributed to Mexico's objectives for the Program. The
     first chapter studies the process of internationalization of
     North American industry through the creation of assembly
     plants in underdeveloped counties to compete in the world
     market, particularly with Japan. The second addresses
     the sociodemographic characteristics of the Mexican border
     region, including its strict dependence on the economy of
     the United States, and the causes that originally moti-
     vated the Mexican government to establish the maquiladora
     program in that area. The third chapter analyzes United
     States' reactions to the program--on the one hand, those
     of North American unions, on the other, those of the
     business community advocating freedom of international
     commerce and resisting the restrictions demanded by the
     unions; and, finally, the work analyzes the Mexican laws
     governing the maquiladora industry, and the results of
     border development based on an industrialization largely
     defined by external factors over which the Mexican
     government has no control.

14. Fernández, Raul A. The United States-Mexico Border: A
     Politico-Economic Profile. Notre Dame, IN: University of
     Notre Dame Press, 1977. 174 pp.

     Study of the political economy of the U.S.-Mexican border
     region as it has developed on both sides of the border.
     The border economy is examined in terms of migration,
     urbanization and the border towns, and the Border
     Industrialization Program. The Border Industrialization
     Program is seen as representing "the entry of the
     multinational corporation into the economic development of
     the border area (and as) . . . a manifestation of a broad
     change in the economic policies of Latin American nations,
     which, not surprisingly, happen to coincide with the 'best
     interests' of the corporation."

15. Fernández-Kelly, María Patricia. For We Are Sold, I and My
    People: Women and Industry in Mexico's Frontier.
    Albany, NY: State University of New York Press, 1983.
    217 pp.

    Study of the role of women in Mexico's border industries.
    Includes chapters on the Border Industrialization
    Program; the characteristics of the work force in Ciudad
    Juárez' assembly plants; the view from inside a maquila-
    dora as experienced by the author in her field research,
    which included employment in an apparel assembly plant;
    cultural changes in Ciudad Juárez brought about by the
    maquiladora program, including those involving union-
    ization and alleged increased prostitution; and an
    ethnographic account of maquiladora work and household
    organization. The author includes a great deal of
    information on individual workers, gathered through
    personal interviews.

16. Fuentes, Annette, and Barbara Ehrenreich. Women in the
    Global Factory. New York, NY, Boston, MA: Institute
    for New Communications, South End Press, 1983. 64 pp.

    The authors discuss the role of women on the "global
    assembly line," providing a framework for viewing the
    employment by multinational corporations of usually
    young, previously unemployed women in assembly plants
    throughout the world. A chapter on women in the
    maquiladoras gives a history of the Border Industrial-
    ization Program and its particular benefits for multi-
    national corporations; discusses the health, economic, and
    social problems affecting maquila women; and discusses
    the role of the Centro de Orientación de la Mujer Obrera
    in Ciudad Juárez (founded in 1970) in serving the needs
    of working women, particularly former maquiladora
    workers.

17. Iglesias, Norma. La flor más bella de la maquiladora.
    Historias de vida de la mujer obrera en Tijuana, B.C.N.
    México, DF: Secretaría de Educación Pública, CEFNOMEX
    (Centro de Estudios Fronterizos del Norte de México),
    1985. 166 pp.; photographs.

    Attempts to describe and analyze the lives of women
    workers in the border maquiladoras during a ten-year
    period of development which the author sees as ending
    with the devaluation of the Mexican peso in February,
    1982. The study, based on the lives of ten women, is
    divided into seven chapters: chapter one describes the
    work routine of the maquiladora, including the fragmenta-
    tion of processes and the high output required; chapter

two discusses working conditions; chapter three describes in detail why the maquiladora industries have chosen as policy to employ mostly women; chapter four describes the characteristics of women who are selected for hiring; chapter five discusses places of origin, migration patterns, and benefits/problems encountered by women working in the maquiladoras; chapter six describes the innumerable political-ideological controls designed by the factory management to increase production, eliminate or at least retard consciousness-raising, and discourage union activity; and chapter eight describes the experiences of a woman worker involved in one of the independent unions that operate in the maquiladoras.

18. Levy Oved, Albert, and Sonia Alcocer Marbán. Las maquiladoras en México. México, DF: Fondo de Cultura Económica, 1983 (1984). 125 pp.

This study examines the phenomenon of multinational assembly plants, the reasons for their development on the United States-Mexican border, and the evolution of the maquiladora, including the special status granted them by Mexican law. It concludes with a detailed study of maquiladoras by economic sector to evaluate their impact on the regions where they are located, and their role in economic and labor developments in Mexico.

19. Seligson, Mitchell A., and Edward J. Williams. Maquiladoras and Migration: Workers in the Mexico-United States Border Industrialization Program. Austin, TX: Mexico-United States Border Research Program, University of Texas at Austin, 1981. 202 pp.

Examines some of the controversies concerning the Border Industrialization Program. Based on personal interviews with 839 maquiladora workers in 82 plants, located in 8 Mexican cities and towns, it provides information on the impact of the Border Industrialization Program on migration in Mexico. It also presents demographic, socio-economic, and attitudinal information on the maquiladora worker.

20. Tiano, Susan. Maquiladoras, Women's Work, and Unemployment in Northern Mexico. East Lansing, MI: WID Working Papers, Michigan State University, No. 43, Feb., 1984. 32 pp.

Working paper discusses the Border Industrialization Program and presents findings of a study on unemployment in the border region. The author uses these data to examine claims in regard to the Border Industrialization Program's impact on unemployment in northern Mexican cities. Among other findings, she concludes that the program does not appear to have enhanced women's labor market situation relative to men's. Rather, the same conditions that weaken women's employment status in other parts of Mexico also operate in the north, despite any job opportunities the program might offer.

21. Zazueta, César. La mujer y el mercado de trabajo en México. México, DF: Centro Nacional de Información y Estadísticas del Trabajo, 1981. 121 pp.

This extremely detailed statistical study analyzes impor- tant variables in assessing female participation in Mexico's labor market. The statistics were taken from the Encuesta de Ingresos y Gastos Familiares, 1975 of the Centro Nacional de Información y Estadísticas del Trabajo. Variables examined include the population of the area of residence (over or under 10,000), marital status, age, education, income of the rest of the family/household, number of children under six years of age in the home, preference for another type of employment, region of residence, and occupation of the head of the household. The author draws a number of conclusions from the statistical analysis, and provides a very interesting framework for a comparison of the women workers in the overall labor market of Mexico with those in the maquiladora industry.

Selected Articles

22. Bustamante, Jorge A. "El programa fronterizo de maquila- doras: observaciones para una evaluación." Foro Internacional, 16:2 (Oct.-Dec., 1975), 183-204.

Classic article provides detailed information on and a framework for evaluating the maquiladora industry. It is based on the author's response to the conclusions of a report entitled La Frontera Norte: Diagnóstico y perspec- tivas, published in April, 1975 by the Secretaría de Industria y Comercio. Much of this information appears in translation in the author's essay "Maquiladoras: A New Face of International Capitalism on Mexico's Northern Frontier" (see next entry).

23. _____. "Maquiladoras: A New Face of International Capitalism on Mexico's Northern Frontier." In Women, Men, and the International Division of Labor, ed. June Nash and María Patricia Fernández-Kelly. Albany, NY: SUNY Press, 1983. Pp. 224-256.

Presents detailed information on the binational region of the U.S.-Mexican border, including demographic and economic patterns. It also outlines the historical context of border development, discusses the maquiladora issue in Mexico, presents a frame of reference for an evaluation of the maquiladora industries program, describes the role of female labor, and raises a variety of questions for researchers, social planners, and policy makers.

24. Chavez L., Eliza. "Las empresas matrices de las maquiladoras mexicanas. Dos estudios de caso de la industria del vestido." In Lecturas del CEESTEM: Maquiladoras. México, DF: Centro de Estudios Económicos y Sociales del Tercer Mundo, 1981. Pp. 61-71.

Discusses the maquiladora assembly plant as part of an industrial process that most often begins and ends at a factory located in the United States. The author examines the apparel industry in the United States and then presents findings based on a study of two California apparel companies that operate maquiladoras in Tijuana. She concludes by forecasting greater development of Mexican maquiladoras by California's industries owing to California's higher labor costs, resulting in turn from greater worker organization and new state legislation to enforce strict compliance with labor codes.

25. Dillman, C. D. "Maquiladoras in Mexico's Northern Border Communities and the Border Industrialization Program." Tijdschrift Voor Economische en Social Geografie, 67:3 (1976), 138-150.

Examines Mexican assembly operations with reference to the: (1) nature and value of output and the mechanisms regulating customs clearance across the international boundary; (2) growth and distribution of maquiladoras, their industry mix and labor force; (3) locational advantages provided by proximity to U.S. manufacturers for whom labor substitution in offshore sites may be feasible; (4) pattern of distribution of parent firms in the United States and their choice of site in the border zone; (5) the Border Industrialization Program's impact upon interaction between Mexican and U.S. border communities;

and (6) prospects for growth and development of the Border Industrialization Program.

26. _____. "Assembly Industries in Mexico: Contexts of Development." _Journal of Interamerican Studies and World Affairs_, 25:1 (Feb., 1983), 31-58.

Examines the contexts of development for the assembly plants set up by multinational companies, especially as related to the locational advantages of the Mexican border zone, and offers socioeconomic perspectives on the internationalization of production in the region. The author discusses the benefits of the Border Industrialization Program for the multinational corporations, and its liabilities for Mexico's economic and regional development.

27. "Faldas tras las máquinas." _Ser Ahí en el Mundo (Revista de Divulgación Científica de la Universidad Autónoma de Baja California_, 1 (Feb.-March, 1985), 53-59.

A report on a research project entitled "Características de la mujer obrera en la Frontera Norte: el caso de Mexicali, Baja California," carried out by Silvia Leticia Figueroa Ramírez and Ana María Avilés Muñoz at the Instituto de Investigaciones Sociales of the Universidad Autónoma de Baja California. It provides a brief history of the integration of women into the labor force of Mexicali, describes working conditions, profiles the working woman, and discusses the integration of work with responsibility for the home. Also included are the findings on training for women in the maquiladoras by two students who prepared their thesis on "La capacitación y el ascenso laboral de la mujer obrera en la industria maquiladora de Mexicali, B.C." Their conclusions indicate that the provision of on-the-job training and its role in job advancement are strikingly different for men and women: women receive less training, and benefit less from what they do receive in terms of promotion.

28. Fernández-Kelly, María Patricia. "Mexican Border Industrialization, Female Labor Force Participation and Migration." In _Women, Men, and the International Division of Labor_, ed. June Nash and María Patricia Fernández-Kelly. Albany, NY: SUNY Press, 1983. Pp. 205-223.

The author states that, "contrary to widespread assumptions, it has now become apparent that in Latin America the majority of migrants are young women." In this essay she outlines "a schema for the conceptualization of migratory processes along the Mexican-American border in the context of its recent industrialization." A major factor in this discussion is the "special dimension that the maquiladora industry has added to the complex picture of migration from the interior of Mexico to its northern border." The essay discusses the characterization of Mexican women migrants to the border region, profiles women in the maquiladoras, and explores the "crucial connections among gender, class, family structure, and occupational alternatives for both men and women along the U.S.-Mexican border in the context of its recent industrialization."

29. _____. "The Maquila Women." In Anthropology for the Eighties, ed. Johnnetta B. Cole. New York, NY: The Free Press, 1982. Pp. 291-297. (Also published in North American Congress on Latin America. N.A.C.L.A. Report on the Americas, 14:5 [Sept.-Oct., 1980], 14-17.)

Details characteristics of the women who work in the maquiladoras, including the distinct differences between those in the electronics sector and those in the apparel sector. It then discusses their educational, work, and family backgrounds. A section on "maquila mythologies" discusses the mystique that surrounds maquiladora work and workers.

30. Gambrill, Mónica-Claire. "La fuerza de trabajo en las maquiladoras. Resultado de una encuesta y algunas hipótesis interpretativas." In Lecturas del CEESTEM. Maquiladoras. México, DF: Centro de Estudios Económicos y Sociales del Tercer Mundo, 1981. Pp. 7-60.

Based on a study of assembly plant workers in Tijuana, B.C., essay includes information on age, education, and work histories; workers' experiences as migrants; and working conditions in the maquiladoras, including salaries, health concerns, and workers' rights.

31. González Salazar, Gloria. "Participation of Women in the Mexican Labor Force." In Sex and Class in Latin America, ed. June Nash and Helen Icken Safa. Brooklyn, NY: J.F. Bergin Publishers, Inc., 1980. Pp. 183-201.

Discusses economic and social factors influencing the role of women in Mexico's work force. Tables provide statistics on women's employment by economic sector, by occupation, by source of income, and by monthly income.

32. Iglesias P., Norma. "El empleo de mujeres en la industria maquiladora." Boletín Informativo Sobre Asuntos Migratorios y Fronterizos (Jan.-Feb.-March, 1983), 8-9.

Discusses issues such as why maquiladoras employ mostly women; whether women are really oppressed by the social and economic situation; the relationship between education and employment; the impact of women's new economic independence resulting from employment; forms of control in the assembly plants; and incentives to increase production.

33. _____. "Las mujeres somos delicadas y pacientes." Fem, 8:39 (April-May, 1985), 52-54.

Discusses the reasons usually given for the heavy preponderance of women workers in the assembly industry, and then examines the justifications given by the workers themselves. More often than not, because of social conditions and the psychological control exerted within the maquiladoras, women workers respond with the same justifications given by the maquiladora managers.

34. Inman, Harry A., and Alejandro Ortíz Tirado. "A Mexican Dividend: 'Las Maquiladoras'." International Lawyer, 9:3 (1975), 431-440.

Details the special terms under which the Border Industrialization Program operates, and then provides legal advice and guidelines (including considerations of the "cost and attitude" of labor) for multinational corporations considering new plants on the U.S.-Mexican border.

35. North American Congress on Latin America. "Hit and Run: Runaway Shops on the Mexican Border." North American Congress on Latin America. N.A.C.L.A.'s Latin America and Empire Report, 9:5 (July-Aug., 1975), 2-30.

Report is extremely useful for its detail on the history, development, and conflicts surrounding the evolution of the maquiladora industry in northern Mexico.

36. _____. "Capital's Flight: The Apparel Industry Moves South." North American Congress on Latin America. N.A.C.L.A.'s Latin America and Empire Report, 11:3 (March, 1977), 2-33.

A case study of the apparel industry in the United States and its movement from its birthplace in the large industrial cities of the Northeast and Midwest to locations

abroad and to other areas of the United States. We
include it here because of this industry's deep
involvement with the maquiladora program in Mexico, and
because it presents many possibilities for comparing and
contrasting the situations for women in the two countries'
apparel industries. In each, women constitute nearly
80 percent of the work force.

37. Peña, Devon Gerardo. "Las Maquiladoras: Mexican Women
     and Class Struggles in the Border Industries." Aztlán:
     International Journal of Chicano Studies Research, 11:2
     (Fall, 1980), 159-229.

     Outlines the events that led to Border Industrialization
     Program; provides a political economic profile of current
     conditions in maquiladora industries in Ciudad Juárez,
     Ciudad Reynosa, Matamoros, and Nuevo Laredo; and
     analyzes the Border Industrialization Program in Nuevo
     Laredo and Tijuana, focusing particularly on the cycles of
     female struggles in the maquiladoras between 1973-75 and
     1979-80.

Selected Periodicals

38. Boletín informativo sobre asuntos migratorios y fronterizos.
     México, DF: Centro de Información Para Asuntos Migra-
     torios y Fronterizos (Ignacio Mariscal 132, Colonia
     Revolución, 06030 México, DF), 1978(?)--. (Irregular,
     may have ceased.)

     Newsletter has a regular section "Noticias sobre maquila-
     doras" in many issues. It has published brief reports on
     a wide variety of issues concerning maquiladoras.

39. Boletín puente/Bridge Over the Border. Tijuana, Baja
     California, México (Calle 4a No. 1848 Desp. 14, Zona
     Centro, Tijuana, Baja California 22000, or P.O. Box 2618,
     Los Angeles, CA 90051), 1:1-- (Feb./April, 1985--).

     First issue of this new newsletter on border issues
     includes several items on maquiladoras, including informa-
     tion on a strike at the Zenith assembly plant in Reynosa,
     across the border from McAllen, Texas; transfers of
     assembly plants from the United States to Mexico; union
     activities; salaries; and health problems affecting women
     working in the maquiladoras.

40. Maquiladora Newsletter.   México, DF: American Chamber of
     Commerce of Mexico, 1972(?)--. (Monthly.)

     Newsletter prepared expressly for the use of maquiladora
     members of the American Chamber of Commerce, A.C. It
     includes articles and statistics on issues relating to
     maquiladoras and incorporates such information as United
     States and Mexican legislation, customs, exchange rates,
     wages, employment, and union activities.

Selected Dissertations

     Additional dissertations can be located through the author
and key word indexes of Dissertation Abstracts International.

41. Carrillo V., Jorge, and Alberto Hernández H. "La mujer
     obrera en la industria maquiladora: el caso de Ciudad
     Juárez." Thesis, Universidad Nacional Autónoma de
     México, 1982. 459 pp.

     Extremely detailed and thoroughly documented study
     presents a history of the development of the maquiladora
     industry in Ciudad Juárez within the framework of the
     industrialization of the entire border region. The extra-
     ordinary growth of industry in this city (the most
     popular location for North American companies) is
     attributed to its location near El Paso and to its highly
     developed urban and industrial infrastructure. The
     thesis reviews the period of expansion of the maquiladora,
     1970-1974; the crisis of 1974-75; and the period of
     recuperation, from 1976 to 1978. A chapter on women in
     the maquiladora work force includes a study of the female
     population of Ciudad Juárez; a profile of the maquiladora
     worker by age, marital status, area of origin, education,
     work experience, and family structure; and conditions of
     work including salaries, requirements imposed by manage-
     ment for obtaining positions in the maquiladoras, and
     health problems resulting from the work situation. A
     final chapter covers labor practices in the maquiladora
     industry in Ciudad Juárez and other border cities. The
     thesis includes an extensive bibliography (pp. 327-406),
     as well as appendixes including the questionnaire used to
     interview 476 maquiladora workers and a wide variety of
     statistical tables. Much of this information appears in a
     book entitled Mujeres fronterizas en la industria maquila-
     dora, published in 1985 by the Secretaría de Educación
     Pública and the Centro de Estudios Fronterizos del Norte
     de México.

42. Fernández, María Patricia. "'Chavalas de maquiladora': A
     Study of the Female Labor Force in Ciudad Juárez'
     Offshore Production Plants." Ph.D. diss., Rutgers
     University, 1980. 402 pp.

     "Explores the characteristics of the female labor force in
     offshore production plants, as well as the international
     economic and political circumstances that have led to the
     transfer of productive stages from highly industrialized
     countries such as the United States to underdeveloped (or
     peripheral) areas such as the Mexican-American border."
     Most of this material is incorporated in María Patricia
     Fernández-Kelly, For We Are Sold, I and My People
     (Albany, NY: State University of New York Press, 1983),
     entry 15, above.

43. Peña, Devon Gerard. "The Class Politics of Abstract Labor:
     Organizational Forms and Industrial Relations in the
     Mexican Maquiladoras." Ph.D. diss., University of
     Texas, Austin, 1983. 607 pp.

     Focuses on the development of organizational forms in the
     maquiladoras, including management systems, and then
     examines female workers' struggles and self-organization.
     The dissertation is based on 223 survey interviews,
     30 hours of oral histories, 20 hours of management inter-
     views, and 10 months of observational field notes.

Selected Unpublished Papers

44. Gambrill, Mónica-Claire. "Empleo via maquiladoras: el caso
     de Tijuana." Paper presented at the Primer Encuentro
     Sobre Impactos Regionales de las Relaciones Económicas
     México-Estados Unidos, Guanajuato/Querétaro, México,
     July, 1981. 13 pp.

     Discusses the effect of the maquiladora industry program
     on the resolution of the problem of unemployment,
     focusing in particular on Tijuana. Major findings include
     that the maquiladoras create a new sector within the labor
     market and that they develop their own pool of laborers.
     This strategy allows them to pay lower salaries, and
     simultaneously aggravates the unemployment problem.

45. Tiano, Susan. "Women Workers in a Northern Mexican City:
     Constraints and Opportunities." Paper presented at the
     Latin American Studies Association, Albuquerque, NM,
     April, 1985. 38 pp.

     Focuses on conditions that affect the labor market status
     of women in assembly processing and service occupations,

and discusses preliminary findings of a study of export processing workers in Mexicali, Baja California. The electronics workers in the author's sample are more likely than garment workers to possess characteristics that give them advantages in the labor market, though these advantages appear to translate into few concrete gains. Other findings contradict claims usually advanced with regard to the economic needs of maquiladora workers, and their migration in order to work in the assembly plants.

46.   Valdéz de Villalba, Guillermina. "Empleo y transferencia de tecnología o mano de obra femenina desechable: el caso de Ciudad Juárez, Chihuahua." Paper presented at the Primer Encuentro Sobre Impactos Regionales de las Relaciones Económicas México-Estados Unidos, Guanajuato/ Querétaro, México, July, 1981. 10 pp.

Study carried out by researchers at the Centro de Orientación de la Mujer Obrera, A.C. in Ciudad Juárez, in conjunction with 300 women working in the maquiladoras from 1980 to 1981. It reports preliminary findings of a six-year study on employment and unemployment of women, particularly those in the electronic and apparel assembly plants. A major aspect of the maquiladoras' female work force is its rapid turnover. Based on a survey of the women involved in the study, the author arrives at a list of characteristics common to women who once worked in the maquiladoras and who have since been laid off or fired.

INDEX OF AUTHORS

NOTES

1.   César Zazueta, La mujer y el mercado de trabajo en México (México, DF: Centro Nacional de Información y Estadísticas del Trabajo, 1981), p. 65.

2.   Jorge A. Bustamante, "Maquiladoras: A New Face of International Capitalism on Mexico's Northern Frontier," in Women, Men, and the International Division of Labor, ed. June Nash and María Patricia Fernández-Kelly (Albany, NY: State University of New York Press, 1983), p. 233.

3.   Ibid., p. 236.

4.   Harry A. Inman and Alejandro Ortíz Tirado, "A Mexican Dividend: 'Las Maquiladoras'," International Lawyer, 9:3 (1975).

5.   Mario Arriola Woog, El programa mexicano de maquiladoras: una respuesta a las necesidades de la industria norteamericana (Guadalajara, Jalisco, México: Instituto de Estudios Sociales, Universidad de Guadalajara, 1980), p. 78.

6.   Eliza Chavez L., "Las empresas matrices de las maquiladoras mexicanas. Dos estudios de caso de la industria del vestido," in Lecturas del CEESTEM: Maquiladoras (México, DF: Centro de Estudios Económicos y Sociales del Tercer Mundo, 1981), p. 62.

7. Jorge Carrillo V. and Alberto Hernández H., La industria maquiladora en México: bibliografía, directorio e investigaciones recientes (La Jolla, CA: Program in United States-Mexican Studies, University of California, San Diego, 1981), p. 7.

8. Arriola Woog, El programa mexicano de maquiladoras, p. 23.

9. María Patricia Fernández-Kelly, "Mexican Border Industrialization: Female Labor Force Participation and Migration," in Women, Men, and the International Division of Labor, ed. Nash and Fernández-Kelly, p. 209.

10. Albert Levy Oved and Sonia Alcocer Marbán, Las maquiladoras en México (México, DF: Fondo de Cultura Económica, 1983 [1984], p. 96.

11. Maquiladora Newsletter, 12:1 (Jan., 1985), 13.

12. Mónica-Claire Gambrill, "Empleo via maquiladoras: el caso de Tijuana," paper presented at the Primer Encuentro Sobre Impactos Regionales de las Relaciones Económicas México-Estados Unidos, Guanajuato, Querétaro, México, July, 1981, p. 3.

13. Ibid., pp. 2, 3.

14. Mónica-Claire Gambrill, "La fuerza de trabajo en las maquiladoras. Resultado de una encuesta y algunas hipótesis interpretativas," in Lecturas del CEESTEM: Maquiladoras, p. 58.

15. Norma Iglesias, "Las mujeres somos delicadas y pacientes," Fem, 8:39 (April-May, 1985), 52.

16. María Patricia Fernández-Kelly, For We Are Sold, I and My People: Women and Industry in Mexico's Frontier (Albany, NY: State University of New York Press, 1983), pp. 50-59.

17. Guillermina Valdéz de Villalba, "Empleo y transferencia de tecnología o mano de obra femenina desechable: el caso de Ciudad Juárez, Chihuahua," paper presented at the Primer Encuentro Sobre Impactos Regionales de las Relaciones Económicas México-Estados Unidos, Guanajuato, Querétaro, México, July, 1981, p. 5.

18. C. D. Dillman, "Maquiladoras in Mexico's Northern Border Communities and the Border Industrialization Program," Tijdschrift Voor Economische en Social Geografie, 67:3 (1976), 143.

19. Inman and Ortíz Tirado, "A Mexican Dividend: 'Las Maquiladoras'," p. 440.

20. Gambrill quoted in Valdéz de Villalba, "Empleo y transferencia de tecnología o mano de obra femenina desechable," p. 5.

21. Levy Oved and Alcocer Marbán, Las maquiladoras en México, pp. 101-102.

22. María Patricia Fernández-Kelly, "The Maquila Women," in Anthropology for the Eighties, ed. Johnnetta B. Cole (New York, NY: The Free Press, 1982), p. 294.

23. Arriola Woog, El programa mexicano de maquiladoras, p. 23.

214   Karen J. Lindvall

24. Norma Iglesias, La flor más bella de la maquiladora. Historias de vida de la mujer en Tijuana, B.C.N. (México, DF: SEP/CEFNOMEX, 1985), p. 116.

25. Carrillo and Hernández, La industria maquiladora en México, pp. 7-8.

26. Ibid., p. 16.

27. Iglesias, La flor más bella de la maquiladora.

28. Ibid., pp. 17-18.

19. LATIN AMERICAN WOMEN AND LIBERATION THEOLOGY: PRELIMINARY EXPLORATIONS

Mina Jane Grothey

This paper is subtitled "Preliminary Explorations" because that is an accurate description of its content. There is much more to be read and explored before anything definitive can be said. Here I look at a broad picture rather than specific issues. I also look at all of Latin America, and not just the situation in a specific country. The development of these issues varies from country to country, and in each country over time.

I begin with the writings of the theologians of liberation. In the works that I have read, there is little mention of the special problems of Latin American women.[1] But first, as other writers point out, one must define the use of the term "woman." The introduction to Five Studies on the Situation of Women in Latin America has a very good discussion of the need to place women within their political, socioeconomic, and cultural situation.[2] The women referred to here are the poor, and the poor are also the subject of the theologies of liberation. The literature on women in Latin America states that if poor men are oppressed, often doubly by both class and race, then women suffer a triple oppression of class, race, and sex. There is actually no need to consult the literature on Latin American women to find this information: works by Latin American women discussing their liberation and its connection with liberation theology cover this basic situation as background material.[3]

All the Latin American writers of liberation speak of the need to change from an unjust society to a just one. As theologians, they feel there is a way to do this through Christianity. Therefore, the Church speaks of a "preferential option for the poor" and the need to overcome oppression. But where does oppression come from, and how can it be combatted? These writers agree that oppression exists, but the root causes and where to work first are open to much discussion. What is the root of oppression? Is it to be found in capitalism and classism? Or in racism? Or sexism which is rooted in the patriarchal structure of society? The answer to this question usually depends on the writer's point of view. Latin Americans tend to see it in capitalism, black theologians see it in racism, and feminist theologians find it in sexism.

Editor's Note. See also the author's "Women in Latin America: A Pathfinder," Volume II, pp. 529-533.

Most agree that there is a need to combat all these "isms," but which should be fought first? Some believe you cannot try to correct one without affecting all. For this reason, many feminists believe that women's liberation should come first. In liberating women, you will also liberate the races, since women are members of all races. The same argument holds for capitalism/classism. Other writers, such as Letty Russell and Nelle Morton, take a broad approach by speaking of human liberation. Elsa Tamez, a Latin American, believes it is wrong to look at a theology of women separately from a theology of liberation. Women's liberation must be viewed as part of liberation theology.[4]

I don't think liberation theologians meant to specifically exclude women; but, as feminist scholars point out, the inclusive assumption that "man" equals "man and woman" is not always interpreted in that manner. Edward Cleary in Crisis and Change: The Church in Latin America Today admits that "a great lacuna in the first formulations of liberation theology was that of the role of women in Latin American culture and in the church."[5] Cleary goes on to point out that the liberation theologians were made aware of this deficiency by women activists in Latin America and through contacts at international conferences. Rosemary Ruether makes the same point: "the theologians of liberation (with the exception of a few who have worked with feminists in the United States . . .) are equally likely to overlook women."[6]

Enrique Dussel, although a liberation philosopher rather than a theologian, does include women when he speaks of liberation. A favorite theme is that of domination-liberation.[7] Within this theme he looks at three relationships: man-woman, father-child, and brother-brother. He also refers to these in terms of the sexual/erotic, the educational or pedagogical, and the political. The first level to address is the erotic, since the man-woman domination is the oldest. But Dussel agrees that all three levels must be worked on at one time. He believes that the liberation of women will include the liberation of men.

Domination, at the erotic level, refers to the domination of women by men in their roles of father, husband, and lover. Women are also actively involved at the pedagogical level—but now they perpetuate the domination. Within the family, it is the mother who teaches society's values to her children. Dussel also uses this level to refer to those who teach in the educational system. At this level, woman contributes to her own domination by transmitting the values that cause her subordination.

At the political level, women often work to perpetuate existing systems rather than seeking to reform a political structure that has brother dominating brother and sister. Many studies on Latin American women remark that, although laws exist to protect them, these mandates are often ignored or abused.

Besides this prominent theme in Dussel's work, he also talks specifically about women and the Church in his Ethics and the

Theology of Liberation.   Chapter 4,   entitled   "Alienation and
Liberation of Woman in the Church: A Treatment of the Erotic in
Theology," addresses the role of religious women and how the
Church has silenced them.   Yet for Dussel "the religious are
essential to the liberation process; we must unleash all the
strengths that our people and our church have if we are not to
become mired in futility in sin."[8]   Dussel sees women's liberation
as an important theme for the theology of liberation.

In looking at women's liberation, a common refrain is that
Latin American women should not look to North American feminism
as a model.   Actually, this refers to two concerns: that North
American feminism is seen as a middle-class phenomenon rather
than a cause of the poor, and that the most radical feminist
statements demand the total equality of the sexes.   It is felt that
the latter would only eliminate the distinctions between male and
female, an outcome that Dussel and other writers see as wrong.
Rather, they feel that a rediscovery of the distinctive in the
female is needed to raise her to equality with the male.

Another author who looks at the feminine, including its
religious aspects, is Leonardo Boff in O rosto materno de Deus.
The second part is devoted to an analysis of the feminine in
anthropology, biology, and philosophy, to prepare the way for a
theological analysis.   Boff posits six basic propositions about the
feminine: (1) The difference of the sexes.   (2) Inclusiveness, by
which he means that although the sexes are different, each contains elements of the other to varying degrees.   (3) Reciprocity,
a term he uses in contradistinction to complementary.   Male and
female do not stand side by side, but face to face.   (4) Histori-
city; as they stand face to face, the modes in which the male and
female elements are realized are necessarily diverse, since there
is no preestablished form for this relationship.   (5) Historic
originality; by the very fact of being different, inclusive, and
reciprocal, each sex can be described by its most salient expressions.   This condition, nonetheless, does not confer exclusivity to
that characteristic.   The feminine includes all that concerns the
dimension of life, of profundity, interiority, mystery, spirituality,
tenderness.   (6) Unity in difference; the different man-woman
yields to the unity that is the human being.   Boff feels that
there will never be a total reconciliation between masculine and
feminine.   There will always be tension.   He describes it as a
dialog of two dimensions: its synthesis is full of this tension that
sustains it, renews it, and constantly deepens it.

In analyzing the feminine in theology, Boff asks the basic
question of what God intended by the "feminine"?   He agrees with
feminist theologians that the Scriptures must be depatriarchalized.
A feminine dimension exists in the Scriptures, but it is often over
looked.   Boff looks for this dimension in the Old Testament where
God is seen as Wisdom, a feminine concept, and even referred to
in maternal terms.[9]   In the New Testament, after the standard

examination of the feminine in relation to Jesus, he proposes that the Holy Spirit is the feminine component of the Trinity and can be equated with the Virgin Mary.[10] The most vital role of Mary in defining the feminine is discussed later.

When one thinks of Latin American liberation theology, the first writer that comes to mind is Gustavo Gutiérrez. In his earliest work in English, A Theology of Liberation, he does not mention women. By 1978, however, his writings take note of their needs. Power of the Poor in History is a collection of his essays from 1973 to 1979. In Chapter 4, "The Historical Power of the Poor" (first published in Spanish in 1978), he notes:

> Certain communities committed to the liberation process have, for some time now, been attempting to develop an elaboration of the faith out of their own experience--an elaboration of which they themselves are the primary historical subject. . . . The same thing is occurring among women in today's society--especially women, who as members of the popular classes, are doubly exploited, marginalized, and degraded.[11]

Although Gutiérrez spends little time on the issue of women, he now realizes that their needs must be taken into account.

The timing of this statement is of interest: 1978, just one year before the Puebla meeting of CELAM. Two occurrences at Puebla dramatize the changing, yet unchanging, attitude of the Church. The first was the presence of women delegates. Most were religious women who Ruether believes were more interested in looking after the interests of their organization, CLAR, than in addressing women's issues.[12] Cleary paints a more optimistic picture when he quotes Archbishop Marcos McGrath, who observed that the Church was making progress by including women delegates and observers.[13] Other women wanted to participate in the meeting, and eventually did so from "outside the walls"--to quote the subtitle of one publication. Gary MacEoin and Nivita Riley describe what happened in Puebla: A Church Being Born.

> Women, too, came from all over North and South America to assert their existence. Called Mujeres para el Diálogo (Women for Dialogue), they identified themselves as a movement rather than a group, operating without an internal hierarchy, democratically making decisions with the aid of a nucleus to help communication and cooperation. The forums held in Puebla were initiated by Betsy Hollants, founder of CIDHAL, a research center on women in Latin American society based in Cuernavaca, Mexico. Assisting Betsy in directing the conference were Rosemary Ruether, U.S. Roman Catholic historian and theologian, a pioneer in the movement for total liberation of women; Victoria

Reyes from Peru, whose primary concern is domestic
help; Ada María Isasi-Díaz, coordinator of the U.S.
Women's Ordination Conference; and theologian Yolanda
Lallande, who performs all the ministries other than
eucharistic in a parish in Cuernavaca, Mexico.

The women came well prepared. Position papers
were distributed to the press, to liberation theologians,
and to the bishops. These dealt with 'human and
liberation theology,' 'theology and religious life,' 'woman
as the key to liberation,' 'the family in our society,'
'status of domestic help in Latin America,' 'ministering
women in grassroots communities,' and many other
pertinent issues. . . .[14]

The women failed in their attempts to obtain a
caucus with the bishops and other official delegates.
They did establish some meaningful relationships with
progressive bishops and other individuals, using these
as liaison to get their messages to the attention of the
conference. This work had positive concrete results.[15]

The positive results referred to above included the Puebla
document's official recognition that "The women are doubly
oppressed and marginalized" (§ 1135). Gutiérrez believes that
the treatment of women in the Puebla document "constitutes without a doubt one of the conference's remarkable contributions.[16]
Rosemary Ruether, in "Consciousness-Raising at Puebla: Women
Speak to the Latin Church," gives a more detailed analysis of
both Mujeres para el Diálogo and the Puebla documents. The
above statement is to be found within the Commission on Laity, as
is an analysis of this marginalization.[17] The emphasis on women
being active in the laity has generated some very interesting
discussions, especially about the Christian base communities.

The activities of women in these communities have generated
many references. Participants include both religious and lay
women who serve as leaders or as part of the group itself. One
of the documents of Women in Dialogue, "Information about New
Ministries and Small Base Communities (Comunidades de Base) in
Brazil," outlines these activities. Although there is great scope
for women's participation, this does not come automatically; it
must be worked for and maintained once accomplished. These
references include few detailed accounts of activities in the base
communities. The National Catholic Reporter for August 17, 1984,
does carry an inspirational account incorporating a few
experiences from a community in Peru.[18]

One interesting note, both in these documents and elsewhere, is that many women approve of this lay activity because it
keeps them closer to the people than they would be as ordained
clergy. The clergy are seen as apart from and above the people.
The attitude of lay practitioners is therefore not anticlerical, but

antihierarchical. One begins to see why the growth and strength of the base communities worries many within the hierarchy of the Roman Catholic Church.

Another definition of these communities comes from Rosemary Haughton, who sees them as a "'wisdom' type of creation."[19] The importance of this statement comes from the view that "God as Wisdom" refers to the feminine side of God.[20] As Haughton points out, "This shift is not from a masculine to a feminine type of ecclesiastical presence, but from a one-sided Church culture to one which may 'marry' masculine and feminine in a Church which lives from within, outwards, but which uses its God-given 'masculine' awareness to discern and support what emerges."[21] This reference to working outward is another way of looking at the base communities, which are often referred to as "grass-roots" communities because they work from the bottom up.

The activities of women in the base communities are just one example of the roles that women, especially in Third World countries, are filling within the Church. These roles include preaching, baptizing, presiding at weddings and funerals, and even giving communion--in fact, most of the duties of the clergy. Cleary states that "something of a revolution has already taken place in practice, if not in ideology." He goes on to say that Latin American women have made greater advances than many women in the United States, Catholic or Protestant.[22] Yet others worry about the split between what actually happens and what the Church says about women in these ministerial roles.[23] In her analysis of Chile, Katherine Gilfeather finds Church reactions tied more to expediency than to a true change of policy.[24] There are not enough men to fill all the roles within the Church, so women have filled the vacuum. One reason given for not officially opening such roles to women is a fear of alienating men, already too few in the Church.

I first saw the term "new Mariology" in Ruether's discussion of Puebla.[25] Prior to this, I wondered what references to Mary could have to do with liberation theology. I was thinking about the traditional symbol of the Virgin Mary as a model of passivity. Boff enumerates these traditional characteristics of meekness, sweetness, piety, and humility. In them, the figure of Mary was viewed not in her own right but only in her connections with Jesus. As mentioned earlier, Boff rather sees a connection between Mary and the Holy Spirit. This connection raises her to the side of her Son Jesus rather than keeping her below him. With such a concept, Mariology can be freed from its current Christocentrism.[26]

According to Ruether, the bishops at Puebla were not "capable of grasping the radicalism of this liberation Mariology." This new view was given further support by statements of the Pope during Puebla, which Gutiérrez reviews in the chapter on "Liberation and the Poor: The Puebla Perspective."[27]

The primary source for the liberation view of Mary is the Magnificat (Luke 1:46-55). The verses most often quoted are "He has put down the mighty from their thrones, and exalted those of low degree. He has filled the hungry with good things; and the rich he has sent empty away" (vv. 52-53). Within his analysis of Mary, Boff devotes a section to the Magnificat. Mary becomes a prophetic figure, full of strength and courage, committed to the messianic liberation of the poor from the historical-social injustices of society. This image in turn gives hope to the oppressed in today's Latin America, many of whom put their faith into practice in the base communities.[28]

As may be imagined, the figure of Mary is also prominent in the writings of feminist theologians. Space prevents me from reviewing all that they have to say, and much of it is similar to the statements above.[29] A word of caution is offered by Mary Daly, who wonders whether it is worthwhile to spend time seeking the liberating and positive aspects of so strong a patriarchal symbol.[30]

The Virgin as a liberation figure has special importance to Latin Americans, as Dussel notes in speaking of the Virgin of Guadalupe. Only when Latin American liberation movements join the power of their religious symbols with their political proposals will the movements reach the soul of the people.[31] Cora Ferro reinforces this idea by taking the symbol back even further into history: the place where Our Lady of Guadalupe is now venerated was sacred to "Tonantzin, the mother-goddess who consoled the oppressed of the Aztec Empire."[32]

So far we have looked at the writings of the theologians of liberation, the inclusion and exclusion of women at Puebla, how women participate in liberation theologies (especially through the base communities), and the power of the "new Mariology." I would like to conclude with a brief glance at the relationship between Latin American liberation theologies and feminist theologies. It should be clear that the two are related since both deal with liberation. There are already articles that discuss this relationship.[33]

The work I mention here is Bread Not Stone, by Elisabeth Schussler Fiorenza. This current work, published in 1984, uses one of the major Latin American liberation theologians, Juan Luis Segundo, as a main source for its discussion of the need for a distinction between the hermeneutics of liberation theology and feminist theology. Liberation theology presents a challenge to academic biblical scholars when it calls for an "advocacy stance." Feminist theology agrees with this stance. But the hermeneutics used do not go far enough for the critical task of feminist theology.[34] The main reason for mentioning this work is to demonstrate that Latin American liberation theology is indeed contributing to feminist theology.

When I began working on this paper, I found little mention
of women in Latin American liberation theologies.   Women are now
starting to find their place as an essential part of this theology.
I am less sure about the relationship between liberation theology
and the roles of women in the Church.   Is liberation theology
giving women a theological basis for these new roles?   To date,
feminist theology has provided this foundation.   Or have women,
with their greater participation in the ministerial roles of the
church, influenced the way that liberation theology looks at the
Church?

This paper raises more questions than it answers.   Many of
the topics here only touched upon are worthy of much fuller
treatment.   For example, I scarcely mentioned the theological
issues of feminism.   Some other areas for future exploration
include the works of writers not mentioned here.   Also, the
effects of the current reentrenchment within the Church merit
close observation.   The situation of individual countries,
Nicaragua for example, should be explored.   Are the different
experiences just variations on a theme?   In looking at Latin
America today, and the important role played by liberation
theologies, we must keep in mind the influence they have on
women in Latin America as well as the role women must play in
the theory and the praxis of liberation theology.

NOTES

1.   I have certainly not read every liberation theologian,
nor all the works of those I have studied.   For a complete list of
works examined, see the bibliography.

2.   Five Studies on the Situation on Women in Latin America
(Santiago, Chile: CEPAL, 1983), pp. 20-23.

3.   An example is "General Schema about the Woman in
Society: Workshop Conclusions," in Women in Dialogue (Notre
Dame, IN: Catholic Committee on Urban Ministry, 1979),
pp. 120-126.

4.   Elsa Tamez, "Woman, Church and Theology," Latin
American Documentation, 14:5 (May/June, 1984), 4.

5.   Edward Cleary, Crisis and Change: The Church in
Latin America Today (Maryknoll, NY: Orbis, 1985), p. 143.

6.   Rosemary Radford Ruether, "Consciousness-Raising at
Puebla: Women Speak to the Latin Church," Christianity and
Crisis, 39 (April 2, 1979), 77.

7.   Enrique Dussel covers this topic in many of his works
including "Domination-Liberation: A New Approach," in The
Mystical and Political Dimension of the Christian Faith, ed. Claude
Geffre and Gustavo Gutiérrez (New York, NY: Herder and
Herder, 1974); Ethics and the Theology of Liberation (Maryknoll,
NY: Orbis, 1978); A History of the Church in Latin America

(Grand Rapids, MI: W. B. Eerdmans, 1982); and in two essays published together, Liberación de la mujer y erótica latino-americana (Bogotá: Editorial Nueva América, 1980).

8. Dussel, Ethics and the Theology of Liberation, p. 110.

9. Leonardo Boff, O rosto materno de Deus (Petrópolis: Vozes, 1979), p. 89.

10. Ibid, p. 96.

11. Gustavo Gutiérrez, Power of the Poor in History (Maryknoll, NY: Orbis, 1973), p. 102.

12. Ruether, "Consciousness-Raising," p. 78.

13. Cleary, Crisis and Change, p. 143.

14. A collection of the documents from this meeting is available in English as Women in Dialogue (Mujeres para el Diálogo), Puebla, Mexico, January 27 to February 13, 1979: Translation of Seminar Sessions Held "Outside the Walls" during CELAM III (Notre Dame, IN: Catholic Committee on Urban Ministry, 1979).

15. Gary MacEoin and Nivita Riley, Puebla: A Church Being Born (New York, NY: Paulist Press, 1980), pp. 86-87.

16. Gutiérrez, Power of the Poor in History, p. 161, n. 7.

17. Ruether, "Consciousness-Raising," p. 77.

18. Mary Beth Moore, "'The Light Came': Living Liberation Theology," National Catholic Reporter, 20:37 (Aug. 17, 1984), 13.

19. Rosemary Haughton, "Is God Masculine?" in Women in a Men's Church, ed. Virgil Elizondo and Norbert Greinacher (New York, NY: Seabury Press, 1980), p. 70.

20. Boff (O rosto materno de Deus, p. 89) discusses God as Wisdom.

21. Haughton, "Is God Masculine?" p. 70.

22. Cleary, Crisis, p. 143.

23. Manuel Alcala, "The Challenge of Women's Liberation to Theology and Church Reform," in Women in a Men's Church, ed. Elizondo and Greinarcher, p. 100.

24. Katherine Gilfeather, "Changing-Role of Women in the Catholic Church in Chile," Journal for the Scientific Study of Religion, 16:1 (1977), 39-54.

25. Ruether, "Consciousness-Raising," p. 79.

26. Boff, O rosto, p. 197.

27. Gutiérrez, Power, p. 139.

28. Boff, O rosto, pp. 196-198.

29. For example, see Rosemary Ruether, Sexism and God-Talk (Boston, MA: Beacon Press, 1983), pp. 152-157.

30. Mary Daly, Beyond God the Father (Boston, MA: Beacon Press, 1973), p. 83.

31. Dussel, Ethics and the Theology of Liberation, pp. 117-118.

32. Cora Ferro, "The Latin American Woman: The Praxis and Theology of Liberation," in The Challenge of Basic Christian

224   Mina Jane Grothey

Communities, ed. Sergio Torres and John Eagleson (Maryknoll,
NY: Orbis, 1981), p. 25.
   33. One example is Elisabeth Schussler Fiorenza, "Feminist
Theolgy as a Critical Theology of Liberation," Theological
Studies, 36 (1975), 605-626.
   34. Elisabeth Schussler Fiorenza, Bread Not Stone (Boston,
MA: Seabury Press, 1984), pp. 137-139.

                           BIBLIOGRAPHY

Agudelo, Maria. "The Church's Contribution to the Emancipation
   of Women." In Women in a Men's Church, ed. Virgil Elizondo
   and Norbert Greinacher. New York, NY: Seabury Press,
   1980. Pp. 124-132.
Alcala, Manuel. "The Challenge of Women's Liberation to Theology and Church Reform." In Women in a Men's Church, ed.
   Virgil Elizondo and Norbert Greinacher. New York, NY:
   Seabury Press, 1980. Pp. 95-101.
Boff, Leonardo. O rosto materno de Deus: ensaio interdisciplinar
   sobre o femenino e suas formas religiosas. Petrópolis: Vozes,
   1979.
The Challenge of Basic Christian Communities. Ed. Sergio Torres
   and John Eagleson. Maryknoll, NY: Orbis, 1981.
Cleary, Edward L. Crisis and Change: The Church in Latin
   America Today. Maryknoll, NY: Orbis, 1985.
Consultation of European Christian Women. Ed. N. Hundertmark.
   Geneva: World Council of Churches, 1978.
Daly, Mary. Beyond God the Father: Toward a Philosophy of
   Women's Liberation. Boston, MA: Beacon Press, 1973.
Dussel, Enrique. "Domination-Liberation: A New Approach." In
   The Mystical and Political Dimension of the Christian Faith, ed.
   Claude Geffre and Gustavo Gutiérrez. New York, NY: Herder
   and Herder, 1974. Pp. 34-56.
_____. Ethics and the Theology of Liberation. Maryknoll,
   NY: Orbis, 1978.
_____. A History of the Church in Latin America:
   Colonialism to Liberation, 1492-1979. Grand Rapids, MI:
   W. B. Eerdmans, 1982.
_____. Liberación de la mujer y erótica latinoamericana:
   ensayo filosófico. Bogotá: Editorial Nueva América, 1980.
Ferro, Cora. "The Latin American Woman: The Praxis and
   Theology of Liberation." In The Challenge of Basic Christian
   Communities, ed. Sergio Torres and John Eagleson.
   Maryknoll, NY: Orbis, 1981. Pp. 24-37.
Fiorenza, Elisabeth Schussler. Bread Not Stone: The Challenge
   of Feminist Biblical Interpretation. Boston, MA: Seabury
   Press, 1984.

_____. "Feminist Theology as a Critical Theology of Liberation." Theological Studies, 36 (1975), 605-626.

Five Studies on the Situation of Women in Latin America. Santiago, Chile: CEPAL, 1983.

"General Schema about the Woman in Society: Workshop Conclusions." In Women in Dialogue. Notre Dame, IN: Catholic Committee on Urban Ministry, 1979. Pp. 120-126.

Gilfeather, Katherine Anne. "Changing-role of Women in Catholic Church in Chile." Journal for the Scientific Study of Religion, 16:1 (1977), 39-54.

González, Maruja. "Oppression of the Latin American Woman: A Political-Economic, Cultural-Ideological Problem." Latin American Documentation, 14:5 (May/June, 1984), 5-8.

Gutiérrez, Gustavo. Power of the Poor in History. Maryknoll, NY: Orbis, 1983.

_____. A Theology of Liberation. Maryknoll, NY: Orbis, 1973.

Halkes, Catharina. "Feminist Theology as a Model of Liberation Theology." In Consultation of European Christian Women, ed. N. Hundertmark. Geneva: World Council of Churches, 1978. Pp. 37-40.

Haughton, Rosemary. "Is God Masculine?" In Women in a Men's Church, ed. Virgil Elizondo and Norbert Greinacher. New York, NY: Seabury Press, 1980. Pp. 63-70.

Laurentin, Rene. "Jesus and Women: An Underestimated Revolution." In Women in a Men's Church, ed. Virgil Elizondo and Norbert Greinacher. New York, NY: Seabury Press, 1980. Pp. 80-92.

Lessa, Marina. "Information about New Ministries and Small Base Communities (Comunidades de Base) in Brazil." In Women in Dialogue. Notre Dame, IN: Catholic Committee on Urban Ministry, 1979. Pp. 85-86.

Lozano Urbieta, Itziar. "Women, the Key to Liberation." In Women in Dialogue. Notre Dame, IN: Catholic Committee on Urban Ministry, 1979. Pp. 53-62.

MacEoin, Gary, and Nivita Riley. Puebla: A Church Being Born. New York, NY: Paulist Press, 1980.

Moore, Mary Beth. "'The Light Came': Living Liberation Theology." National Catholic Reporter, 20:37 (Aug. 17, 1984), 13.

Morton, Nelle. "Towards a Whole Theology." Lutheran World, 22:1 (1975), 14-22.

"La Mujer latinoamericana: la praxis y la teología de la liberación." Servir, 16:88/89 (1980), 589-621.

The Mystical and Political Dimension of the Christian Faith, ed. Claude Geffre and Gustavo Gutiérrez. New York, NY: Herder and Herder, 1974.

Philosophy of Religion and Theology. Comp. J. McClendon.
  Tallahassee, FL: American Academy of Religion, Philosophy of
  Religion and Theology Section, 1974.

"Reflections for a Church of Liberation." In Women in Dialogue.
  Notre Dame, IN: Catholic Committee on Urban Ministry, 1979.
  Pp. 101-102.

Ruether, Rosemary Radford. "Consciousness-Raising at Puebla:
  Women Speak to the Latin Church." Christianity and Crisis,
  39 (April 2, 1979), 77-80.

_____. Liberation Theology. New York, NY: Paulist
  Press, 1972.

_____. New Woman, New Earth: Sexist Ideologies and
  Human Liberation. New York, NY: Seabury Press, 1975.

_____. Sexism and God-Talk: Toward a Feminist Theology.
  Boston, MA: Beacon Press, 1983.

Russell, Letty M. "Liberation Theology in a Feminist Perspec-
  tive." In Philosophy of Religion and Theology, Comp.
  J. McClendon. Tallahassee, FL: American Academy of
  Religion, Philosophy of Religion and Theology Section, 1974.
  Pp. 18-30.

Segundo, Juan Luis. The Liberation of Theology. Maryknoll,
  NY: Orbis, 1976.

_____. A Theology for Artisans of a New Humanity.
  Maryknoll, NY: Orbis, 1973.

Tamez, Elsa. "Woman, Church and Theology." Latin American
  Documentation, 14:5 (May/June, 1984), 3-5.

_____. "Women: A Latin American Approach." Mid-
  stream, 21 (July, 1982), 333-337.

"Woman: The Workshop of Life, the Builder of the New Society."
  Latin American Documentation, 14:5 (May/June, 1984), 1-13.

Women in a Men's Church, ed. Virgil Elizondo and Norbert
  Greinacher. New York, NY: Seabury Press, 1980.

Women in Dialogue (Mujeres para el Diálogo), Puebla, Mexico,
  January 27 to February 13, 1979: Translations of Seminar
  Sessions Held "Outside the Walls" during CELAM III. Notre
  Dame, IN: Catholic Committee on Urban Ministry, 1979.

20. A SURVEY OF THE CRITICAL LITERATURE ON FEMALE FEMINIST WRITERS OF HISPANIC AMERICA

Enid F. D'Oyley

Feminists, suffragettes and bluestockings, courtesans and doyennes of literary salons, nuns and abbesses, and, in the beginning, poets--these are some of the women who first rebelled against male hegemony in their desire to define their place in society and to seek self-determination, self-fulfillment, and authenticity. Politicization of these age-old strivings is a recent phenomenon.

Gerda Lerner, in "Politics and Culture in Women's History: A Symposium,"[1] distinguishes between "women's rights" in the sense of achieving civil and political equality, and "women's emancipation" in the sense of a broader striving for freedom from oppressive restrictions imposed by sex. A sampling of the critical literature on feminist writers of belles lettres in Latin America reveals that much of their brand of "feminism" is primarily concerned with "women's emancipation," with a consciousness of being "the other" in a male-dominated society, rather than with achieving civil and political equality. Like most generalizations, however, there are exceptions, for "the assumption that it is possible to generalize about women writers, or even about Latin American writers, is sexist since no specialist would presume to encompass in a single category Latin American or Hispanic male writers."[2]

The critical works included in this survey fall within the category of feminist criticism, notwithstanding that "una crítica literaria feminista . . . es difícil definir porque hay pocos modelos que señalar como ejemplo sobre todo en lengua española."[3] Such an observation did not prevent Beth Miller from elaborating what she considered should be the focus of feminist criticism. First, the ideology or perspective should be one of radical feminism, directed at the study and abolition of sexual stereotypes which have deep historical and sociohistorical roots and which have erroneously appeared natural and immutable. Furthermore, and like Marxist criticism, feminist criticism should view literature from a sociological or sociohistorical perspective, and employ the methods already existing or applicable in non-feminist literature.

Miller was to discuss at greater length the problems surrounding the application of feminist criticism to Latin American writings, in the "Introduction: Some Theoretical Considerations," to Women in Hispanic Literature: Icons and Fallen Idols.[4] The major problems she saw resided in:

1.   The ambivalence of the women writers themselves toward the issue of feminism.   Though conscious that they are a breed apart, they still yearn for recognition by their male counterparts, and seek acceptance in the mainstream literary histories and criticisms written by male critics--an honor granted a rare few women poets, usually the dead ones.   Nearly all Latin American "poetisas," a term used condescendingly by male critics, are relegated to the realm of "minor," and thence to oblivion.   Here the critic may be overreacting by identifying the culturally charged "poetess" of English, which may or may not be used patronizingly, with "poetisa"--a perfectly legitimate Spanish term. She may also be assigning "poetisa" to the same category as "pobre monjita," or "damita intellectual," diminutives used to refer to Sor Juana Inés de la Cruz and to which the feminist critic Electa Arenal objects.[5]

Interestingly enough, Anita Brenner and Luisa Josefina Hernández held the same low opinion of their fellow female writers--the latter having no "respecto alguno por las obras de las escritoras en México. . . .   Tal vez con excepción de dos de ellas," they are "escritoras mediocres" or "terribles."[6]   Elena Poniatowska claims that "en México ha existido solo una gran poeta, Sor Juana Inés de la Cruz . . . Nadie (hombre o mujer) la ha igualada."[7]

2.   The absence of a substantial body of theoretical works applying feminist perspectives to the study of Latin American literature.   Despite awareness of the works of foreign feminists through translations,[8] for example, Michèle Mattelart, La cultura de la opresión femenina, and interest in the works of Virginia Woolf, Simone de Beauvoir, and Erica Jong, to name but a few, many Latin American feminists are still reluctant to accept the radical feminism of North American scholars.   The North Americans, revolutionary in their approach, know they run the risk of being branded intellectual charlatans by their male colleagues.   They are nevertheless questioning traditional methods of evaluating literature and proposing new frames of reference, for example, by studying the role of gender in literary history.[9]

The great divide between North American and Latin American feminists, according to Beth Miller, is the difference in ideological approach.   In general, the latter tend to endorse socialist feminism.   The dialectic then becomes dependent Third World countries dominated by imperialists, usually the United States and/or multinational corporations, rather than a male/female dichotomy.   Women are no more oppressed than the economically exploited Latin American male, and changing the social and economic order is the primordial task.   Perhaps because of that attitude, recent North American publications on Latin American writers, while providing the latter with the international exposure they crave, are simultaneously viewed as one more aspect of imperialism--that is, of cultural domination.[10]

3. The question of whether there is a separate female literary tradition, a specifically female heritage or line, an identifiable female style. To open the debate, Beth Miller referred to the statement made by the poet Griselda Alvarez that poetry has no gender. "No hemos querido intencionadamente titular Antología de poesía femenina porque . . . nunca hemos creído que exista poesía femenina y poesía masculina, es decir, poesía hormonal, ya se incline al estrógeno o a la testosterona."[11] Other critics nonetheless postulate that there are gender-linked differences, that women's literature differs from men's not because of biological determinants but because women's experiences differ from men's in nearly every society. This perspective would confirm the belief that a common and discernible sensibility exists in women's poetry, if only because women write out of their own experience as women. By reading other women's works, attitudes may be absorbed and bonds created.

Beth Miller takes the laudable position that, rather than entangling herself in this web of definitions, a sounder approach is to focus on each work's content, themes, attitudes, thought and statement, persona, poetic or narrative stance, and allusions.

4. The risk of biographical and bibliographical error confusing even the most basic facts. This bugbear in literary scholarship is prone to affect the study of Latin American women writers for several reasons: they often write in greater isolation than their male counterparts; they are often unrecognized in their lifetime; because their works are usually not available in translation, they are inaccessible to a non-Spanish speaking audience. Living in obscurity, working in obscurity, dying in obscurity, women writers leave behind very little to help the scholar reconstruct a life or reevaluate a work.

These forgotten or ignored women writers have found a champion in Beth Miller. Armed with interviews[12] (see Appendix A, a sample questionnaire), wanting to "sacar a luz algunas tendencias en la literatura hecha por mujeres," she rescues from oblivion "la mujer escritora" who "sigue marginada . . . como en la época de los Contemporáneos," despite the fact that opportunities for the creative woman have somewhat improved.[13]

Easily the most theoretical and scientific of current researchers, Miller utilizes the techniques of the social scientist—interviews, random surveys to present the authors to a wider audience—to provide the framework for future studies. Her interest is mainly literary history, not textual criticism.[14]

In 1976, it was impossible to find substantial articles in print applying feminist perspectives to Hispanic literature, Beth Miller wrote in her Introduction to Women in Hispanic Literature: Icons and Fallen Idols.[15] Since then, thanks to the feminist movement, "el interés por la obra de las autoras se ha acrescentado notablemente desde los años sesenta."[16] If the interest in feminism is fostering "sexism" in literature by creating a marginal subcategory, she justifies her position by pointing out the thousands of books and academic courses dedicated exclusively to men.

Other critics have since accepted the challenge by producing in-depth studies of specific works, such as Lucía Fox-Lockert's Women Novelists in Spain and Spanish America.[11] This work includes studies on thirteen Latin American women novelists: Gertrudiz Gómez de Avellaneda: Sab (1841); Clorinda Matto de Turner: Aves sin nido (1889); Mercedes Cabello de Carbonera: Blanca Sol (1889); Teresa de la Parra: Ifigenia (1924); María Luisa Bombal: La Amortajada (1908) translated as The Shrouded Woman (1948); Silvina Bullrich: Bodas de cristal (1941); Clara Silva: La sobreviviente (1951); Marta Brunet: María Nadie (1957); Rosario Castellanos: Balún Canán (1957); Beatriz Guido: Fin de fiesta (1958); Elena Garro: Los recuerdos del porvenir (1963); Luisa Josefina Hernández: La cólera secreta (1964); Elena Poniatowska: Hasta no verte, Jesús mío (1969). These novelists-- one Cuban, two Peruvian, one Venezuelan, two Chilean, two Argentinian, one Uruguayan, and four Mexican--"best represent awareness of feminine ideals."[18] They are studied under headings of family, social class, sexuality (i.e., the interaction between the sexes), and the message. The novels articulate the woman's point of view, and in so doing reveal basic aspects of Latin American culture--in Fox-Lockert's view, because "these writers use their feminine protagonists as mouthpieces for their own hopes and frustrations."[19] The latter assumption, however, is dangerous. No one would confuse the actor with the part he or she plays, and it is likewise false to think of the author and the characters as one, to confuse the persona with the person.

False assumption notwithstanding, Fox-Lockert does a commendable job in attempting to interpret the world of each of these novels. Each work reflects the spirit of the age in which it is written, so its fictional world becomes a microcosm of the society at large. Sab, the male slave, is equated with "woman" enslaved by the tyranny of a male dominated society; the exploitation of the Indians in Aves sin nido is seen in its larger context of sexual exploitation; and so on. Whether slave or Indian, rich socialite or poor working-class female, the protago- nists of these novels live in an oppressive society. However, and as the author concludes, they are able to break through suffering to discover within themselves the power of their own individual- ity, as well as hope for a better world.

Complete works on individual authors have also appeared including: María Rosa Fiscal, La imagen de la mujer en la narrativa de Rosario Castellanos; Lucía Guerra-Cunningham, La narrativa de María Luisa Bombal: una visión de la existencia femenina; Esther Melón de Díaz, La narrativa de Marta Brunet; Marjorie Agosín, Los desterrados del paraíso: protagonistas en la narrativa de María Luisa Bombal; and Perla Schwartz, Rosario Castellanos: Mujer que supo latín. . . .[20]

The works enumerated above are significant mileposts in feminist criticism. They deal with the problem of women in Latin American literature by reevaluating the author's works, debunking old myths, and emphasizing elements formerly ignored. Agosín's work, for example, tackles the problem of how to treat the heroine in the twentieth-century novel. In patriarchal societies like Latin America, women are seen as supporting characters helping a man to change the world, never as the initiators of change. When women appear in the novels, they are presented as stereotypes fitting into roles designated by society: daughter, wife, mother, Madonna/prostitute. How can an author present authentic female protagonists in the fictional world when no prototypes exist in the actual society in which she lives? Or should the author create protagonists of heroic proportions, figures that are larger than life, who make things happen rather than have things happen to them—female protagonists as women should be, not as they are?

Bombal solved the dilemma by creating female protagonists who, like the traditional hero, are always on a quest. This might be mythical, physical, or spiritual, though it usually involved the search for love or to find the meaning of life. The quest has traditionally been used to symbolize a desire for change, an escape from prevailing circumstances. Unlike most heroes, Bombal's heroines do not return triumphant. They end up as defeated, alienated beings, living in a dreamworld of their own creation, incapable of functioning in the real world, and resigned to an old age devoid of memories, enthusiasm, or a past.

In La Narrativa de María Luisa Bombal: una visión de la existencia femenina, Lucía Guerra-Cunningham considers the ideological and esthetic influences (French and Nordic rather than Latin American) which shaped Bombal as a writer. She also discusses the image of women in Latin American society and the conflicts that arise between the being (woman) and the world (the values of the society in which she lives). Each work is then analyzed from a particular perspective. La Amortajada is seen as "El retorno a las raíces primordiales de lo femenino";[21] La Ultima Niebla as "Ensueño y frustración en la existencia femenina";[22] El Arbol as "Liberación y frustración,"[23] wherein the music of three different composers symbolizes different stages in the protagonist's development: Mozart—the innocence and social marginality of the young, the spontaneous joy of youth; Beethoven—the frustration and annihilation of the feminine essence which coincides with marriage discovered to be loveless; and Chopin—the search for love. Agua y Tierra is seen as a definition of the feminine archetype,[24] and Islas Nuevas as its degradation;[25] Trenzas, the loss of paradise;[26] and La Historia de María Griselda, belleza fatal versus belleza maravillosa.[27]

María Rosa Fiscal has analyzed Rosario Castellanos's treatment of women from a historical-sociological perspective.
Castellanos (1925-1974) witnessed the transformation of an
agrarian, semifeudal Mexico into a quasi-industrialized society,
while also carrying the memory of a semifeudal Mexico which still
survived in the rural state of Chiapas where she grew up.
Castellanos stood on the threshold of a new Mexico; a Mexico of
change, shouting liberty, justice, law, land; a Mexico of violent
struggle and upheavals. While looking forward to this land of
educational and agrarian reform, and anticipating the recognition
of women's importance in the workplace of an industrialized
society, she nevertheless looked backward as well. Thus, her
images of Chiapas, the microcosm of a colonial Mexico of quiet
streets, huge latifundias, exploited peons, and bored women
subjected to all the strictures of "proper conduct" imposed in a
feudal society.

Her female protagonists reflect this polarity--the new Mexico,
and its new woman, active, individualistic, self-determined; the
opposed, colonial Mexico, whose women lack identity and follow
the preordained paths of marriage and maternity or shameful
spinsterhood (one of her "formas de muerte"),[28] in either case
wilting under the weight of benevolent despotism. Each chapter
is introduced by a quotation from a work by Castellanos.
Chapter 1 has the catchy title "¿Y cúal es mi lugar, señor, entre
actos?" taken from Salomé, a dramatic poem; chapter 2, "Formas
de muerte" from the poem "Satisfacción no pedida" in the collection El uso de la palabra; chapter 3, "En los labios de viento he
de llamarme/árbol de muchos pájaros" from "Poema 2," in Dos
Poemas. Literature, dubbed by her "the use of the word,"
becomes for Castellanos the instrument for influencing social
reality, and thus her vehicle for change. Her writing cannot be
escapist literature, fostering a "salon culture." Rather, it must
explore the human condition which is almost never entertaining or
pleasant. The writer must be "engaged."[29]

The work by Perla Schwartz, Rosario Castellanos: Mujer que
supo Latín . . . (the title taken from one of Castellanos's works
which is derived from a popular saying--"mujer que saber latín ni
tiene marido, ni tiene buen fin") continues in the same vein.
However, it is more strongly biographical, and it analyzes the
psychological effects of a solitary childhood and an overprotective
environment. Castellanos first turned to literature for escape,
and only then became a committed writer striving for the
intellectual, social, and economic liberation of women.

The International Women's Year, 1975, witnessed a conference sponsored by the Latin American Literary Review at
Carnegie-Mellon University to "promote women writers and their
works, primarily in the United States, where they have been
heretofore virtually unknown."[30] Writers like Carlota O'Neill and
Ofelia Machado Bonet spoke about the need to enlighten Latin

American women, and about the discrimination they face at every level in the workplace. Mercedes Valdivieso spoke of her novel La Brecha (1965), which deals with divorce among upper middle class Chileans. This work was attacked by the press for openly discussing a woman's rejection of motherhood and for exploring the feeling of being trapped in a loveless marriage.

The essays in the conference collection cover a wide spectrum, encompassing varying critical approaches and both male and female critics. Martin Taylor, for example, offers a historical overview of "Women Intellectuals in Chilean Society."[31] He focuses on education, politics, and literature, and notes that new women writers--Gabriela Mistral and Marta Brunet--were victimized by that society. One was forced into exile, the other forced to stifle her sexuality. John C. Miller presented a paper on "Clorinda Matto de Turner and Mercedes Cabello de Carbonera: Societal Criticism and Morality."[32] Matto de Turner, novelist, journalist, and founder of newspapers for women, represented traditional moral values which saw women and the family as the fulcrum of society.[33] While she would be considered conservative from a twentieth-century perspective, she was nevertheless publicly censured, excommunicated, and forced into exile because of her "liberal" tendencies. She was particularly attacked for advocating marriage for the clergy, who her novels Aves sin nido (1889) and Indole (1891) depicted as corrupt, immoral, and not living up to their vows of celibacy. Mercedes Cabello de Carbonera wrote about Peru's decaying upper-class society in Blanca Sol (1888), Las consecuencias (1880), and El conspirador (1892). She spent her last years in a mental institution.

Also included among the conference papers are: "Soledad Acosta de Samper, Life and Early Literary Career of the Nineteenth Century Colombian Writer";[34] "Elena Poniatowska's Hasta no verte, Jesús Mío (Until I See You, Dear Jesus),"[35] which presents the world of the lower-class working woman who is shown in a reversal of the male/female role in Mexican society; "María Angélica Bosco and Beatriz Guido: An Approach to Two Argentinian Novelists between 1960 and 1970";[36] "Argentine Women in the Novels of Silvina Bullrich" by Corina S. Mathieu;[37] "Three Female Playwrights Explore Contemporary Latin American Reality: Myrna Casas, Griselda Gambaro, Luisa Josefina Hernández";[38] "A Thematic Exploration of the Works of Elena Garro";[39] "Nellie Campobello: Romantic Revolutionary and Mexican Realist";[40] "Feminine Symbolism in Gabriela Mistral's 'Fruta'";[41] and "Teresa de la Parra, Venezuelan Novelist and Feminist" by Ronni Gordon Stillman.[42]

Teresa de la Parra's feminist stance is best reflected in Ifigenia: Diario de una señorita que escribió porque se fastidiaba (1924), the partly autobiographical novel of upper-class Venezuelan society at the turn of the century. The critic notes particularly that this work "is a valuable contribution to the cultural anthropology of Spanish America."[43] De la Parra was also denounced in her time, and her novel criticized as "Voltairean, treacherous and extremely dangerous in the hands of contemporary young ladies."[44] Yet the novelist affirmed that boredom, aimlessness, and sacrifice on the altar of marriage for the sake of economic security were the enemies of feminine virtue, not books, work, and exposure to life.[45] In 1975, the International Women's Year, she was thoroughly vindicated. An exhibition celebrating the event was mounted in her honor.[46]

And these female authors, did they consider themselves feminists? Or were they writing to indulge their taste for literature, creating a plausible story because they were bored (viz. Teresa de la Parra) or because they perceived it as a career (viz. Clorinda Matto de Turner, the first Peruvian woman to earn a living from her writing)? Writing was an elegant pastime for upper-class women in nineteenth-century Latin America, an example being Soledad Acosta de Samper. Yet she was atypical because of the scope of her intellectual and cultural development; her prolific literary production included more than one hundred and fifty works. Daughter of a Colombian diplomat and an Englishwoman, she was educated abroad in Halifax, Canada, and knew French, English, Spanish, Italian, Swedish, German, Danish, and Russian.

Acosta began her literary career translating the works of Alexander Dumas and George Sand for El Neo-Granadino (a newspaper edited by her husband). She was always interested in women's issues, particularly those involving the need to educate women to earn a living so they would not be forced into loveless marriages for economic security. Her educational objectives led her to write historical novels to teach women about their country's history, as well as works like La mujer en la sociedad moderna,[47] which provided role models through biographies of women from throughout history, whether in Europe or the Americas, who had led exemplary lives and contributed to society.

La mujer en la sociedad moderna also contains Acosta de Samper's theory about literature, particularly the function of the novel and the role of male and female within society. While

> la parte masculina de la sociedad se ocupa de la política, que rehace las leyes, atiende al progreso material de esas repúblicas y ordena la vida social . . . ¿No será muy bello que la parte femenina se ocupase en crear una nueva literatura? una literatura sui generis, americana en sus descripciones . . . una literatura tan hermosa y tan pura que pudieran figurar sus obras en todos los salones de los países en donde se habla la lengua de Cervantes . . . que elevaran las ideas de cuantos las leyesen, que instruyesen y que al mismo tiempo fueran nuevas y originales . . . En esta

literatura de nuestros ensueños no se encontrarían
descripciones de crímenes y escenas y cuadros que
reflejaran las malas costumbres importadas a nuestras
sociedades por la corrompida civilización europea . . .
pues . . . la novela no debe ser solamente la descrip-
ción exacta de lo que sucede en la vida real . . . ; la
novela puede interesar a pesar de ser moral, y debe
pintar gráficamente la existencia humana y al mismo
tiempo lo ideal, lo que debería ser, lo que podrían ser
los hombres y las mujeres si obraran bien.[48]

Can Acosta de Samper be considered "feminist," since her
values are traditional, moralistic, idealistic, and the very opposite
of what most twentieth-century "feminists" advocate? Yet she was
interested in women's problems, founded newspapers directed to
women (e.g., La Mujer),[49] and always asserted that women were
as intelligent as men.

In the twentieth century, the profession of writing is open
to all social classes. Are the attitudes of contemporary Latin
American writers any different from those of their earlier
counterparts? Are they more feminist? Sidonia Carmen
Rosenbaum, writing in 1945, thought not.[50] She claims that most
of Latin America's female poets, novelists, and essayists are not
feminists, because the feminist movement which was strongest in
Nordic countries with Protestant traditions never really took root
in Spanish America. What do the authors say of themselves?[51]

Elena Poniatowska (b. 1933 in Paris). Mother Mexican,
father Polish. Novelist, journalist, living in Mexico since 1942:
"Me parece absurda decir que no soy femenista . . . igual
trabajo, igual salario etcétera. . . ."

Leonora Carrington (b. 1917 in England). Short story
writer, novelist, artist, living in Mexico since 1942: "¿Qué
persona cuerda puede no serlo? Claro que soy feminista."

Esther Seligson (b. 1941 in México, DF). Novelist, poet:
"Todo ese movimiento del 'Women's Lib' . . . no me interesa . . .
para mí, el artista no tiene sexo. . . . En el fondo el mexicano
es muy débil hacia el sexo feminino y basta que sepas coquetear,
basta que no seas demasiado fea, para que no te pongan
obstáculos. Así que no creo que en México las mujeres que
quieren publicar tengan ninguna dificultad por el hecho de ser
mujeres."

Emma Godoy (b. 1918 in Guanajuato). Poet, dramatist,
novelist, essayist: "No se puede hablar de hombres y mujeres en
la literatura. Ambos son andróginas . . . las mujeres hemos sido
engañadas. . . . La liberación femenina es más bien liberación
masculina. . . . Yo no quiero derechos . . . quiero que me
devuelvan mis privilegios. . . . Este movimiento feminista . . .
fue creado . . . para la mujer inglesa del tercer sexo, pero no
apropriados para la mujer latina. . . ."

And from Colombia, Fanny Buitrago and Albalucía Angel speak:[52]

Buitrago: "There isn't a feminist feminist movement because Colombian women are very self-indulgent . . . and despite her screaming and shouting . . . is fascinated [in] . . . having a man at her side . . . having that all important prestigious last name her husband will give her . . . have a man who will maintain them with the best of everything . . . they nourish machismo, but they live beautifully from it."

Angel: "I hope there isn't even a feminist movement in Colombia, with all its screaming, but rather . . . a study of vindication for the woman. . . . Man is really the complement, man is the great friend, the antipode, the antagonist. . . . I don't think we can make an Amazon society. Never!"

Why, then, do feminist critics consider the authors to be feminists, even though some wrote up to three centuries ago, and even though many of the contemporary authors--while exposed to the full force of the twentieth-century Women's Movement--reject it in principle?

Undoubtedly the primary cause lies in the mere act of being a female writer, of being a woman intellectual in a society where dumb and beautiful is more highly valued than bright. Woman's proper role, as the ornamental, decorative being, is to revolve around man--the center of the universe. The female's place is firmly fixed, in the home. In writing, women reject the role into which they are cast. By so doing, they commit an act of rebellion. Ergo, they are feminists. Sor Juana Inés de la Cruz (1651-1695), Mexican poet and playwright, the first of a line of Latin American poets and the "last of the great seventeenth century Hispanic Baroque writers"[53] thus becomes a fit subject for feminist critics. Child prodigy, intellectual without peer, she switched from court to convent to find the freedom for her intellectual pursuits.

Recent studies on Sor Juana from a feminist perspective include Electa Arenal, "The Convent as Catalyst for Autonomy: Two Hispanic Nuns of the Seventeenth Century"; Celia de Zapata, "Two Poets of America: Juana de Asbaje and Sara de Ibáñez";[55] Mirta Aguirre, Del encausto a la sangre: Sor Juana Inés de la Cruz;[56] and Tarsicio Herrera Zapién, López Velarde y Sor Juana, feministas opuestas y cuatro ensayos sobre Horacio y Virgilio en México. And Margery Resnick and Isabelle Courtivron, in Women Writers in Translation: An Annotated Bibliography, 1945-1982,[57] mention Sor Juana as one of several "silenced" writers: her offense, daring to write about profane matters and indulging her interest in secular studies. When English readers were surveyed to find what they wanted in translation, the poetry of Sor Juana ranked at the top of 825 listed titles. The lack of translations of Latin American female writers, according to Beth Miller, is one of the major problems facing feminist critics.

Until the 1970s, when feminist criticism became fashionable, the critical works on Sor Juana saw her primarily as a gongorista.[58] Feminist criticism has shifted the focus away from the poetry's structure and language, and toward its content. It has likewise focused on Sor Juana's famous autobiographical letter to the Bishop of Puebla, who had written under the name Sor Filotea to reprimand her for pursuing profane studies. Sor Juana's Respuesta a Sor Filotea de La Cruz (1691) is considered the most important document on seventeenth-century feminism, and this letter fully displays the magnitude of her learning. She employs irony to confound the skeptics who would belittle the intellectual capabilities of women. In so doing, she defends the right of women to learn, to think, and to reflect. Sor Juana has become an inspiration for feminists and nonfeminists, male and female. Her place in the annals of Hispanic literature is assured, women writer though she was.

A second reason for including authors within the file of feminist criticism seems to include their selection of themes and their statements as they develop a plot. Gertrudis Gómez de Avellaneda (1814-1873), Cuban expatriate in Spain, romantic poet, dramatist, novelist, essayist, editor of La Gaceta de Mujeres (a Spanish newspaper) and founder of El Album Cubano (1860) (directed solely at women), thus becomes a favorite. Her unconventional life-style, romantic as some of the works she wrote, contravened all codes of behavior for the nineteenth-century Spanish society in which she spent the greater part of her life. She won acclaim in her lifetime and came to be called "La Avellaneda," though she was also denied admittance to the Real Academia de Lenguas in 1853. Her letters protesting the negative decision, made solely because she was a female writer, are well worth reading.

Her literary production, too, is considered feminist in some of its themes. For example, racial equality is equated with sexual equality in Sab. This work, written in 1836 and published in 1841, and thus predating Uncle Tom's Cabin, is generally regarded as the first abolitionist novel. In the words of Beth Miller, "From a historical and feminist perspective, probably the single most important thing Avellaneda achieved was endurance."[59]

Contemporary authors have been no less outspoken in selecting themes formerly considered taboo. Marta Brunet, for example, deals with homosexuality and feminine aggressiveness; and Esther Seligson explores the sexual aggressiveness of active females in the style of Erica Jong. More prevalent themes deal with love and marriage. One archetypical sequence concerns girls groomed for marriage, but then forced into loveless unions for economic reasons. Many old patrician families have fallen on hard times, and rich immigrants from any social class may marry into them to prop them up. On the other hand, the rejection of marriage and motherhood by upper-class women constitutes a rejection of the values of a moribund society.   Hence birth control and abortion are openly discussed.   Lower-class women without beauty or fortune have no place in society.   They are the prey, the María Nadies of society, the Jesusa in Hasta no verte, Jesús mío.

The works I have included in this study were, with a few exceptions, published after 1974.   This is the cut-off date for Meri Knaster's Women in Spanish America: An Annotated Bibliography from pre-Conquest to Contemporary Times.   Although still not complete, this is by far the most comprehensive bibliography to date.   Knaster's work focuses on secondary source material, but also considers some primary material and refers to books, chapters in books, articles, pamphlets, and doctoral dissertations. It does not include newspaper articles, except when they are reprinted in periodicals or other publications, or articles from the popular press, Sunday magazines, and the like.

Knaster treats women under such headings as the Arts, Literature, Mass Media and Folklore, Education, Magic, and Politics.   The section on literature considers women as writers, readers, and characters, and deals with themes from all literary forms.   Of particular interest is a list of nineteenth-century newspapers which were directed specifically to a female audience, and which sought to educate them and to provide an outlet for their literary productions.[60]   These newspapers are a treasure trove of women's writings.

Twentieth-century feminists have followed their predecessors in founding periodicals and newspapers.[61]   Letras femeninas, for instance, is directed toward the female academic; while Fem is more populist and aggressive than Búcaro Americano, and seemingly against everything that Búcaro Americano advocated in terms of women's education.   Yet its purpose remains the same: to raise women's consciousness and to illustrate women's achievements through the ages.   (See Appendixes B and C).

Knaster's bibliography includes much more than literature as it considers Latin American women.   As the compiler explains, she also incorporates "works which address themselves to female questions, to contemporary women's issues."[62]

In conclusion, I would like to quote from a letter to the Editor in The New York Times Book Review, Jan. 13, 1985.

> "Women's Literature" may be a concept founded upon a false analogy with the undeniably existent hyphenated literatures . . . Afro-American, French-Canadian . . . produced by a minority culture.   Such cultures define themselves as apart from the host culture in certain respects or have such definitions forced upon them for historical reasons.   But what is the minority culture that women's literature belongs to? . . .   Naturally, women often write about the difficulty of woman's

estate, yet that does not make theirs a literature apart. Think of all the men writing about the perils and hardships of being men. . . . Life is probably sufficiently hard for both sexes without setting up a competition through the segregation of writing by sex.[63]

And I must ask, "Do we have a category called 'Masculine Literature'?" So the circular argument continues.

Appendix A

QUESTIONNAIRE FOR THE INTERVIEWS

From Beth Miller, "Testimonios: Seis escritoras Mexicanas frente al feminismo," Mujeres en la literatura (México, DF: Costa-Amic, 1978)

Interrogantes comunes

I. Sobre su vida y carrera.
    (¿Cómo y cuándo empezó a escribir? ¿Qué educación tuvo? ¿Recibió ayuda o estímulo de otras mujeres o solamente de hombres? ¿Ayudó alguna vez profesionalmente a otras mujeres? ¿Cree que el ser mujer le ha hecho más difícil su carrera? ¿Se ha tropezado con invalidantes prejuicios sexuales por parte de colegas o críticos masculinos?)

II. Sobre sus obras.
    (¿Cree usted que los lectores pueden identificar como femeninas sus obras?) ¿Cree que existan diferencias entre obras literarias escritas por hombres y por mujeres? ¿Cree que algunas de sus publicaciones hubieran sido mejor o de diferente modo recibidas de haber estado escritas por un hombre? ¿Se considera usted feminista? ¿Existe femenismo en sus obras?)

III. Sobre sus opiniones personales y profesionales acerca de otras escritoras. (En general, cree usted que las escritoras en México tienen dificultades a causa de su sexo, para publicar sus obras o presentarlas en teatro, o bien para lograr una reputación literaria? ¿Cree que una mujer pudiera ocupar la posición de Octavio Paz en las letras mexicanas, de prestigio inmenso, influencia y poder? ¿Puede nombrar algunas otras escritoras a quienes verdaderamente admire, mexicanas o de otros países latinoamericanos? ¿Cuáles piensa que son las de primera categoría?)

Appendix B

Contents of <u>Búcaro Americano</u>; <u>Periódico de la Familia</u>, 1:1, 1ª época (Buenos Aires, 1 de Febrero, 1896)

Directora: Clorinda Matto de Turner

The title page has a miniature surrounded by a garland of flowers of Leonor Tezanos Pinto de Uriburu.

"Bautismo" (article)

The most important act in the life of man is naming him. Naming a child is like Matto's naming her "periódico," which she will baptize with the waters of her own inspiration and in which she will present to the public the children of her thoughts. This publication is the son of her pain, born in the ostracism to which the pain of the death of a beloved brother condemns her.

She will follow the mode established through ancient usage of calling to the baptismal font good fairies and bad (<u>encantadoras y hechiceras</u>) in order to bring good luck. She will select three fairy godmothers, one Argentine, one Uruguayan, one Peruvian-- three nationalities that symbolize sky, flower, the heart--three personalities as varied as the colors at dawn. To them she entrusts the fate of this "son of thought and ideas," to them the solution of the great problem. They will select the name: Búcaro Americano.

<u>Búcaro Americano</u>, as its name implies, gathers together the rich flowering of American literature. But this is not its only objective; there is something more transcendental at the root of its mission, that is: "la educación de la mujer en el rol que la depara el movimiento del progreso universal para que pueda cumplir satisfactoriamente los deberes que esa misma corriente evolutiva la señala," not only as mother and wife, "cargos fáciles de desempeñar" because the heart directs them, but also as mother-in-law, stepmother, daughter-in-law, sister-in-law, and friend. These are difficult stumbling blocks from which to save herself if "el cerebro ilustrado" and "la voluntad educada" do not participate directly in "su modo de ser."

We shall not ignore social movement(s), nor elegant fashion as it is not possible to separate woman from fashion since she would lose her brilliance.

Engravings will occupy our attention also, because both kinds of art, that is, poetry and painting, produce the same impression and evoke the same sentiments by presenting appear- ance as if it were reality to create pleasing illusions. Painting and poetry linked together give graphic form to beauty. We have selected the form of miniature engravings by taking into con- sideration the taste of women who have a preference for all that is delicate, they being <u>mujeres mimadas</u> (pampered creatures), and bearing in mind that these pages will be turned by the gloved hands of the eternal artist.

"Leonor de Tezanos Pinto de Uriburu" (biography)
    Courtesy and affection cause us to inaugurate <u>Búcaro Americano</u> with the portrait of the worthy wife of the Chief of State. . . . She was born in Peru of Argentine parents, was well educated, and grew up "aspirando la atmósfera de las virtudes del hogar que preparan a la dignificación del matrimonio y a la sublima maternidad." Then to Lima came Don José E. Uriburu, diplomat. She preferred him to all her suitors. They wed, and it was not long before she followed him to Argentina, where he became president of "la primera nación de América del Sur." She, as the president's wife, knew how to be exquisitely tactful--an art required in high places in order to command respect and maintain the affection and warmth of society. If it is in the salons and the theaters that beautiful Argentine ladies shine, it is in the home, "el templo azul," where the matron discharges her function. Her virtues are thus reflected within her country and outside it as well. Few women know how to be <u>presidenta</u>, and vanity and pride have been the downfall of many women in high places. La señora de Uriburu has succumbed to neither, and because of that we present her as a model and offer to her our homage, repeating that modesty is the most brilliant diadem that a woman, born to be sweet and good, can wear.

"Fragmentos" (poem; 7 stanzas) by Dorita Castell de Orozco, 1896, Montevideo

      Triste es también mirar en claro día
      El bosque, el mar, el cielo, la llanura . . .

"Las obreras del pensamiento en la América del Sur" (lecture) given by the author [Clorinda Matto de Turner] in the Ateneo in Buenos Aires, December 14, 1895.
    Women and all that they have achieved over the centuries are of interest. In the <u>Vedas</u>, woman is silent and resigned. Ever since she has passed through history repeating the magical words "libertad" and "derecho," from classical times to modern, and in both Greco-Roman tradition and Judeo-Christian religion. Yet the benighted and the egotists, interested in preserving woman as instruments of pleasure and passive obedience, keep her hidden in the bedchamber, without realizing that divorce is born from absolute equality between man and woman. The struggle has begun. Vigorous and healthy bodies, studying the social conditions of the period, understand that to put off the enlightenment--"la ilustración"--of woman is to retard the enlightenment of humanity. The foremost sociological principle is

"el trabajo con libertad dignifica; el trabajo con esclavitud humilla." If you want to reign over bodies of slaves and uncultured minds you have examples in history--"degradad a la mujer" (degrade woman) "pervertid su sentido moral" (corrupt her moral sensibilities), and soon you will have "el hombre envilecido" (debased man) without the strength to fight despotism, because woman is the soul of humanity. Redemption from all slavery and the triumph of all great ideas have required blood. Only the cause of woman's enlightenment has needed nothing more than patience and the heroism of silence, followed by audacity on the pedestal of perseverance. Today we can affirm that thousands of women give not only their sons to the country but also prosperity and glory. "Estas son las obreras del pensamiento." As many as 4,000 work in the Civil Service; more than 3,000 as journalists, writers, and translators; nearly 4,000 as clerks in banks and commercial houses. Others find a place in education, medicine, and so on. One must not be alarmed at this shattering of stereotypes. "Es que la mujer toma posesión de sus derechos. . . . Las mujeres que escriben" are "verdaderas heroínas." From Argentina, one sees Policarpa Salvarrieta and Juana Manuelita Gorriti, the latter respected not because she was the wife and mother of presidents but because she is a writer; from Uruguay, Dorita Castell de Orozco, Adela Castell, Casiana Flores, Lola Larrosa, author of the novels, El lujo, Los esposos, and so on. (The list continues with authors from Paraguay, Bolivia, Ecuador, Colombia, and other countries.)

Feminine journalism is indebted to Carolina Freyre de Jaimes, who founded El Album in Peru, and continued it in Bolivia. It was the vehicle for the writings of many women writers . . . in it can be found short novels like El regalo de boda, Memorias de una redusa as well as poetry, ". . . La enumeración, aunque sea incompleta," serves to remind us that "las obreras del pensamiento" are true heroines who have to "luchar contra la calumnia, la rivalidad, el indiferentismo y toda clase de dificultades para obtener elementos de instrucción." They even run the risk of being old maids (quedarse tías) because "los tontos" are afraid of educated women: "la mujer está en lucha abierta entre la ceguera que amenaza y la luz que es preciso dilatar."

"A Federico" (poem) by Carolina Freyre de Jaimes, January, 1896

"A mi hija Pilar 'El día de su boda'" (essay) by Nicanor Bolet Teraza

"Los Ojos" (poem) by Adela Castell, Montevideo, 1896

"Economía Doméstica" (essay)

On thrift and the sin of ostentation among the poor: "El lujo es un deber en los ricos porque representa el fomento de las grandes industrias donde trabajan miles de gentes pobres . . . es decir el lujo de los ricos es el pan de los pobres."

"Social" (a column in the format of a letter) by Azul del Monte

It begins: "Mis queridas lectoras, salud." The purpose is to review social life, "las fiestas de grande novedad," and current fashion, "asunto de alta importancia en los salones y transcendental para nosotros, porque es preciso declarar en voz alta lo que pensamos en secreto desde niñas . . . que ellos nos tratan conforme nos ven, confesando que El Arte en el vestir realza la belleza y modifica la deformidad. . . ."

These fashions will be the latest from Paris, with reports supplied by Baronesa Blanc, Búcaro Americano's Paris correspondent. Her first letter is given below. News about Buenos Aires: it is deserted, and most families have gone to their summer residences. The writer then lists the fabrics preferred by the elegant, well-dressed women: muslin, crepe, tulle, "bengaline diagonal," silk.

Theater News: La Verbena de la Paloma is playing at La Comedia Theater. La viuda de González (zarzuela) is at the Odeon. La Dolores, the latest work by Bretón, is on everyone's lips. The Society "Proteccionista Intelectual," nearly 800 members strong, laid a plaque at the sepulcher of former member and Uruguayan writer Lola Larrosa de Ansaldo, who died tragically at thirty-eight. Clorinda Matto de Turner spoke about her achievements. (Clorinda Matto de Turner's speech is given in full.)

Wedding News follows, and the section ends with an anecdotal advertisement promoting a special face cream, "Crema Clori de Madamoiselle La Valière": "Ninguna mujer instruída ignora que . . . fue la dama de Louis XIV, que con su rostro de azucena y su espiritualidad sin igual, enloqueció de amor al rey . . . al extremo de obligarle, cierto día, a beber, de rodillas a sus pies, el agua que le dió en el hueso de ambas manos juntas." Her beautiful complexion was due to the cream she used, the secret recipe for which she gave to the Abbess of the convent of Cluny. "La droguería de los señores Cometti y Cía de la calle Perú 337 acaba de hacer un gran pedido de esta crema al fabricante de París y tan luego como llegue comunicaré la noticia a las distinguidas señoras."

Letter from Baronesa Blanc dated Paris, January 1896

End of Vol. 1, No. 1.)

Appendix C

Fem

A Sample of the contents of Fem; Publicación feminista trimestral (México, Nueva Cultura Feminista, 1976--) 1:1 (Octubre-Diciembre 1976)

Director: Alaíde Foppa and Margarita García Flores

Editorial Board: Elena Poniatowska, Lourdes Arizpe, Margarita Peña, Beth Miller, Elena Urrutia, Marta Lamas, Carmen Lugo.

Fem proposes:

1. to point out from different angles what can and ought to be changed in the social conditions of women: it invites analysis and reflection. Research material and rational and verified arguments will be used, not emotional ones.

2. to try to reconstruct a history of feminism unknown to many, and to pass on information about what is happening in this field today, particularly in Mexico and the rest of Latin America.

3. not only to publish information and essays but to be a vehicle for the literary creations of women who write in a feminist mode and who contribute to the knowledge of that new being (woman) who is free, independent, and productive, as the women of today are showing themselves to be. Works of men who share the same ideals will be included.

4. not to be attached to any group, but to be open to all who pursue the same objectives.

5. Fem considers that women's struggles cannot be dissociated from the struggle of the oppressed. The hope is to create a new world.

Contents

Illustrations of reclining women in the nude.

Translation of fragments of Donne Mie entitled "El arte de amar" by Dacia Maraini (pp. 4-7).

"Anatomía no es destino" (essay) by Alaíde Foppa (pp. 8-9).

"Del trabajo invisible al trabajo visible" (essay) by Elena Urrutia (pp. 14-15).

"Castillo en Francia" (short story) by Elena Poniatowska (pp. 16-17).

"Margaret Randall: no soy una feminista radical" (interview) by Beth Miller (pp. 23-26).

"¿Beneficia el desarrollo económico a la mujer?" (essay) by Lourdes Arizpe (pp. 27-34).

"María Langer: ideología y psicoanálisis" (essay) by Carmen Lugo (pp. 35-38).

"Condicione a su marido" (essay) by Luis González de Alba (pp. 39-42).

Translation of conversation between Sartre and Simone de Beauvoir: "Sartre: la lucha femenina podría socavar la sociedad" (pp. 43-47; 49-51).
List of best-sellers published by Grijalbo (p. 48):
  El Grupo by Mary McCarthy. A novel full of revelations about the condition of women. A great novel about social conditions in the thirties.
  Nuevas Cartas Portuguesas/Las Tres Marías. An implacable denunciation of the feminine mystique of the twentieth century.
  París fué ayer (1925-1939) by Janet Flanner.
  Mi destino de mujer by Martha Richard. The biography of an extraordinary woman who knew how to live ahead of her time.
  Retrato de un matrimonio by Nigel Nicholson. Biography of Vita Sackville-West and Harold Nicholson, a couple of writers who led scandalous lives. An extraordinary vision of the Victorian period.
  Mirar y pasar by Taylor Caldwell. A memorable and nostalgic re-creation of North American society at the beginning of the century.
Two pages of advertisements:
Modas (p. 58):
    Al desvestirse . . .
    ¡Quede bien vestida!

    Oración de las niñas solteras
    Ahora que me voy a acostar
    deseo un hombre que cantar.
    Si bajo mi cama
    ya estuviera . . .
    ojalá, ni una sola
    de mis palabras se perdiera.
  (p. 59)
    Toda mujer ideal tiene varios secretos . . .
    ¡Conózcalos!
    La mujer ideal siempre viste
    elegantemente, sabe de
    todo, es excelente madre, esposa
    amante y ejemplar, genial,
    inteligente, culta, sociable.
    Esta mujer no
    nace así, ¡lo aprende todo!
    Aprenda usted también
    y dé su primer paso obteniendo
    su copia de "La Mujer
    Ideal" de Vanidades
    en su puesto de revistas favorito
    "La Mujer Ideal"

de Vanidades
contiene artículos que
la ayudarán a . . .
* Ser más bella
* Vestir bien a todas horas
* Resolver sus problemas
  de decoración
* Sorprender a todos
  con platos especiales
* Conocer del
  arte latinoamericano
* Descubrir los
  autores de nuestra América
* Saber más de los
  hombres y del amor
* Explorar su sexualidad
* Ser una madre inolvidable
(On the same page)

bien
venidos
por última vez
estereotipos
de la
feminidad
(Signed by:)   ML y MGF
(Drawing of a woman wearing an undergarment)
¡Luzca un bello Busto!

índice

NOTES

1. Gerda Lerner, "Politics and Culture in Women's History: A Symposium," in Feminist Studies, 6 (Spring, 1980), 50.
2. Beth Miller, "Introduction," Women in Hispanic Literature: Icons and Fallen Idols (Berkeley, CA: University of California Press, 1983), p. 8.
3. Idem, Mujeres en la literatura (México, DF: Fleischer Editora, 1978), pp. 7-8.
4. Idem, "Introduction," Women in Hispanic Literature, pp. 2-5, esp. pp. 5, 9.
5. Electa Arenal, "The Convent as Catalyst for Autonomy: Two Hispanic Nuns of the Seventeenth Century," in Women in Hispanic Literature: Icons and Fallen Idols, pp. 181-182.
6. See the response of Luisa Josefina Hernández in "Testimonios: Seis escritoras frente al feminismo," Mujeres en la literatura, p. 85.
7. See the response of Elena Poniatowska in ibid., p. 90.
8. See Beth Miller, "Introduction," p. 11 n. 16. Michèle Mattelart, La cultura de la opresión femenina (México, DF: Era, 1977), is one of several works available in translation to which Miller attributes a definite ideological stance. See also Miller, "Introduction," p. 12 and n. 18.
9. Ibid., p. 10 n. 15. The author cites Cheri Register, "American Feminist Literary Criticism: A Bibliographical Introduction," in Feminist Literary Criticism, ed. Josephine Donovan (Lexington, KY: University Press of Kentucky, 1975), pp. 1-28; and Jane Williamson, New Feminist Scholarship: A Guide to Bibliographies (Old Westbury, NY: Feminist Press, 1979).
10. Miller, "Introduction," p. 13. Miller cites Gabriel Zaíd, "La nueva ley de Malthus," Como leer en bicicleta (México, DF: Joaquín Mortiz, 1975), pp. 11-12, as an example of ironic treatment of this theme.
11. Griselda Alvarez, Diez mujeres en la poesía mexicana del siglo XX (México, DF, Complejo Editorial Mexicano, 1974), p. 7.
12. See Appendix A. "Interrogantes Comunes" was the questionnaire given to the six Mexican women writers that were interviewed (Miller, "Testimonios . . . ," p. 78).
13. Ibid., "Prólogo," 26 autoras del México actual (México, DF: B. Costa-Amic editor, 1978), p. 9.
14. Idem, "A Random Survey of the Ratio of Female Poets to Male in Anthologies: Less-Than-Tokenism as a Mexican Tradition," in Latin American Women Writers: Yesterday and Today, Selected Proceedings from the Conference on Women Writers from Latin America, March 15-16, 1975, ed. Yvette E. Miller and Charles M. Tatum (Pittsburgh, PA: Latin American Literary Review, 1977), pp. 11-17, esp. pp. 11-12, in which Miller points out that in Las cien mejores poesías mexicanas modernas, ed. Antonio Castro Leal (1939; 2d ed. México, DF: Porrúa, 1945),

only one of one hundred poems was written by a female poet. A larger anthology, La poesía mexicana moderna, ed. idem (México, DF: Fondo de Cultura Económica, 1953), presented only a slightly higher average, 13:115. Mexican women poets, however, received recognition from their male counterparts during International Women's Year with the publication of Poetisas mexicanas siglo XX, ed. Hector Valdés (México, DF: Universidad Nacional Autónoma de México, 1976). Seventeen women poets were included.

15. Beth Miller, "Introduction," p. 25.

16. Idem, "Prólogo," p. 7.

17. Lucía Fox-Lockert, Women Novelists in Spain and Spanish America (Metuchen, NJ, and London: The Scarecrow Press, 1979). For full bibliographical citations of works listed in the text, see attached bibliography.

18. Ibid., p. 1.

19. Ibid.

20. Other works exist: e.g., Tarsicio Herrera Zapién, López Velarde y Sor Juana, feministas opuestas, y cuatro ensayos sobre Horacio y Virgilio en México (México, DF: Porrúa, 1984), cited in Boletín Bibliográfico Mexicano, 44:371, (julio-agosto de 1984), 55-56. I have not seen this work. Also: Velia Bosch, Esta pobre lengua viva. Relectura de la obra de Teresa de la Parra a medio siglo de las Memorias de Mamá Blanca (Caracas: Ediciones de la Presidencia de la República, 1979), and Michael H. Handelsman, Amazones y artistas. Un estudio de la prosa de la mujer ecuatoriana, 2 vols. (Guayaquil: Casa de la Cultura Ecuatoriana, 1978). Handelsman's work focuses on the contribution of women writers to the literature of Ecuador and the position that women occupy in the society. The two women writers traditionally referred to in Ecuadorian letters are Marietta de Veintemilla (1958-1907) and Blanca Martínez de Tinajero (1897). Handelsman proves that other worthy authors also exist. See his "Introduction" to Vol. 1, pp. 11-12.

21. Lucía Guerra-Cunningham, La narrativa de María Luisa Bombal. Una visión de la existencia femenina (Madrid: Editorial Playor, 1980), pp. 75-105.

22. Ibid., pp. 43-74.

23. Ibid., pp. 107-131.

24. Ibid., pp. 135-150.

25. Ibid., pp. 151-168.

26. Ibid., pp. 169-182.

27. Ibid., pp. 183-198.

28. See the title of Chapter 2 in María Rosa Fiscal, La imagen de la mujer en la narrativa de Rosario Castellanos (México, DF: Universidad Nacional Autónoma de México, 1980), pp. 50-71.

29. Ibid., p. 80.

30. Yvette E. Miller, "Introduction," Latin American Women Writers: Yesterday and Today, p. 1.

31. Martin C. Taylor, in ibid., pp. 18-24.

32.   John C. Miller, in ibid., pp. 25-32.
33.   See Appendix B. Sample contents of Búcaro Americano. Periódico de la familia, 1:1, 1ª época (Feb. 1, 1896), ed. Clorinda Matto de Turner (Buenos Aires). Excerpts are from pp. 1, 4, 15, 16.
34.   Harold E. Hinds, in Latin American Women Writers: Yesterday and Today, pp. 33-41.
35.   Charles M. Tatum, in ibid., pp. 49-58.
36.   Esther A. Azzario, in ibid., pp. 59-67.
37.   Corina S. Mathieu, in ibid., pp. 68-74.
38.   Gloria Feiman Waldman, in ibid., pp. 75-84.
39.   Gabriela Mora, in ibid., pp. 91-97.
40.   Dale E. Verlinger, in ibid., pp. 98-103.
41.   Carmelo Virgilio, in ibid., pp. 104-114.
42.   Ronni Gordon Stillman, in ibid., pp. 42-48.
43.   Ibid., p. 42.
44.   Ibid., p. 43.
45.   Ibid.
46.   The publication which resulted is La mujer en las letras venezolanos. Homenaje a Teresa de la Parra en el Año Internacional de la Mujer, 5-26 de octubre de 1975 (Caracas: Imprenta del Congreso de la República, 1976). Her birthday, October 5, was selected for the opening of the exhibition. She was again honored in 1979 at the first congress of Venezuelan writers with the publication of Homenaje a Teresa de la Parra. Memoria del primer congreso venezolana de escritores, 5-6-7 de octubre de 1979 (Valencia y Puerto Cabello, Estado Carabobo: Ediciones de la Presidencia de la República, 1982). Papers in her honor include Elena Dorante, "Ifigenia o la crítica a la falsa identidad de la mujer," pp. 179-182; Elena Vera, "El concepto de la libertad en María Eugenia Alonso y el arte como escóndite," pp. 183-187. María Eugenia Alonso is the female protagonist of Ifigenia.
47.   Soledad Acosta de Samper, La mujer en la sociedad moderna (Paris: Garnier, n.d. [c. 1895]).
48.   Ibid., pp. 381 ff. esp. p. 388.
49.   La Mujer (1878), founded by Doña Soledad Acosta de Samper, was the first Colombian periodical edited and sustained entirely by women. See Harold E. Hinds, in ibid., p. 35.
50.   See Sidonia Carmen Rosenbaum, Modern Poets of Spanish America: The Precursors--Delmira Agustini, Gabriela Mistral, Alfonsina Storni, Juana Ibarbourou (New York, NY: Hispanic Institute, 1945), pp. 11-21.
51.   Excerpts that follow are from Beth Miller, 26 autoras del México actual: Poniatowska, pp. 301-321, esp. p. 320; Carrington, pp. 97-111, esp. p. 103; Seligson, pp. 347-355, esp. p. 352; Godoy, pp. 223-236, esp. pp. 228, 234, 235.
52.   Raymond Williams, "An Interview with Women Writers in Colombia," in Latin American Women Writers: Yesterday and Today, pp. 155-161.

53. Arenal, The Convent as Catalyst for Autonomy, p. 164.

54. Ibid., pp. 147-183.

55. Celia de Zapata, "Two Poets of America: Juana de Asbaje and Sara de Ibáñez," Latin American Women Writers: Yesterday and Today, pp. 115-126.

56. Mirta Aguirre, Del encausto a la sangre. Sor Juana Inés de la Cruz (La Habana: Casa de las Américas, 1975).

57. See Diane Marting in Margery Resnick and Isabelle de Courtivron, Women Writers in Translation: An Annotated Bibliography, 1945-1982 (New York, NY, and London: Garland Publishing Co., 1984), pp. 227-230.

58. Notable exceptions: Pilar de Oñate, El feminismo en la literature española (Madrid: Espasa Calpe, 1935) cited in Arenal, The Convent as Catalyst, p. 172 n. 27; also Anthology of Mexican Poetry, trans. Samuel Beckett, comp. Octavio Paz, pref. C. M. Bowra (London: Thames and Hudson, 1958), p. 204, cited in Arenal, p. 174 n. 30.

59. Beth Miller, "Gertrude the Great: Avellaneda Nineteenth Century Feminist," in Women in Hispanic Literature: Icons and Fallen Idols, pp. 200-214, esp. p. 203.

60. See Appendix B.

61. See Letras Femeninas founded by Victoria E. Urbano (Boulder, CO: Asociación de Literatura Femenina Hispánica, 1975); also Fem; Publicación feminista trimestral, directed by Alaíde Foppa and Margarita García Flores (México, DF: Nueva Cultura Feminista, 1976). The editorial board consists of Elena Poniatowska, Lourdes Arizpe, Margarita Peña, Beth Miller, Elena Urrutia, Marta Lamas, Carmen Lugo. For a sample of the contents of Vol. 1, no. 1, see Appendix C.

62. Meri Knaster, Women in Spanish America: An Annotated Bibliography from Pre-Conquest to Contemporary Times (Boston, MA: G. K. Hall & Co., 1977), pp. xiii, 40.

63. Julian Moynahan, "Letters: Women in the Mainstream," The New York Times Book Review, Jan. 13, 1985.

BIBLIOGRAPHY

Acosta de Samper, Soledad. La mujer en la sociedad moderna. Biblioteca contemporánea. Paris: Garnier, n.d. [c1895]. xi, 429 pp.

Agosín, Marjorie. Las desterradas del paraíso, protagonistas en la narrativa de María Luisa Bombal. Senda de Estudios y Ensayos. New York, NY: Senda Nueva de Ediciones, 1983. 126 pp.

Aguirre, Mirta. Del encausto a la sangre. Sor Juana Inés de la Cruz. Cuadernos Casas, 17. La Habana: Casa de las Américas, 1975. 92 pp.

Ahern, Maureen, and Mary Seale Vázquez, eds. Homenaje a Rosario Castellanos. Valencia: Albatros-Hispanófila ediciones, 1980. 174 pp.

Alvarez, Griselda. Diez mujeres en la poesía mexicana del siglo XX. Colección Metropolitana. México, DF: Complejo Editorial Mexicano, 1974. 151 pp.

Asociación de Escritores Venezolanos, comp. Homenaje a Teresa de la Parra. Memoria del Primer Congreso Venezolano de Escritores 5-6-7 de octubre de 1979, Valencia y Puerto Cabello, Estado Carabobo. [Valencia]: Ediciones de la Presidencia de la República, 1982. 382 pp.

Asociación de Escritores Venezolanos and Banco Central de Venezuela, comp. La mujer en las letras venezolanas. Homenaje a Teresa de la Parra en el Año Internacional de la Mujer 5-26 de octubre de 1975. Caracas: Imprenta del Congreso de la República, 1976. 382 pp.

Bosch, Velia. Esta pobre lengua viva. Relectura de la obra de Teresa de la Parra a medio siglo de las Memorias de Mamá Blanca. Caracas: Ediciones de la Presidencia de la República, 1979. 278 pp.

Búcaro Americano; Periódico de la familia, 1:1, 1ª época (Feb. 1, 1896), dir. Clorinda Matto de Turner. Buenos Aires, 1896--.

Fem; Publicación feminista trimestral 1:1 (oct.-dic., 1976), dir. Alaíde Foppa and Margarita García Flores. México, DF: Nueva Cultura Feminista, 1976--.

Fiscal, María Rosa. La imagen de la mujer en la narrativa de Rosario Castellanos. Cuadernos del Centro de Estudios Literarios. México, DF: Universidad Nacional Autónoma de México, 1980. 123 pp.

Flores, Ángel, and Kate Flores, comp. Poesía feminista del mundo hispánico (desde la edad media hasta la actualidad). Antología crítica. La creación literaria. México, DF: Siglo Veintiuno, 1984. 285 pp.

Fox-Lockert, Lucía. Women Novelists in Spain and Spanish America. Metuchen, NJ, and London: The Scarecrow Press, 1979. 347 pp.

Guerra-Cunningham, Lucía. La narrativa de María Luisa Bombal. Una visión de la existencia femenina. Colección Nova Scholar. Madrid: Editorial Playor, 1983. 205 pp.

Handelsman, Michael H. Amazonas y artistas. Un estudio de la prosa de la mujer ecuatoriana. 2 vols. Colección Letras de Ecuador, 70, 71. Guayaquil: Casa de la Cultura Ecuatoriana, 1978. 125 pp. 120 pp.

Herrera Zapién, Tarsicio. López Velarde y Sor Juana, feministas opuestas y cuatro ensayos sobre Horacio y Virgilio en México. México, DF: Porrúa, 1984. 187 pp.

Knaster, Meri. Women in Spanish America: An Annotated Bibliography from Pre-Conquest to Contemporary Times. Boston, MA: G. K. Hall, 1977. liii, 696 pp.

Luque Valderrama, Lucía. "La novela femenina en Colombia." Tesis para optar al grado de doctor en Filosofía, Letras y Pedagogía. Bogotá: Pontificia Universidad Católica Javeriana, 1954. 248 pp.

Melón de Díaz, Esther. La narrativa de Marta Brunet. Colección UPREX. Serie: Estudios Literarios. [San Juan]: Universidad de Puerto Rico, Editorial Universitaria, 1975. 268 pp.

Miller, Beth. Mujeres en la literatura. México, DF: Fleischer editora, 1978. 145 pp.

Miller, Beth, ed. Women in Hispanic Literature: Icons and Fallen Idols. Berkeley and Los Angeles: University of California Press, 1983. 373 pp.

Miller, Beth, and Alfonso González. 26 autoras del México actual. México, DF: B. Costa-Amic, 1978. 463 pp.

Miller, Yvette E., and Charles E. Tatum, eds. Latin American Women Writers: Yesterday and Today. Selected Proceedings from the Conference on Women Writers from Latin America, March 15-16, 1975 sponsored by the Latin American Literary Review/Carnegie-Mellon University. Pittsburgh, PA: Latin American Literary Review, 1977. 199 pp.

Resnick, Margery, and Isabelle de Courtivron. Women Writers in Transition: An Annotated Bibliography, 1945-1982. Garland Reference Library of the Humanities v. 288. New York, NY, and London: Garland Publishing Co., 1984.

Rosenbaum, Sidonia Carmen. Modern Women Poets of Spanish America: The Precursors--Delmira Agustini, Gabriela Mistral, Alfonsina Storni, Juana Ibarbourou. New York, NY: Hispanic Institute, 1945. 273 pp.

Schwartz, Perla. Rosario Castellanos, mujer que supo latín. . . . Los pueblos y el tiempo, 2. México, DF: Editorial Katún, 1984, 159 pp.

Valdes, Héctor, comp. Poetisas mexicanas siglo XX. México, DF: Universidad Nacional Autónoma de México, 1976.

III. Puerto Rico: Hidden Colony, Hidden Citizens

21. LA HISTORIA DE LOS TRABAJADORES EN LA SOCIEDAD PRE-INDUSTRIAL: EL CASO DE PUERTO RICO, 1870-1900

Gervasio Luis García

"¿Qué investigas?"
"Los orígines del movimiento obrero en Puerto Rico."
"¿Marcha bien?"
¡Qué va! Me he topado con grandes dificultades."
"Imagino que la principal debe ser que no había obreros."

Así, más o menos, transcurrió el inicio de una conversación con un condiscípulo francés cuando comencé a investigar la historia del movimiento obrero puertorriqueño. Desde la óptica europea, hablar de "obreros" en el contexto de una sociedad pre-industrial era arriesgado porque quizás estiraba el término más allá de su contenido tradicional. Recuerdo el diálogo porque me obligó a definir el concepto, y demostró la necesidad de aclarar las premisas que soportarían la estrategia de la investigación futura.

Si nos atenemos a la definición más precisa de la palabra, un obrero es el que vende su fuerza de trabajo por un salario. En ese sentido existían muy pocos habitantes dignos de ese nombre en el Puerto Rico decimonónico. Sin embargo, cualquier plan de investigación sobre los orígenes del movimiento obrero exige mostrar cómo se adquiere esa categoría, descubrir el proceso en el que esclavos, jornaleros, artesanos—y hasta propietarios—se transforman en proletarios modernos. No se trata de una elucubración semántica sino de la elucidación de unos términos que orientarán la búsqueda de unas fuentes particulares y determinarán en gran medida las conclusiones del trabajo.

En esa onda, el investigador en vez de perseguir obreros puros buscará en los libertos que viven la transición de la esclavitud al trabajo libre, o en los agregados expulsados de las haciendas por el avance incontenible del cultivo azucarero, los primeros gérmenes de la proletarización de los trabajadores de la tierra. Estos procesos no son rectilíneos, y es probable que en sus primeras etapas tropecemos con casi-proletarios. Un buen ejemplo es el del cortador de caña durante las primeras etapas de la revolución técnica en el azúcar. Este trabajaba nominalmente por un salario, pero raras veces lo tocaba en moneda sonante sino en vales, fichas o en mercancías de la tienda del hacendado. Divorciado de la tierra e instalado fuera del perímetro de la propiedad productiva, parecía transformarse en un trabajador libre dependiente exclusivamente de un salario. Pero su libertad

de movimiento y contratación se diluyó a la hora de gastar el
sueldo, y en el endeudamiento sempiterno que lo ató a los
hacendados.

Otra diferencia significativa existe entre movimiento obrero y
clase obrera. En más de un texto los autores los dan equivocada-
mente como idénticos, pero en la práctica suelen marchar a pasos
diferentes. Mas no son cuerpos distintos: el movimiento es parte
de la clase y si no se comprende la segunda, el primero resulta
inescrutable. Es decir, son inseparables y el estudio de uno
lleva al otro. Hablar de la respuesta obrera--del sector organizado de la clase--a los alegatos burgueses esconde el hecho de
que muchos trabajadores son apáticos, o suscriben los valores de
las capas dominantes. Es tarea del historiador mostrar cuán
representativo es el movimiento de la clase entera o de sus
sectores, y hasta dónde llega el apoyo callado de los obreros a los
grupos más conscientes enfrascados en acciones deliberadas. En
última instancia, será el conocimiento de la vida cotidiana del
trabajador--salario, costo de la vida, tamaño de la familia,
esparcimiento social, etc.--lo que dará la clave para explicar el
origen y el desarrollo de los movimientos obreros modernos.

El esclarecimiento de esos y otros supuestos teóricos resuelve
parcialmente el complejo problema de "reconstruir las experiencias
individuales y colectivas" de las masas y las minorías. Al
principio, la consulta de los ficheros de las bibliotecas y los
catálogos de los archivos es descorazonante si buscamos únicamente testimonios de proletarios conscientes. En esa primera
etapa de la investigación no pretendamos encontrar actas de
reuniones, discursos impresos, pliegos de demandas, tratados
teóricos y mucho menos libros de extracción obrera. En realidad,
se trata de descubrir una "literatura sin lectores" dirigida a una
minoría alfabetizada y divulgada casi siempre en periódicos y no
en volúmenes encuadernados. Sus primeras huellas aparecen, por
lo general, en la prensa comercial (noticias sobre la inauguración
de un casino de artesanos, la fundación de una sociedad de
socorros mutuos, etc.) y luego en periódicos obreros de vida
breve. Estos seguramente son brazos de un cuerpo obrero débil
que a duras penas publica un solo número y expira pronto. Para
el historiador, la consulta de estos periódicos natimuertos es útil
porque en el primer número suelen justificar su existencia y
proclamar sus anhelos. Respecto al siglo XIX, no siempre se
conoce el alcance de la agrupación, ni la ideología del grupo
editorial que desaparece sin dejar otro rastro.

Es también en la prensa comercial donde aparecen las
primeras noticias de actos masivos espontáneos como las protestas
contra el alza de los impuestos y las huelgas por aumentos súbitos
de los precios. Sus móviles son claros, pero no es evidente el
tejido organizado ni es fácil detectar un liderato que parece
anónimo e invisible. Más adelante, en el siglo XX, éstas y otras
actividades obreras son precedidas de volantes y hojas sueltas

que las anuncian. Por lo general, estos materiales no atraen la atención de los archiveros, los bibliotecarios y de muchos historiadores, pero en el Archivo General de Puerto Rico se encuentra una rara colección de ellos que datan de los primeros años del presente siglo.

En el caso de Puerto Rico, no es sino hasta después de 1898 que encontramos documentos internos del movimiento obrero tales como las actas de reuniones. Estas no aparecieron en el baúl abandonado de un líder fallecido o desterrado, ni entre los documentos confiscados por la policía durante una redada, sino en la prensa obrera de la época. En vista de las comunicaciones difíciles, los escasos recursos económicos y propagandísticos y los deseos de la organización obrera de divulgar sus trabajos a un amplio público, el periódico obrero sirvió como una carta informativa y publicó las actas de las reuniones de la Federación Libre en las que aparecieron acuerdos importantes y debates reveladores de corrientes encontradas. Con su ayuda, los historiadores han calibrado la amplia democracia que reinó en el seno de la directiva obrera durante sus primeros años.

Ahora bien, las huelgas, los periódicos y las discusiones ideológicas de las organizaciones obreras son manifestaciones de acciones intencionadas fácilmente identificadas por los investigadores. Es, sin lugar a dudas, una búsqueda necesaria pero insuficiente, porque no siempre contiene los mecanismos que las enmarcan ni los resortes lejanos que las detonan. Por eso no hay historia obrera sin contexto económico, social y político. Es decir, las actividades obreras son el encuentro de decisiones, de actos controlables, con procesos independientes de la voluntad de los trabajadores. Sería exagerado decir que la historia obrera es tres cuartas partes economía y una cuarta parte movimiento obrero. Pero igualmente desenfocado sería hacer la historia de los trabajadores al margen del desarrollo económico. La meta del historiador es establecer los vínculos entre ambos, las correlaciones imprescindibles entre lo que hacemos y los complejos factores, frecuentemente imperceptibles, que nos provocan a actuar.

Por ejemplo, las uniones y los sindicatos obreros surgen con el fin primordial, pero no siempre exclusivo, de proteger y aumentar el poder adquisitivo de los salarios y mejorar las condiciones de trabajo. Estos propósitos se expresan en proclamas y programas, mítines y marchas, huelgas e insurrecciones. Pero si una biblioteca o un archivo desea facilitar la investigación de estos acontecimientos, además de capturar los documentos de estos chispazos, deben trascenderlos y recoger el resto del todo. Así, las huelgas se comprenden adecuadamente si contamos con información sobre la tensión entre los salarios y el costo de la vida cotidiana. La fuerza y la debilidad de las uniones de cortadores de caña partirá de la naturaleza estacional del cultivo. El desarrollo desigual del movimiento obrero y el surgimiento de las "aristocracias" proletarias, los explican sus posiciones privilegiadas en el proceso productivo y su poder de regateo como trabajadores especializados. La disposición a una lucha organizada y el desarrollo de unos valores y una "moral" obrera se nutren de una larga tradición de gestiones y de vida como proletarios. La fácil o difícil organización de los trabajadores dependerá del tamaño del grupo en los centros de trabajo o de la concentración o dispersión geográfica.

Es decir, las listas de precios y salarios, las descripciones y los estudios de los cultivos, las estadísticas industriales, los censos que revelan las edades y los oficios así como el tránsito del campo a la ciudad del trabajador y su familia, no son el decorado de la vida obrera sino la vida misma, tan importantes como los actos luminosos y oficiales.

Alguien objetará que las estadísticas y los informes los emiten los gobiernos o las clases propietarias, prejuiciando así la materia prima del historiador. A ellos les recuerdo que el oficio del historiador consiste en darle sentido a una información fragmentada y "cargada," de origen proletario o propietario. Además, los documentos de procedencia obrera no son más confiables que los de los patronos: las fuentes que emiten los trabajadores también magnifican o esconden matices importantes de la realidad.

En verdad, los testimonios de los obreros y los propietarios son parte de una sola realidad: la sociedad dividida en clases que pugnan por defender sus ideales y sus intereses. La conducta de una clase ayuda a explicar los proyectos de la otra. Por tal razón, no es contradictorio ni repugnante sino imprescindible conocer la historia de los trabajadores y sus organizaciones a través de los documentos emitidos por los dueños del poder y la riqueza. Van de la mano el periódico de la Federación Libre y la revista de la Asociación de Agricultores, las luchas legislativas del Partido Socialista y los discursos de José de Diego y otros líderes del Partido Unionista, los fiestones de los obreros y los bailes formales del Casino de Puerto Rico. Del estudio de los contrastes, las imitaciones y los préstamos ideológicos y culturales, saldrá una realidad menos sencilla pero más rica y menos monótona.

Si lo que preocupa es ser fiel a los hechos, la preferencia de las estadísticas y los métodos cuantitativos no resolverá el falso problema de la amenazada "objetividad," tan anhelada por los redactores de manuales de investigación. A veces se privilegian los fríos números como antídoto del subjetivismo escondido en la prosa de otras fuentes. A estas alturas no vale la pena resucitar el debate superado sobre el choque entre lo cuantitativo y lo cualitativo porque sabemos de sobra cuan subjetivas y deformadas pueden ser las estadísticas. Basta recordar que en nuestro país las estadísticas son del color del partido oficial o de los tonos de la oposición. La solución no está en ser un historiador daltoniano sino en descubrir los principios ideológicos, cualitativos, que llevan a celebrar o a deplorar las circunstancias inmediatas con el apoyo de unas estadísticas convenientes.

Por otra parte, al enfrentar las dificultades que surgen en la reconstrucción de las vidas individuales y colectivas de los trabajadores, una de las más formidables es la validez de la muestra estudiada. En este caso la fuerza del número, la frecuencia de unas conductas y la repetición de unos patrones ayuda a reducir el margen de error de los juicios cualitativos. De la misma manera, los errores que siempre se cuelan en las estadísticas se diluyen cuando se proyectan en largas series indicadoras de tendencias, más que de precisiones matemáticas.

En el caso de Puerto Rico, es igualmente importante incorporar al análisis las fuentes emanadas en las metrópolis. El historiador encerrado exclusivamente en los archivos nacionales no podría precisar siempre el origen de las iniciativas internas. Es incongruente afirmar que Puerto Rico fue y es una colonia--una de las pocas cosas en que la mayoría de los puertorriqueños está de acuerdo--y a la vez ignorar el peso metropolitano en la sociedad puertorriqueña. Sería igualmente chocante concluir que toda nuestra historia ha sido determinada únicamente desde afuera.

Otro problema no menos complejo la plantea el aparente divorcio entre el centro y la periferia, entre el Estado y los trabajadores marginados de los suburbios. Hoy el aparato gubernamental parece omnipresente (aunque siempre se habla de economías subterráneas y de subculturas invisibles), pero la sociedad del siglo XIX da la impresión de que consiste de mundos yuxtapuestos, de anillos que nunca se tocan. Sin embargo, sospecho que los desclasados de la sociedad suburbana entran y salen del sistema mayor en la medida en que éste los necesita, o desarrolla nuevos medios para incorporarlos plenamente. Sus vidas son miserables precisamente porque el Estado no puede absorberlos en pie de igualdad, y los expulsa o los atrae arbitrariamente. El caso de los jornaleros de Utuado ilustra el proceso de inserción paulatina de la población trabajadora en la órbita oficial.

Los desafíos que encuentra el historiador en los ejemplos mencionados arriba no comparan con el mayúsculo problema de explicar por qué los obreros no piensan ni actúan política e ideológicamente de acuerdo a sus orígenes e intereses de clase. Los obreros crean las riquezas, pero no las controlan; son la mayoría, pero siguen los símbolos políticos y las metáforas culturales de la minoría propietaria. A pesar de los intentos de crear sus propios partidos, militan o se alían a los partidos de la burguesía dominante. En fin, su proverbial debilidad ideológica y su dificultad para aglutinar voluntades desde una posición subordinada todavía no ha sido descifrada plenamente por los historiadores.

En conclusión, es claro que para investigar la historia obrera a partir de las preocupaciones de este seminario se imponen varios pasos importantes:

1. una colaboración más estrecha entre historiadores, bibliotecarios y archiveros. Ayudará mucho una mayor especialización en problemas históricos de la clase obrera, más que en épocas y áreas geográficas.

2. recopilar fuentes que muestren los procesos de largo aliento con ayuda de estadísticas generales, sin olvidar los testimonios de los trabajadores concretos. En palabras de Fernando Picó: estudiemos la tuberculosis sin olvidar a los tuberculosos.

3. aspirar a un enfoque multidimensional. Integrar al estudio de los movimientos obreros la historia política, ideológica y cultural del resto de la sociedad.

4. mostrar a los trabajadores en sus relaciones conflictivas o armoniosas con la clase propietaria.

5. sacar del anonimato a la mujer trabajadora; pero en vez de confinarla a los "womens studies" urge sumarla al análisis de la red de relaciones de la sociedad y de la historia.

6. recordar, en palabras de Naomi Bliven, que ". . . mediante el estudio del trabajo aprendemos a respetar las capacidades del prójimo."

Fuentes

Las Primeras Organizaciones

La historia de los orígenes de la clase obrera y sus organizaciones apenas comienza. Hasta hoy la fuente que más información ha rendido sobre la creación de casinos de artesanos, sociedades de socorros mutuos y cooperativas son los periódicos comerciales. Entre 1870 y 1898 aparecen esporádicamente noticias de sus actividades en el Boletín Mercantil, La Democracia y La Correspondencia. En la Colección Puertorriqueña de la Biblioteca José M. Lázaro de la Universidad de Puerto Rico pueden consultarse los estatutos de un buen número de sociedades de socorros mutuos formadas en varios pueblos durante las últimas dos décadas del siglo XIX.

Salarios

Todavía no contamos con suficiente información sobre salarios y precios que permita elaborar largas series. Respecto a los salarios, la consulta sistemática y rigurosa del Fondo de Obras Públicas (ramos de caminos, construcción y reparación de edificios, prestaciones de trabajo, etc.) del Archivo General de Puerto Rico (AGPR) seguramente arrojará frutos valiosos. Igualmente los presupuestos municipales, que aparecen en los fondos de varios pueblos y en el ramo de "Municipios" del Fondo de los Gobernadores españoles del mismo Archivo.

Los libros de contabilidad como los de la Hacienda Mercedita de Ponce (localizados en la oficina matriz de las Empresas Serrallés) y los de la Hacienda Pietri de Adjuntas (algunos en el AGPR) también ayudarán a reducir la enorme ignorancia que tenemos sobre los salarios imperantes a fines del siglo XIX.

Precios

Los precios de los productos de consumo cotidiano han corrido igual suerte. La Gaceta de Puerto Rico, periódico del gobierno colonial español, publicó intermitentemente durante la segunda mitad del siglo XIX los precios máximos del pan y de la carne impuestos por el Ayuntamiento de San Juan a los comerciantes de la Capital. Pero en vista de que la política de control de precios no fue aplicada constantemente, la información fragmentada no permite construir una estadística sin grandes lagunas aunque sirve para comparar precios de distintas épocas. Las actas del Ayuntamiento de San Juan (depositadas en el AGPR) dan noticia de las controversias internas en torno al problema de control de los precios. Tal vez los libros de contabilidad de las empresas comerciales como Roses y Compañía, de Arecibo (custodiados en el Centro de Investigaciones Históricas de la Facultad de Humanidades de la Universidad de Puerto Rico), añadirán datos importantes. A partir de 1912, el Negociado del Trabajo incluyó en sus informes anuales abundante información de precios y salarios.

Emigración Interna y Proletarización

El tránsito de los trabajadores del campo a la ciudad y el surgimiento de los barrios obreros merece un estudio más intenso. Algunos censos de pueblos, como los de Ponce, dan informaciones vitales tales como oficio, edad, número de años en el vecindario, tamaño de la familia, analfabetismo, etc. A pesar de que no todos los censos municipales son tan informativos como los de Ponce, ayudarán--junto a la consulta de los libros parroquiales, planillas de riqueza rural y el catastro de fincas--a reconstruir el itinerario de los campesinos expulsados de sus tierras o seducidos por la esperanza de una vida mejor en la ciudad. Dado el volumen de los casos a estudiar, se impone escoger muestras que hagan manejable la investigación con ayuda de la computadora. Por otra parte, la proletarización del campesino es mostrada por Fernando Picó, Libertad y servidumbre el el Puerto Rico del siglo XIX.[1] Este proceso ocurre también en los campos de caña de azúcar. Al respecto, véase Andrés A. Ramos Mattei La hacienda azucarera: su crecimiento y crisis en Puerto Rico (Siglo XIX).[2]

Prensa y Literatura Obreras

La mejor orientación bibliográfica de periódicos, revistas y libros de y sobre los obreros de fines del siglo XIX y comienzos del XX es la de A. G. Quintero Rivera, Lucha obrera en Puerto Rico.[3] En la Colección Junghams del AGPR aparecen hojas sueltas y periódicos obreros importantes, así como en la hemeroteca de la Colección Puertorriqueña de la Biblioteca José M. Lázaro de la Universidad de Puerto Rico.

Las manifestaciones culturales de los trabajadores han sido investigadas por Ricardo Campos, "Apuntes sobre la expresión cultural obrera en Puerto Rico,"[4] ponencia mecanografiada presentada en la Conferencia sobre historiografía puertorriqueña, 1974. Rubén Dávila también investiga el tema en su libro de próxima aparición El derribo de las murallas.

La Perspectiva Metropolitana

En los últimos años, el Centro de Estudios Puertorriqueños de la City University of New York se ha destacado por su interés en añadir la perspectiva de las estrechas relaciones del movimiento obrero puertorriqueño y el norteamericano. Destacan, por ejemplo, la recopilación de la correspondencia de Samuel Gompers y William Green relacionada con el movimiento obrero puertorriqueño entre 1901 y 1925; las resoluciones sobre Puerto Rico presentadas en las asambleas anuales de la American Federation of Labor; los artículos, editoriales e informes laborales que aluden a Puerto Rico y que aparecieron en el American Federationist durante las primeras dos décadas del siglo XX; y una selección de documentos del Bureau of Insular Affairs encontrados en los National Archives.

El History Task Force del Centro de Estudios Puertorriqueños también ha contribuido mucho al conocimiento de la emigración de los trabajadores puertorriqueños a los Estados Unidos. (Véase, Labor Migration under Capitalism. The Puerto Rican Experience[5] y Sources for the Study of Puerto Rican Migration: 1879-1930.[6])

Por otro lado, falta descubrir la dimensión española de la historia obrera puertorriqueña. Todavía ignoramos si existieron contactos con las distintas agrupaciones de los trabajadores de España. Al presente contamos con el diario de sesiones de las Cortes españolas y con otros fondos procedentes del Archivo Histórico Nacional que ayudan a comprender mejor las ideologías y las decisiones de los que trazaron la política colonial. (María de los Angeles Castro, Guía descriptiva de los fondos documentales existentes en el Centro de Investigaciones Históricas.[7])

NOTAS

1.   Fernando Picó, Libertad y servidumbre en el Puerto Rico del siglo XIX (Río Piedras, PR: Ediciones Huracán, 1979).

2.   Andrés A. Ramos Mattei, La hacienda azucarera: su crecimiento y crisis en Puerto Rico (Siglo XIX) (San Juan, PR: CEREP, 1981).

3.   A. G. Quintero Rivera, Lucha obrera en Puerto Rico (San Juan, PR: CEREP, 1971), pp. 153-161. (Hay traducción al inglés.)

4.   Ricardo Campos, "Apuntes sobre la expresión cultural obrera en Puerto Rico," City University of New York, 1974. (Typewritten.)

5.   Labor Migration under Capitalism. The Puerto Rican Experience (New York, NY, and London: Monthly Review Press, 1979).

6.   Sources for the Study of Puerto Rican Migration: 1879-1930 (New York, NY: Centro de Estudios Puertorriqueños, 1982).

7.   María de los Angeles Castro, Guía descriptiva de los fondos documentales existentes en el Centro de Investigaciones Históricas (Río Piedras, PR: Universidad de Puerto Rico, Recinto de Río Piedras, Oficina de Publicaciones de la Facultad de Humanidades, 1984).

22. FUENTES PARA LA HISTORIA DE LAS COMUNIDADES RURALES EN PUERTO RICO EN LOS SIGLOS 19 Y 20

Fernando Picó

En los últimos diez años he estado trabajando en las fuentes de la historia rural de Puerto Rico, especialmente del siglo 19. He tratado de consultar todas las fuentes accesibles para el estudio de un gran centro cafetalero, Utuado, y para la historia de un municipio tabacalero y ganadero de la costa, Camuy. Ultimamente estoy estudiando la historia de un barrio periférico de Río Piedras, Caimito, que hasta hace muy poco tiempo estuvo dedicado a la producción de frutos menores y alguna caña de azúcar.

Estas investigaciones han estado dirigidas a explorar el desarrollo de las comunidades en un marco mucho más amplio que el de su producción agrícola. He pretendido trazar las etapas en el desarrollo de las condiciones de vida y de trabajo de los que han formado parte de estas comunidades, aunque su participación en la producción haya sido mínima o nula. En un esfuerzo por identificar los rasgos salientes de las mentalidades, he querido estudiar las observancias religiosas, las solidaridades, las historias familiares, y la intervención del estado en la vida cotidiana. En otras palabras, me he querido aproximar al modelo de historia "global" o "total" de la que han hablado los historiadores franceses de la escuela de Annales.

Al tratar de hacer las investigaciones, me he topado con una enorme dificultad. Las fuentes disponibles no son necesariamente las más idóneas. De la enorme cantidad de documentos que los organismos administrativos, judiciales, y eclesiásticos, y las familias y las corporaciones generaron, ha llegado hasta nosotros una menguada fracción.

Para darles una idea de lo que ha significado el proceso de atrición de los materiales para la historia de Puerto Rico, basta con señalar las experiencias concretas que ha tenido la documentación del municipio de Utuado, que para fines del siglo 19 llegó a ser el segundo municipio más poblado de Puerto Rico. Existe una copia del inventario del archivo municipal en 1838, casi un siglo después de la fundación de Utuado (1739). Básicamente el archivo consistía entonces de la correspondencia con la gobernación, los expedientes fiscales de subsidios y gastos públicos, los padrones de terrenos, listas de milicias urbanas y de electores para el más reciente ayuntamiento constitucional, matrículas de esclavos y material análogo. También se notan los cuadernos de juicios y de protocolos notariales, ya que el teniente a guerra o alcalde tenía que actuar como juez de paz y como juez cartulario:

Un Registro Protocolo que contiene ochenta y nuebe instrumentos públicos jurídicos de los años desde 1754 hasta 1799 inclusibe.

Otro ydem ydem de Testamentos, codicilos e inventarios desde 1748 hasta fin de 1837.

Un legajo con diez y ocho sumarios y causas criminales.

Otro idem con cuarenta y ocho causas civiles desde el año de 1803 hasta fin de 1837.[1]

De todo esto, en la actualidad queda muy poco: los padrones de terrenos de 1833 y 1837 y un fragmento del de 1827; los cuadernos de juicios verbales de 1838 y de Protocolos Notariales de 1831, 1832, 1833 y 1838; una copia de un padrón de vecinos de alrededor de 1828; una copia de una matrícula de esclavos de la década del 1820; fragmentos de subsidios y de gastos públicos de la época. Los protocolos notariales y el cuaderno de juicios verbales probablemente deben su supervivencia al hecho de que en fechas posteriores fueron trasladados a otros archivos, el de Protocolos Notariales del Distrito de Arecibo, y el del Tribunal Superior de Arecibo.

Un inventario del archivo municipal de Utuado en 1867 nos muestra un archivo municipal mucho más desarrollado y en vías de sistematización.[2] La documentación generada por el municipio es entonces mucho más abundante. Los legajos comienzan a encuadernarse en volúmenes numerados y organizados temáticamente. Hay una contabilización más estricta de las obligaciones fiscales, y un empeño en documentar los reclamos del municipio en la reorganización de la vida cotidiana. Sobre esta documentación pudo haberse basado una historia abarcadora de las personas y la tierra entre 1812 y las vísperas del Grito de Lares en 1868.

Pero de todo ese material inventariado entonces, y del que las próximas décadas acumularon, hoy día nos quedan sólo restos, remanentes de un naufragio del archivo municipal en las tormentas reales y metafóricas del último siglo. Cuando Luis de la Rosa acudió con otros miembros del personal del Instituto de Cultura de Puerto Rico a Utuado, a principios de los 1970, para recoger el archivo municipal, que por ley pasaba a formar parte de las colecciones documentales del Archivo General, nadie conocía de la existencia del antiguo archivo municipal de Utuado. Cuando estaban ya a punto de irse, un conserje los abordó: "¿Ustedes están buscando papeles viejos? Vengan." Los llevó a una húmeda covacha donde se guardaban los ataúdes de pobres. Allí, roídos por ratones, polillas y comején, acartonados por la humedad, en pedazos, en hilachas, estaban los antiguos documentos de Utuado.

En este caso fueron los ratones y los insectos quienes decidieron qué nos iba a quedar para hacer la historia del siglo 19. Las personas hacía tiempo ya que se habían desinteresado de esa historia. Y en fin de cuentas, no son tanto los azotes tropicales, la humedad y los depradadores, como la indiferencia de sus custodios lo que continuamente reduce y elimina las fuentes disponibles papa la historia de nuestra sociedad.

Y no es que no haya conciencia histórica en el país, sino que hay una conciencia histórica deformada. El que se pierdan estos materiales no ha espantado a los responsables, porque estos siempre han creído que lo que es importante, lo que es Historia con mayúscula, es lo que se guarda en Washington o en España, lo que tiene la firma de los próceres, lo que habla de batallas y de tratados diplomáticos, lo que tiene los sellos y las rúbricas del poder. La concepción de que la historia de Puerto Rico la constituyen una serie de iniciativas y decisiones hechas afuera y arriba tiene como corolario lógico el que ese montón de papeles viejos sólo tiene escasa importancia histórica.

Así es que la mayor dificultad con que se topa un historiador de Puerto Rico que se afana por las fuentes, es la concepción teórica de la historia que tienen los supuestos custodios de esas fuentes. Pero para que no se piense que eso es meramente una concepción anacrónica y ya rebasada de lo que constituyen las fuentes históricas, tomemos otro ejemplo de la historia de Utuado.

Sabemos que en distintos períodos entre 1880 y 1930 se publicaron 11 periódicos distintos en Utuado.[3] De esos 11 periódicos, tras diez años de búsquedas e indagaciones, yo no he encontrado un solo ejemplar. En distintas ocasiones en que he hablado, pública y privadamente, con bibliotecarios sobre este tema, les he urgido a que se dediquen, cada cual en su área geográfica, a coleccionar y preservar las muchas y diversas publicaciones periódicas que hoy día se hacen en Puerto Rico sobre política, religión, cultura, deportes y negocios. Y es una de las decepciones del investigador en Puerto Rico constatar que la misma dificultad que tenemos hoy en localizar los materiales impresos de hace sesenta años, la tendrán nuestros sucesores dentro de sesenta años tratando de localizar las de hoy día.

Uno de los fenómenos religiosos campesinos más interesantes de principios de este siglo en la zona central de Puerto Rico fue la aparición de los Hermanos Cheos, predicadores itinerantes. De la literatura religiosa que generaron, ¿cuánto nos queda? Y cuánto más quedará dentro de ochenta años de todas estas comunidades religiosas rurales de presente, sectas, comunas, e iglesias centradas alrededor de un líder carismático?

El problema con las fuentes de nuestra historia rural, sin embargo, no sólo reside en la preservación de los testimonios contemporáneos. Hay fuentes que se han preservado pero que por una u otra razón permanecen inaccesibles a los investigadores. En algunos casos se trata de custodios celosos de la documentación; en otros, de masas de material no catalogadas; y en otros casos todavía se trata de la falta de un instrumental metodológico adecuado para analizar las fuentes. Detrás de cada una de estas limitaciones se discierne el perfil de alguna distorsionada concepción de lo que es el trabajo del historiador. Las prioridades que tienen el acopio de fuentes de origen privado y la catalogación de fuentes públicas en el Archivo General de Puerto Rico reflejan una concepción de lo que es historia. El entrenamiento metodológico que reciben los historiadores refleja también las concepciones teoréticas todavía vigentes. Distintas teorías de la historia implican metodologías distintas.

Hablemos, sin embargo, de lo que hay y de las posiblidades de trabajo que se ofrecen, y en primer lugar de las fuentes accesibles.

Las Fuentes Accesibles

Las Fuentes Impresas

Para la historia de las comunidades rurales de Puerto Rico las principales fuentes impresas son la Balanza Mercantil, la Gaceta del Gobierno de Puerto Rico, y los muchos otros periódicos de la época, cuyos nombres y fechas de edición Pedreira recoge en El periodismo en Puerto Rico; las publicaciones, que se hacen frecuentes desde la década de los 1880, sobre los problemas de la agricultura en Puerto Rico[4]; la Revista de Agricultura, Industria y Comercio revistas análogas, que se publican especialmente desde la década de los 1920; las obras literarias que de una manera u otra inciden sobre los problemas del campo; y la abundante cantidad de discursos y ensayos políticos que han proliferado en torno a la temática rural en Puerto Rico.

El repositorio básico para mucho de este material es la Colección Puertorriqueña de la Biblioteca General de la Universidad de Puerto Rico. Hay también un acopio considerable de publicaciones periódicas y ocasionales sobre asuntos agrarios en la Biblioteca de la Estación Experimental Agrícola, de la Universidad de Puerto Rico en Río Piedras, y en otras bibliotecas de agencias públicas e instituciones docentes o culturales del país.

Las Fuentes Manuscritas

Mucho más heterogéneas, y con grandes posibilidades para la realización de investigaciones innovadoras, son las fuentes manuscritas. De la enorme gama de ellas examinemos aquí las más importantes para la historia de nuestra sociedad agraria.

Protocolos Notariales.--La obligación de agrupar en un mismo cuaderno o tomo todas las escrituras notarizadas en cada año natural ha provisto a los historiadores latinoamericanos con una maravillosa mina de información. Compraventas de terreno y de esclavos, permutas, obligaciones hipotecarias, testamentos, escrituras de manumisión y de aprendizaje, laudos de árbitros, arrendamientos de terreno, formaciones y disoluciones de sociedades comerciales, fianzas, apremios y protestas, cartas de reconocimiento de dote, divisiones de bienes hereditarios, promesas de venta y otras formas de contrato, proveen al investigador con un cuadro bastante rico de las relaciones económicas prevalecientes en la sociedad rural desde su tránsito al monocultivo hasta la disolución del régimen agrario del azúcar y del café.

En Puerto Rico los protocolos más antiguos que se conservan son los de Coamo, de la década de los 1760. Para Guayama y algunos otros municipios se han conservado desde la década de los 1790. Desgraciadamente el archivo de protocolos del distrito judicial de Mayagüez (en el oeste) desapareció en un accidente hace muchos años. En general los protocolos del área sur, más seca, se han conservado en mejores condiciones que los del área norte y este.

Padrones de tierra.--La obligación de pagar derechos sobre la propiedad, establecida por la cédula real de 1778 que concedía la titulación de la tierra en Puerto Rico, resultó en la formación anual de padrones de terrenos. Los más antiguos que se conocen son posteriores a la organización independiente de la Intendencia. Aunque pocas copias de padrones de tierras han sobrevivido en los archivos de la gobernación,[5] en los archivos municipales por lo general se han encontrado copias u originales del período entre 1820 y 1868. Con ellos se ha podido examinar la estructura de la tenencia de la tierra titulada en distintas áreas.

Planillas de riqueza.--Para las últimas tres décadas del siglo 19, en vez de padrones de terrenos, existen en algunos archivos municipales, como el de Manatí, planillas de riqueza. Estas permiten apreciar la calidad de la tierra y la rentabilidad de sus cultivos.

Las "Galletas de Hacienda."--Es éste el nombre expresivo con que se conocen los Registros de Tasación y Contribución sobre la Propiedad. El fondo de Hacienda en el Archivo General tiene una extensísima serie de libros anuales para cada municipio desde 1902, con los contribuyentes sobre la propiedad inmueble, la extensión de sus propiedades, su rentabilidad, y la cuota asignada de impuestos. Idealmente esta fuente haría posible examinar la estructura de la propiedad agraria en Puerto Rico hasta mediados de este siglo.

El Registro de la Propiedad.--Fundado en mayo de 1880, el Registro de la Propiedad tardó bastantes años en incorporar a sus libros la mayor parte de la propiedad inmueble titulada de Puerto Rico. Para las muchas propiedades que se registraron en las últimas dos décadas del siglo 19, el Registro de la Propiedad provee al historiador la oportunidad de examinar las vicisitudes de una unidad productiva: sus traspasos, obligaciones hipotecarias, arrendamientos, divisiones, servidumbres públicas, y mejoras. El Registro constituye el complemento ideal a una investigación basada en protocolos notariales para el período previo al 1880. Requiere práctica en su manejo, ya que es necesario saber cuando una propiedad se inscribió originalmente para poder localizarla en el Registro. Hay un centro del Registro para cada dos o tres municipios.

Los Registros de Antigua Anotaduría.--Esta es una de las fuentes que mayor peligro corre en perderse. Antes de la fundación del Registro de la Propiedad, se mantenía constancia en las cabeceras de los distritos de las obligaciones que pesaban sobre las propiedades inmuebles por gravámenes de censos, capellanías o hipotecas. Como con frecuencia los propietarios rurales hipotecaban sus estancias o haciendas en las notarías de ciudades costeras, donde tenían sus sedes las más importantes sociedades comerciales acreedoras, no basta con un examen de los protocolos notariales de un municipio dado para averiguar los patrones de crédito y de financiamiento disponibles para las unidades de producción agrícola. Estos registros se descontinuaron después de la fundación del Registro de la Propiedad; en vez, se hicieron anotaciones en las páginas de éste, con referencias, cuando pertinentes, a los "registros de antigua anotaduría." Con el tiempo estos últimos quedaron obsoletos. No se han recogido en el Archivo General de Puerto Rico, y no hay ningún catálogo de las copias que han sobrevivido a la destrucción o a la apropiación individual.

El Catastro de Fincas Rústicas.--A principios de la década de los 1890 el gobierno instituyó un inventario sistemático de la propiedad inmueble en cada municipio. Los catastros de fincas rústicas y de fincas urbanas fueron el resultado. Al presente los catastros se encuentran en el Archivo General de Puerto Rico. Cada página contiene datos sobre la cabida de una propiedad, sus colindantes, el uso que se le está dando en ese momento a las tierras, y las edificaciones, si alguna, que contiene.

Listas fiscales y administrativas.--Para muchos municipios en el período de las primeras décadas del siglo 19, sólo se dispone de listas de vecinos hechas para el cobro de subsidios y gastos públicos, o listas de hombres entre los 16 y los 60 años como miembros de las milicias urbanas. Estas fuentes, analizadas cuantitativamente, pueden rendir mucha información. En el Fondo de los Gobernadores Españoles de Puerto Rico, serie Municipalidades, y en el Fondo de Diputación Provincial se hallan numerosas copias. En los Archivos Municipales, también en el Archivo General, por lo general sobrevive un grupo reducido de originales para cada municipio entonces existente.

Censos.--Aunque el gobierno español y la Iglesia Católica, con distintos fines, llevaron a cabo censos de los habitantes de Puerto Rico antes del siglo 19, estas fuentes se hallan en archivos españoles. Para el siglo 19, sin embargo, se ha conservado un gran número de ellos tanto en los fondos derivados de la administración central, como en los archivados en los municipios y luego trasladados al Archivo General. De especial interés para el historiador de las comunidades rurales son los censos persona por persona. Hay uno para el pueblo de Patillas, del año siguiente de su fundación, en la serie Censo y Riqueza del Fondo de Gobernadores Españoles, donde también se encuentra un número considerable de censos parecidos para otros municipios en fechas posteriores. Uno de los primeros censos simultáneos y exhaustivos que llevó a cabo el gobierno fue el de la Nochebuena de 1860 (24 a 25 de diciembre). Hasta la fecha se han encontrado completos o parciales los expedientes de ese censo para Utuado, Camuy, Guaynabo y Naranjito.[6]

Un complemento interesante de los censos de persona a persona lo constituyen los expedientes de variaciones, o de entradas y salidas, que los alcaldes, al menos desde la década de los 1830, remitían a la gobernación, para dar cuenta de las altas y las bajas de la población de su término.

Recientemente se ha hecho accesible, en micropelícula, el conjunto de las planillas originales del Censo Federal de 1910, que es, hasta la fecha, el único censo federal de Puerto Rico cuya data cruda pueda ser examinada por los historiadores. No sólo para la historia demografía, sino también para múltiples aspectos de la historia social de la ruralía, este censo promete ser un semillero de información.

Los Registros Parroquiales.--Muchos historiadores latino-americanos han demostrado ya las enormes posibilidades que ofrece el examen sistemático de los libros de bautismos, defunciones, y matrimonios de las parroquias católicas antes del establecimiento del registro civil.[7] En Puerto Rico queda muy poco del siglo 17.[8] Para el siglo 18 están los registros de San Juan, San Germán, Mayagüez, Arecibo, Coamo, Bayamón, Guaynabo, Río Piedras, Guayama y varios otros municipios más. En distintas ocasiones se han hecho inventarios de los archivos parroquiales.[9] Des-graciadamente, hasta el presente sólo se han microfilmado y puesto a disposición de los investigadores en la Universidad de Puerto Rico los registros parroquiales de Añasco, Hormigueros e Isabela. Según informes del vicario de pastoral de la diócesis de Ponce, monseñor Herminio de Jesús, esa diócesis ha emprendido un proyecto de microfilmación de sus registros.

Juicios Verbales y Juicios de Conciliación.--Los juicios verbales eran litigios de menor cuantía en que el alcalde, y a partir de mediados de los 1860, el juez de paz, adjudicaba con el consejo de los "hombres buenos", es decir, los representantes de las partes. En los juicios de conciliación las partes sometían sus diferencias para lograr una avenencia; el juez no dictaminaba. En uno y otro caso la solución dictada o convenida adquiría fuerza legal. En los 1860, muchos propietarios buscaban el dictamen de un juicio verbal para así amarrar a los agregados, arrendatarios o pequeños agricultores vecinos, al pago con trabajo de sus deudas.[10]

Estos expedientes, cuyas copias se pueden hallar tanto en los fondos municipales como en los judiciales, documentan la multitud de conflictos y diferencias que agitaban la vida rural:

promesas incumplidas de matrimonio, ofensas de palabras, incumplimientos de contratos de arrendamiento, diferencias de colindancias, invasiones de terreno, divisiones de herencia, conflictos de contabilización de tareas o de valorización de cosechas, etc. Son magníficas fuentes para la historia de las mentalidades.

Fuentes Policiales.--Todavía no se ha hecho una indagación sistemática de las fuentes policiales del siglo 19. Hay remanentes de ellas en algunos archivos provenientes de los municipios, y por lo general datan de las últimas dos décadas del siglo 19. En ellas se patentizan los agudos conflictos sociales de la época. Para el siglo 20, las series de Querellas, Circulares y Libros de Novedades de la Policía proveen preciosa información cotidiana sobre la vida de la ruralía.

Libros de Cuentas de Haciendas y Casas de Comercio.--El Archivo General de Puerto Rico tiene un grupo reducido de colecciones particulares que incluyen libros de cuenta de haciendas y casas de comercio de la segunda mitad del siglo 19 y las primeras décadas del 20. El Centro de Investigaciones Históricas de la Universidad de Puerto Rico ha recibido los libros de Roses y Compañía, gran sociedad comercial del área de Arecibo. Hay un número reducido de libros en manos de particulares, pero por lo general el acceso no está institucionalizado.

El nivel de ganancias de las casas comerciales, la extensión de su crédito, la variedad de las mercancías disponibles, los patrones de consumo, los ritmos de producción, los costos de transporte, y todos los otros problemas relacionados a la agricultura y al comercio rural, aguardan investigaciones detalladas de estas fuentes.

Correspondencia de alcaldes y gobernadores.--En los fondos de Gobernadores Españoles y de Diputación Provincial del Archivo General se encuentran rezagos de lo que debió de haber sido una riquísima veta de documentación. Hay originales de los oficios de los alcaldes, y borradores de las respuestas que se les mandan. Algunos fondos municipales, como el de Río Piedras (San Juan B), conservan los oficios de los gobernadores. Es interesante notar en estas fuentes los múltiples esfuerzos por conservar el vulnerable orden público y la recurrencia de los problemas monetarios y fiscales.

El Fondo de Obras Públicas del Archivo General.--Los expedientes generados por planificación, trazado, construcción y reparación de carreteras, caminos vecinales y puentes, como los expedientes de concesiones de terrenos baldíos, permisos de uso de agua, censos y capellanías pertenecientes a las órdenes mendicantes, construcción de edificios públicos y religiosos, y de la construcción del ferrocarril, ofrecen un abanico de posibilidades para la investigación. Es interesante, en particular, el desarrollo de la infraestructura de comunicaciones que vincula la producción agrícola a los centros de exportación y que integra a los habitantes de Puerto Rico en un solo sistema de comunicaciones.

Querellas de Migrantes.--En los fondos provenientes del Departamento del Trabajo hay una interesantísima sub-serie en la documentación guardada por el Negociado de Empleos y Migración. Se trata de las cuarenta y seis cajas de Querellas de Obreros Migrantes, con expedientes de los años 1949 en adelante. Los obreros contratados en programas auspiciados por el gobierno de Puerto Rico para la recolección de vegetales y otros productos en fincas de Estados Unidos, con frecuencia se toparon con dificultades de incumplimiento de contrato, y dirigieron sus reclamos al gobierno de Puerto Rico. Estos expedientes no sólo documentan la gran emigración de trabajadores rurales en la década de 1950, sino que también muestran los contextos específicos de los obreros que emigraban. Con frecuencia los expedientes contienen cartas de los familiares del emigrante, y otra documentación valiosa para recrear el universo mental del trabajador que se iba a Michigan o New Jersey con la esperanza de "mejorar".

Fuentes No Documentales

La historia agraria puertorriqueña no se limita al uso de fuentes escritas. El historiador, en la medida de lo posible, debe aprovechar la existencia de otras fuentes: las de la historia y la tradición oral, los remanentes de edificios y estructuras y máquinas usadas en la ruralía, las colecciones de riles y fichas, sustitutos de la moneda menuda en muchas haciendas, la iconografía, la música, y los propios contornos naturales del agro, que delatan los usos y abusos previos de la tierra.

Las Fuentes Todavía Inaccesibles

Pero si son abundantes las fuentes accesibles a los historiadores de las comunidades rurales en Puerto Rico, quedan todavía bastantes fuentes documentales sin explorar.

El material demográfico, tanto en registros parroquiales como en el registro demográfico civil y en los censos no examinados del siglo 19, ofrece una veta importante a los investigadores. Mucho de este material permanece sin inventariar en los archivos municipales no catalogados. De particular importancia serían los censos de barrios en los cuales se podría observar la evolución de la estructura del hogar. Para los registros parroquiales, la prioridad debiera ser una microfilmación exhaustiva de todos los libros anteriores al 1885 (fecha de la formación del Registro Demográfico). De particular prioridad son los libros de defunciones o entierros, que por haber permanecido inactivos han sufrido más deterioro.

Hay una gran cantidad de material de los archivos de los gobernadores en el siglo 20 que todavía permanece inaccesible a los investigadores, pues no se ha acometido su catalogación, y sólo excepcionalmente se ha permitido su consulta. De particular interés es la colección documental de Luis Muñoz Marín, para la cual la Fundación Luis Muñoz Marín está construyendo un archivo y estableciendo un inventario. Es de esperar que para inicios de 1987 el Archivo Muñoz Marín esté en operación en los terrenos de su antigua residencia en Trujillo Alto.

Uno de los filones más preciosos para la historia social aguarda todavía el que se le dé paso a los investigadores. Me refiero a los fondos de los tribunales superiores en el Archivo General y en el Centro Judicial de San Juan, y el todavía inaccesible fondo del Tribunal Superior de Humacao. Los expedientes civiles, criminales, administrativos y demográficos en estos fondos ayudarán a los investigadores en múltiples tareas de historia de la mujer, de la propiedad y del orden público, de las mentalidades, y de los percances electorales, huelgarios y de índole masiva-popular que en determinadas coyunturas de nuestra historia han sido significativos. Hasta el presente están disponibles los fondos de los tribunales superiores de Ponce y Aguadilla, cuya índole es preponderantemente civil. Los de Arecibo, Guayama, y Mayagüez, ordenados cronológicamente e inventariados en fecha reciente, todavía no están disponibles a la consulta, por falta de facilidades en el Archivo General.

De mayor urgencia es la valorización de las fuentes de origen privado que a diario se pierden y se desperdigan en nuestro país. Los papeles de las casas de comercio no han sido sistemáticamente buscados y solicitados por el Archivo General. Tampoco se ha indagado con suficiente persistencia en archivos privados del exterior el material correspondiente a las relaciones de negocio con Puerto Rico. Un ejemplo de las posibilidades que este esfuerzo reportaría lo constituyen las indagaciones de Andrés Ramos Mattei en Glasgow sobre la fabricación de equipo para las centrales de azúcar en las últimas décadas del siglo 19. Si tuviéramos el beneficio de esfuerzos análogos en Estados Unidos, España y Francia, podríamos entender mejor los engranajes de la producción agrícola tropical con el gran comercio internacional, y la aportación técnica de la revolución industrial a los cambios fundamentales en la estructura de la producción agraria.

Los archivos privados de la correspondencia de personajes políticos de las últimas nueve décadas, con frecuencia contienen material alusivo a los problemas agrarios y su tematización política. Pero debemos ensanchar la concepción de lo que se considera valioso en la correspondencia privada del pasado, para abarcar todos los testimonios significativos para la historia de las mentalidades. La correspondencia privada no tiene que ser de orden político o económico para aportar a la comprensión de fenómenos sociales de larga duración.

Uno de los archivos más prometedores, pero todavía inaccesible, a la investigación sobre la historia de las mentalidades sería el archivo del arzobispado de San Juan. La correspondencia entre los párrocos y los obispos es un barómetro de los cambios

sociales, cuyo valor va mucho más allá que la especificación de las
etapas en el desarrollo de las experiencias religiosas.

Conclusión: Perspectivas de la Investigación sobre las Comunidades Rurales en la Próxima Década

Si la investigación sobre las comunidades rurales en Puerto
Rico logra hacer suficiente mella en la conciencia social y en las
prioridades propuestas de los custodios de las fuentes, en la
próxima década podremos disponer, con mayor certidumbre y
conveniencia, de fuentes más amplias para la tarea historiográfica.
Al presente, sólo se puede predecir con seguridad que en los
próximos años los fondos judiciales jugarán un papel crucial en la
historia social. Los expedientes de testamentarías harán posible
el precisar la estructura de las fortunas de estancieros y hacendados. En los juicios verbales, se documentará mejor el trabajo
por endeudamiento. La posición de la mujer en la sociedad rural
quedará más clara al trasluz de las fuentes contenciosas que se
afanan por definir el alcance de sus derechos y de sus reclamos.
La violencia rural, documentada y precisada, se podrá entender
mejor en función de las coyunturas económicas y políticas.
Sistemas de solidaridad hasta el presente intuídos, pero no
explicados, quedarán expuestos. Claro está que todas estas
predicciones, tan galanamente hechas, dependen de un avance en
las metas que se fijen los investigadores, pero no es difícil ver
que la disponibilidad de unas fuentes y la vigencia de unas
inquietudes no tardarán en hacer juego.

Otro frente de avance, necesario para la mayor comprensión
de los valores articulados por nuestras sociedades rurales, lo
constituyen las fuentes de origen eclesiástico. Hasta el presente,
el mayor uso de los libros parroquiales ha sido el de documentar
los principales cambios demográficos. Pero se le pudieran hacer
preguntas de otra índole a las partidas de bautismos, entierros y
matrimonios. La microfilmación de estas fuentes haría más fácil
los estudios comparativos de observancias religiosas; las tasas de
receptores de sacramentos al morir; los lapsos de tiempo entre
nacimiento y bautismo; las nomenclaturas; los patrones de
compadrazgos; las expresiones, a largo plazo, de la consanguini-
dad; las expresiones de secularización y de atomización de la vida
familiar; los movimientos migratorios internos; inclusive la
incidencia de homicidios y suicidios. Es posible también que otras
fuentes eclesiásticas para la historia social se lleguen a valorizar
más; la literatura religiosa popular,[11] la iconografía, la correspondencia eclesial, y el propio Boletín Eclesiástico de la Iglesia
Católica, así como los informes anuales, libros de memorias y
revistas de las distintas denominaciones de raíz protestante que se
han establecido en Puerto Rico.

Finalmente, la perspectiva de que un mayor número de colecciones particulares se hagan disponibles a la investigación se
acentúa con la creciente conciencia de su valor documental. Estas

apoyarán los estudios de microhistoria económica que complementarán los grandes planteamientos teóricos de nuestros historiadores.

La coyuntura presente es, pues, de esperanzas y bríos.

NOTAS

1. Archivo General de Puerto Rico (AGPR), Fondo de los Gobernadores Españoles de Puerto Rico, caja 359. Oficio del alcalde José Colomer y Comas, acompañado del inventario del archivo de Utuado.

2. AGPR, Fondo Municipal de Utuado, caja provisional. "Ynventario de los documentos que ecsisten en los archivos de esta Alcaldía."

3. Ver el listado de los periódicos puertorriqueños de ese período en Antonio Pedreira, El periodismo en Puerto Rico, tomo 5 de Obras Completas.

4. Ver, por ejemplo, José Ramón Abad, Puerto Rico en la Feria-Exposición de Ponce en 1882, 2a. ed. facsimilar por Emilio Colón (Río Piedras, PR, 1967); Fernando López Tuero, La reforma agrícola (San Juan, PR, 1891); Ramón Morel Campos, El porvenir de Utuado (Ponce, PR, 1897).

5. Para un gran número de municipios, hay copia de los padrones de terrenos de 1860 en el fondo de Obras Públicas, serie Propiedad Pública.

6. Los de Utuado y de Camuy están en los respectivos fondos municipales, y los de Guaynabo y Naranjito en la colección Junghanns del Archivo General. Sobre el fragmento de Guaynabo hay un estudio, "Guaynabo en 1860," de Carlos Rodríguez Villanueva, publicado en Anales de Investigación Histórica, VIII (1981).

7. Ver Claude Morin, "Los libros parroquiales como fuente para la historia demográfica y social novohispana," Historia Mexicana, XXI (1972), 389-418.

8. Generoso Morales Muñoz, en el Boletín de Historia Puertorriqueña (1948-49), publicó los más antiguos fragmentos de los registros parroquiales de San Juan.

9. Ver Lino Gómez Canedo, Los archivos de Puerto Rico (San Juan, PR, 1965). Mario Rodríguez León, O.P., planea una publicación para completar y poner al día el inventario.

10. Ver por ejemplo el siguiente caso: En 9 de abril de 1863 don Melitón Maestre, como apoderado de los Sres. Bagué Hermanos de Utuado, demanda a Gabino Rivera por 49 pesos 3 reales de plazo vencido. Rivera reconoce la deuda y ofrece pagar a razón de "tres días de trabajo semanales o su importe en metálico". La oferta es aceptada. (Tribunal Superior de Arecibo, Civil, Utuado, caja 241 A, sin título, Juicios Verbales de 1863, 38 r-v).

11. Ver la reciente publicación en microficha de Valentina Borremans, CIDOC Collection: The History of Religiosity in Latin America, ca. 1830–1970, on Microfiche (Zug, Suiza: Inter Documentation Company, 1985).

IV. Aspects of Social, Political, and Ideological Change

23. DOING RESEARCH ON POPULAR RELIGION AND POLITICS

Daniel H. Levine

Introduction

These brief reflections are personal and programmatic. The personal side arises from a fresh look at my own recent fieldwork in Venezuela and Colombia. I discuss here the general character of that research and argue that the specific issues and problems it addresses form part of a broad rethinking of the entire field. This process of redefinition and reformulation is apparent in research now underway in Latin America, Africa, Asia, Europe, and the United States. The programmatic component consists of a few related suggestions for improving the quality of both field-work and documentation, and for setting such work more fully in the context of central theoretical concerns.

A definition or two may help. The term "popular religion" is notoriously ambiguous, and subject to considerable academic debate as well as political and ecclesiastical struggle. In my own work, "popular religion" refers above all to the religious ideas, beliefs, practices, and organizational expressions of poor people-- the populus, however defined in a particular social order.

That definition has several notable implications for field research. First, it suggests that "the popular" will be found wherever popular expression and organization, of any kind, are linked to central institutions. In this case, our focus is the institutions of religion and politics. We are not dealing with isolated primitives, much less with a somehow pure, natural, or spontaneous product of indigenous belief.

Second, while popular groups are indeed linked to institutions, they cannot be understood as simple extensions of the programs that institutions and their leaders create and seek to project. Popular groups come to institutions with needs and agendas of their own: the relationship is dialectical, not one-way. Popular groups are thus never wholly malleable, mere clay for elites to mold.

Finally, this definition suggests that, while elements of social differentiation like class (which receives so much attention) are

Author's Note. The fieldwork discussed here was carried out between 1981 and 1983 in Venezuela and Colombia. Support was provided by the Horace H. Rackham School of Graduate Studies of the University of Michigan and also by the National Endowment for the Humanities through Research Grant # RO-20271-82.

important, they are not determining. It is false and misleading to identify popular religious groups entirely with the social class base of their membership. Catholic radicals often do this, asserting that such groups "arise from the people alone" and hence can be understood apart from the churches. This misrepresents the origins of such groups, and distorts our understanding of the motivations of members and the meaning that they give to action. Social class must be set against the continuities provided by institutional membership and by the cultural formations surrounding religious belief and practice.

My own recent research has focused on links between popular religion and politics (e.g, Levine, 1986). Working in peasant and urban slum communities in Venezuela and Colombia, I have searched for continuity and change in the everyday life of religion and politics, and explored the linkages between change at the community level and institutional and national patterns. These concerns suggest a meaning for "politics" which goes beyond the formal institutions of government and partisan dispute, to embrace a politics of everyday life. Ideas of power and authority thus help structure characteristic patterns of personal and organizational activity. The linkage between these ideas and patterns and "high politics" is an empirical question, whose exploration provides much of the theoretical interest of the work.

Issues and Problems in Fieldwork

The working definitions sketched out above help structure my own fieldwork in a few practical and concrete ways.

1. They offer a structure for identifying organized groups. I work within the structural net provided by the Catholic Church. By locating organized life within this framework, I can then examine connections up and down a chain stretching from neighborhood to parish, diocese, nation, and so on. At the same time, having an organizational foundation within the Church provides a concrete reference point for tracing connections horizontally to more explicitly political issues, movements, and organizations.

2. This approach places ideas and behavior in contexts that are real and meaningful to participants. We can then examine the formation, career, orientation, and commitments of specific groups: people participate in them both because they want to belong to the group per se and because they identify with its program. Membership is valued in and of itself, as well as for programmatic reasons. The first facet often provides a basis for solidarity and mutual support, upon which evolving objectives and commitments can effectively rest.

3. My own research relies fundamentally on interviews, supplemented by extensive documentary and organizational analysis. The interviews offer a window into personal and group

motivations--into the meaning of action to specific participants. Documentary and organizational analysis, in combination with an intensive group and site (i.e., local) history, provide the indispensable framework for understanding group life. Combining analyses of this sort also helps bring competing agendas within the institutional church to light (e.g., Jesuits vs. bishops), and thus brings greater sense to variations between the structure and orientation of different movements.

Unlike traditional anthropological fieldwork, my own research is not based on extensive residence in given communities. I have sacrificed such depth in order to visit several communities in two nations, and to shuttle back and forth between local and national, grass roots and institutional levels.

4.   This approach has theoretical as well as methodological value. A major issue in recent studies of religion and politics has been how best to grasp the meaning of action to participants, or how to see the world in the categories they themselves use. It is all too easy for researchers to accept either the agenda of elites (who, after all, usually produce the written record which comes to us), or to assume that the categories which interest scholars are also those which move the actors themselves. To overcome these problems, the traditional texts of analysis must be reexamined, and then enriched with a systematic look at organized social life and at such cultural expressions as songs, festivals, passion plays, and the like (e.g., Berryman, 1984; Comaroff, 1985; Fields, 1985; Ileto, 1979; Mainwaring, 1985).

5.   In Latin America, as elsewhere, understanding popular meanings and aspirations is a major concern of scholars of religion and politics. It likewise attracts elites and activists in the churches and in political institutions of all kinds. The proper understanding of religion and politics is, in this sense, funda- mental to the analysis of masses and minorities for several related reasons. First, and most obviously, many of the poor--who are, after all, the majority--are religious. This does not necessarily mean that they go to church regularly, or that they even "belong" to religious groups. They may simply see the world, and their place within it, in terms derived from religion.

Second, the institutions of religion, and most obviously Latin America's Catholic Church have, over the past ten or fifteen years, struggled to define, reach, and orient the poor. This process subsumes several facets: defining who the poor are and explaining their poverty (are they peasants, workers, "the humble," the poor in spirit?); then defining what texts should go to the poor (who selects the texts for community Bible study, who records and distributes the cassettes, who runs the copiers and the mimeograph machines?).

Third, it is important to realize that the radicalized groups that attract so much public attention (e.g., base communities in Central America or Brazil) are neither very numerous nor in any sense typical. Their significance lies in their centrality, not their representative character: they clearly occupy a crucial position in the process of religious and political change. They have become central by providing a shield for activities prohibited or drastically restricted in society at large, and by giving emerging religious concepts a practical medium for everyday expression (see Levine, 1986, and the studies collected there; see also Mainwaring, 1985).

6.   Fieldwork on this general topic entails a number of concrete problems. The first and most basic involves location and access. It is often very difficult to find and reach groups, and access is uncertain even under the best of circumstances. Poor communications, erratic and unreliable transportation, the people's demanding work schedules, and a widespread reserve with outsiders all impede access in rural areas. In urban areas, frequent moves and the rapid growth of sprawling shantytowns make communication and simple transportation almost as hard. Careful preparation and institutional legitimation help. I carried a letter from the Vicar General of one rural diocese, was legitimated by Jesuit advisers in another, and in urban areas worked wherever possible with zonal coordinators, progressing from contact to contact.

There are also notable problems of evidence. Documentation is very sporadic. Many dioceses, parishes, movements, and small communities print study guides, flyers, and programs of different kinds. But, in my experience, centralized archives do not exist: documentation is often a catch-as-catch-can process. A number of religious orders in Latin America do keep archives, as do missionary groups like Maryknoll in the United States. There are also a great many Latin American religious journals, appearing on a more or less regular basis, which deserve to be rescued from seminary libraries for more general use (see Lernoux, 1980; Levine, 1985).

The only way I know to deal with the problem of documentation is to strive for various kinds of evidence, keeping a firm grip on the way any particular statement or document fits into a larger whole. This requires interpretation, and interpretation is the final problem I want to mention. Effective interpretation requires a number of precautions, including careful attention to institutional agendas, to the language ordinary people use, and to the structure and reconstructed history of groups and localities. These necessarily imperfect measures provide the best possible sources for any interpretation which aspires to rise above the terms of the formal agenda from which elites construct the written record we know as history.

Programmatic Notes

1.   The strategy here outlined in general terms is intended to allow systematic analysis of the links between everyday life and

larger structures, without reifying such elements as class, culture, or institutions.

2. Such analysis is absolutely essential if we are to cast the structures of Latin American religion and politics in terms of real people, rather than abstractions or "the people" in general. Real individuals and groups think, feel, evaluate, and act in concrete and often contradictory circumstances. We are concerned with this real life, lived by real people.

3. We cannot, however, simply abandon general categories, or assume that each individual is unique. This would be foolish and self-defeating. Rather, we must reconstruct individual and collective experience by relating the categories uncovered in popular discourse to the "objective" structures of class, power, and meaning in which popular groups create their lives.

4. This perspective requires us to look closely at the sources of cultural transformations, and at the linkages between different levels and forms of expression. Ideas and culture thus appear not as disembodied, ethereal manifestations but rather as norms, concepts, and ways of seeing and making sense of the world. All of these emerge within the context of structures and institutions, and all are shaped by them. Ideas acquire ordered social power through their relationships with these structures, and with the needs and agendas of emergent classes and groups.

5. I have phrased the matter in this way because, while stressing the need for cultural analysis, I want to avoid the very notable errors of the "political culture school." This approach saw culture as a homogeneous and static determinant of behavior, but paid very little attention to either its structure or to the conflicts arising within and around it. I, for one, do not want to overcome the blinders of classical liberal or Marxist analysis-- which made cultural issues largely epiphenomenal--simply to fall into the opposite error.

6. Religion is particularly relevant to the contemporary scene, both as a source of ideas, organizations, leadership, and commitments, and as a critical arena of struggle. If recent experience in Latin America (or, indeed, throughout the world) teaches us anything, it is surely that we must abandon conventional assumptions about the relationship between modernization and secularization, which presume an inevitable decline in religion's public salience. The Latin American experience offers innumerable examples of creative syntheses of religion and politics, syntheses that find special vitality at the level of grass roots organizations and popular religious expression.

7. We must also shed the assumption that religious ideas, strategies, and organizations are epiphenomenal, the mere by-products of social, economic, and political interests somehow more rational and real. Religion (ideas, practices, and groups) clearly creates interests of its own. As noted earlier, the bonds and

values arising from religion have independent implications for politics.

8.   I believe that careful attention to <u>organized</u> social life helps uncover the autonomous logic and dynamic of religious change.   Participants may find satisfaction in group membership per se, just as they may in organizing and carrying out the specific agendas that the group establishes for itself.

9.   Research must grasp this point if we are to comprehend the real sources of motivation and commitment at issue in religion and politics today.   Most of the groups that have captured the headlines, such as the base communities in Central America, began as religious organizations and were later radicalized by experience.   They arose from religious motives.   Religious values and the experience of membership and solidarity within religious groups underlie their subsequent capacity for sustained action, and give moral conviction to their commitments.

10.   The problem for scholars is to document the lives and perspectives of ordinary people in an effective and faithful way. The changing issues of religion and politics provide the context, but it is concrete individuals, groups, and movements that breathe life into the process.   Ordinary people have a central role to play, and their ideas are as vital to analysis and under-standing as the more easily documented positions of elites and formal institutions.   It is difficult to combine so many kinds and levels of reality, but the task is essential if we are to grasp the process of change in all its richness and to achieve durable, reliable understanding.   While the task is hard, it is not impossible.   George Eliot's words may guide us as we work:

> We need not shrink from this comparison of small things with great, for does not science tell us that its highest striving is after a unity which shall bind the smallest things with the greatest?   In natural science, I have understood, there is nothing petty to the mind that has a large vision of relations, and to which every single object suggests a vast sum of conditions.   It is surely the same with the observation of human life.   (<u>The Mill on the Floss</u> [New York, 1983], p. 287).

BIBLIOGRAPHY

Berryman, P.   <u>The Religious Roots of Rebellion: Christians in the Central American Revolutions</u>.   Maryknoll, NY: Orbis Books, 1984.

Comaroff, J.   <u>Body of Power, Spirit of Resistance</u>.   Chicago, IL: University of Chicago Press, 1985.

Fields, K.   <u>Revival and Rebellion in Colonial Central Africa</u>. Princeton, NJ: Princeton University Press, 1985.

Ileto, R.   Pasyon and Revolution: Popular Movements in the
    Philippines, 1840–1910.   Manila: Ateneo de Manila University
    Press, 1979.
Lernoux, P.   "The Latin American Church," Latin American
    Research Review, 15:2 (1980), 201–211.
Levine, D.   Popular Religion, the Churches, and Political Conflict
    in Latin America.   Chapel Hill, NC: University of North
    Carolina Press, 1986.
_____.   "Religion and Politics: Drawing Lines, Under-
    standing Change."   Latin American Research Review, 20:1
    (1985), 185–201.
Mainwaring, S.   The Catholic Church and Politics in Brazil,
    1916–1985.   Stanford, CA: Stanford University Press, 1985.

24. THE LITERATURE OF OUTSIDERS: THE LITERATURE OF THE GAY COMMUNITY IN LATIN AMERICA

Robert Howes

The purpose of this paper is to give an overall view of the literature published by, for, and concerning the gay community in Latin America. It concentrates on works of fiction and non-fiction which deal explicitly with homosexuality, whether they are written by homosexuals or heterosexuals, and the literature produced by gay groups and movements. By homosexuality I mean erotic love and sexual relations between individuals of the same sex, whether men or women. For the sake of brevity I refer to any works on this subject as gay literature or gay publications.

The perception of homosexuality exists on two levels. In the first place it is a very intimate and personal matter: what it means to the individual to be gay, to be attracted to members of one's own sex, or to fall head-over-heels in love. But it is also a social and political matter: the individual lives in the wider community and is deeply affected by the attitudes of others towards homosexual behaviour. And the dynamics of prejudice or tolerance have ramifications which spread throughout the social system.

Gay literature reflects these perceptions in many different ways. On the one hand, it is a means of self-expression for the individual, reaching out to other gays and helping to break down the isolation and loneliness in which many gay people find themselves. On the other hand, it moulds the patterns of social interactions between gays and the wider community, reflecting either attempts by elements of the majority to explain and control--if not suppress--homosexual behaviour; increasingly in recent years, efforts by gay people to assert the validity of a gay identity to society at large.

Author's Note. I should like to express my gratitude to the many people who have provided me with material and advice, with particular thanks to João Antônio Mascarenhas, Luiz Mott, and Oscar Delepiani. The opinions expressed are, of course, my own responsibility.

Editor's Note. See also the author's "Select Bibliography of Latin American Publications Dealing with Homosexuality," Volume II, pp. 580-591.

Unlike most ethnic, religious, or cultural minorities, gays are not born into a community. The term "gay community" represents an aspiration rather than a fact. But gay literature is a powerful vehicle for forming a gay community. The novelist L. P. Hartley once wrote "The past is a foreign country: they do things differently there."[1] For gay people the response to that is--well, yes and no. Looking back over the past we note changing interpretations of homosexuality, and yet we can also see the same basic feelings and forms of behaviour recurring over the years. There is a sense of continuity with the past. For any community it is important to know that is has a history. Gay publications help to create a community in the present. Equally important, they are essential elements in forming a community which spans the passage of time, based on a shared culture.

Gay Literature in Latin America: General Characteristics

Works dealing with homosexuality have been published in Latin America since the late nineteenth century and have covered a wide variety of forms and disciplines. The main categories are imaginative literature, that is, fiction, poetry and drama; memoirs; scientific, medical, legal, and academic publications based on research; and polemical literature and publications issued by gay groups for the gay community. I discuss these categories in general terms before going on to survey the gay literature of the main Latin American countries.

The portrayal of homosexual characters has a long history in the Iberian Peninsula, beginning with the satirical entremeses "El marión" and "Los mariones" by the seventeenth-century Spanish playwright Luis Quiñones de Benavente, and continuing with the naturalist novel O Barão de Lavos by the Portuguese writer Abel Botelho, which was first published in 1891.[2] In Latin America the explicit portrayal of gay characters began with Aluísio Azevedo's novel O cortiço and Adolfo Caminha's Bom-Crioulo, published in 1890 and 1895, respectively.

There has been, to my knowledge, no overall study of the treatment of homosexual characters in Latin American literature, but there are a number of anthologies and studies which act as useful pointers. The most accessible to North American readers are two anthologies of Latin American gay fiction in translation, published in San Francisco by Gay Sunshine Press: Now the Volcano (1979) and My Deep Dark Pain Is Love (1983). Both were edited by Winston Leyland. These two anthologies are the essential starting point for identifying Latin American writers who have written on gay themes; they include writers from Mexico, Brazil, Colombia, Argentina, Cuba, and Chile.

There are two pioneering anthologies of Brazilian writings with a gay theme: Histórias do amor maldito (1967) and Poemas do amor maldito (1969), edited by Gasparino Damata and Walmir Ayala. The editors have drawn their net quite widely and include stories such as "Pìlades e Orestes" by Machado de Assis, where the homoerotic element is only lightly touched upon. It illustrates both the richness to be found in imaginative literature and the difficulties of defining a gay publication. Two anthologies of erotic fiction, Zero zero sexo: o erotismo no romance brasileiro contemporâneo (1967), edited by Edilberto Coutinho, and El cuento erótico en México (1975), edited by Enrique Jaramillo Levi, contain some stories involving gay characters.

There have been few studies on Latin American gay writing, but three should particularly be mentioned. Alfredo Villanueva analyses the treatment of gay characters in a number of Spanish American novels in "Machismo vs. Gayness: Latin American Fiction," an article published in Gay Sunshine in 1976. In his final conclusions he says, "Some authors have seized upon homosexuality as a metaphor for the expression of particular religious or metaphysical ideas about the nature of reality and its relationship to creativity. Homosexuals [in the novels analysed] usually belong to highly visible groups which are by nature also quite marginal. No one has dealt with the homosexual within the social mainstream."[3] These observations provide a useful point of reference, although they are less true now than when the article was published, and they apply more to Spanish American than to Brazilian literature. Nevertheless, and perhaps for this reason, Spanish American novels have had a wider appeal. Two in particular have achieved international acclaim: José Lezama Lima's Paradiso and Manuel Puig's El beso de la mujer araña. Other studies of gay writing are Luis Canales, "O homossexualismo como tema no moderno teatro brasileiro" (1981) and Karl Reinhardt, "The image of gays in Chicano prose fiction" (1981).

Non-fiction works which deal with homosexuality cover a wide range of disciplines from history and anthropology to medicine, psychiatry, law, and criminology. Historical research, which may cover all these fields in its search for materials, is only in its early stages in Latin America. Two overall views of the position of gays in Latin American culture and society are E. A. Lacey, "Latin America: Myths and Realities" (1979), and Peter Fry, "Da hierarquia à igualdade: a construção histórica da homossexualidade no Brasil" (1982).

Brazilian anthropologist Luiz Mott has searched Inquisition records in the Torro do Tombo in Portugal for documents on trials for sodomy in Brazil and is currently writing up the results. He has also compiled a bibliography on homosexuality in Brazil (see Volume II, pp. 592-609). Francisco Guerra's The Pre-Columbian Mind (1971) analyses the varying attitudes towards homosexuality and sodomy amongst the indigenous peoples as described by the Spanish chroniclers, whilst the anthropologist Peter Fry reviews the literature on homosexuality and the Afro-Brazilian cults in a paper in his book Para inglês ver (1982). A constant subject of research is male homosexual behaviour. Works published over the years by doctors, lawyers, criminologists, sociologists, and journalists provide valuable evidence of the continuity of the homosexual sub-culture.

Finally, there are the publications produced by the gay liberation groups, a relatively recent phenomenon of gays talking openly and directly to gays. Most of these publications take the form of leaflets or serials which are often published very irregularly owing to the financial, social, and personal pressures faced by the publishers. The most notable was the Brazilian journal Lampião, which was published regularly for three years from 1978 to 1981. Details on current publications are given below.

I conclude this section with two general points. Firstly, throughout this paper I have used the words gay and homosexual to refer to both male and female homosexuals. In point of fact, however, the vast majority of the publications I have seen refer to gay men; the amount produced by and for lesbians is relatively small. It may be that there is a wealth of material relating to lesbians in Latin American feminist publications with which I am not familiar. However, my impression is that there is not a great deal of material, perhaps because lesbians have either lacked the financial or organisational means to produce their own publications, or have concentrated their efforts on the feminist movement. Wherever I have been able to find any, however, I have included references to lesbians in the following sections.

The second point concerns the relationship between homosexuals and the Left. This is a recurring theme throughout the literature, and has been brought to prominence by the treatment of gays in post-revolutionary Cuba. The fundamental conflict is between, on the one hand, gay activists who regard homosexuality as subversive of the existing social order and therefore revolutionary, together with left-wing activists who happen to be homosexual and wish to be able to live openly as such as a matter of personal honesty; and, on the other, traditional left-wingers who regard homosexuality either as a bourgeois deviation on a level with prostitution and therefore counter-revolutionary or, at best, as a diversion from the fundamentally important issue of the class struggle. The issue emerges in works both of fiction and non-fiction, as is discussed in the following sections.

Brazil

Brazil figures prominently in this paper both because it is the country I know best and because it has a very rich and varied gay literature and culture. A forthcoming book by João Silvério Trevisan, to be published in London by Gay Men's Press, will probably become the main introduction to gay life in Brazil for English-speaking readers. The book, provisionally and somewhat inelegantly entitled Perverts in Paradise, discusses all aspects of Brazilian gay life and culture and covers history, the

Inquisition, the Brazilian Indians, psychiatry, transvestism, literature, the theatre and television, the gay movement and relations with the Left, cruising, AIDS, Carnaval, and candomblé. A book intended for the general reader rather than academic scholars, it nevertheless contains much factual information and beautifully conveys the exuberance of gay life in Brazil. A smaller but useful introduction which has already been published is Peter Fry and Edward MacRae, O que é homossexualidade (1983).

The best introductions to Brazilian gay literature are the anthologies edited by Gasparino Damata and Walmir Ayala, and the article on the theatre by Luis Canales, which have already been mentioned. Any review of Brazilian literature, however, must start with Adolfo Caminha's novel Bom-Crioulo, first published in Rio de Janeiro in 1895. The novel tells the story of a black sailor, Bom-Crioulo, who falls in love with and seduces a white cabin-boy, Aleixo, who is serving on the same warship. They set up home together in a room rented from a Portuguese washer-woman, Dona Carolina, in the Rua da Misericordia in Rio de Janeiro. All goes well until Aleixo is seduced by the washer-woman and loses interest in Bom-Crioulo. Isolated in a naval hospital, Bom-Crioulo is wracked by feelings of love, jealousy, and despair which finally drive him to the tragic dénouement.

Bom-Crioulo is a remarkable novel because of the sober, dis-passionate style in which it is told and for the open, objective way in which the author--who was almost certainly heterosexual--describes and accepts his hero's homosexuality. Although Caminha is generally numbered among the Brazilian naturalists, there are no attempts in the novel to find scientific or patho-logical explanations for Bom-Crioulo's condition. Both author and character accept it as a fact of life. Bom-Crioulo emerges as a tragic hero, consumed and ennobled by a great passion. The novel is one of the high points of nineteenth-century Brazilian literature, and it is still relevant and readable today. An English translation was published by Gay Sunshine Press in 1982.

Other early Brazilian novels which contain references to homosexuality are Aluísio Azevedo's O cortiço (1890), whose minor characters include three classic homosexual stereotypes: the dirty old man, Botelho, who touches up a student; the effeminate Albino who spends most of his time among the washerwomen; and the predatory lesbian prostitute, Léonie. Raul Pompeia's O Atheneu (1888) contains some veiled references to emotional and sexual relationships amongst the pupils of the boarding school which gives the book its name.

The setting of a boarding school is taken up again in Paulo Hecker Filho's novelette Internato (1951), and the question of homosexuality is treated quite explicitly. While by no means great literature, Internato seems to be the first of the modern wave of Brazilian literature in which homosexuality forms the central theme and is openly referred to. A prolific writer who has dealt with the subject in several works is Walmir Ayala. His play Nosso filho vai ser mãe (1965) is a plea for tolerance of homosexuals; his novel Un animal de Deus (1967) also has a homosexual theme.

The other editor of the two anthologies mentioned earlier, Gasparino Damata, is also the author of a book of short stories, Os solteirões (1976), which describe realistically the lives of homosexual men in Rio de Janeiro. The characters are of various social classes, but the stories tend to concentrate on the relationships of mutual but unequal exploitation between older, richer, and more powerful men and their young, poor, but desired partners. The stories are told in a lively, colloquial style while the narrator adopts a dispassionate although slightly sad and disenchanted attitude. The story "Muro de silêncio," which describes the end of a relationship between a middle-class man and a marine, is particularly evocative.

Other writers who have published novels or short stories with gay themes are Aguinaldo Silva, Caio Fernando Abreu, Roberto Freire, João Silvério Trevisan and Darcy Penteado. Darcy Penteado, who is prominent as an artist and a spokesman for gay rights as well as a writer, has published a novel, Nivaldo e Jerônimo (1981), which recounts the vicissitudes of a love affair between a left-wing activist who becomes a guerrilla in the Araguaia and a good-looking but apolitical younger man. The story is highly idealised and begs many questions as to what would happen in reality, but it has its charm as a vision of what the relationship between gays and the Left might be.

A more pessimistic view on this subject emerges from the memoirs of a left-wing guerrilla, Herbert Daniel, Passagem para o próximo sonho (1982). Written in exile in Paris, where the author was working as an attendant in a gay sauna, the book gives a critical account of his activities as an urban guerrilla in the late 1960s and early 1970s, and describes the hostile reaction he faced when he tried to discuss the question of homosexuality at a meeting of Brazilian exiles in Paris.

An important book of memoirs is A queda para o alto (1982) by Sandra Mara Herzer, alias Anderson Herzer or Bigode, in which the author describes the brutal conditions she faced in the state orphanages in which she was brought up. It is not clear whether Herzer was a lesbian or a female to male transsexual, but the book represents a graphic testimony of the problems encountered by women in the poor classes.

Turning now to academic and scientific works, particular mention should be made of the theses written by medical students, which are valuable sources of information about social conditions in Rio de Janeiro and other cities. Of relevance to this paper are José Ricardo Pires de Almeida, Homossexualismo: a libertinagem no Rio de Janeiro (1906) and Jorge Jaime,

Homossexualismo masculino (1947). In the 1930s, research was
carried out by Leonidio Ribeiro, one of the leading exponents of
forensic medicine in Brazil. The dubious implications of this
research are discussed in Mariza Corrêa, "Antropologia e medicina
legal: variações em torno de um mito" and Peter Fry, "Febrônio
Indio do Brasil: onde cruzam a psiquiatria, a profecia, a homossexualidade e a lei." Much of the recent research has been
carried out by anthropologists and the results, including the
papers mentioned above, have been published in Caminhos
cruzados: linguagem, antropologia e ciências naturais (1982) and
in Peter Fry, Para inglês ver: identidade e política na cultura
brasileira (1982).

This brings us to the literature of the gay liberation movement. This sprang up rapidly in the late 1970s under the
influence of similar movements in North America and Western
Europe, and following the political liberalisation instituted by
Brazil's military regime. At one stage there were twenty-two gay
groups functioning in Brazil, but the number has now dropped to
five. Leila Míccolis in Jacarés e lobisomens: dois ensaios sobre a
homossexualidade (1983) includes a detailed history of the
Brazilian gay movement from 1978 to 1982 as well as a list of gay
journals from the 1960s to the 1980s. There is also a general
survey of the gay movement, Os homoeróticos (1983), by the
journalist Délcio Monteiro de Lima. However, this is so full of
factual errors and wild sweeping statements unsubstantiated by
any supporting evidence as to be practically valueless. An
interesting essay on the attitudes of gay activists towards the
political implications of camping it up (fechação) is Edward
MacRae, "Os respeitáveis militantes e as bichas loucas" (1982).
Relations between the gay liberation movement and left-wing
political parties are discussed in Hiro Okita, Homossexualismo: da
opressão a libertação (1981?), and in various papers in Sexo e
poder (1979), edited by Guido Mantega. During the November,
1982 elections, leaflets aimed at attracting gay voters were issued
by Leonel Brizola's Partido Democrático Trabalhista and Lula's
Partido dos Trabalhadores; a collection of these is now in the
British Library, London.

The most important gay journal by far was Lampião, which
was published regularly each month from April, 1978 to June,
1981, with a total of thirty-eight issues. It was published by a
collective of gay writers and activists which was formed as a
result of the visit to Brazil by Winston Leyland, the editor of Gay
Sunshine Press, when he was collecting material for the anthology
Now the Volcano. Lampião was printed in tabloid newspaper
format, and sold on the newsstands in Rio and other large cities
as well as by subscription. It contained a variety of
well-researched articles, interviews with prominent gay personalities, information on the activities of gay groups and the gay

movement, and various other items, all produced in a lively, professional journalistic style.

In September, 1978, the Ministry of Justice attempted to prosecute Lampião for corrupting public morals and good mores. Following protests both within Brazil and from abroad, the case was shelved in January, 1980. Lampião made a large contribution to the upsurge of the Brazilian gay movement, and its pages provide a valuable record of the movement. They also offer an important source of information on popular urban culture (in which gays play a prominent role)--an area which has been largely neglected by academic researchers. Lampião ceased publication with its June, 1981 issue owing to financial difficulties and dissension amongst the editorial board. The editor, Aguinaldo Silva, then brought out a new publication, Pleiguei, which had a more consumerist style. It folded after four issues.

Several of the gay groups in Brazil have produced publications, some of which continue to appear--albeit rather irregularly. In São Paulo the Grupo Somos published a journal, O corpo, containing news, comment, articles, and short stories (three issues from 1982 to 1983). The Grupo Outra Coisa published O bandeirante destemido: um guia gay de São Paulo (1981), a well-produced and amusingly illustrated guide to the gay scene in São Paulo. In the same city the Grupo Ação Lésbica Feminista continues to publish Chanacomchana at irregular intervals. This is one of the few publications produced by and for lesbians, and contains political comment, theoretical articles, interviews, personal testimonies, and poetry.

The only other group currently publishing in Brazil is the Grupo Gay de Bahia, based in Salvador. This is the most active Brazilian group, and it coordinated the campaign to have article 302.0 of the International Classification of Diseases (which classifies homosexuality as a Sexual deviation and disorder) declared null and void in Brazil. The GGB publishes a mimeographed "Boletim" which appears irregularly and which contains analytical articles as well as news items from Brazil and around the world. It for some time collected newspaper reports on gays who had been murdered, and it published an analysis of this information in its issue no. 10 of January, 1985. The GGB has also been appointed by the International Gay Association to act as an information centre for all the Latin American groups, and now publishes the "Informativo del Secretariado Latino-Americano de Grupos Homosexuales" (S.L.A.G.H.) in a format similar to the "Boletim." The "Informativo" is written in what the editors themselves admit to be "portuñol"! In 1982 the GGB held a poetry competition and published the best entries in a small booklet entitled 24 poemas gays (1982). The cover has a picture of two men kissing, designed in the style of literatura de cordel booklets; the picture has been taken up and reproduced in gay publications around the world.

The other side of gay polemics is illustrated by a book written by Reuel P. Feitosa, O avesso do amor (1978), which strongly condemns homosexuality from a traditional, religious standpoint. The Pope's views on the subject are well known, but it would be interesting to know if liberation theology has had anything positive to say on the matter.

Brazil may not be exactly a pervert's paradise, but gays are an accepted, if not particularly respected, part of life, at least in the large cities. The easy-going tolerance of Brazilian attitudes, coupled with an underlying amoral realism, is nicely captured in a short story by the gay writer Darcy Penteado, "Bofe a prazo fixo." A young worker in São Paulo who desperately needs money to get married is introduced, through the good offices of his cousin, to a rich, elderly homosexual. They have a sexual relationship and Angelo, the worker, earns enough money to meet all his commitments. After he gets married they give up sexual relations but remain friends and, when he has his first child, he invites his ex-lover to be the godfather. "Afinal todo bom pai deve garantir desde cedo o futuro dos filhos" ["After all, every good father should early on guarantee the future of his children"].[4]

Cuba

Cuba has many similarities to Brazil in terms of climate, ethnic composition, and cultural background, and yet the position of gays is markedly different. Cuba is one of the few countries in the world where the treatment of homosexuals has had major political and international repercussions. The increasing pressure to conform exerted on Cuban writers and intellectuals (many of them gays) in the mid-1960s, and the UMAP labour camps to which many gays were sent in the period 1965-1967, were major factors contributing to the international intelligentsia's disenchantment with the Cuban Revolution.[5] The Mariel exodus in 1980, with its large gay component, was a blow to the prestige of the Cuban government; the wounds have been reopened by the recent film Improper Conduct, directed by Nestor Almendros and Orlando Jiménez Leal.

It is difficult for an outsider to know how much the campaigns against homosexuals are the result of the internal political and ideological dynamics of the Revolution, and how much they reflect traditional Cuban attitudes. A Cuban-born criminologist who was brought up in the United States, Luis Salas, comments that "A great amount of criticism has been leveled at Cuba as a result of its treatment of homosexuals. An interesting feature of this criticism is that the bulk has come from members of the U.S. New Left, rather than from conservative Cuban exiles or Americans."[6]

A number of writers have described and commented on the treatment of Cuban homosexuals since Fidel Castro took power.

Guillermo Cabrera Infante gives a very personal account of what happened to writers and intellectuals in the 1960s in a lengthy article, "Bites from the Bearded Crocodile," published in the London Review of Books in 1981. The poet José Mario details the repercussions of American poet Allen Ginsberg's visit to Cuba, and his own imprisonment in a labour camp, in an article published in 1969. Carlos Alberto Montaner chronicles the effect of the campaign against gays and reproduces the text of the Declaración del Primer Congreso Nacional de Educación y Cultura, 30 April 1971, condemning homosexuality, in the chapter "Sexo malo" of his book Informe secreto sobre la Revolución Cubana (1976).

An important and relatively objective source on the day-to-day situation of gays is Luis Salas, Social Control and Deviance in Cuba (1979), especially Chapter 4, "Sexual Deviance: Homosexuals and the Revolution." The main radical American writer on the subject is Allen Young, who recorded his growing disillusionment with the Revolution because of its treatment of homosexuals in Gays under the Cuban Revolution (1981) and earlier articles.

Cuban attitudes towards homosexuality are explored in the section "Los cubanos y el homosexualismo" of the literary review Mariel, no. 5, founded by exiles who left in the boatlift in 1980. The American gay press of the period had many articles on the number of gays amongst the refugees, and there is a telling photograph in the Brazilian magazine Visão showing slogans painted on the house of someone who left the country. These read "Vende Patria. ¡Que se vayan! Traidor. Aquí vivió un traidor homosexual. H.P. ¡Viva Fidel!" The word "Homosexual" is written in the largest letters.[7] In December, 1981 El caimán barbudo published an article, "Western" by Rodolfo González Almaguer, which ridiculed the gay movement in the United States as a sign of American decadence and weakness.

The recent film Improper Conduct, which explores the treatment of gays after the Revolution, has led to both attacks by supporters of the Cuban Revolution and heart searching amongst gay socialists.[8] It remains to be seen whether the Cuban authorities significantly change their attitudes. A gay Spanish sympathiser of the Revolution who visited Cuba recently, while not trying to minimise or excuse the repression of gays, saw some signs that the government is beginning to change its mind.[9]

Turning to literature now, a number of Cuban writers have dealt with homosexuality in their works. But whereas Brazilian writers tend to give a realistic or humorous picture of gay people and their everyday lives, Cuban writers have taken an altogether more profound and serious view of the subject. Perhaps this reflects the greater pressures which gays experience in Cuba.

The most famous work which has homosexuality as a major theme is José Lezama Lima's novel Paradiso (1966). This vast celebration of bourgeois life, with its baroque imagery, contains a lengthy philosophical disquisition on homosexuality and a number of explicit sexual scenes. The novel as a whole is not necessarily a defence of homosexuality since the gay proponent, Foción, later goes mad; but the theme alone was sufficient to cause it problems. Shortly after it was published, Paradiso was withdrawn from the bookshops on the grounds that it was pornographic. Orders from higher up soon led to it being put back on sale but, as far as I know, there have been no later Cuban editions since the first one of 1966, although it is one of the great Cuban novels of the twentieth century.[10]

Rivalling Paradiso in its esoteric language and imagery is Severo Sarduy's Cobra (1972), which has a transvestite as its main character (I think!). More accessible and moving is Reinaldo Arenas' Arturo, la estrella más brillante, published in 1984 but written in 1971, which describes the feelings and thoughts of a young homosexual imprisoned in a labour camp.

Finally, for its historical interest, one should mention the novel El ángel de Sodoma by Alfonso Hernández Catá, a minor Cuban writer who spent most of his life in Spain. It is set in Europe and tells the story of a young aristocratic homosexual who is riddled with shame and guilt, and commits suicide rather than besmirch the family name. The first edition was published in Madrid in 1928.

Mexico

My information on the literature of the other Spanish-speaking countries is relatively limited, and I should be glad to receive any further leads. Of particular interest in Mexico is the number of periodicals which have been published by gay liberation groups. These include Nuestro cuerpo (1979), published by the Colectivo Mariposas Negras del Frente Homosexual de Acción Revolucionaria; Nuevo ambiente (1981), published by the Grupo Lambda de Liberación Homosexual; Política sexual (1979?) of the Frente Homosexual de Acción Revolucionaria; and ¡Y qué! (1984-85), which is currently being published in Tijuana. There was also a publication for lesbians, Amazona (1979?), published by the Colectivo de lesbianas del Frente Homosexual de Acción Revolucionaria in Mexico City, which I have not seen.

The behaviour of Mexican gay men has been studied by two American Ph.D. students, Joseph Michel Carrier, "Urban Mexican Male Homosexual Encounters: An Analysis of Participants and Coping Strategies" (1972); and Clark Louis Taylor, Jr. "El Ambiente: Male Homosexual Social Life in Mexico City" (1978), with related articles published in academic periodicals. There is a work by Ramón Valdiosera Bermán, El lesbianismo en México (1973) but, judging from the compiler's annotations to the bibliography, the subject has been treated in an unsympathetic, sensationalist way from a male viewpoint.[11]

The Gay Sunshine anthology <u>Now the Volcano</u> included a short memoir by the poet and dramatist Salvador Novo which vividly describes his sexual adventures in the 1920s. This tradition was carried on into the 1960s and 1970s by the hero of the novel <u>Las aventuras, desventuras y sueños de Adonis García, el vampiro de la Colonia Roma</u> (1979) by Luis Zapata. This work, written in a highly colloquial style, won the Grijalbo Prize and has been translated into English with the title <u>Adonis García: A Picaresque Novel</u> (1981). Another work which describes the Mexican gay world is <u>El vino de los bravos</u> (1981) by Luis González de Alba.

Argentina

Argentina had one of the earliest gay liberation groups in Latin America, the Frente de Liberación Homosexual de la Argentina, which produced at least two publications, <u>Homosexuales</u> (1973) and <u>Somos</u> (1974). Its manifesto was published in English in <u>Gay Sunshine</u> in 1972. The group was subsequently wiped out by the military dictatorship. The repression is chronicled in "Sufoco na Argentina," published in <u>Lampião</u>, no. 21, February 1980 and "Dossier: Argentine, exil et repression," published in the Parisian gay journal <u>Masques</u>, no. 11, Autumn 1981. Gay groups are being re-established in Argentina following the restoration of democracy and, despite continuing difficulties, have begun publishing again. <u>Diferentes</u> (1984) is a discreet magazine oriented towards the middle-class consumer, and I have seen recent references to <u>Postdata</u>, published by the Grupo Federativo Gay, and <u>Sodoma</u>, published by the Grupo de Acción Gay, both in Buenos Aires.

Two monographs of interest are Carlos Da Gris, <u>El homosexual en la Argentina</u> (1965), which appeals for tolerance and understanding towards gays; and Paco Jamandreu, <u>La cabeza contra el suelo</u> (1975), the memoirs of a gay fashion designer who makes no bones about his homosexuality.

Of Argentinian writers who have written on a gay theme, the best known internationally is Manuel Puig, who broaches the topic of the Left and homosexuality in <u>El beso de la mujer araña</u> (1976). This consists mainly of dialogues between the two main characters, an effeminate homosexual and a heterosexual Marxist political prisoner; it strongly conveys the development of the relationship between the two.

Chile

The earliest novel with a gay theme written by a Spanish American writer which I have been able to trace is the work of a Chilean novelist, Augusto Goeminne Thomson, who wrote under the pseudonym Augusto d'Halmar. His novel <u>La pasión y muerte del cura Deusto</u>, first published in Madrid and Buenos Aires

around 1924, is set in Seville and tells the story of the relationship between a Basque priest and a young gypsy. José Donoso's
El lugar sin límites (1967) has as its central character
La Manuela, an aged transvestite queen who runs a brothel. The
novel conveys the conflicting feelings of scorn, attraction, fear,
and dependency between La Manuela, the macho Pancho Vega, and
the local landowner, Don Alejo.

Information on gay life in Chile is hard to come by, but a
certain amount can be found in A first report on the situation of
gays in Chile, prepared and researched by the Riksförbundet för
sexuellt likaberättigande, Sweden, for the 2d annual conference of
the International Gay Association in 1980.

Colombia, Venezuela, Guatemala

Colombia was the country of publication of Ventana gay,
which recently ceased publication. Although I have not seen a
copy, I am told it was one of the largest and best-produced of
Latin American gay publications. A small bulletin, De ambiente
(1985), is currently being produced by the Colectivo de Orgullo
Gay in Bogotá. Colombia was one of the few Latin American
countries which specifically legislated against homosexuality; this
is mentioned in Lisandro Martínez Z., Derecho penal sexual
(1977). A Colombian anthropologist, Manuel Lucena Salmoral,
records a case of berdache, that is, a man assuming a woman's
role in tribal life, among the Guahibo del Tomo Indians in the
Revista colombiana de antropología (1966/69).

Until recently, Venezuela had a well-produced gay journal,
Entendido, but this has now ceased publication. Finally, from
Guatemala, Hugo Carrillo's play La calle del sexo verde (1959)
contains a scene between a worldly-wise gay man and a gay
adolescent.

United States

The United States has played a considerable role in the
development of Latin American gay literature, both because of the
large number of Latinos living in the United States and the close
links between the United States and the countries further south.
The American gay movement has provided a powerful model for
groups in Latin America, as in other parts of the world, and the
word "gay" or "guei" is widely used, particularly in Brazil.

Publications produced in the United States are able to take
an overall view of the whole of Latin America. The literary
anthologies and translations published by Gay Sunshine Press in
San Francisco have already been mentioned. A very useful
source of information on gay liberation groups and their
publications is the bulletin Paz y liberación, published at
irregular intervals in Houston, Texas, in English, Spanish, and
Portuguese.

A number of publications are published by and for the Latino population in the United States. A well-produced journal is Sin fronteras, published in English in Denver, Colorado, and aimed at gay Latinos and lesbian Latinas. Its issue no. 2, Winter, 1985, was devoted to Nicaragua. According to Paz y liberación, the Gay & Lesbian Latinos Unidos group in Los Angeles publishes a newsletter called Unidad in English and Spanish. In 1980, the Tsunami Press of Seattle issued a collection of lesbian-feminist articles in Spanish and English under the title Salir a la luz como lesbianas de color/Coming Out Colored-- Maya Chumu.

The image of gays in Chicano novels has been analysed in a paper by Karl Reinhardt, which has already been mentioned. One of the leading gay writers in the United States, John Rechy is also counted as a Chicano writer, although this is not apparent to English readers of his gay novels such as City of Night (1963), Numbers (1967), The Sexual Outlaw (1977), and Rushes (1979).

Finally, news items and articles about Latin America regularly appear in the North American and European gay press. Papers which have printed reports on Latin America include Gay Community News (Boston, MA), The Body Politic (Toronto), Gay Times/Him Monthly (London), and Gai pied, Masques, and Homophonies (Paris). The International Gay Association has had a considerable influence in encouraging Latin American gay groups and publishes news about them in its Bulletin, issued by the Information Secretariat (c/o RFSL, Box 350, S-10124 Stockholm, Sweden).

Libraries and Gay Literature

Most research libraries specialising in Latin America should have at least some of the main literary and academic works discussed above, which can generally be acquired through the regular book trade or similar channels. Much more problematic are the publications of the gay groups. Two major collections of these are:

The Labadie Collection	Canadian Gay Archives
711 Harlan Hatcher Library	Box 639, Station A
The University of Michigan	Toronto, Ontario
Ann Arbor, MI 48109	Canada M5W 1G2

Annotations of their serials holdings are included in the bibliography.

The publications of gay groups can usually only be obtained directly from the groups themselves, or from gay or community bookshops. The groups are mostly small, short of funds, and suffering from the personal and social pressures inherent in assuming a gay identity. The gay movement in Latin America seems to be at a low ebb at the moment--groups tend to collapse quite frequently, and publications appear at irregular intervals. For this reason I have not generally given the addresses of groups and publications, but instead would refer those interested to the following publications, which give reasonably up-to-date information on groups, publications and addresses:

Sin fronteras, P.O. Box 1551, Denver, CO 80201, USA. (Subscription for one year, $10);

Paz y liberación, P.O. Box 600063, Houston, TX 77260, USA. (Subscription for four issues, $3);

Informativo del S.L.A.G.H. (Seretariado Latino-Americano de Grupos Homosexuales), SLAGH, Caixa Postal 2552, 40.000 Salvador, Bahia, Brazil. (No subscription rate given, but I suggest a donation of $5. The Boletim do Grupo Gay da Bahia can be obtained from the same address; I suggest a similar donation.)

In writing to Latin American gay groups, care should be taken only to use the initials and not the full name of the group in order to avoid problems with the mail. Enquiries should be accompanied by personal correspondence, and a donation or subscription.

In this paper I have not touched upon the vexed question of pornography. Gay publications, however, of whatever type, face harrassment and censorship at any stage in their circulation. Too many people in authority still regard the very mention of homosexuality as obscene. The British Customs and Excise is currently conducting a campaign against imported gay books. Amongst the books seized and which must therefore be considered as officially banned in Britain are the two Gay Sunshine anthologies, Now the Volcano and My Deep Dark Pain Is Love, which contain original material by such important Latin American writers as Manuel Puig, Reinaldo Arenas, and Salvador Novo. The directors of Gay's the Word, London's main community bookshop, have been charged with conspiring to evade the prohibition on importation of indecent or obscene material. The trial is likely to be a major test of censorship and civil liberties in Britain.[12]

I hope that this paper has illustrated something of the richness and variety of Latin American gay literature. It is a preliminary draft, and makes no claim to being comprehensive. I should welcome any further information which anyone can supply for the final version. In the meantime, I hope that it will encourage librarians and others to preserve, explore, and promote Latin America's gay literary heritage.

Postscript

Since writing this paper, my attention has been drawn by Professor Wayne Dynes to two further articles which provide useful guides to gay fiction and novels with homosexual characters: Stephen Wayne Foster, "Latin American Studies, Part I, Homosexuality in Central American Fiction, 1894-1927; Part II,

Augusto D'Halmar and 'El amor oscuro'," published in The Cabirion and Gay Books Bulletin (New York, NY) in 1984; and Kessel Schwartz, "Homosexuality as a Theme in Representative Contemporary Spanish American Novels," published in the Kentucky Romance Quarterly in 1975. I have incorporated many of the works mentioned in these articles and the publications referred to in the main paper into the bibliography, using the entries in NUC where I have not been able to consult a copy of the work myself.

A forthcoming monograph in the Gai Saber series, no. 5, edited by Stephen O. Murray and Wayne Dynes, will be devoted to Latin American gay literature. A new lesbian journal, Al margen, published by the Grupo de Autoconciencia de Lesbianas Feministas, has recently begun to appear in Lima.

NOTES

1.   L.   P.   Hartley,   The   Go-between   (Repr., Harmondsworth: Penguin Books, 1971), p. 7.

2.   Luis Quiñones de Benavente, "Entremés famoso: Los Mariones" and "Entremés del Marión," in Emilio Cotarelo y Mori, ed., Colección de entremeses, loas, bailes, jácaras y mojigangas desde fines del siglo XVI a mediados del XVIII, Tomo I, vol. 1 (Madrid: Bailly-Bailliere, 1911), pp. 595-598 and 722-725; Abel Botelho, O Barão de Lavos, 2d ed., rev. (Porto: Livraria Chardron, De Lello & Irmão, 1898).

3.   Alfredo Villanueva, "Machismo vs. Gayness: Latin American Fiction," Gay Sunshine, 29/30 (Summer/Fall, 1976), p. 22.

4.   Darcy Penteado, "Bofe a prazo fixo," in his Teoremambo (São Paulo: Cultura, 1979), pp. 91-95; trans. as "Part-time Hustler" in My Deep Dark Pain Is Love . . . (San Francisco, CA: Gay Sunshine Press, 1983), pp. 241-244.

5.   UMAP = Unidades Militares de Apoyo a la Producción.

6.   Luis Salas, Social Control and Deviance in Cuba (New York, NY: Praeger, 1979), p. 150.

7.   See Gay Community News (Boston, MA), 7:44, 47, 48 (May-June, 1980); New York Native, 35 (April 12-25, 1982), 14, 35; Gay News (London), 191, p. 12; 196, pp. 7, 18; The Body Politic (Toronto), 65 (Aug. 1980); Gai pied (Paris), 19 (Oct. 1980), 14-15; Visão, 29:43 (Nov. 24, 1980), 32-33.

8.   Leaflet "Improper Conduct: A Proper Reply," distributed by the Britain-Cuba Resource Centre before the showing of the film at the 28th London Film Festival, Nov., 1984; Lesbian and Gay Socialist (London), Spring, 1985, p. 21.

9.   Garbi, "Cuba: primer 'territorio libre de América Latina' (ven y verás . . .)," Gay hotsa (Bilbao) 26 (Feb.-March, 1985), no page nos.

10. "Entrevista: Cintio Vitier," Areíto, 27 [1981], 30-34, esp. p. 33.

11. Meri Knaster, Women in Spanish America: An Annotated Bibliography from Pre-Conquest to Contemporary Times (Boston, MA: G. K. Hall, 1977), p. 271, item 1080.

12. Leaflets, "Gay's the Word and H.M. Customs. The seized titles," Oct. 1984; "Update," no. 3, May 1985, both issued by the Defend Gay's the Word Campaign, London. Adolfo Caminha's novel Bom-Crioulo of 1895 was also seized.

25. PERU AND THE 1985 ELECTORAL CAMPAIGN

Nancy E. van Deusen

January through April of 1985 were politically dynamic months in the history of Peruvian elections, as four chief political party candidates vied for the presidency. The contenders were Alan García Pérez for the Partido Aprista Peruano (PAP, more commonly referred to as APRA), with a social democratic platform; Alfonso Barrantes Lingán, representing the leftist coalition party Izquierda Unida (IU); Luis Bedoya Reyes, who formed a conservative coalition party, Convergencia Democrática (CODE), on the bases of the Partido Popular Cristiano (PPC) and the Movimiento de Bases Hayistas (MBH); and Javier Alva Orlandini, from the moderately conservative Acción Popular (AP). It was the first time in decades that two consecutive democratic presidential elections were held successfully and legitimately; the preceding vote had taken place in 1980. The only president-elect in the history of the sixty-one-year-old Partido Aprista Peruano, Alan García Pérez, is expected at this writing to be inaugurated on July 28, 1985. APRA is likely to win a majority in the House of Representatives and Senate as well.

Campaign strategists applied sophisticated methods learned from countries such as the United States and Germany in the 1985 elections. Television was utilized to a great degree in the metropolitan areas of Lima, Cuzco, Arequipa, and Trujillo. Radio, a more traditional medium, was used principally in the rural highlands and the lowlands. Printed pamphlets, brochures, and other materials were distributed in the mail, at rallies, individually by campaign workers, and through campaign headquarters. Banners, paintings with campaign slogans, and propaganda literally papered over Lima and other areas of Peru. Polls were taken weekly by various organizations to gauge voter sentiments.[1]

Changes in the use of the media can be traced to previous elections. If the elections of 1983 (for mayor of Lima) and 1985 are compared with those held in 1980, it is evident that candidates shifted away from the public arena of personal contact in Lima and other major cities, and relied more heavily upon television. Fernando Belaúnde Terry, Acción Popular's 1980 candidate for president, successfully utilized television to promote an image of working with the masses. Belaúnde's advertisements did more than merely denigrate the other candidate or espouse party ideology, and this worked to his advantage. Yet television was not used as extensively as in the 1983 and 1985 elections. Television now reaches most sectors of the urban Lima population, from the very wealthy and middle classes to the materially deprived inhabitants of the pueblos jóvenes (urban slum districts). While oratorical facility had been a requirement for previous campaigns, politicians were now demonstrating charisma, communication skills, and the ability to argue effectively in televised interviews and debates. Political talk shows with a format similar to the North American "Nightline" cropped up in the last year. Both presidential and congressional candidates appeared frequently to exhibit their rhetorical prowess before Lima audiences.[2]

Completely accurate figures are not yet available for expenditures of each political party. Nonetheless, several journals have attempted to estimate some of the campaign costs. The weekly Oiga, for example, analyzed each party's expenses for the various types of media employed during the campaign (table 1).

Table 1

CAMPAIGN COSTS IN THE 1985 PRESIDENTIAL ELECTION
(in U.S. dollars)

	Newspapers, magazines	Television, radio	Political rallies*	Placards, pamphlets	Total
APRA	800,000	1,800,000	1,000,000	140,000	3,740,000
CODE	450,000	1,100,000	500,000	150,000	2,220,000
IU	350,000	400,000	450,000	20,000	1,220,000
AP	200,000	500,000	800,000	120,000	1,620,000

Source: "Cuánto gastaron en la campaña electoral," Oiga, 224 (April 15, 1985), 16-17.

*Includes location, security, equipment, and mobility costs.

Some expenses in table 1 may be exaggerated or underestimated. Tallies of the number of publicity spots and the amount of TV time may provide a better indication of party expenditures.[3] Misrepresentation of costs may be attributed to the fact that each party maintains political connections with particular families who run the numerous dailies and television stations. According to Oiga, it is likely that APRA did not have to pay costs for advertisements in the two dailies La República and Hoy, whereas Izquierda Unida benefited from its close association with La República and El Diario de Marka. Acción Popular probably received reduced rates on Channel 4, and APRA on Channel 5.[4] Generally, radio time and other forms of media are less expensive, but campaign officials from Izquierda Unida and APRA both confirmed that more time was invested in television than other media for the Lima area.[5]

Outside Lima, candidates relied heavily on radio, local party organizations, and personal visits. Alfonso Barrantes, on a campaign excursion to Puno where television is not commonly found, mocked its excessive use. He said:

> Nosotros no tenemos equipos de televisión que inmortalicen estas multitudes y que nos graben estas manifestaciones para romperle los ojos con imágenes a quienes dicen que el pueblo no nos respalda. ¿Saben por qué no tenemos esos equipos? Porque como nuestro compromiso no es con todos los peruanos, los que tienen las cámaras de televisión no se sienten representados ni comprometidos con nosotros. . . .[6]

Alan García, very popular for his youth and his ideas for major changes, traveled more than any other presidential candidate, especially during the last ten days of the campaign in April. All the candidates knew that television had its limits outside the major urban centers and that, in the end, personal contact provided the most impressive way to communicate their political message.

In Lima's mayoral campaign of 1983, television and radio advertisements became paramount in associating party ideologies with representative images. Acción Popular, in an effort to taint the popular appeal of Izquierda Unida candidate Alfonso Barrantes, created an ad that subliminally suggested associations between IU and the Maoist terrorist group Sendero Luminoso (the Shining Path), which at that time had created a wave of panic in both Lima and the department of Ayucucho. In the 1985 presidential, senatorial, and congressional elections, television spots were equally important in conveying a kind of party image. Alan García was shown letting a dove fly out of his hand before an excited crowd (the dove and star are legendary symbols in the party's history), while the vals criollo "Mi Perú" played in the background. Music was employed successfully on both television and radio. Whether consciously or unconsciously, Peruvians identified themselves culturally with a specific candidate who chose a jingle set to huayno, vals criollo, or Afro-Peruvian music in campaign advertisements. The APRA party even produced a 45 rpm recording of songs used in Alan García's campaign!

Not only was music incorporated into campaign propaganda but each political candidate developed slogans with a kind of universalist appeal. People were at once to think that they belonged to a particular and unique socioeconomic group, and that they also belonged to the political unity that is Peru--coast, sierra, and selva. In the 1983 mayoral campaign, Barrantes used the slogan "una Lima para todos" to convey this idea of unity as he proposed to "democratize" the city and its people. In 1985, Alan García used the simple statement "mi compromiso es con todos los peruanos" in his speeches, television and radio advertisements, and street propaganda. Alfonso Barrante's slogan for the presidential campaign "justicia, paz y vida" was an attempt to disassociate the party from Sendero Luminoso and communism. Luis Bedoya (CODE) used a map of Peru as his image, and played upon his previous experience as mayor of Lima to convince voters that "Bedoya puede y debe ser Presidente." Television spots showed a concerned Javier Alva (AP), with a group of laborers, insisting that Peruvians recognize the laborers' accomplishments-- begun by outgoing-president Fernando Belaúnde Terry--and adding "que la obra no se detenga." The slogan "Peruanicemos al Perú" was adopted by AP to reflect the universality of their program as well.

The polls taken from January through April were not always reliable measures of public opinion. Nonetheless, secondary sources overflowed with their findings. Fernando Tuesta Soldevilla, author of the interesting work entitled El Nuevo rostro electoral; las municipales del '83, commented:

> Lamentablemente la importancia asignada, que se hizo evidente por la profusión de ellas, está más relacionada con la intención de influir que con la tarea de informar. Las empresas Peruana de Opinión Pública (POP), Datum, Inter-Gallup, y en menor medida Rivhi Internacional fueron las que llenaron los medios de comunicación con sus encuestas. Este nuevo elemento de la escena electoral se presentaba ante el electorado como protegido por una aureola de carácter científico, por el contorno de sus cifras, la proyección de sus resultados y la supuesta imparcialidad de sus pregun- tas. Supuestamente, su interés residía en el carácter de vaticinio y apuesta respecto al resultado final, lo que moviliza a todas las capas sociales a prestarle su atención y probablemente a persuadir sobre sus preferencias.[7]

Like television, which tended to present technologically slick, packaged advertisements to impress viewers, polls in Lima often claimed to be accurate and impartial. In fact, a precise methodology was often lacking, and the questions were framed in a tendentious manner.[8]

Voters received pamphlets and brochures at political rallies and through the mail. One negative result of this was a months- long congestion in the Lima post office, aggravated by a major workers' strike. Some individuals received propaganda in the middle of May which was postmarked from February (the election was April 14th!). The initial intent in sending this literature may have been negated by its tardy delivery. Nonetheless, these pamphlets are valuable to collect: they reflect particular candi- dates' views on how to solve Peru's multitudinous problems.

Apathy among Peruvian voters in 1985 was quite high; but then one only has to walk down Avenida Abancay, in the center of Lima, to see the absolute destitution that preponderates. It is no wonder that people listened with jaded ear as the candidates promised to transform the current, precarious economic situation. I am nonetheless convinced that propaganda influenced voters both negatively and positively, if only because it was apparent everywhere. If researchers in the United States are to understand how the campaign functioned in 1985, and to what extent literature influenced prospective voters, librarians should attempt to collect both printed and nonprinted source materials.

I have thus far attempted to describe this year's electoral campaign in Peru. I now assess whether materials representative of each party are available. Political propaganda, in printed and nonprinted form, could be acquired by contacting propaganda officials for the different political parties, as well as journalists who have private archives and who permit the reproduction of their papers. For instance, El Comando Nacional de la Campaña de Apra ran an expensive and well-organized campaign--and donated a variety of material to the Nettie Lee Benson Latin American Collection. Materials were also collected from campaign officials for Acción Popular and Izquierda Unida. Making contacts was time consuming and often frustrating, but the results were well worth "pounding the pavement."

Two hours of video tape acquired from Hugo Otero, campaign director for APRA, included twenty minutes from the initiation of the APRA campaign on "El Día de la Fraternidad," February 24, 1985; a special program dedicated to the problems of Puno; nine minutes of a speech in Huáraz, considered one of Alan García's finest discourses during the campaign; and edited versions of other television spots. This primary source material is noteworthy not only for its research value but also because the party itself had the foresight to collect the televised material for its own archival purposes.

Photographs are valuable for capturing the image of personal contact between each candidate and the voters. More than forty photographs of Alan García in Cuzco, Machu Picchu (an important national symbol), Arequipa, Ayacucho, Chimbote, and Lima's pueblos jóvenes depict scenes typical of the campaign. Other photos show candidate Alan García with local APRA officials in Piura and other locations. Images of walls splattered with paper and paint in the final, frenzied days of the campaign enlarge our notion of what each individual voter experienced on a daily basis. Thirty-five such photographs capture the reality of a Lima papered and painted over with propaganda of presidential and congressional candidates.

Each party produced documents and printed material that reflected its ideology and campaign strategies. Copies of these were also donated to the Benson Latin American Collection. El Comando Nacional de la Campaña de APRA distributed a pamphlet called Activismo político; guía para el activista, which was geared toward the voter who reads very little. The print was quite large, and the work contained sketches to capture the reader's attention. The commission also printed a Manual de organización del área ejecutiva; objetivos de la campaña, which included diagrams of the organizational structures on national, departmental, provincial, zonal, and district levels. Acción Popular's campaign commission wrote a Manual del personero de Acción Popular, which summarized the electoral statutes and explained Peru's preferential vote. A slim periodical entitled El Perú como doctrina was issued twice. Izquierda Unida prepared a synthesis of the Plan de gobierno de Izquierda Unida; Perú 1985-1990. Eduardo Ballón, in charge of propaganda for the Izquierda Unida campaign, contributed other internal documents with information about tactics and projections for the campaign. (These were written in November of 1984.) Other campaign-related material acquired for the Benson Collection includes a book published by the Consejo Unitario Nacional Agrario (CUNA) entitled Los Partidos y el Agro; 1er. Forum Nacional: futuro inmediato del agro nacional, with expositions by Nils Ericson (representing Acción Popular), Alan García, and Alfonso Barrantes.

Shifting trends in the use of the media in the 1983 and 1985 election campaigns demonstrate that published sources cannot provide thorough coverage of Latin American politics. Since nonpublished materials are difficult to acquire through regular channels such as blanket order dealers, carefully planned acquisition trips synchronized with important political events will become increasingly important. In the last five years, several South American countries have negotiated the transition from military dictatorships to popularly elected social democracies. Uruguay, Argentina, Brazil, Bolivia, and Peru are examples. While books and other published materials are usually available no matter what type of government is in power, printed and audio-visual materials that reflect political processes and transition have not been so easily accessible. The Peruvian elections of 1985 provide an interesting case study of the increasing sophistication in the media, the different types and uses of campaign literature, and the availability of these materials for those who are willing to make the necessary personal contacts.

NOTES

1.   Examples of polls taken are found in the following sources: "Ultima encuesta," Caretas, 35:838 (Feb. 18, 1985), 14; "Cifras y opiniones en Lima," Debate, 7:31 (March, 1985), 8-17; "¿A qué aspira cada partido?" Oiga, 5:222 (April 8, 1985), 10-11.

2.   An article by Lorena Ausejo y Gabriel Ortiz de Zevallos, "La batalla de las promesas," Debate, 7:32 (May, 1985), 52-55, also treats images and slogans in the campaign.

3.   Publicity spots were totaled from January to April, 1985. The results were: Spots (S); Time in seconds (T). CODE 3,515 (S), 108,400 (T); AP 2,700 (S), 103,203 (T); APRA 1,737 (S), 49,808 (T); IU 760 (S), 20,600 (T). ¿"Quién gastó más en publicidad electoral?" Visión política, April 28, 1985, p. 2.

4.   "El costo de la campaña electoral," Oiga, 224 (April 22, 1985), 16.

5.   Hugo Otero, Jefe de Propaganda, APRA, Conversation with author, Lima, Peru, May 14, 1985; Eduardo Ballón, Jefe de Propaganda, IU, Conversation with author, Lima, Peru, May 21, 1985.

6.   "Los mitines de Barrantes," Quehacer, 34 (April, 1985), 50.

7.   Fernando Tuesta Soldevilla, El nuevo rostro electoral: las municipales del 83 (Lima: Centro de Estudios y Promoción del Desarrollo, 1985), p. 89.

8.   See Rafael Roncagliolo, "Las encuestas políticas: validez y límites," Quehacer, 34 (April, 1985), 64-70; and his earlier book, ¿Quién ganó? Elecciones 1931-1980 (Lima: DESCO, 1980).

26. BOOKS AND THE NICARAGUAN REVOLUTION

Charles L. Stansifer

Revolutions are born of internal ferment and they inevitably arouse conflicting interpretations, both internally and in other nations. (I am speaking of a revolution as a primarily political upheaval accompanied by violence and profound social change.) As the winners justify the course they took, and the losers gather in exile to analyze their errors and uncover conspiracies, the conflicting interpretations spawn reflection, analysis, and eventually books.

Revolutions in the Old World--the English, the French, the Russian--have caused controversy in the international arena and have given rise to various theories, some now classic, of revolu-tion.[1] Revolutions in the New World--the American, the Mexican, the Cuban--are often measured against the classical European revolutionary yardstick. The Nicaraguan Revolution of 1979, the current generation's focal point for inter-American political controversy, although taking place in a smaller spatial setting and involving fewer people than most commonly studied revolutions, is currently provoking an outpouring of literature, scholarly and otherwise.

It does not seem to matter that Nicaragua is a small country. In the case of other revolutions, especially the American, French, and Russian, the depth of the controversy and the quantity of literature seem proportional to the power of the affected country. The Mexican Revolution began in 1910, when Mexico had approxi-mately 15 million people and Latin American studies in the United States was in its infancy. It nonetheless provoked an appropriate amount of controversy and writing; it was Latin America's first genuinely revolutionary upheaval; it was extremely violent; it persisted for years; and it occurred in the very shadow of the United States. Castro's revolution swept Cuba in 1959, when that country had only 6.5 million inhabitants. Interest was high both because of Cuba's proximity to the United States, especially the East Coast's universities and publishing houses; and because United States academia was in the process of producing a cadre of Latin Americanist scholars interested in the region's internal dynamics.

Nicaragua, which erupted twenty years later, numbered only 2 million--one-third Cuba's population in 1959--and a far smaller proportion of Nicaragua's population could read and write. Nicaragua, despite its relative distance from the United States (compared with Mexico and Cuba), and despite having so few inhabitants, has engendered a volume of literature comparable with that inspired by the Mexican and Cuban revolutions, especially if we remember that only six years have elapsed since the Sandinista victory.[2]

It is, of course, well to note that a revolution can take place on too small a stage. The Grenadan Revolution of 1979–1983 seems handicapped in its ability to inspire scholarly literature by its limited scope--the island counts fewer than 100,000 inhabitants.

There are several useful ways to quantify, classify, analyze, and judge the literature of the Nicaraguan Revolution. Specific questions may help to illustrate the problem. Which nationalities have been most prolific in their writings? How do the Nicaraguan, North American, and Russian interpretations differ-- that is, if generalizations can be made about writers from specific countries? What disciplines have dominated in analyses of the Nicaraguan Revolution, and what methodologies have been brought to bear? Are the studies built on a sound database, and how does the Nicaraguan database compare with that for other Latin American revolutions? I address these questions in a somewhat impressionistic manner, since I cannot say that I have read thoroughly every book on the Nicaraguan Revolution.

Let us look first at the nationalities of authors of books on Nicaragua. In this manner I focus first on the principal books on the Nicaraguan Revolution, and at the same time touch on some of the other questions I have posed. It will probably come as no surprise to learn that the greatest number of books on the Nicaraguan Revolution have been written by Nicaraguans. If we stretch the Revolution's time frame to include the florescence of Augusto César Sandino, then the predominance of Nicaraguan production is beyond question. The Sandinista government has naturally made a special effort to recapture the words and deeds of its greatest hero. This is reflected within Nicaragua by the nomenclature of institutions, from the Asociación Sandinista de Trabajadores de Cultura to the Policía Sandinista, by special exhibitions at the National Archives and the Banco Central, and by books on Sandino.

The truth, however, is that few new books on Sandino have been published by Nicaraguans. Gregorio Selser's Sandino, general de hombres libres, one of the most comprehensive books on Sandino written before 1979 (the first edition appeared in 1955), has been revised and reprinted in Havana, Montevideo, and the United States--but not in Nicaragua.[3] Selser is an Argentine journalist now living in Mexico, and his work continues to be the most popular single-volume book on Sandino.

The most substantial contribution to an understanding of Sandino is Sandino: El pensamiento vivo, a two-volume collection of Sandino's writings edited in 1984 by Nicaragua's current vice-president, Sergio Ramírez Mercado.[4] The first, one-volume edition of this book was published in 1974 by the Editorial de las Universidades Centroamericanas. The second edition, which is more than twice the size of the first, reflects the efforts of the Instituto de Estudio del Sandinismo to locate and preserve documentation concerning the revolutionary hero.

In 1983, Edelberto Torres Rivas, eminent Nicaraguan educator and author of a popular biography of Rubén Darío, published what at first glance appears a monumental biography of Sandino. However, the book, entitled Sandino y sus pares, has more information on the pares than on Sandino.[5] Still, this work's 320 pages on Sandino, of 810 pages total, may well provide the best synthesis of his life currently available in Spanish.

The Sandinistas have engaged in several efforts to place Sandino in perspective, specifically for the purpose of showing that the fight against imperialism has been a steady one since the 1920s. Works such as Humberto Ortega's Cincuenta años de lucha sandinista exemplifies this concern. Beyond them, I know of no other significant contribution to the history of Sandino's fight against the United States Marines.[6]

No other historians of other nationalities have added significantly to our knowledge of the 1927-1934 period either. We are still dependent on the well-known United States historians Neill Macaulay (The Sandino Affair) and Richard Millett (Guardians of the Dynasty) for information and interpretation.[7]

A number of memoirs and specific accounts by Nicaraguans concern the Sandinista insurrection and subsequent victory, but none is truly outstanding as literature, and we still lack a synthesis. Probably the best personal account of the struggle is La montana es más que una inmensa estepa verde (1982), by Omar Cabezas Lacayo, which won an award from the Casa de las Américas in Havana.[8] A close second is François Pisani, Nicaragua, journal d'un témoin de la révolution sandiniste (1980), which focuses on the struggle during June and July, 1978.[9] The low quality of most revolutionary memoirs is disappointing because, although the raw material to reexamine the days of Sandino appears to be missing, Nicaragua overflows with information on the insurrection. The most remarkable set of data is the collection of oral histories assembled by the Comisión de Historia shortly after the victory, and now held by the Instituto de Estudio del Sandinismo. Unfortunately, so far as I know, no work based on these data has yet been published.

The best synthetic accounts of the revolution by non-Nicaraguan authors have been written by North American political scientists. John Booth's The End and the Beginning contains the best narrative of the Sandinista insurrection, has the most comprehensive analysis of the problems besetting the Somoza dynasty prior to its fall, and reveals the best grasp of the secondary literature.[10] Thomas Walker's Nicaragua in Revolution has the most comprehensive coverage of various aspects of the revolution--sports, economics, role of women, and so on--but is marred by a pro-Sandinista bias.[11] It is an edited volume, and it exemplifies the strengths and weaknesses of this genre. Walker's new Nicaragua: The First Five Years, recently released by Praeger, promises to be more extensive, more balanced in coverage, and perhaps more neutral than the first volume. Three other books by non-Nicaraguans, Triumph of the People by the Englishman George Black, Nicaragua: la révolution sandiniste by the Frenchman Henri Weber, and La revolución nicaraguense by the Argentine Carlos Vilas, are also useful syntheses of the Sandinista Revolution. They, like the Walker books, tend to be unabashedly sympathetic to the Sandinista government.[12] The Vilas volume was published first in Spanish in Havana and Buenos Aires (1984) and then in English (1985). Although quite sympathetic to the Nicaraguan government, it is superior to Booth in its analysis of the working classes and their response to Somoza and revolutionary change. Since Vilas worked for the Nicaraguan Ministry of Planning, he had access to socioeconomic data available to few other writers.

Walker, Weber, Black, and Vilas are all favorable to the revolution. If you add to this list of syntheses The Nicaraguan Revolution (1981), by Richard Fagen; La Nicaragua: le modèle sandiniste (1981), by Jean Michel Caroit and Veronique Soule; and the edited volume Nicaragua: glorioso camino a la victoria (1982), by P. Fedoseev and J. Grigulevich, the inevitable conclusion is that virtually all the synthetic accounts are sympathetic to the Sandinistas.[13] This tempts one to draw a parallel with classic revolutionary theory: after the violence subsides, internal and external perceptions of the revolution are generally favorable. So are the books.

Another category of literature is notable for its absence. With all the focus on the background to the Sandinista insurrection, it is surprising to find so little solid reading material on the Somoza dynasty. Nicaraguan writers are understandably repulsed by the subject, but few others have stepped into the breach. Potboilers such as Bernard Diederich's Somoza (1981), Richard Elman's Cocktails at Somoza's (1981), and Eduardo Crawley's Dictators Never Die (1979), suggest that the subject does not as yet attract serious scholars.[14] Diederich and Elman are North Americans, Crawley an Argentine. (A few dissertations under way at United States universities may give rise to more substantial analysis at a later date.) I do not want to leave this topic without referring to one of the rare Russian contributions to the story of the Nicaraguan revolution. However, The Agony of Dictatorship, by Oleg Konstantinovitch Ignat'ev and Genrykh Borovik, is an all too predictable Marxist interpretation of the ills of Nicaragua, with a flimsy documentary basis. It cannot be considered serious scholarship.[15]

The counterrevolution, now in its fourth year, has generated a wealth of periodical commentary but as yet few books.

Nicaragua under Siege (1984), edited by Marlene Dixon and Susanne Jonas; and Nicaragua: The Price of Intervention (1985), by Peter Kornbluh, are two examples of North American books extremely critical of the Reagan administration.[16]

Measuring studies of the Nicaraguan Revolution by disciplinary coverage produces no surprises. Political scientists and sociologists, who would be expected in the vanguard of the analytical army, are indeed out in front. Several of the best books among those mentioned are by political scientists--Walker and Booth, for example. Chapter authors in Walker's two edited volumes are primarily political scientists, with a scattering of other social scientists and journalists. Political scientists from the United States constitute the majority among the fifteen Latin Americanists who completed a book-length report on the Nicaraguan elections of November, 1984 for the Latin American Studies Association. Economists from the United States have contributed many article-length analyses of the Nicaraguan Revolution, mostly focusing on agrarian reform and international commerce. They have yet to produce a book-length study.

It would be too much to review all the books treating specific aspects of the Nicaraguan Revolution, but it is worthwhile to note that the Nicaraguan literacy crusade of 1980 has been carefully studied by a number of authors. Among the Nicaraguan government's many books on the crusade is Y también enséñenles a leer, by Carlos Alemán Ocampo.[17] It captures the exhilaration of the young brigadistas during the crusade in excerpts from diaries and field notes. A similar book, published in English, is And Also Teach Them To Read by Sheryl Hirshon (one of the few North American brigadistas) and Judy Butler, a writer for the North American Congress on Latin America.[18] Valerie Miller's Between Struggle and Hope: The Nicaraguan Literacy Crusade was published late in 1985.[19] Since Miller is an education specialist who was an adviser to the literacy campaign, the book promises a more detailed analysis of methodology and results.

Historians for the most part have not entered the competition, apparently preferring to wait for the evidence to sift and the dust of controversy to settle. Nevertheless, one of the best studies of Sandinista ideology is by a young historian, David Nolan, of the University of Miami. His M.A. thesis, The Ideology of the Sandinistas and the Nicaraguan Revolution, was published in 1984.[20] Although somewhat tainted by an anti-Sandinista bias in the later chapters, it remains the most thorough study of its subject. It also contains excellent biographical sketches of Sandinista leaders and a detailed chronology of the Revolution.

Novelists and short story writers, as well as literary critics and literary historians, have yet to make their mark. Some works nonetheless exist. Antonio Skarmeta, a Chilean novelist and screenwriter who lives in exile in Germany, has published La insurrección.[21] Perhaps the most interesting book of Nicaraguan cultural life since the Revolution is El alba de oro: la historia viva de Nicaragua by Sergio Ramírez, Nicaragua's foremost politician-intellectual.[22] El alba de oro (1983) is a collection of Ramírez' speeches and writings from both before and after the Revolution.

In an interview in Havana in February, 1982, Ramírez was asked why Nicaragua had produced so few storytellers (narradores). His response was: "Nuestra realidad literaria ha sido eminentemente poética . . ." and he proceeded to name five or six of the best-known literary figures of Nicaragua, all of whom are primarily poets.[23] Indeed these poets, and many more, have been published in books, pamphlets, and magazines since the Revolution. However, it would not be easy to single out any book of Nicaraguan poetry since 1979 as particularly exemplary of the revolution. Incidentally, one of the first books published by Nicaragua's Ministry of Culture after the Sandinista victory was Nuestro Rubén Darío, an anthology of the great modernist's nationalist, anti-imperialist poetry selected by Nicaragua's leading literary critic, Ernesto Mejía Sánchez.[24]

Before leaving this section on poetry it is well to mention that one great contemporary Nicaraguan poet, Pablo Antonio Cuadra, has recently begun to publish some of his works in San José, Costa Rica. There he is cooperating with the Libro Libre publishing house in bringing out his Obra poética completa. The first volume of a projected eight-volume set was published in 1983, the second in 1984.[25]

Those who attempt to understand and explain the Nicaraguan revolution face severe handicaps on one hand and some clear advantages on the other. Nicaragua possessed less reliable data about prerevolutionary society than either Cuba or Mexico. The situation has changed but little since 1979. The database in a country with 50 percent illiteracy--Nicaragua's situation in 1979-- cannot be secure. Since 1979, the Nicaraguans have been more concerned with making the revolution work than with documenting it. Since 1981, when the counterrevolution first began to affect internal affairs, shortages of paper and ink, not to speak of manpower, have seriously limited the production of data. Censorship, which began at the same time, has both restricted the flow of information and discouraged criticism. Book production in Nicaragua has declined owing to unavailability of printing supplies and equipment, discouragement of private publishing, censorship, preoccupation with the war with the contras, and the general economic decline.

On the positive side, despite repeated crises and a siege situation, most Nicaraguan government offices remain accessible to foreign researchers of all political inclinations. Nicaraguans, believing that their cause depends on support from groups in the United States and Western Europe, have been far more open to researchers than Cuba was during the first six years of its revolution. Because published data often are not available, interviews must substitute--albeit at some risk to accuracy. The thirst for information about Nicaragua by private interest groups in the United States, by Congress, and by the public at large encourages research, as does the controversial nature of the American government's undeclared war against the Sandinistas. The very nature of this information demand, however, opens the field to amateurs and, sad to relate, propagandists. It even converts some scholars into publicists.

There are additional reasons why the Nicaraguan Revolution has generated a fair share of books in English. North American universities boast a mature corps of scholars with deep experience in Latin America. It has been relatively easy for them to divert their attention to Nicaragua. Richard Fagen, a Cuban specialist who has written extensively on the Nicaraguan revolution, is but one example. Moreover, knowledge of previous Latin American revolutions has both sparked curiosity about the Nicaraguan revolution and provided a baseline for scholarly comparison.

Judging by the number of books published on the Nicaraguan Revolution, one must conclude that the Sandinistas have converted a small country with little strategic significance per se into a source of continuing, major international controversy.

NOTES

1.   See especially Crane Brinton, Anatomy of Revolution, rev. ed. (New York, NY: Vintage Books, 1965).

2.   To get an idea of the quantity, see John A. Booth, "Celebrating the Demise of Somocismo: Fifty Recent Spanish Sources on the Nicaraguan Revolution," Latin American Research Review, 17:1 (1982), 173-189. See also Ralph Lee Woodward, Jr., Nicaragua (Santa Barbara, CA: Clio Press, 1983), a volume in the World Bibliographical Series.

3.   Gregorio Selser, Sandino, general de hombres libres (Buenos Aires: Ediciones Pueblos de América, 1955).

4.   Sergio Ramírez Mercado, ed., Sandino: El pensamiento vivo, 2d ed., rev., 2 vols. (Managua: Editorial Nueva Nicaragua, 1984).

5.   Edelberto Torres Rivas, Sandina y sus pares (Managua: Editorial Nueva Nicaragua, 1983).

6.   Humberto Ortega Saavedra, Cincuenta años de lucha sandinista (Medellín: Ediciones Hombre Nuevo, 1979).

7.   Neill W. Macaulay, Jr., The Sandino Affair (Chicago, IL: Quadrangle Books, 1967); Richard Millett, Guardians of the Dynasty: A History of the U.S.-Created Guardia Nacional de Nicaragua and the Somoza Family (Maryknoll, NY: Orbis Books, 1977).

8. Omar Cabezas Lacayo, La montana es más que una inmensa estepa verde (Havana: Casa de las Américas, 1982). This book is now available in translation: Fire from the Mountain: The Making of a Sandinista, intro. by Carlos Fuentes (New York, NY: Crown, 1985).

9. François Pisani, Nicaragua, journal d'un témoin de la révolution sandiniste (Paris: Encre, 1980).

10. John A. Booth, The End and the Beginning: The Nicaraguan Revolution (Boulder, CO: Westview Press, 1982).

11. Thomas W. Walker, ed., Nicaragua in Revolution (New York, NY: Praeger, 1983).

12. George Black, Triumph of the People: The Sandinista Revolution in Nicaragua (London: Zed Press, 1982); Henri Weber, Nicaragua: la révolution sandiniste (Paris, François Maspero, 1981); and Carlos María Vilas, Perfiles de la revolución sandinista (Havana: Casa de las Américas, 1984).

13. Richard R. Fagen, The Nicaraguan Revolution: A Personal Report (Washington, DC: Institute for Policy Studies, 1981); Jean Michel Caroit and Veronique Soule, La Nicaragua: le modèle sandiniste (Paris: Le Sycomor, 1981); P. Fedoseev and J. Grigulevich, eds., Nicaragua: glorioso camino a la victoria (Moscow: Academy of Sciences of the USSR, 1982).

14. Bernard Diederich, Somoza and the Legacy of U.S. Involvement in Central America (New York, NY: E.P. Dutton, 1981); Richard Elman, Cocktails at Somoza's: A Reporter's Sketchbook of Events in Revolutionary Nicaragua (Cambridge, MA: Apple-wood Books, 1981); Eduardo Crawley, Dictators Never Die: A Portrait of Nicaragua and the Somozas (New York, NY: St. Martin's Press, 1979).

15. Oleg Konstantinovitch Ignat'ev and Genrykh Borovik, The Agony of Dictatorship: Nicaragua Chronicle, trans. from Russian by Arthur Shkarovsky (Moscow: Progress, 1980).

16. Marlene Dixon and Susanne Jonas, eds., Nicaragua under Siege (San Francisco, CA: Synthesis Publications, 1984), and Peter Kornbluh, Nicaragua: The Price of Intervention (Washington, DC: Institute for Policy Studies, 1985).

17. Carlos Alemán Ocampo, Y también enséñenles a leer (Managua: Editorial Nueva Nicaragua, 1984).

18. Sheryl Hirshon with Judy Butler, And Also Teach Them To Read (Westport, CT: Lawrence Hill, 1983).

19. Valerie Miller, Between Struggle and Hope: The Nicaraguan Literacy Crusade (Boulder, CO: Westview Press, 1985).

20. David Nolan, FSLN: The Ideology of the Sandinistas and the Nicaraguan Revolution (Coral Gables, FL: Institute of Interamerican Studies, University of Miami, 1984).

21. Antonio Skarmeta, La insurrección (Hanover, NH: Ediciones del Norte, 1982). This book is also available in

English: The Insurrection, trans. Paula Sharp (New York, NY: Persea Books, 1983).

22. Sergio Ramírez Mercado, El alba de oro: la historia viva de Nicaragua (México, DF: Siglo Veintiuno, 1983).

23. Ibid., p. 305.

24. Ernesto Mejía Sánchez, ed., Nuestro Rubén Darío (Managua: Ministerio de Cultura, 1980).

25. Pablo Antonio Cuadra, Obra poética completa, Vol. I, Canciones de pájaro y señora; Vol. II, Cuaderno del sur, canto temporal (San José: Asociación Libro Libre, 1983-1984).

Part Three

Images and Realities in Nontraditional Formats

INTRODUCTION

We now turn from our opening preoccupation with the metaphysical and intellectual aspects of studying Latin America's
masses and minorities--how images are formed, communicated, and
perpetuated; how scholars work to refine existing images through
new questions, techniques, and resources--and from our subsequent focus on the bibliographic basis for more particular
research questions. We here consider resources on--and of--the
masses and minorities. These materials have tended to fall
outside our collecting concerns and, until recently, outside a
substantial segment of organized scholarship.

This part is divided into three sections. The first considers
the creation and appropriation of nonprint media by the masses.
Cuba's revolutionary cinema and the region's pervasive and
enduring music are our specific topics. Next come three papers
on expressions of the minimally literate, focusing on chapbooks,
music (the tango form), and the <u>fotonovela</u>. Finally, a student of
the Latin American elite considers both opera and the process by
which it may be studied. As these authors demonstrate, the
analysis of "nontraditional" materials can significantly enhance our
appreciation of Latin American masses and minorities. Equally
important, it can complement and enrich the rather monochromatic
perspective engendered by exclusive reliance on the printed
word.

D.C.H.

I. Nonprint Media and the Semiliterate Masses

27. THE MOVIES AND THE MASSES IN CUBA

Patricia Aufderheide

Cinema is both attractive and elusive as a primary source of information on modern societies. It is a dominant form of communication in the twentieth century. Entertainment features have become the major popular art form, transmogrifying enduring myths and narratives, and shaping the characters and stereotypes of industrial culture. Industrial and training films pervade working life. Commercials fuel the society of the consumer. Cinema has become a major medium of abstract and narrative art. Even television is dominated by the film medium: mainstream television has been modeled on film, and most works shown on television--even the commercials--are still produced on film.

And yet cinema also poses enormous difficulties in research and in use. The storage problems can be nightmarish. Film on nitrate stock ages quickly and poses a fire hazard, as recent fires destroying substantial early holdings at the U.S. National Archives and in Mexico City have demonstrated. Commercial studios have, with the exception of Disney, taken only casual care of their heritage, and resist preservation and archiving by third parties. Information retrieval is in the dark ages: much of what we know is drawn from the trade magazines of the period, which were not necessarily accurate. Even current films can be hard to track down, with distribution companies often holding only a few titles, and films frequently passed from company to company within the course of a year. Trying to locate a film that has not found a distributor often means being at the right film festival at the right time.

Cinema also poses a challenge of interpretation, because the relation between a film and its audience, not to mention between a film and the public or the social context in which it was made, is far from transparent. Tell a Hollywood producer whose teen movie just bombed about supply and demand. Ask yourself whether you get an accurate sense of Puerto Rican culture from Fort Apache, the Bronx, or of the oil business from Dallas. Assessing the relation between cinema and society is what keeps film departments in universities fueled with course topics, and replete with professors using sociological, semiotic, and historical tools to attack the problem.

In Latin America, the relationship between cinema and society is defined as well by the influence of American film production and distribution on the national industry. The U.S. Motion Picture Export Association, under the leadership of Jack Valenti, has deftly maintained a controlling interest in screen time all over Latin America for U.S.-made films. Even without

327

Valenti's expertise in negotiating favorable terms for the North American products, it would still be true that "Hollywood movies" are tremendously popular with Latin American audiences, and shape their expectations for what cinema is and for what they like in movies.

Cuba is a place where many of these messy variables, to use the language of American sociology, can be controlled. And it is a place where cinema offers some unique advantages as a primary document of life over the last twenty-six years.

Cuban film was born, as one Cuban screenwriter put it, "without original sin." Although some production facilities existed before the Revolution, there was no national film industry. There was, however, a tremendous appetite for movies. Among intellectuals, fascination with film--and particularly with the postwar experience of Europe's national cinemas, in which neorealism in a variety of personal styles expressed the tensions and conflicts of nations reconstructing themselves--formed the basis for small student groups. These film societies were also debating societies on the political issues of the day. People like Santiago Alvarez and Tomás Gutiérrez Alea enthusiastically participated.

At the time of the Revolution, however, none of the film-society buffs who had organized screenings, hosted the likes of Italian neorealistic Cesare Zavattini, and held forums on national identity and cinema art had ever actually made a movie. Their chance came with the 1959 founding of the Cuban Institute for the Art and Industry of Film (ICAIC). The film society boys (and it was almost entirely a male group) became film producers.

The mandate of ICAIC was simple but global. It was charged with capturing the unrolling revolution as experienced by the majority of Cubans, and to present it to Cuban audiences both as document and example. To this day, ICAIC is respon-sible first and last to its audience. It makes no educational or training films, nor does it work with the television service. Its products go directly to theaters, and indirectly to television through a program that screens selected films, usually classic and international features. Success is measured in greatest part by box office appeal and by international film deals--in short, by public approval.

The institute bureaucratically must answer to the vice-minister of culture, who is himself a filmmaker and one-time film society organizer. Internally, it is structured according to activity--newsreel production, documentary, and features. Priorities and budgets within each division are established by the entire working team, albeit with a certain amount of ad hoc decision making and personalism of the kind that comes from having a small organization that operates more like a workshop than an industry. (There still is no film school in Cuba, although an international school was established in 1986, so ICAIC continues to function, as it did in the early days, as a training school cum production house. Newcomers work on newsreels first, then graduate to documentaries, and eventually rise to features.) It has a hierarchical management structure, and the workers are represented by a fairly strong union. Management and workers are bound together by a mutual concern to keep ICAIC autonomous from outside control, but the union has also had open clashes with ICAIC management. These have particularly involved the enforcement of salaries and working conditions long mandated by the government, but equally long ignored.

Totally contained within one building at the corner of 24th and 12th in the chic Havana neighborhood of Vedado, ICAIC can be a hectic place even when filmmakers are not caught up in the annual New Latin American Film Festival, begun in 1979 as a showcase for Latin American independent (and often, therefore, socially or politically critical) film. But it is also friendly, a place where people respond quickly to genuine interest. Both its frantic and friendly qualities come from the same source: ICAIC people, by and large, are working at something they love. Being a successful filmmaker in Cuba is not much of a stepping-stone to anywhere else in politics. While it is a prestigious occupation, celebrity does not bring out the kind of fan pathology it does in the United States. It may get you your own videocassette recorder at home and some international trips, but you are unlikely to become rich. It does give you the prestige and perks of professional status. So Cuban moviemakers do what they do because they are dedicated to it, and because they like it. They are artists in a popular medium.

Cuban film, because of its peculiar slot in the social and political structure, has been a unique expression of a society undergoing rapid, self-conscious change. It is interesting for its form and its content, as well as its reception.

Ever since its first days, ICAIC has churned out a weekly 9-minute newsreel to be shown in theaters. Within a year, it also began producing long-form documentaries. By 1968, it had produced enough features for a retrospective, held first in Paris and then at New York's Museum of Modern Art. That retrospective, featuring Memories of Underdevelopment by Tomás Gutiérrez Alea and Lucia by Humberto Sólas, among others, made a big international splash; Cuban film was widely regarded in aesthetic circles as an exciting adventure in a form that incorporated documentary style into fiction (Memories) and merged the psychological and social (Lucia).

But Cuban features, at three to six per year, comprise only a small part of the total annual production. (ICAIC is responsible as well for selecting and distributing some 100 to 150 films for Cuba's theaters, including its "mobile theaters," from international suppliers. It buys from all around the world, except the United States, which continues its blockade. Filmmakers from the

United States occasionally donate copies, and U.S. films are seen on television when taped from satellite cable transmissions.) For Cubans, Cuban film is much more oriented to the documentary, and that is where Cuba has shown its greatest stylistic vigor and innovation.

The father of Cuban documentary is Santiago Alvarez, who from his early days as a radio programmer saw his mission as using the popular media as political weapons. He was assigned to produce the newsreels in 1959, and he made them far more than a record of weekly political speeches. He continues to head the documentary division, although he no longer personally constructs the newsreels. Alvarez is responsible for the unique record of Cuban history that ICAIC's nearly complete newsreel collection affords.

Two features mark Alvarez's work. It is boldly ideological, describing not only events but also their social and political meaning. This can entail retracing history, identifying a political enemy, or explaining the differences between socialist and capitalist "propaganda." However, his films are never top-down didactic, but always designed as a series of bold provocations to a viewer's preconceptions, forcing the viewer to complete the thought initiated by the screen and the sound track. Stylistically, Alvarez's films are marked by what has been called "nervous montage," a presentation of information through visual images and sound, eschewing narration. Sequences typically mix and match news clippings, stills, news footage, words within newspaper headings, cartoons, and captions that both pose questions and make controversial statements. In part, the fact that ICAIC works almost exclusively in 35 mm and is chronically short of film stock explains the use of montage and its minimal experimentation with cinema verité. But for Alvarez, at least, montage is a natural result of his "cinema of synthesis," in which chronicling an event is only the beginning of the documentary filmmaker's responsibility to explain its meaning.

Alvarez's subjects have included politics, particularly the heroic episodes of the early years (e.g., defense of the Bay of Pigs), international issues (e.g., Vietnam), and profiles of Fidel and other leaders. However, as the revolution has become the daily life of new generations, ICAIC documentaries and newsreels have spanned subjects that range from the art and music of the island (big sellers on the international market) to the national debate over sex roles and responsibilities (provocative favorites for the national audience). Sports and sporting events have been the subject of some of the most popular documentaries, including the elegant, even poetic Something More than a Medal, about the Pan-American games.

Public response to the documentaries and the newsreels is positive. Feature-length documentaries have drawn lines as long as those for features, and when asked to recall Cuban films people will usually include a documentary title in the mix. Newsreels do not suffer the scorn they do in other places, which is not surprising given that they are not tainted by official obscurantism. Officials of ICAIC told me that when newsreels do not arrive on time, and features are screened without them, the audiences complain. This may be true; my own reactions mixed respect with mild curiosity, but included no raging desire.

Alvarez's style is direct, angry, and built around dramatic moments in what he calls the best "fiction" of all--real life. At the start of his 1969 film Departure at 6 p.m., a 41-minute film about mobilization for a massive sugar cane harvest, he placed captions reading: "You are going to see / a film that is / Didactic / Informative / Political / and . . . Pamphleteering!" Perhaps it is a style particularly appropriate for his generation, and perhaps it is a highly personal expression. In any case, younger documentarians are experimenting with a diversity of documentary styles, including reenactment and verité filmmaking. One filmmaker, Luis Bernaza, has even made a hilarious send-up of stuffy documentaries in his El Piropo, which surveys sexual attitudes in modern Cuba through the many kinds of offhand remarks men make to (and about) women passing by in the street.

If one can see, in documentary, the passing of an era in which political headlines were also the major meat of films, the same thing holds for fiction features. The Institute marked its twenty-fifth anniversary by producing six features in one year, all of them concerning the conflicts of daily life during the second generation of the revolution.*

The films included contemporary drama, historical drama, situation comedies, and a musical. Each was stylistically distinct, even highly personal, as an expression of a director's style. A common thread, however, was their concern with sex roles. All the films assumed sex roles to be social facts, not merely biological ones; all of them treated the personal and the political as separate but related realms. The films met with varying levels of public success. None was a disaster; but, interestingly, it was two comedies--both made by young men who grew up with the revolution--which made the biggest hit.

Cuban films have in the past been more than entertainment. They have been seen as triggers for discussion and action. Portrait of Teresa, by Pastor Vega, concerned a woman hard-pressed to maintain her obligations as a worker, mother, and wife. Her husband's jealousy--we are never sure whether his suspicions that she is having an affair are correct--precipitates crises in the family and at work. The film came out after the

---

*See my article "Red Harvest," American Film, (March, 1984).

Cuban government had passed the so-called Family Act mandating, among other things, equality in domestic responsibilities between man and wife. The law had given legitimacy to women's complaints, but it was Portrait of Teresa that provided public, vivid validation of the problem. The film became a touch point in community and workplace discussions, and remains one of the first films Cubans mention as a noteworthy Cuban product. (It also did well internationally.)

The Cuban film industry may be unique in its autonomy, its centralization, the quality of its record keeping, and its explicit mission to use cinema art to chronicle a changing society. As a state-controlled cinema, it is interesting for its subject matter and for its reception.

It is difficult for North Americans to get a good sense of any of these issues, however, owing to the U.S. government's blockade. Some films are available from two distributors: New Yorker Films, 16 W. 61st St., New York, NY 10023; and Cinema Guild, 1697 Broadway No. 802, New York, NY 10019. It is also possible to sample the documentary work of Santiago Alvarez from a retrospective exhibition put together by Young Filmmakers Video Arts, 4 Rivington St., New York, NY 10002. Young Filmmakers has also published a catalog of the exhibit, with extensive notes.

But in one sense all this work provides a badly skewed view of Cuban society, biased toward the entertainment features and toward the pioneering period of the documentary. For an understanding of the social tensions and textures of today's Cuba, the ordinary annual production of documentaries provides a rich pool of information. These materials are available for screening at ICAIC. International visitors to ICAIC deal with Pastor Vega, an equable and elegant man who has several efficient helpers. The Institute is almost bureaucracy free, and if a visitor can adjust to the production schedule's demands on the filmmakers, ICAIC people are usually glad to oblige.

A journal, called Cine Cubano, is published by ICAIC more or less regularly. It is a pleasant jumble of criticism (usually not intellectually rigorous, but not flackery either), interviews, and production information. Cine Cubano is hard to get in the United States, even at the Library of Congress, but full runs are available on the Island.

It is possible, even easy, to travel to Cuba. One must have a work-related reason to visit, or relatives on the Island, but no particular proof is required. I have carried documentation of my assignments, but no one ever wanted to look at it. You do need money; the chartered flights from Miami are expensive. And you need patience--both in Havana and in Miami there are almost inevitable, usually inexplicable, delays associated with security. It would be sensible to budget some extra time beyond work obligations, not least because Cuba is a pleasant tropical island, but I have never seen the beaches that Italians and Canadians keep going to when I am staying at one of the Havana hotels.

The study of relationships between Cuban cinema and society is an international concern. Such people as Michael Chanan from England, Guy Hennebelle from France, and Peter Schumann from Germany have become experts on Cuban cinema; in this country, Julianne Burton at the University of California, Santa Cruz knows Cuban cinema well.

Many of the most interesting questions, however--those dealing with the evolving relationship between the Cuban public and Cuban cinema--have yet to be investigated. The answers may help us understand the role of cinema in mass society in other places as well.

28. THE CURRENT STATE OF BIBLIOGRAPHIC RESEARCH IN LATIN AMERICAN ETHNOMUSICOLOGY

John M. Schechter

This paper examines the current status of bibliographic research in Latin American ethnomusicology, with special attention to materials pertaining to the region's urban popular music. The discussion begins with a statement of the rationale for acquiring ethnomusicological materials, followed by a summary of major repositories of field recordings and printed sources in the United States and Latin America. The report subsequently evaluates the major bibliographic tools currently at our disposal. I make references to three bibliographic compilations: "Selected Bibliographic Sources in Latin American Ethnomusicology"; "Doctoral Dissertations in Latin American Ethnomusicology: 1965-1984"; and "A Selected Bibliography on Latin American Urban Popular Music" (see Volume II, pp. 664-682).

The central role of music in Latin America, particularly among its masses and minorities, cannot be overstated. To think of American culture is to form conceptual images of mass media, consumerism, and high technology. To ponder Latin American culture is to call up mental pictures of mass media, yes; but also an immense collage of ritual behavior--periodic and aperiodic, large-scale and small-scale, urban and rural. Musical perform-ance is ever-present in these prescribed, formalized actions. The Latin American case is subsumed under the following universal principle, stated by Norma McLeod: "Wherever else it may appear, music is always connected with ritual."[1] Major blocks in the Latin American ritual collage include life-crisis rites--those marking physiological or social transition, such as a child's wake or a wedding; rituals of affliction, such as the healing ceremony of a shaman; and cyclical rituals, such as Semana Santa processions or agricultural fertility rites.

With this ubiquity of music making a quintessential ethno-graphic fact, it behooves a mainstream Latin American library collection, including the collection at an institution not directly supporting ethnomusicological research, to seek out ethno-musicological materials. Since the discipline of ethnomusicology focuses on living musical traditions, whether propagated by mass media or by ritual, and since living musical traditions are integral

---

Editor's Note. The author's three bibliographies were distributed during the panel session "The Music of Latin American Masses and Minorities."

to Latin American culture, the library wishing to document that culture must provide materials falling under the rubric of ethnomusicology.

The librarian contemplating an expansion of his or her holdings in Latin American ethnomusicology might wish to know of those institutions in this country and in Latin America where collection development has already taken place. The student of ethnomusicology is fortunate to have significant resource centers that place both printed and aural sources at her or his disposal. In the United States, the Archive of Folk Culture of the Library of Congress qualifies as a substantial repository for field recordings from a number of Latin American countries. Originally termed "The Archive of American Folk-Song," renamed "The Archive of Folk Song" in 1955, and given its present designation in 1981, the Archive of Folk Culture boasts field recordings from Trinidad, Peru, and the U.S.-Mexican border region. Its "An Inventory of the Bibliographies and Other Reference and Finding Aids Prepared by the Archive of Folk Culture" (1984) serves as an introductory guide both to these field recordings and to selected bibliographies and internal Finding Aids. Of particular relevance to our subject, the document "Folklife and Ethnomusicology Archives and Related Collections in the United States and Canada" (LC Folk Archive Reference Aid no. 2, April 1984) lists these archives, with addresses, in alphabetical order by state or province. Its last page has a list of other directories helpful in locating archival resources in ethnomusicology and folk life.

The Archives of Traditional Music at Indiana University stands among the finest American university collections of field and commercial recordings, and includes a significant body of material from Latin America. The Archives were originally built by George Herzog. Herzog early worked as an assistant in the Berlin Phonogramm archiv, an institution founded in 1900 by Carl Stumpf and Otto Abraham principally to store cylinders prepared by German ethnomusicologists. The Indiana Archives holds 7,000 cylinder recordings made between 1895 and 1938, and thousands of later recordings made with discs, wires, open-reel tapes, and cassettes. It produces a newsletter, Resound: A Quarterly of the Archives of Traditional Music, and is currently headed by Anthony Seeger. Dr. George List, who succeeded Herzog as Director of the Archives in 1954, pursued extensive research in Colombia; thus, the Colombian holdings are particularly strong. In 1982, Ronald Smith, an ethnomusicologist teaching at Indiana University, published a selective listing of its commercial and field recordings from Guatemala, Honduras, El Salvador, Surinam, Venezuela, Colombia (post-1964), and Panama. The listing includes item, collector, and archives accession number.[2]

Recording with cylinders was underway in Latin America by 1905, when the medical doctor-architect-anthropologist Robert

Lehmann-Nitsche captured music of the Tehuelche Indians.[3] One can find an informative review of the active cylinder recording of diverse Latin American indigenous groups during the first thirty years of this century in a paper published in 1972 by Isabel Aretz.[4] Aretz's teacher Carlos Vega pioneered Latin American ethnomusicological field research; today, many of his recordings, as well as copies of all field material recorded by whatever means from 1940 on, are to be found in the Fonoteca Nacional of the state-sponsored Instituto Nacional de Musicología "Carlos Vega," (founded by Vega in 1931) in Buenos Aires. The current director is Ercilia Moreno Chá. This rich archive contains recorded music of the indigenous and folk cultures of Argentina, Bolivia, Chile, Ecuador, Paraguay, Peru, Uruguay, and Venezuela, along with a collection of musical instruments. The "Carlos Vega" Institute has produced long-playing discs--the product of Institute-sponsored field research--as well as mono-graphs and anthologies.[5]

Isabel Aretz heads another major Latin American archive and ethnomusicological study center, the Instituto Interamericano de Etnomusicología y Folklore (INIDEF), in Caracas. The institute is an important repository of field-recorded music and ethnographic data from Central America, the Caribbean, and con-tinental South America.[6] A number of North and South American scholars have served apprenticeships at INIDEF. The Instituto, under Aretz's editorship, has published the Revista INIDEF since 1975.

Less well-known than INIDEF, but growing in importance and founded by former INIDEF student Carlos Alberto Coba A., is the sound archives of the Instituto Otavaleño de Antropología, Otavalo, Ecuador. Carefully cataloged are numerous recordings of music and folkloristic data from Ecuador's Sierra and Oriente regions. The Otavalo Institute has published an extensive series of works on Ecuadorian anthropology and folklore in its Colección Pendoneros. One of the volumes is Coba Andrade's 1980 Litera-tura Popular Afroecuatoriana, which documents texts of black folklore genres from both highlands and coast. Sarance is the journal published by the Instituto Otavaleño de Antropología.

Before closing this discussion of repositories with close looks at two collections of special value--the Belfer Audio Laboratory and Archive of Syracuse University, and the Benson Latin American Collection of The University of Texas at Austin--I must mention several relevant items to be found in the Latin American issue of Ethnomusicology, the Journal of the Society for Ethno-musicology, 10:1 (January, 1966), edited jointly by Gilbert Chase and Bruno Nettl. The lead article is "Mesomusic: An Essay on the Music of the Masses" by Carlos Vega, a study I return to later. It is followed by papers on various aspects of the musical cultures of several indigenous groups--Motilone, Kwaikèr, Araucanian, and Yaqui. George List concludes his articles on

"Ethnomusicology in Colombia" and "Ethnomusicology in Ecuador" with bibliographical references and sections entitled "Deposited Field Recordings." The latter lists, by individual archive (including the Archives of Traditional Music of Indiana University), field recordings made and deposited. List remarks, in the Colombia essay, that the Instituto Colombiano de Antropología, in Bogotá, holds the largest collection of recordings of Colombian traditional music.[7] Isabel Aretz has an early report, "Notes on Ethnomusicology in Venezuela," in which she summarizes ethnomusicological activity in that country up to about 1965.[8]

One need hardly comment on the enormous value of the printed materials on ethnomusicological and related subjects in the Benson Latin American Collection. My own dissertation research benefited most from the Benson Collection's extraordinary collection of hard-to-find books and manuscripts from the sixteenth to nineteenth centuries. These sources enabled me to establish the needed historical and ethnographical depth for modern ritualistic practices such as the child's wake observance.[9] But the Benson Collection goes beyond the contents of its Rare Books Room: it has painstakingly acquired dissertations, monographs, and journals pertinent to Latin American ethnomusicology.

By contrast with the Benson Collection, the Belfer Audio Laboratory and Archive of Syracuse University, completed in 1982, contains only aural materials. The enormous collection--more than 250,000 phonodiscs (from the Bell Collection; see below), 3,000 cylinders, and 3,000 to 5,000 tapes--originated in 1963 as the Thomas A. Edison Re-recording Laboratory. The present edifice, adjacent to the Bird Library, is the first building in the world designed specifically for the preservation and restoration of audio materials. In a September, 1982 interview with Walter L. Welch, the program's first curator and director,[10] and William Storm, the Belfer Archive's current director, Storm noted that a major goal of the center was to prepare usage (rerecorded) forms of various cylinder and tape collections from around the world.[11] The Belfer Audio Laboratory and Archive falls under the administration of the Director of Libraries of Syracuse University. As of the fall of 1982, microfilm-cataloging of the Belfer Collection of discs was still underway.

Of special interest for our purposes is Belfer's collection of discs acquired from the brothers Joseph and Max Bell, entrepreneurs who operated in prerevolutionary Havana and in New York City.[12] They acquired an enormous body of discs, many reflecting Caribbean and Caribbean-derived popular genres. (These discs, mostly 45 rpm, had not yet been microfilm-cataloged by the fall of 1982, when I began processing them.) The Belfer Collection's Latin American popular music 45s number, by William Storm's estimation, between 30,000 and 40,000.[13]

Insofar as these discs had not yet been cataloged, I began this process during my 1982-83 tenure as a postdoctoral fellow at

Syracuse University. I decided to catalog only those 45s having Latin American songs or by Latin American artists. The discs are shelved in alphabetical order by record company and in numerical order within each company. Among the musical genres I cataloged were the following: rancheras, merengues, boleros, porros, guarachas, valses, pasillos, chachachás, pachangas, merecumbes, aguinaldos, seises fajardeños, plenas, tango-boleros, pasodobles, mambos, guaguancós, sones montunos, charangas, guajira sones, plechangas, calypsos, bossa novas, bombas, bembés, seises jíbaros, tangos, paseos, danzones, seises milongas, huapangos, canciones, polkas, and salves. I surveyed the discs of 32 record companies, and examined recordings by some 60 to 70 different ensembles. The 57-page discography I compiled (which is available upon request) barely scratched the surface of the Latin popular music 45-rpm disc collection: I cataloged discs of companies only perhaps halfway through the letter "A."

This 45-rpm collection of primarily Caribbean and Caribbean-derived musics is enormously important for students of Latin American urban popular music--whether from the perspective of musical genre (notably, genre-hybridization); in terms of ensembles, individual artists, and record companies; or for the historical development of the whole gamut of Caribbean musics.

This discussion of the Belfer 45-rpm holdings leads me to the general question of scholarly attention to Latin American urban popular musics. The definition provided by Gérard Béhague in his introductory paragraph to the article "Latin America. IV. Popular Music" in The New Grove Dictionary of Music and Musicians[14] clearly enunciates what musicologists intend by this phrase:

> The term "popular music" is understood here to represent musical repertories and genres emanating primarily from urban areas, and disseminated through sheet music, radio and television, and commercial recordings. Implicit in urban popular music are commercial promotion of composers and performers, the orientation of genres to particular social groups, and the relative sophistication of musical arrangements. Popular music is used primarily for entertainment, but it may also involve socio-political participation and criticism. Rather than going through emphemeral fashion cycles, popular music should be considered as changing more rapidly than other repertories because of the complexity and heterogeneity of urban cultures and the ready exchange of information among practitioners.

Of fifty-two dissertations in Latin American ethnomusicology from the period between 1965 and 1984, only eight--those of Béhague, Lampman (not explicitly directed to Latin American popular music), Lashley, Ramírez, Reyes Schramm, Singer, Solís, and Stigberg--center on, or involve to some degree, Latin American popular music (see Volume II, pp. 673-678). Advanced scholarly activity in Latin American ethnomusicology--if one may use doctoral dissertations as one criterion--has clearly focused on folk and indigenous music, and above all on indigenous cultural manifestations.

A number of voices have nonetheless cried out for greater attention to popular music. Charles Seeger's contributions to the development of Latin American musical scholarship have been documented by Malena Kuss.[15] As early as 1946, in his introductory essay to the "Music" section of the Handbook of Latin American Studies (9:1943 [published in 1946), p. 446), Seeger lamented the lack of scholarship on the subject:

> One area of prime importance has been knowingly slighted here, that of popular or commercial music, música populachera. Once ignored on principle by the serious student, it has recently been recognized as the only music idiom in which the New World has distinguished itself . . . some way of handling this twentieth century wonder child must be found by musicology. . . .

Willard Rhodes, an early pioneer in the Society for Ethnomusicology, wrote in 1956 that the emerging discipline of "ethnomusicology" should encompass the study of popular music.[16] In 1966, Carlos Vega laid theoretical foundations for the study of the music of the masses--what he termed, "mesomusic":

> the aggregate of musical creations (melodies with or without words) functionally designed for recreation, for social dancing, for the theatre, for ceremonies, public acts, classrooms, games, etc., adopted or accepted by listeners of the culturally modern nations . . . mesomusic, then, coexists in the minds of urban groups along with fine-art music, and participates in the life of rural groups along with folk music.[17]

Little further research was undertaken in the following decade, prompting Robert Stevenson in 1978 to bemoan that "No facet of Latin American music more urgently awaits bibliographic control than the popular product-fed urban radio, television, and concert-going publics . . . yet it is the popular products that constitute the reality of Latin American music to millions. . . ."[18] Bruno Nettl's introductory essay to the anthology Eight Urban Musical Cultures: Tradition and Change stated the case more bluntly in the same year: ". . . there is a more important cause for the neglect of urban music. Ethnomusicologists, the scholars who have been most involved in the study of non-Western musics, have for most of their field's short history avoided studying the music of cities as such."[19]

Soon thereafter, in 1980, Harold Hinds, Jr., assessed the "new" research frontier of Latin American popular culture. He sustained the lament that Latin American popular music was a large field as yet little worked. He reiterated his judgment in a similar bibliographic essay, four years later: "Writing on Latin American music continues to be dominated by studies of folk, colonial and art music."[20]

Testing Hinds's statement against the published literature confirms that very little on popular music appeared before 1973, with increased scholarly attention only dating from the late 1970s and early 1980s (see Volume II, pp. 679-682).

Bibliographic resources for Latin American popular music remain similar to those for other Latin American musics. They center on the bibliographic citations provided at the conclusion of specific essays, articles, and books, supplemented by standard bibliographic references in music. Gérard Béhague concludes his essay on Latin American Popular Music in The New Grove (X:534) with a bibliography of pre-1974 sources, most of them monographs. Béhague likewise incorporates a short bibliography on Brazilian urban popular music, and a selected discography, in his 1973 study of the recent evolution of this form.[21] And Béhague's 1975 bibliographic essay on Latin American music annotates several studies of Brazilian and Mexican popular music from the 1970s.[22] The same author's bibliographic essay on research in Ecuadorian, Peruvian, and Brazilian ethnomusicology concludes with a selected bibliography on publications, several of which deal with popular music in Brazil.[23]

The generative force of Gérard Béhague in the arena of Latin American urban popular-music scholarship is irrefutable. His was the first doctoral dissertation[24] I know to respond to the calls of Seeger and others by paying popular music serious scholarly attention, and he continues to publish in the sphere of Brazilian popular music.[25] His earnest commitment has been conveyed to at least three of his students, who have published on popular musical culture in Mexico and Brazil.[26] Finally, the journal he founded in 1980, and which he currently edits--Revista de Música Latinoamericana/Latin American Music Review--has included at least one article on Latin American popular music in nine of its ten issues.[27]

As an introduction to the broader topic of bibliographic sources in Latin American Ethnomusicology per se (see Volume II, pp. 664-672), I suggest the reader consult first the several bibliographies found in The New Grove, both in the broad "Latin America" article (X:515, 522, 528, and 534) and in the articles on individual Latin American countries. Second, the two articles by Dale Olsen in the 1980 anthology edited by Elizabeth May, Musics of Many Cultures: An Introduction--"Symbol and Function in

South American Indian Music," and "Folk Music of South America, A Musical Mosaic"--should be consulted.[28] These essays conclude with helpful broad bibliographies, discographies, and filmographies on the ethnomusicology of South America's indigenous and folk cultures.

Malena Kuss's article on Charles Seeger, referred to above, provides (in her note 30) a helpful summary of bibliographic sources for the study of Latin America's living folk, popular, and indigenous musical traditions. She cites, among other sources, the biennial "Music" section of the Handbook of Latin American Studies (in the "Humanities" volumes), and the "Current Bibliography [Discography, and Filmography]" of Ethnomusicology. Ethnomusicology's unannotated "Current Bibliography, etc." is perhaps the most important bibliographic reference tool for Latin American ethnomusicology. In the first place, this "Current Bibliography" appears three times per year, in contrast to the Handbook's annotated "Music" section which is only published once every two years. Equally important, the Ethnomusicology compilation does not rely on the scanning of a single scholar, but rather utilizes bibliographic citations submitted by any and all scholars on a continuous basis, as well as listings located by the "Current Bibliography" staff. The "Dissertations and Theses" listing in the same periodical, compiled by Frank J. Gillis, keeps the reader current on this new scholarship in the ethnomusicology of Latin America, as well as other areas of the world.

Two other indispensable sources for materials on Latin American Ethnomusicology are The Music Index and RILM (Répertoire International de Littérature Musicale), both of which may be found in "Selected Bibliographic Sources in Latin American Ethnomusicology" (Volume II, pp. 664-672). The Music Index, appearing first in monthly fascicles and ultimately bound as annual volumes, indexes more than 225 periodicals from around the world by subject and author. It is relatively current, and the monthly fascicles are published only some eight months behind actual publication dates. Disadvantages include the use of author's first initial only and, for dissertations, reference only to the page in Dissertation Abstracts, without the year, institution, subject major, or dissertation adviser. RILM aims at comprehensive bibliographic coverage. Unlike The Music Index, which appears soon after the articles it indexes, each RILM fascicle carries the publication date of the articles, books, and reviews annotated inside it. Its quarterly fascicles appear some five years after the date on the journal front cover. As an example, the latest RILM fascicle to appear is that covering January–April, 1980.

This paper must conclude with an acknowledgment of a very recent and most significant publication for our topic, Malena Kuss's late 1984 "Current State of Bibliographic Research in Latin American Music."[29] She there remarks that "with exceptions,

Latin America's art and ethnomusic are inextricably bound."[30] This observation is supported by doctoral dissertations including Béhague's, and Kuss's own. Her comment also demonstrates the inevitable precariousness of our topic: bibliographic sources for Latin American ethnomusicology and historical musicology will inevitably overlap, owing to the integration of the two bodies of music. Given this bibliographic dilemma, the world of Latin American musical scholarship anxiously awaits Malena's forthcoming comprehensive volume, <u>Latin American Music: An Annotated Bibliography of Reference Sources and Research Materials</u>. This work will surely testify to the already sizable amount of research that has been undertaken in both Latin American ethnomusicology and Latin American music in general.

As Kuss has stated, and as I hope this presentation will further substantiate, "the vast amount of existing documentation [in Latin American music] should eradicate the misconception that, in 1984, research materials are inadequate or insufficient for a comprehensive, relevant, and accurate account of the music practiced and produced in Latin America from its pre-Columbian past to the present."[31] No one can question that the present, living musical traditions of Latin America will continue to live, or that these traditions will continue to be documented through the eyes, ears, and pens of ethnomusicologists.

NOTES

1.   Norma   McLeod,   "Ethnomusicological   Research   and Anthropology," <u>Annual Review of Anthropology</u>, 3 (1974), 108.

2.   Ronald R. Smith, "Latin American Ethnomusicology: A Discussion of Central America and Northern South America," <u>Revista de Música Latinoamericana/Latin American Music Review</u> <u>(LAMR)</u>, 3:1 (Spring/Summer, 1972), 8-14.

3.   Isabel Aretz, "Colecciones de Cilindros y Trabajos de Musicología Comparada Realizados en Latinoamérica durante los primeros Treinta Años del Siglo XX," <u>Revista Venezolana de Folklore</u> 4, 2ª época (Dec., 1972), 54.

4.   Ibid.

5.   A current pamphlet, <u>Publicaciones</u>, is available from the Instituto Nacional de Musicología "Carlos Vega."

6.   Smith, "Latin American Ethnomusicology," p. 7.

7.   George List, "Ethnomusicology in Colombia," <u>Ethnomusicology</u>, 10:1 (Jan., 1966), 71.

8.   Charles Seeger discussed repositories of field recordings of Latin American musics as early as 1946; see his introductory essay to the "Music" section of the <u>Handbook of Latin American Studies</u>, 9 (1943), 447.

9.   For one postdissertation product of this research, see John M. Schechter, "<u>Corona y baile</u>: Music in the Child's Wake of

Ecuador and Hispanic South America, Past and Present," LAMR, 4:1 (Spring/Summer, 1983), 1-80.

10. See Walter L. Welch, "Preservation and Restoration of Authenticity in Sound Recordings," Library Trends, 21:1 (July, 1972), 83-100; and, with Oliver Read, From Tin Foil to Stereo: Evolution of the Phonograph, 2d ed. (Indianapolis, IN: Howard W. Sams, 1976).

11. Clients of the Belfer Audio Laboratory and Archive have included the Musée de l'Homme, Paris; The Bernice P. Bishop Museum, Honolulu; and the Indiana University Archives of Traditional Music.

12. Interview with Walter Welch and William Storm, Belfer Audio Laboratory and Archive, Sept. 27, 1982.

13. Ibid.

14. 20 vols. (London: Macmillan; Washington, DC, 1980), X, 529.

15. See Malena Kuss, "Charles Seeger and Latin America: Themes and Contributions," Revista Interamericana de Bibliografía/Inter-American Review of Bibliography, 30:3 (1980), 231-237.

16. Willard Rhodes, "On the Subject of Ethno-musicology," Ethnomusicology Newsletter, 7 (April, 1956), 1-9.

17. Carlos Vega, "Mesomusic: An Essay on the Music of the Masses," Ethnomusicology, 10:1 (Jan., 1966), 3.

18. Robert Stevenson, "Music" section of the Handbook of Latin American Studies, 40 (1978), 536.

19. Bruno Nettl, "Introduction," in B. Nettl, ed., Eight Urban Musical Cultures: Tradition and Change (Urbana, IL: University of Illinois Press, 1978), p. 4.

20. Harold E. Hinds, Jr., "Latin American Popular Culture: Recent Research Trends and a Needs Assessment," Journal of Popular Culture, 18:1 (Summer, 1984), 62; the earlier article by the same author is "Latin American Popular Culture. A New Research Frontier: Achievements, Problems and Promise," Journal of Popular Culture, 14:3 (Winter, 1980), 405-412, esp. p. 409.

21. Gérard Béhague, "Bossa and Bossas: Recent Changes in Brazilian Urban Popular Music," Ethnomusicology, 17:2 (May, 1973), 209-233.

22. G. Béhague, "Latin American Music: An Annotated Bibliography of Recent Publications," Yearbook for Inter-American Musical Research, 11 (1975), 190-218.

23. G. Béhague, "Ecuadorian, Peruvian, and Brazilian Ethnomusicology: A General View," LAMR, 3:1 (Spring/Summer, 1982), 17-35.

24. G. Béhague, "Popular Musical Currents in the Art Music of the Early Nationalistic Period in Brazil, circa 1870-1920," Ph.D. diss., Musicology, Tulane University, 1966. 288 pp. (Dis. Abst. 27:05A, p. 1390; UM No. 6610751.)

25. See. G. Béhague, "Brazilian Musical Values of the 1960s and 1970s: Popular Urban Music from Bossa Nova to Tropicalia," Journal of Popular Culture, 14:3 (Winter, 1980), 437-452; also, "Interpenetration of Traditional and Popular Musics in the City of Salvador, Bahia [Brazil]," in D. Heartz and B. Wade, eds., Report of the Twelfth Congress [International Musicological Society]: Berkeley 1977 (Kassel: Bärenreiter; Philadelphia, PA: American Musicological Society, 1981), pp. 298-300.

26. David Stigberg: "Jarocho, Tropical, and 'Pop': Aspects of Musical Life in Veracruz, 1971-1972," in B. Nettl, ed., Eight Urban Musical Cultures: Tradition and Change (Urbana, IL: University of Illinois Press, 1978), pp. 260-295; also "Urban Musical Culture in Mexico: Professional Musicianship and Media in the Musical Life of Contemporary Veracruz," Ph.D. diss., University of Illinois at Urbana-Champaign, 1980. 408 pp. (Dis. Abst. 41:06A, p. 2349; UM No. 8026603); also "Mexican Popular Musical Culture and the Tradition of música tropical in the City of Veracruz," Studies in Latin American Popular Culture, 1 (1982), 151-163.

See Ralph Waddey, "Viola de Samba and Samba de Viola in the Recôncavo of Bahia (Brazil)." In two parts: [Part I]: Viola de Samba], LAMR, 1:2 (Fall/Winter, 1980), 196-212; Part II: Samba de Viola, in LAMR, 2:2 (Fall/Winter, 1981), 252-279.

See William Gradante: "'El Hijo del Pueblo': José Alfredo Jiménez and the Mexican canción ranchera," LAMR, 3:1 (Spring/ Summer, 1982), 36-59; also "Mexican Popular Music at Mid-Century: The Role of José Alfredo Jiménez and the canción ranchera," Studies in Latin American Popular Culture, 2 (1983), 99-114.

27. See the following studies, all in LAMR:

Theodore Solís, "Muñecas de Chiapaneco: The Economic Importance of Self-Image in the World of the Mexican Marimba," 1:1, 34-46;

Manuel H. Peña, "Ritual Structure in a Chicano Dance," 1:1, 47-73;

Ralph Waddey, 1:2 (see n. 26);

Rina Benmayor, "La 'Nueva Trova': New Cuban Song," 2:1, 11-44;

Ralph Waddey, 2:2 (Part II of the 2-part article; see no. 26);

William Gradante, 3:1, 36-59 (see n. 26);

Larry Crook, "A Musical Analysis of the Cuban Rumba," 3:1, 92-123.

Marina Roseman, "The New Rican Village: Artists in Control of the Image-Making Machinery," 4:1, 132-167;

Roberta L. Singer, "Tradition and Innovation in Contemporary Latin Popular Music in New York City," 4:2, 183-202;

Ruben George Oliven, "A Malandragem na Música Popular Brasileira," 5:1, 66-96;

Jorge Duany, "Popular Music in Puerto Rico: Toward an Anthropology of Salsa," 5:2, 186-216.

28. The full citation of the anthology is Elizabeth May, ed., Musics of Many Cultures: An Introduction (Berkeley, CA: University of California Press, 1980); the Olsen articles are on pp. 363-385 and 386-425, respectively.

29. Malena Kuss, "Current State of Bibliographic Research in Latin American Music," Fontes Artis Musicae, 31:4 (Oct.-Dec., 1984), 206-228.

30. Ibid., p. 211.

31. Ibid., p. 215.

II. The Literary Forms of the Minimally Schooled

29. THE SOUL OF THE PEOPLE: THE TANGO AS A SOURCE FOR ARGENTINE SOCIAL HISTORY

Donald S. Castro

Shortly before World War I, at a reception held by Czar Nicholas II for foreign diplomats accredited to his court, the Czar greeted each diplomat personally in a reception line. As his aide whispered the name of each, the Czar then greeted him as if he knew him personally. When the aide whispered the name of the Argentine Ambassador, the Czar exclaimed, "Ah yes, the tango!" If this story is true, it seems to show that even in distant St. Petersburg, Argentina was already closely identified with the tango. In the Hollywood films of the 1920s, Argentina was identified not only with tangos but also with gauchos. The same held true in Paris. In fact, these two images of Argentina eventually became one, with gauchos dancing tangos. It therefore seems reasonable that both of these cultural phenomena should be studied by scholars interested in Argentina. While this has been true in the case of the gaucho, very few American scholars have used the tango as a source for research into the Argentine reality. Perhaps this has been in part because the tango is popular culture and not yet truly respectable as a source for research.

The use of popular culture as a research source for social scientists has only recently come into its own. The pioneering research journal in this area, the Journal of Popular Culture, was not established until 1967.[1] Its primary focus is the United States and Western Europe, with occasional special issues devoted to other world areas. Studies in Latin American Popular Culture (SLAPC) was recently created (1982) to fill a geographic void not met by the older journal.[2] These journals have had the therapeutic effect of encouraging both social scientists and scholars in the humanities to look to popular culture sources as new research tools. This focus has helped inspire my study of the Argentine tango.

While it can be said with great assuredness that the Argentine tango is "popular culture," one is hard-pressed to come up with a facile definition of what "popular culture" is. Several contributors to one issue of the Journal of Popular Culture joined with the editor in attempting to develop a consensus on the term.[3] Many of those engaging in this quest have come to the field from a background in folklore and/or literature. These individuals include Ray Brown, the founding editor of the Journal of Popular Culture, who offered the following as a "viable definition" of popular culture: ". . . all those elements of life which are not narrowly intellectual or creatively elite and which are generally though not necessarily disseminated through mass media."[4]

The implication of this definition is that popular culture is mass culture. This is also explicit in the definition provided by Bruce Lohof, who stated that popular culture consists of the "cultural artifacts which are recognized by a significant percentage of the population";[5] or by Arthur Asa Berger, who suggested that popular culture is "the culture of the people . . . which appeals to large numbers of people."[6]

By these definitions, it seems that there must be some process for disseminating culture to large numbers of people before it can become mass culture. Consequently, before the invention of technologies for mass communications (e.g., the electronic media) in the early twentieth century, popular culture could only exceptionally have been the same as mass culture. In the Argentine context, such exceptions might be demonstrated through the example of José Hernández's epic poem Martín Fierro, which was read to large numbers of people in public readings in pulperías (bar-general stores) throughout the rural areas. Tom Kando, in his article in the Journal, confirms this view when he states "mass culture consists of cultural elements traditionally not included in high culture and transmitted by the printed press, the electronic media or by other forms of mass communication."[7]

The creation of SLAPC has not necessarily clarified our understanding of what popular culture can be. Its editors do, nonetheless, provide the following guide for contributors:

> By popular culture we generally do not mean cultura popular or folk culture. By popular culture we do mean--and this is only the most tentative of definitions--some aspect of culture which is accepted by or consumed by significant numbers of people. Acceptance or consumption may take the form of (1) widely held artifacts such as symbols, beliefs, and myths, or (2) direct participation as a viewer of, reader of, listener to, or some other sensory response to some aspect of popular culture.[8]

The Argentine tango clearly falls within this definition. However, it has had a long germination into what we now consider the tango. In its process of change, it has evolved from folk culture (SLAPC's cultura popular) to mass culture. This transition brings into play elements of folk culture, popular culture, and mass culture, and helps make the tango something further reaching than any specific category. In its earliest stage (1880-1890), it was most likely folk culture; in its next stage, as a defined dance (tango-danza), it could be defined as popular culture (1890-1917); when the tango became more than just a dance in a formalized way (tango-canción), after 1917, its evolution coincided with the beginnings of the electronic media of films and radio. By the 1930s, the popularity of sound films and radio made the tango-canción (tango-song) accessible to wide numbers of people. It could by then be properly classified as mass culture.

In considering the tango as a source for Argentine history, one must first recognize that Argentine acceptance of the tango as a cultural form has been class determined. In its earliest stages, the tango was clearly associated with the underclasses or the lumpen proletariat. The upper classes (primarily the men) joined the lower classes in their appreciation of the tango, and the tango environment of the bordello. The tango provided upper-class males with an escape from the social and moral restrictions of their class. To the elite male, the tango experience was similar to that of upper-class whites in New York who went to Harlem to do what was described in the song "Putting on the Ritz." For the lower classes, however, the tango was an expression of frustration and alienation. Only after World War I did the middle classes become tango-involved, and it was not until the late 1920s that all classes came to accept this form. These changes are clearly reflected in the tango lyric, and in the places where tangos were played--shifting from bordello to nightclub. In sum, the tango is very much a social document.[9]

The tango is also a source for urban history because it includes as a basic subtheme the geographic setting of a city, Buenos Aires. The tango, though generally associated with Argentina, is not truly an expression of Argentina in either the terms of its origins or its thematic worldview. The tango is intrinsically a part of the port city and capital of Argentina, Buenos Aires. This study is consequently space-bound by what Argentines would consider to be porteño. The scope of the research is also time-bound, in accord with the tango's stages of development as an identifiable cultural expression in the porteño environment.

The changes in tango themes as it evolved from the suburbio (outskirts of city) to downtown Buenos Aires at once reflect the creole's perception of the world about him and the rising cultural ascendancy of the immigrant.[10] The basic themes of the tango, in order of their development, fall into nine categories: the countryside, the suburbio, the city, love, the world of men/women (el ambiente), satire (la chachada), the life of a prostitute (el mundo ludiro), philosophies of life, and social protest.[11]

The theme of the countryside (el tema campesino) centers on the recently urbanized creole's nostalgia for his country home, or the settled city dweller's pining for a romanticized, rural long ago. This theme also recreates in a musical form the duelo criollo (creole duel), as well as recounting the wisdom of the volk. This first type of theme is exemplified in "El Entreriano" (The Man

from Entre Rios) (ca. 1897) by the creole Rosendo Menizábal.
(This was the pseudonym used by Anselmo Rosendo, 1868-1913,
who is credited with writing the first identifiable tango criollo.)

The theme of the arrabal or orillero (terms largely synonym-
ous with suburbio) includes subcategories that focused on the
patio of the conventillo (porteño tenement house), the barrio or
neighborhood, the changing demography of the city, and the like.

The theme of the city--its districts (barrios), its streets, its
events, its personalities, the docks, harbor and port facilities,
and above all the melancholy of individuals lost in its immense
anonymity--is perhaps the one with which we are most familiar.
This familiarity largely derives from the tango "Mi Buenos Aires
querido" (My Beloved Buenos Aires), immortalized by Carlos
Gardel (Charles Romuald Gardes, 1890-1936). The love theme
covers the full range from pure honest love (of mother, the
home, and children) to pure sex. Within this theme lies the
subtheme of betrayal, so important in the tangos "Amargura"
(Bitterness) and "El día que me quieras" (The Day That You
Love Me) immortalized as well by Carlos Gardel.[12]

The theme of the world of men and women is significant
because of the male's sexual dominance in the tango lyric. Women
are very secondary characters: whether as chinas (mistresses),
or prendas (skirts), they are little more than hembras (female
animals), rather than three-dimensional beings. The sense of
machismo permeates the tango. Also tied to this theme are lyrics
treating the lives of prostitutes, pimps, whores, and the petulant
lady's man, el compadrito. The massive influx of primarily male
immigrants, compounded by the creole male's resentment toward
the immigrant male who competed for the affections of Argentine
women, led to a male-dominated society with a tragic sense of
sex, a nostalgia for home, and a wistful desire for pure love.[13]

Other, interrelated themes involve social criticism and satire,
both of particular interest to the social historian. Social dis-
content, and radicalism within Buenos Aires' growing working
class, coincided with the development of the tango. The early
tango period (1890-1917) was characterized by the rise of radical
working-class movements, general strikes, and urban disruptions.
Working-class feelings of betrayal by the middle class and the
economic dislocations of the Depression characterized the era of
the tango as song (1920-1943). The culminating period of the
tango's evolution, between 1943 and 1955, coincided with the
ascendancy of Juan Perón.[14]

Since the primary source for this investigation was the tango
lyric, collections of tango lyrics published in Argentina proved
particularly useful. The chief publishing house on tango topics,
Ediciones Corregidor, has published a great deal of material by
Argentine authors. Notwithstanding the quantity of publications,
Argentine authors have done very little on the tango as a source
for history. Eminent literary figures like Jorge Luis Borges

(Evaristo Carriego, especially Chapter XI, "Historia del tango")[15] and Ernesto Sábato (Tango: Discusión y Clave)[16] have written on the tango.

Some direct participants have also written about their involvement in the evolving tango form, or about others with whom they worked during their careers. Perhaps the most prolific of these is the tango lyricist Francisco García Jiménez, who has written a number of books on the tango and two biographies of Carlos Gardel.[17] The importance of the tango as a symbol of porteño culture is clearly demonstrated by the monumental La historia del tango (18 volumes as of 1985), put out by Ediciones Corregidor. This multivolume work covers topics including male vocalists, leaders of tango orchestras, female vocalists, the 1920s, the role of the electronic media (movies and radio), the tango in the popular theater, and--in one whole volume--Carlos Gardel.[18] Some Argentine social scientists, such as Julio Mafud (Sociología del tango, 1966) have used the tango as a vehicle for research into the reality of porteño society. Others have considered it as part of broader studies, as in Florencio Escardo's Geografía de Buenos Aires (1966).[19] Obviously, Argentine authors recognize the significance of the tango to the history of Buenos Aires. Escardo's study is only one of many. Perhaps the most important are the monographs by Andrés Carretero on the porteño folk types associated with the tango (El compadrito y el tango: El hombre de la argentina comercial, 1964), and by Blas Matamoro, La ciudad del tango: tango histórico y sociedad (1969).[20]

The importance of the tango is also reflected in the number of records and tapes produced in Argentina, whether of new tangos or rereleases. Collections include the tangos of Carlos Gardel, Ignacio Corsini, Ada Falcón, and others. They are particularly useful because they contain complete discographic citations for these great tango interpreters.[21] Numerous sources, both primary and secondary, are available for research on the tango.

There are also important facilities available to the researcher in Argentina. The two most important are the specialized libraries of the Sociedad de Artistas y Compositores, SADAIC (Society of Artists and Composers), and the Academia Porteña de Lunfardo (the Porteño Academy of Lunfardo), both in Buenos Aires. The SADAIC, in essence the musicians' union headquarters, is an excellent locale to talk to old-timers who were active in the tango era of the 1930s. It also has comfortable facilities in which to carry out research and study. The Academia is a fine source on the tango lyric, much of which was written in Lunfardo. It has a file of its members, some of whom are possible sources of information on the tango's linguistic attributes.

Lunfardo is as closely related to Buenos Aires as the tango. Its history bears close similarities as well. Lunfardo, originally the argot of Buenos Aires' criminal classes, provided a secret way for criminals to communicate with one another. The origins of the language are as obscure as those of the tango but, when words were first associated with the tango, they were most often in Lunfardo. As the tango became more acceptable, so did Lunfardo change from the language of criminals to a more generalized slang acceptable to even the middle class. To some, Lunfardo grew into something very special, even unique, so that an academy could be established for its study and perpetuation. It was a language that the porteño could claim with honor and pride. Research on the tango requires a good command of this argot, or at the very least access to Lunfardo dictionaries. José Gobello and Eduardo Stilman, in addition to compiling numerous works on the tango, have also worked together to produce several helpful works on Lunfardo. These have been invaluable in determining the meaning of many tango lyrics.[22]

Research materials on the tango are not readily available in the United States. For traditional primary and secondary sources, the major research libraries, or those accessible through interlibrary loan systems, are of course useful. However, many collections are driven by the particular interests of local campus scholars, or by active area studies bibliographers. Materials falling outside their specializations are not necessarily readily available. For a scholar at a small university or college, access is especially critical: given the costs of specialized collections, their campus libraries are generally inadequate. In many cases, research in areas outside the mainstream is difficult if not impossible within the United States. My own research on the tango has been based almost exclusively on a personal library, my record and tape collection of Argentine materials, and my direct research in Argentina.

The tango is not the only popular expression useful for understanding Latin American history and popular culture. In the Argentine case, the circus and the popular theater (sainete criollo, teatro de revistas) are likewise important for understanding contemporary society. Almost nothing is known of the circus, either in Argentina or the United States. The teatro de revistas (similar to our vaudeville theater) is another area for studying Argentine values and social mores. While very little research has been carried out, there are enough theater plays to support studies of the sainete and its significance in Argentina's sociopolitical history. All of these sources require study, review, and use. They, like the tango lyric, are mirrors of the porteño and Argentine souls.

> Tango: eres un estado de
> alma de la multitud.

> Tango: you are the mirror
> of the multitude's soul.

NOTES

1. Ray B. Brown, ed., Journal of Popular Culture (Bowling Green, OH: Bowling Green State University). First published in the summer of 1967.

2. Harold Hinds, Jr., and Charles M. Tatum, eds., Studies in Latin American Popular Culture (Las Cruces, NM: New Mexico State University, 1982--).

3. Journal of Popular Culture, 9:2 (Fall, 1975).

4. As quoted in Donald Dunlop, "Popular Culture and Methodology," Journal of Popular Culture, 9:2 (Fall, 1975), 375-383. Ray B. Brown's original comments were in Brown and Ronald J. Ambrosetti, eds., Popular Culture and Curricula (Bowling Green, OH: Bowling Green University Popular Press, 1970), p. 11.

5. Bruce Lohof, "Popular Culture: The Journal and the State of the Study," Journal of Popular Culture, 6:3 (Spring, 1973), 456.

6. In Arthur Asa Berger, Popular Culture (Dayton, OH: Pflaum Standard, 1973), p. 8.

7. "Popular Culture and Its Sociology: Two Controversies," Journal of Popular Culture, 9:2 (Fall, 1975), 440.

8. Frontispiece advice to contributors in each edition.

9. For a discussion of the social classes see Donald S. Castro, "Popular Culture as a Source for the Historian: The Tango in its Era of the Guardia Vieja," SLAPC, 2 (1983), 70-85.

10. Creole (or criollo) in Argentina pertains to the native-born as opposed to immigrant. It also could mean mestizo, especially in a cultural sense of nativistically American.

11. Castro, "Popular Culture," pp. 76-78.

12. Donald S. Castro, "Popular Culture as a Source for the Historian: ¿Porqué Carlos Gardel? The Tango in the 1920s-1930s," unpublished manuscript.

13. Donald S. Castro, "Popular Culture as a Source for the Historian: The Tango in its Epoca de Oro, 1917-1943," unpublished manuscript.

14. Ibid.

15. Obras Completas, Vol. 1 (Buenos Aires: Emecé Editora, 1966).

16. Buenos Aires: Editorial Losada, S.A., 1963.

17. One of the biographies is a collaborative work with Gardel's first singing partner: Vida de Carlos Gardel [as told by José Razzano] (Buenos Aires: Editorial Crismar, 1951). This was first printed in 1946.

18. Carlos Gardel is the only vocalist honored with one volume dedicated exclusively to him. Other volumes are projected in this most ambitious series. The editors and authors read like a who's who of tango lyricists and include Jorge Rivera, Blas Matamoro, and José Gobello, among many others.

19. Buenos Aires: Editorial Universitaria de Buenos Aires. This is really a sociogeographical study of the city. The tango is also described as part of a larger study in Juan José Sebreli, Buenos Aires: Vida cotidiana y alienación (Buenos Aires: Ediciones Siglo Veinte, 1979).

20. Both these works are significant contributions to the study of the tango. The Carretero book was published in Buenos Aires by Ediciones Pampa y Cielo; the Matamoro book by Editorial Galerna.

21. While there are many record collections of Gardel's songs, the one used in this study was Carlos Gardel: Album Homenaje en el XXVIII Aniversario de su Desaparición (Buenos Aires: Odeon, Serie Coleccionista OLP No. 311, 1963). This includes a very complete discographic record of all Gardel recordings by title and number.

22. José Gobello has published a number of books on Lunfardo, and he is a corresponding member of the Academia Porteña del Lunfardo. Among his best known works are: Lunfardo (Buenos Aires: Editorial Freeland, 1953); Breve diccionario lunfardo (Buenos Aires: Editorial Freeland, 1959); and Vieja y nueva lunfardia (Buenos Aires: Editorial Freeland, 1969). Eduardo Stilman has also written extensively on both the tango and Lunfardo. One particularly useful work of his is Antología del verso lunfardo (Buenos Aires: Editorial Brújula, 1965).

SELECTED BIBLIOGRAPHY ON THE ARGENTINE TANGO

I. Primary Sources

Tango Anthologies

Centeya, Julian. Primera antología de tangos lunfardos. Buenos Aires: Librería/Editorial Astral, 1967.

Flores, C., E. Cadicamo, E. S. Discépolo, et al. Tangos antología, 2 vols. Ed. Idea Vilarino. Buenos Aires: Centro Editor de América Latina, 1981.

Gobello, José, and Jorge A. Bossio. Tangos, letras y letristas. Buenos Aires: Editorial Plus Ultra, 1979.

Gobello, José, and Eduardo Stilman. Las letras del tango de Villoldo a Borges. Buenos Aires: Editorial Brújula, 1966.

Jedesco, Luis Osvaldo, ed. Cancionero [by various song-writers], 9 vols. Buenos Aires: Torres Agüero, Editor, 1977-78.

República Argentina, Instituto Nacional de Musicología "Carlos Vega." Antología del Tango Rioplatense: Desde sus comienzos hasta 1920. Vol. I, 1984. Coordinated by and under the general supervision of Jorge Novati. Three-record set plus book (153 pp.). Other volumes projected.

Sareli, Jorge. El libro mayor del tango, 2 vols. México, DF: Editorial Diana, 1974.

Tango Contemporaries

Bozzarelli, Oscar. Ochenta años de tangos platenses. La Plata: Editorial Osbaz, 1972.

Cadícamo, Enrique. El desconocido Juan Carlos Cobián. Buenos Aires: Ediciones SADAIC, 1972. Written by a friend and colleague of Juan Carlos Cobián; more a personal reminiscence than a biography.

_____. Poemas del bajo fondo. Buenos Aires: A. Peña Lillo, Editor, n.d. [1976].

Canaro, Francisco. Mis bodas de oro con el tango y mis memorias, 1906-1956. Buenos Aires: CESA Talleres Gráficos, 1956. Famous tango orchestra leader.

Corsini, Dr. Ignacio. Ignacio Corsini, Mi Padre. Buenos Aires: Todo es historia, 1979.

Discepolín (Enrique Santos Discépolo). ¿A mí me la vas a contar? Discepolín y sus charlas radiofónicas. Buenos Aires: Editorial Freeland, 1973. Radio talks broadcast in 1951 by one of the most famous tango lyricists.

De Caro, Julio. El tango en mis recuerdos: Su evolución en la historia. Buenos Aires: Ediciones Centurión, n.d. Noted tango dance band leader in the 1920s, 30s, and 40s.

García Jiménez, Francisco. Carlos Gardel y su época. Buenos Aires: Ediciones Corregidor, 1976. García Jiménez is a noted tango lyricist. His career dates from the 1920s.

_____. Estampas de tango. Buenos Aires: Rodolfo Alonso, ed., 1968.

_____. El tango, historia de medio siglo 1880-1930. Buenos Aires: Editorial Universitaria de Buenos Aires, 1964.

_____. Vida de Carlos Gardel, cantada por José Razzano. Buenos Aires: Editorial Crismar, 1951. (First edition 1946.)

II. Secondary Sources

Books

Astarita, Gaspar J. Pascual Contursi, vida y obra. Buenos Aires: Ediciones La Campana, 1981.

Barcia, José. Tangos, tangueros y tangocosas. Buenos Aires: Editorial Plus Ultra, 1976.

Bates, Hector, and Luis J. Bates. La historia del tango: Sus autores, Vol. I. Buenos Aires: Talleres gráficos de la Compañía General Fabriel Financiera, 1936. Only one volume published.

Borges, Jorge Luis. Obras Completas. 3 vols. Buenos Aires: Editores Emecé, 1965-1966. Especially Evaristo Carriego, first published in 1930.

Briand, René. Crónicas del tango alegre. Buenos Aires: Centro Editor de América Latina, 1972. Part of the series: La historia popular: Vida y milagros de nuestro pueblo.

Campos, Isabel María del. Retrato de un ídolo: Vida y obra de Carlos Gardel. Castelar (province of Buenos Aires): Albores Editores, 1955.

Cantón, Darío. Gardel, ¿a quién le cantas? Buenos Aires: Ediciones de La Flor, 1972. First published in 1962.

Carella, Tulio. Tango--mito y esencia. Buenos Aires: Centro Editor de América Latina, 1966.

Carretero, Andrés M. El compadrito y el tango. El hombre de la Argentina comercial. Buenos Aires: Ediciones Pampa y Cielo, 1964.

Castillo, Catulo, ed. Buenos Aires: Tiempos Gardel, 1905-1935. Buenos Aires: Ediciones "El Marte," 1966.

Cerruti, Raúl Oscar. El tango: Su relación en el folklor musical y ubicación en la cultura argentina. Resistencia (Chaco): Universidad Nacional del Nordeste, 1967.

Couselo, José Miguel, and Osiris Chierico. Gardel: Mito-realidad-ubicación y antología. Buenos Aires: A. Peña Lillo, Editor, 1964.

Dos Santos, Estela. Las mujeres del tango. Buenos Aires: Centro Editor de América Latina, S.A., 1972. Part of the series: La historia popular: Vida y milagros de nuestro pueblo.

Escardo, Florencio. Geografía de Buenos Aires. Buenos Aires: Editorial Universitaria de Buenos Aires, 1966.

Ferres, Horacio. El libro del tango: Crónica y Diccionario: Arte popular de Buenos Aires, 2d ed. Buenos Aires: Antonio Tersol, Editor, 1980. First edition published in 1970.

Franco-Lao, Meri. Tiempos de tango: La historia, el ambiente, los personajes, los textos, pasado y destino. Buenos Aires: América Norildis Editores, SAICFI, 1977. First printed in Italian in Milan in 1975.

Galasso, Norberto. Discépolo y su época. 2d ed. Buenos Aires: Ediciones Ayacucho, 1973. First printed in 1967.

Gobello, José. Conversando tangos. Buenos Aires: A. Peña Lillo Editores, S.A., 1976.

Lara, Tomás de, and Inés Leonilda Roncetti de Panti. El tema del tango en la literatura argentina. Buenos Aires: Ediciones Culturales Argentinas, 1961. Officially printed by the Argentine Ministry of Education and Justice.

Mafud, Julio. Sociología del tango. Buenos Aires: Editorial Americalee, 1966.

Marambio Catán, Carlos. 60 años de tangos. Buenos Aires: Editorial Freeland, 1973.

Martínez Estrada, Ezequiel. La cabeza de Goliat. Buenos Aires: Editorial Nova, 1957.

Matamoro, Blas. Carlos Gardel. Buenos Aires: Centro Editor de América Latina, 1971.

_____. La ciudad del tango: Tango, historia y sociedad. Buenos Aires: Editorial Galerna, 1969.

Milkewitz, Harry. Psicología del tango. Montevideo: Editorial Alfa Montevideo, 1959.

Morena, Miguel Angel. Historia artística de Carlos Gardel. Buenos Aires: Ediciones Corregidor, 1983.

Natale, Oscar. Buenos Aires, negros y tango Buenos Aires: A. Peña Lillo Editor, 1984.

Portogalo, José. Buenos Aires: Tango y literatura. Buenos Aires: Centro Editor de América Latina, 1972. Part of the series: La historia popular: Vida y milagros de nuestro pueblo.

Priore, Oscar del. El tango de Villoldo a Piazolla. Buenos Aires: Crisis, 1975.

Puccia, Enrique Horacio. El Buenos Aires de Angel G. Villoldo, 1860-1919. Buenos Aires: Películas Impulso, 1976.

Puertas Cruse, Roberto. Psicopatología del tango. Buenos Aires: Editorial SOPHOS, 1959, Originally written in March, 1948.

República Argentina. Senado de la Nación. El tango y Gardel. Buenos Aires: 1975.

República de la Banda Oriental del Uruguay. Concejo Departamental de Montevideo. Homenaje a Carlos Gardel. Montevideo: Dirección de Artes y Letras, 1966.

Rivera, Jorge, B. Matamoros, José Gobello, et al. La historia del tango. Buenos Aires: Corregidor Editores, 1977-1985. 18 Vols.

Rossi, Vicente. Cosas de negros: Los orígenes del tango y otros aportes al folklore rioplatense. Rectificaciones históricas. Córdoba: Editora Imprenta Argentina, 1926.

Sebreli, Juan José. Buenos Aires, Vida cotidiana y alienación. Buenos Aires: Ediciones Siglo Veinte, 1979.

Sierra, Luis Adolfo. Historia de la orquesta típica: Evolución instrumental del tango. Buenos Aires: A. Peña Lillo, Editor, 1966.

_____. Tango. Buenos Aires: Todo Es Historia, 1976. Part of the series Todo es Historia.

Silbido, Juan. Evocación del tango, biografías ilustradas. Buenos Aires: Fondo Nacional de las Artes, 1964.

Silva, Federico. Informe sobre Gardel. Montevideo: Editorial Alfa, 1971.

Stilman, Eduardo. Historia del tango. Buenos Aires: Editorial Brújula, 1965.

Ulla, Noemi. Tango, rebelión y nostalgia. Buenos Aires: Jorge Alvarez, Editor, 1967.

Vidart, Daniel. El tango y su mundo. Montevideo: Ediciones Tauro, 1967.

_____. Teoría del tango. Montevideo: Ediciones de la Banda Oriental, 1964.

Magazines, Journals, Films, and Record/Tape Collections

Ada Falcón. Yo no sé qué me han hecho tus ojos. Buenos Aires: EMI 14198. Music from 1929 to 1940.

Azucena Maizani. La nata gaucha en versiones inéditas. Buenos Aires: Surco, Industrias Musicales, 145142.

Bernárdez, Francisco Luis. "Menosprecio del centro y alabanza del arrabal," La Nación (March 28, 1954, 2d section, "Acaulidades y Entrenamientos," p. 1.

Cendanes, Daniel. Buenos Aires Tango (revista bimestral), 1-14 (Nov.-Dec. 1970 - April-June 1974). No. 5 dedicated to Carlos Gardel, May-June 1971.

Francisco Canaro. Los Indispensables de Canaro: Francisco Canaro (intérprete) y su orquesta típica. Buenos Aires: EMI 14323. Music from 1935 to 1953.

Historia de la orquesta típica Víctor (1925-1930). Serie "Tango de Ayer." Buenos Aires: RCA Victor TAMS-4801.

Humberto Ríos, Director and Producer. The Tango Is a History. Black and white. 57 minutes. México, 1983.

Instituto Argentino de Estudios de Tango (de Buenos Aires). Estudios de tango: Revista de historia, crítica y polémica, 1-11 (Jan. 1971 - Aug. 1974).

Juan Schroder, Producer. Carlos Gardel, historia de un ídolo. Black and white. 88 minutes. Estudios Baires, Buenos Aires, 1966.

Julio de Caro. Toda Corazón, Julio de Caro y su orquesta típica. Serie "Tango de Ayer." Buenos Aires: RCA Victor TAMS-4805. Music dates from 1924 to 1928.

Radaelli, Sigrido, ed. Testigo: Revista de literatura y arte. Buenos Aires: Vol. I (Jan.-Mar. 1966).

Revista Gente. Special edition, "Carlitos Gardel." (June 2, 1977). Buenos Aires: Editorial Allalinda, S.A., 1977.

Laurence Hallewell and Cavan McCarthy

Origins

Our English word "chapbook" is a coinage of the last century: the Oxford English Dictionary gives its first use as of 1824. But the idea of cheap books for the masses is far older, predating even the introduction of movable type. As soon as minimal literacy was sufficiently widespread, it became economically worthwhile to mass-produce simple devotional texts such as the Biblia pauperum, printed from carved wooden blocks. In Portugal, the priority of such block books over letterpress may be as much as twenty-two years: there are rumors of block books at Leiria in 1465, and typography did not arrive (at Faro) until 1487. With the advent of movable type, these "little books" increased in both quantity and range. It is difficult to date the earliest because our knowledge of how and to whom fifteenth-century books were distributed remains inadequate. The titles and formats that eventually characterized chapbooks, livres de colportage, "market literature," livros de cego, folhetos de feira-- all terms based on distribution methods--were almost certainly at the beginning sold to much wealthier customers. The 1505 German version of Amerigo Vespucci's report to Lorenzo de' Medici, recounting his 1501 voyage to Brazil, has been cited as an early example of the news-item type of chapbook. However, its being a pamphlet of close to the right size (some 6 x 4.5 inches), with characteristic woodcut illustration, is hardly proof that it was produced for cheap sale to a mass market.

By the middle sixteenth century, however, the fulminations of lawgivers make it clear that both news and entertainment were reaching the wide public in chapbook form. The Reformation had played a part by fostering literacy, but generally each purchaser acted on behalf of a group of illiterate kith and kin. The text had to be designed for reading aloud, a characteristic still evident in this material in Brazil today.

News circulated in broadsheets (Spanish, hojas sueltas; Portuguese, folhas volantes), and also in short pamphlets of up to 16 pages. Longer works of up to 64 pages in a single gathering were destined for entertainment. Many of the more popular stories circulated throughout Europe. Those of the Carolingian cycle appeared in the fifteenth century (e.g., Four

---

Editor's Note. See also the authors' "Bibliography of Brazilian Chapbook Literature," Volume II, pp. 683-707.

Sons of Aymon at Lyons in 1480, and at London in 1488) in their original up-market versions, and were quickly adopted by the chapbook trade. Some were still being reprinted in Brazil in the 1950s.

The natural concern of the colonial powers to keep their overseas possessions in a state of tutelage, and free from unproductive distractions, led early to restrictions on the export thither of such trivia. Spain legislated a total ban on an American trade in vain works, "como son de Amadis," in April, 1531, but to little effect. Chapbook histories of the Princess Magalona, among other such forbidden titles, were smuggled into America in quantity even before the end of the sixteenth century.

Brazil seems to have been less favored: there is no evidence for this type of literature arriving there for almost another century and a quarter. This may reflect the long persistence of Tupi-Guaraní as the "língua geral do Brasil." One authority, Antônio Houaiss,[1] even links the chapbook's strong association with the Northeast of the country to the supposition that it was precisely there that Portuguese first supplanted Guaraní in everyday use. The earliest extant Brazilian bookseller's catalog, that of the Bahian Manuel da Silva Serva from 1811, has a whole section of "Papéis pertencentes a notícias, proclamações e tudo quanto pertence às Guerras, Tragedias e Novelas." Many of these were evidently chapbooks: an Entrada de Napoleão ao inferno, for instance, at 60 reis; or the very traditional Historia do Roberto do Diabo (the legendary life of William the Conqueror's ne'er-do-well eldest son), at eighty. Fifty years later, Portuguese chapbooks were still being imported by the Rio de Janeiro bookshop of B. L. Garnier, leading one researcher to confuse this Parisian (and originally Norman) Garnier with the early eighteenth-century namesake, chapbook-publishing family founded by Pierre Garnier of Troyes.

The first chapbooks to be published in Brazil were printed by the Impressão Régia in 1815. These were histories of the constant Magalona (first printed at Toledo in 1498), and of the damsel Theodora, as shrewd as she was fair. They were originally printed at Seville in 1519, but had been known in Spain for three centuries preceding, and traced back, via the Moors, to the Thousand and One Nights. The idea of producing such literature as a useful fill-in was taken up by other printers, so much so that not to have printed a Magalona became in popular superstition sufficient explanation for a printer's commercial failure--even that of Monteiro Lobato's book-publishing house in the São Paulo of 1925.

The onset of industrialization was accompanied by a proliferation of cheap newspapers and magazines, and a decline in street hawking, country fairs, and rural peddling. This and a gradual sophistication of popular taste[2] have eroded and finally destroyed the chapbook market almost everywhere outside Latin

America. Chapbooks in the United States declined as newspapers became cheaper and more plentiful in the early nineteenth century, and failed to survive the Civil War. In England, the repeal of the newspaper tax in 1855 was a serious blow, although one chapbook publisher hung on in London until 1901. The French livres de colportage (so-called from their display in trays hung from the chapmen's necks) were still sufficiently vigorous at midcentury for Napoleon III to be alarmed by their failure to endorse his regime with sufficient enthusiasm--he had them investigated by a special commission, and a censorship imposed.[3] But they too died out during the Third Republic. The "picturesque trade" survived longer in the underdeveloped south of Europe--Andalusia and the Mezzogiorno--but it is found no more even there. At Elvas, in southern Portugal, a few reprints of long-established texts were still on sale in the early 1970s, but no new material, it seems, was being written.

In the first detailed account of chapbooks in Brazil, by the literary critic Sylvio Romero in 1879, very similar reasons were advanced for anticipating their rapid disappearance there.[4] In fact, however, Romero was writing just as the printing press was spreading into the small towns of the sertão, preparing the way for the chapbook's finest flowering in Brazil. For the next half century, Brazilian production was in the ascendant. It reached its Golden Age during the Vargas years, from 1930 to 1954.

In Europe, many traditional oral ballads found fixed form by being printed as chapbooks. Margaret Spufford, writing on English chapbooks, has much to say about the interaction (for the worse) between the two. She would have it that the chapbook effectively destroyed England's authentic, spontaneous ballad tradition.[5] There is a connection between the ballad and the chapbook in Brazil, too, but one of a different and far healthier nature. The most notable transatlantic transplantation of the Portuguese ballad tradition occurred where Portuguese linguistic influence was strongest: in the backlands of the Northeast. According to Candace Slater's Stories on a String, "the first great school of cantadores, the Escola do Teixeira, emerged toward the end of the eighteenth century in the Paraíban interior"[6] in the small town from which it took its name. The cantadores recited spontaneously composed narrative poetry (cantar is semantically closer to Virgil's "Arma virumque cano" than to our English "sing"), to the accompaniment of the guitar-like viola.[7] It was only natural that they should seek to retell the chapbook stories in verse as soon as these began to circulate in the outback. Such rhymed versions quickly achieved print, following the arrival of the press. Chapbooks in prose, even for the relation of current news events, are now practically unknown in Brazil. The first great name among chapbook versifiers was Silvano Pirauã de Lima, but the first "popular poet" to be published on a large scale was Leandro Gomes de Barros, a native of Teixeira who moved to the state capital Parahyba do Norte (now João Pessoa) and began publishing in 1889. (He later wrote for publication by his son-in-law Pedro Werta Batista Guedes of Guarabira, a small town in the hills fifty-seven miles northwest of João Pessoa.)

By 1911 there were at least two established bookshops in João Pessoa specializing in chapbooks: the Centro de Publicações, with agents in Recife and Lisbon (!); and the Livraria Popular, owned by Pedro Werta's brother Francisco das Chagas Batista. Batista had made the money needed to open his quite substantial shop by a mere nine years' hawking chapbooks at country fairs. Even more successful was João Martins de Athayde, a former Amazonian rubber tapper, who set himself up as a chapbook publisher in Recife on the strength of having bought Leandro's copyrights from the poet's widow in 1921.[8] He gathered about him a number of poets whom he treated like the apprentices and journeymen of a medieval artist's workshop, dividing the work up among them and publishing the joint product under his own name as "editor proprietário." After dominating the chapbook industry during its most prosperous years, he was in 1948 incapacitated by a stroke. He then sold out to José Bernardo da Silva, his agent in Juazeiro do Norte. Juazeiro was the home of Padre Cícero, an unfrocked priest who died there in his nineties in 1934, and whose enormous popularity had made the small town in upstate Ceará a center for pilgrimage so important that by the time of his death it had become the virtual capital of the sertão. Juazeiro was particularly renowned for its trade in the region's traditional handicrafts: leather goods, firearms, and chapbooks. Silva, with his Tipografia São Francisco, was thus the natural successor of Athayde as the country's leading chapbook publisher. The business was continued after Silva's death by his daughters, albeit under the management of a former apprentice, Expedito Sebastião da Silva.[9]

The most important Paraíban publisher of the 1950s was Manoel Camilo dos Santos, a cantador who began publishing in Guarabira in 1942, moved to Campina Grande (second city of the state) in 1953, and in 1957 gave his then quite substantial business the name Estrella [sic] da Poesia. Although he was ruined by the expenses of an ill-advised candidacy for local political office in 1961 or so, his son-in-law José Alves Pontes was able to purchase the original business in Guarabira (of which he had been manager). José's Tipografia Pontes continues and, because of the low costs in the rural Northeast, prints for the Rio de Janeiro poet and chapbookmonger Apolônio Alves dos Santos. Another important publisher of the 1950s, who suffered a serious reverse in the early 1960s, was João José da Silva of Mostardinha, Recife. He sold both his business name, Editora Luzeiro, and his copyrights to the former Editora Prelúdio of São Paulo, for whom he is now the Pernambucan agent.

Academic Interest

Sylvio Romero's early interest in chapbook literature was exceptional. Not until the Modernist[10] movement of the 1920s gave a nationalist and nativist direction to Brazilian art and literature was there any other scholarly concern. Luís da Câmara Cascudo, today the grand old man of Northeastern folklore, published his first book on the subject in 1939. Little else of significance occurred until the 1950s, when the Casa de Rui Barbosa (the Rio home, now museum, of the Bahian republican jurist) set up a small center for chapbook research. This was followed, from the early 1960s, by a steady growth in academic studies, particularly by French Brazilianists. Raymond Cantel was the outstanding pioneer.

Outside researchers introduced the Spanish term "literatura de cordel" as a generic term for what its practitioners, more concerned with specific categorization, had known as (according to size) folhas volantes, folhetos, or romances de feira. The name cordel, referring to the frequent custom of displaying the chapbooks like Christmas cards along lengths of string, was resented and remains unacceptable to traditionalists. "Quem te falar em cordel/ é estudante ou turista/ que trata nosso folheto/ como produto de artista," in the words of one poet.[11] But most chapbook professionals see themselves as businessmen catering to consumer preference, rather than as artists who can afford to indulge their own inclinations. So the term prescribed by researchers, journalists, and middle-class collectors is now generally--if reluctantly--accepted. But this only applies to the folhetos themselves: the people involved are still poetas populares (if authors), or folheteiros (if publishers or vendors).

As recently as 1972, the Aurelião[12] could still define cordel as "de pouco ou nenhum valor literário." By 1975, the dictionary's author (or his publishers) felt obliged to substitute the nonjudgmental "romanceiro popular nordestino." In these last few years it has come to be seen as something to be esteemed and fostered as a phenomenon authentically, typically, and, one might almost say, exclusively Brazilian: the equivalent of America's apple pie, or perhaps (a closer analogy) English change ringing. Cordel is included in university literature courses. The Catholic University of Rio de Janeiro was averaging almost one dissertation a year on it by the late 1970s, and it was even the theme chosen for the Fifth National Conference of Teachers of Portuguese[13] in 1978. Almost every cultural institution of note in the Northeast, and many elsewhere in Brazil, has developed some program to investigate, sponsor, or encourage cordel. The federally funded Joaquim Nabuco Social Science Institute in Recife has been interested since at least 1971, when it ran a competition to find the best cordel illustrator. Its Museu do Homem do Nordeste includes an impressive display of cordel. The Federal University of Paraíba set up its Programa de Pesquisa em Literatura Popular in July 1977, and now has a sizable number of publications to its credit. A number of research publications have also come from Natal's José Augusto Foundation, a cultural organ of the state of Rio Grande do Norte. In Salvador, the Fundação Cultural of the state of Bahia has a program to actually publish folhetos, as have a number of other institutions.

This rising interest in cordel has also resulted in motion pictures and television shows, and the genre has been used or imitated in the theatre (e.g., Ariano Suassuna's Auto da compadecida), in the novel (in ways ranging from Jorge Amado's Tereza Batista cansada de guerra to João Guimarães Rosa's epic Grande sertão, veredas) and, inevitably, in poetry, where (for instance) João Cabral de Melo Neto's haunting Vida e morte severina conforms almost completely to the cordel norm, save in length and publication format. Outside interest has become so great that one eighty-year-old popular poet, asked whether cordel was on its way out, replied ruefully, "Depende . . . Em literatura tá ganhando terreno. Tá perdendo é na leitura."[14] Another practitioner told a newspaperman interviewing him that so many researchers had sought him out that he had long ago tired of repeating his life story. "Então comecei a mudar minha biografia. Foi um sucesso medonho."[15]

Illustrations

One evident result of this academic and official interest, beside the imposition of the term "cordel," lies in the matter of illustration. Medieval blockbooks lent themselves to illustration, and it was technically easy to include woodcuts in the printing of letterpress chapbooks. Although many were crude, quite high standards were sometimes achieved: Thomas Bewick himself began as a chapbook illustrator. In Brazil, however, although the Impressão Régia's Magalona and Teodora had woodcut frontispieces, most early folhetos were solid text. The practice of putting a simple illustration on the cover developed slowly, at the beginning of this century. Nowadays some sort of cover picture is almost de rigueur, though the illustration need not necessarily be a woodcut. Halftone blocks, bought secondhand from newspaper offices, and however inappropriate, are often preferred for the appeal of their apparent sophistication. If an ancient photograph of Clark Gable and Vivien Leigh on the outside of O prince João sem medo appears incongruous to the middle-class folklorist, this is because he allows his totally irrelevant sense of history to intrude on what for the normal reader is contemporary or timeless.

But photographs have none of the esthetic appeal that led David Bland in his History of Book Illustration to categorize cordel woodcuts, "of a curiously archaic appearance similar to French medieval etchings," as practically the only Brazilian book illustration worthy of mention. Unfortunately, the influence of outsiders (particularly when holding competitions or subsidizing publication) has been strong enough to encourage the use of woodcuts, and to extend them to subjects for which they are no longer considered suitable by the consumer. Readers expect them only in tales of obvious fantasy (to depict the Devil or anthropomorphic animals, for instance). At least one commentator, Liêdo Maranhão,[16] insists that this interference has actually prejudiced sales. On the other hand, some printmakers have found it more rewarding to give up cordel work and instead cater to the middle-class art market.

A curious coincidence about cordel is that, whereas most of the important poets and publishers are still, at least in their origins, from Paraíba, the outstanding illustrators seem all to come from the neighboring state of Pernambuco. José Soares da Silva ("Dila"), perhaps the most talented, is from Caruaru (the state's major inland city). José Francisco Borges ("J. Borges"), who continues to illustrate cordel despite an international reputation as a printmaker, is from nearby Bezerros. And José Costa Leite is from Condado, a small town in the far west of the state.

Subjects

Robert Mandrou, describing the themes treated by seventeenth-century livres de colportage, talks of

> une culture complexe où sont juxtaposées . . . au moins trois traditions de classes dominantes: d'abord les survivances de la culture féodale médiévale, romans de chevalerie, chansons de geste héritées d'un lointain passé et point encore oubliées, alors même que la noblesse a cessé depuis longtemps de se conformer collectivement et individuellement a ces idéaux chevaleresques. En second lieu, la continuité beaucoup plus vivante de la culture cléricale, telle que théologiens et clercs de tous ordres l'ont constituées au long du Moyen Âge, telle qu'elle tente de se renouveler encore depuis la Réforme; enfin et surtout, la culture bourgeoise, laïcisée en grande partie, bourrie de richesses de l'héritage gréco-romain retrouvée . . .[17]

Thomas Frost, cited by Margaret Spufford,[18] gives the "prominent favourites" among early nineteenth-century English chapbooks as "Friar Bacon and Dr. Faustus . . . the Seven Champions of Christendom, some selections from the Arabian Nights and an abridgement of the Memoirs of Baron Trenck."

This is not far different from what Sylvio Romero found in Brazil in the 1870s: "A história da donzela Theodora, A imperatriz Porcina, A formosa Magalona, O naufrágio de João de Calais, juntamente com Carlos Magno e os doze pares de França, O testamento do galo e da galinha, e, agora, nos últimos tempos, os poemas do poeta popular João de Sant'Anna de Maria sobre a

guerra do Paraguai."[19]   Even in 1953, Câmara Cascudo could
describe the Doze pares de França as "até poucos anos o livro
mais conhecido pelo povo brasileiro do interior," and João Severo
da Silva of Bayeux (a suburb of João Pessoa) could find it worthwhile in the 1960s to issue a new sequel to João de Calais.

The traditional stock of stories is continually renewed from
the literature of the elite; see, for instance, Pat Roger's account
of chapbook drawings on eighteenth-century English classics in her
(his?) Literature and Popular Culture.[20]   Candace Slater gives
Brazilian examples of versions of José de Alencar's Iracema and
Bernardo Guimarães's A escrava Isaura from the last century, and
Jorge Amado's Gabriela and Tereza Batista from this.   However,
she suggests that such cordel adaptations are only commercial
successes when consumer interest has been aroused by versions
on film or television.[21]

And of course the strife-torn sertão, land of bandits and
mystics, has its own folk heroes, who form the subject of
innumerable folhetos: Padre Cícero Rômão (already mentioned);
the Robin Hood figure of Antônio Silvino (who, being a
repentista--ballad singer--himself, as well as an outlaw, was
largely the author of his own folk-image); and the great bandit
chief of the 1930s, Lampião, whose cordel personality, according
to Dila,[22] is an amalgam of no fewer than twelve reis de cangaço
(kings of outlawry).

Fully a third of a chapbook collection formed by the
seventeenth-century English diarist Samuel Pepys consists of
"small merry books."   Brazilian cordel has its corresponding
share of humor.   One old favorite tells of a hick from Minas who
visits Rio and is conned into "buying" a trolley car.   Bawdy
humor constitutes a category of its own, the literatura de
safadeza, some of which has been anthologized by regular trade
publishers for the middle-class market: for example, Uns
fesceninos, edited by Oswaldo Lamartine de Faria, illustrated by
Poty and issued in a limited edition by Artenova in 1970.   Most of
this depends on skillful use of double entendre, as in O encontro
de velha que vendia tabaco com o matuto que vendia fumo,
employed in the defense of traditional values, or at least with
implicit acceptance of them.   Real pornography, crudely
expressed, anonymously written, and clandestinely distributed,
does however exist.[23]

But so, on the other hand, does improving and devotional
literature, the equivalent of Margaret Spufford's "little godly
books": Biblical tales, lives of the saints, and counsels against
violence or the perils of Demon Rum.   The Devil himself makes
frequent appearance, as our accompanying bibliography
(Volume II, pp. 683-707) confirms.   More often than not he is
treated humorously, although the very humor may mask a deep-
seated fear.   The novelist Guimarães Rosa was sufficiently
impressed by the "sertanejo's" ambiguous attitude toward Satan to

make it the basic theme of his cordel-inspired Grande Sertão, veredas, well conveyed by the novel's English title, The Devil to Pay in the Backlands.

News has always been an attractive subject for the ballad writer and his customers,[24] and many folhetos relate natural disasters (As novas calamidades das chuvas em Timbaúba or As enchentes de Vitória e os horrores de várias cidades da região), horrendous crimes (O pai que forçou a filha na Sexta-feira da Paixão), technological triumphs (O homem chegou na lua) or political events, both Brazilian (from Brazil entrou, Alemanha perdeu a Guerra to A vitória de Tancredo Nevez [sic] e a derrota de Paulo Maluf) and foreign (Libertação dos refréns americanos do cativeiro do Iran). Any event of importance generally gives rise to several rival versions (Eleições diretas já from Apolonio Alves dos Santos, Queremos diretas já from Leonardo . . .). Self-styled "poeta-repórter" José Francisco Santos kept a file of lives of the famous which he could rush into print, after adding a suitable last verse, as soon as he heard of their death. His Morte de Juscelino Kubitschek was on the streets within twenty-four hours of the former president's fatal car crash.

Whatever the subject, cordel remains a very traditional medium. Its physical format has barely changed in five centuries. The choice of verse form in Brazil is quite circum-scribed, and although one account[25] lists seventeen different types, the bulk of cordel is composed in verses of sextilhas or décimas (six or ten heptasyllabic lines). The poem can still even start with a Homeric invocation: "Santa musa dos poetas mandai-me rima altaneira," complete with archaic use of the second person plural of respect. And the basic values and outlook expressed remain very traditional, too.

But all this does not imply unthinking endorsement of the status quo. Criticism of abuses of economic or political power, and of the impact of government policy on the poor, is a frequent--and dangerous--cordel subject. Abraão Batista's A corrupção no Ceará brought him before a military court, and he was abruptly dismissed from his teaching job when he wrote a folheto on a murder case involving some important people. Worse befell Cuica do Santo Amaro, a "poeta popular" whose output included such topics as O que dizem da polícia, Porque falta luz na cidade, and O câmbio negro e as misérias da Bahia: he was the victim of an unknown assassin shortly after the 1964 military coup d'état. José Francisco Soares, in a 1978 interview by the newsweekly Istoé, went so far as to attribute the decline in sales to the fact that customers looked for criticism of the ills of daily life, which no one dared cater to. The increase since then in cordel with titles like A dor qui mas doi no pobre é ador da umilhação, Delf[i]m e Decreto 2045, A crise e a carestia matando o povo de fome, and even O filho de Satanas no Colégio Eleitoral is a welcome sign that the post-1979 Abertura is now curtailing

repression of even the lower classes in the outback. Unfortunately, the police have always looked upon the balladmonger as a
vagabond, making police harrassment an occupational hazard even
when the material itself is innocuous. As recently as 1981, João
José da Silva ("Azulão"), a poeta with a national reputation, was
arrested in Nova Iguaçu (a working-class suburb of Rio de
Janeiro) just for trying to sell his folhetos.

Despite this, the popular appeal of cordel remains strong
enough for commercial firms, fundamentalist sects, and
government agencies to appreciate its value for publicity and
propaganda. Quite a few cordel poets are themselves willing to
compose "sob encomenda." The results range from O movimento
estudantil e as duchas Erasmo em São Paulo, lauding public
security chief Erasmo Dias's brutal suppression of students in
1977; through O papa-léguas da Itapemerim, endorsing a long-
distance bus line; and Pé de dinheiro do Banorte, advertising a
bank; to O prefeito Desafio que mudou Caruaru, in praise of the
local mayor; Carta aos trabalhadores da cana, sponsored by
various Roman Catholic organizations seeking to unionize
sugarcane workers; and Um pequeno agricultor que se tornou
fazendeiro, commissioned by EMBRAPA (the federal agricultural
research institute) to explain and encourage better farming
methods.[26]

Cordel Today

In the 1940s, José Bernardo da Silva's Tipografia São
Francisco was producing 300,000 folhetos a month, in print runs
of 12,000 per title. A decade later, the market was still large
enough for the suicide of President Vargas (a folk hero in the
Northeast) to give rise to sixty rival cordel accounts, in a total
of two million copies. By the 1970s, however, the Tipografia
São Francisco, then the largest folhetaria in the Northeast, was
down to 40,000 copies a month. Its smaller rivals were each
printing barely a tenth as much.

Many factors have contributed to the decline. We have
already mentioned the post-1964 repression and its limitations on
freedom of expression. At least as serious has been the way
production and distribution costs have risen faster than the
general rate of inflation. Between 1972 and 1975, for instance,
the manufacturing cost of a thousand-copy, 32-page edition went
from US$27 to US$65. Works larger than this were virtually
priced out of existence, and we now find the same thing happening to 32-page editions: "os folhetos de 8 a 16 páginas aqui já
estamos vendendo a Cr$500,oo e os de 32 pag. a 700,oo quando
tem, pois quase não existe mais."[27] The spread of the super-
market has also had its effect, eroding the importance of the open
market where cordel has always reached its public. A greater
availability of other media--radio, television, illustrated
magazines, and even recorded sound--has increased competition

for the consumer's limited income, and helped change his taste. Above all, the almost continuous fall in income since 1964 has made it more and more difficult for consumers to buy anything beyond absolute necessities.

The Tipografia São Francisco, which latterly took to using the imprint Lira Nordestina, was sold in 1984 to the state government of Ceará. The new owner has turned it into a museum of cordel, although apparently with the intention of publishing at least a few reprints of older titles. The other main Juazeiro publisher, Manoel Caboclo e Silva of the Folhetaria Casa dos Horóscopos, recently lost the son who would have taken over the business, and tried to sell out. No buyers seem to have come forward, and he now seems resigned to closing down and retiring.[28] Rodolfo Coelho Cavalcante, the founder and chief sustainer of the industry's professional association, the Ordem Brasileira dos Poetas da Literatura de Cordel, and himself among the most prolific of cordel authors, lost his best sales location when Salvador's main market burned down in 1984 (described in his ballad O incêndio do Segundo Mercado Modelo, da Bahia).[29] No longer able to do enough business to continue, he has taken a full-time job with the hope of saving enough to eventually return to cordel publishing. One Paraiban folheteiro, who used to travel regularly from fair to fair to sell his products, concluded in 1980 that, with escalating costs (even of fairground stall rents), he could no longer cover his expenses. He gave up his business to open a bar.

Some poets, and some of their customers, have reacted to "progress" by retreating into a more fanatical conservatism. Particularly prevalent is that type of Protestant fundamentalism that rejects anything pleasant in life as sinful. Several have abandoned their vocation upon conversion to the creed of one of the American missions. Younger folk, on the other hand, have tended to become self-conscious about liking something so old-fashioned and unsophisticated, and hardly any are being attracted into the industry. As a result, the Northeast now has fewer than sixty active popular poets, all but eight of whom are in their fifties or older.[30]

The decline in consumer demand is particularly evident in cordel's traditional northeastern heartland. This may reflect in part the fact that the poor have suffered there even more, economically, than elsewhere in Brazil. Until recently, the legal minimum wage was always set at a lower level in the north than in the south of the country. Nonetheless, living costs are almost certainly higher: in 1982 Recife had the nation's highest urban cost of living. The proportion of workers who are cheated of even the legal minimum is also undoubtedly higher in the Northeast. Nor must we forget that the region is only just recovering from one of the more severe of its terrible periodic droughts, in which wide-scale famine was only averted through massive federal aid. Apolônio Alves dos Santos returned from a buying expedition to Juazeiro do Norte, Campina Grande, and Guarabira in November 1984 empty-handed: "não encontrei nada de folhetos," he wrote. "Portanto tenho que me segurar com um pouquinho que ainda tenho; a nossa literatura está ficando por decadência, isto por causa dos altos preços de materiais e mão de obra, de forma que os pequenos industriais não teem condições de continuarem."[31]

Apolônio is a bricklayer who writes and sells folhetos in his spare time in the São Cristovão open-air market in the Zona Norte of Rio de Janeiro. The biggest markets for cordel now lie in the working-class industrial districts of the great cities of the south. But so many of the consumers there are nordestino immigrants who, presumably, buy it mainly to help assuage their saudades de pátria (homesickness), that one fears for the survival of such interest beyond the present generation.

The resultant concern among intellectuals, anxious to preserve what is now fashionable to regard as an important element of the national culture, has led to increasing institutional attempts to foster cordel. In one instance, that of the Casa das Crianças de Olinda (an orphanage), many popular poets' copyrights were purchased. To the authors' great annoyance, only a few titles were ever printed: apparently a change of personnel led to a change in the institution's policies. How far folhetos that do get officially published, or otherwise subsidized, can be regarded as authentic, remains a moot point. The foreign librarian needs at least to be aware of the situation, and to be ready to make any necessary distinctions in his acquisition policies.

A rather different question of authenticity is posed by the products of the present owners of the Luzeiro imprint. These contain perfectly genuine cordel balladry: besides preprinting copyrights bought from João José da Silva, the firm employs the important popular poet Manoel d'Almeida Filho as editorial consultant to advise on new material. But Luzeiro's publications are produced in São Paulo, by modern offset lithography on normal-quality book paper in an oversize format (18.5 x 13.5 cm, compared with the traditional 16 x 12), with glossy polychrome illustrated covers, and in editions of 5,000 copies (or more) for nationwide distribution . . . and at a price, to boot, hardly above that of their hand-composed rivals. Modern methods apply even to their publishing decisions: any title failing to sell 5,000 copies in a year ceases to be reprinted.

For most cordel enthusiasts, such mass-production methods industrialize and decharacterize their beloved literature, whose traditional rough appearance reflects its humble origins and proves its authenticity. Their outrage has been so strong that, in 1976, Rodrigo Coelho Cavalcante--the industry's spokesman--felt obliged to publish a vigorous defense of Luzeiro. By its success, he claimed, it was actually making it possible for popular poets and their poetry to survive.[32] Not only can the firm afford to pay royalties, but the more sophisticated appearance of its publications, and its more orthodox and commercially reliable business methods, have made its products an acceptable item for display in supermarkets. Perhaps the most important consideration for the foreign library purchaser is that, with its nationwide distribution, Luzeiro can no longer furnish the type of information about consumer tastes and attitudes in specific localities which may be surmised from the content of traditional cordel, with its much more limited radius of distribution from the place of publication. Even this, however, is an uncertain generalization. Publications from Bahia are seldom sold in Recife, nor those of Pernambuco and Paraíba in Salvador. All, however, may turn up in Rio.

Ironically, Luzeiro has a good claim to be not only a traditional cordel publisher that made good but also the country's oldest surviving one. Its founder, José Pinto de Souza (1881-1950), was a Portuguese immigrant who started the firm in 1915, in his own name, to publish Brazilian versions of Portuguese cordel. He began issuing Brazilian originals some fifteen years later, when the collapse of Brazil's currency in the Depression made foreign publishing rights prohibitively expensive. The name was changed to Prelúdio two years after his son and stepson inherited the business, and it became Luzeiro in 1973. It now has almost a hundred titles in print (out of a total output in excess of five hundred titles). It nonetheless remains a family firm, and far from the "multinacional de cordel" depicted by some of its detractors. Recently some other firms, such as the Livraria Bahiana of Salvador, have paid it the compliment of copying its methods.

There is also a growing number of popular poets who make their work available on LP discs rather than in any form of print. Many have taken to the airwaves, even if this is no more than twenty minutes at 5:45 a.m. on some small-town radio station.

For the ordinary, man-in-the-street consumer of cordel poetry, there is no merit in outmoded technology or business methods--unless they keep prices down. We have already mentioned the consumer preference for halftone photographs over woodcuts. In the golden age of cordel, many publishers were hardheaded businessmen running successful enterprises which they eventually sold for considerable sums.[33] The French livres de colportage were, by the standards of the time, comparatively big business; and Spufford gives details of fortunes made in the English chapbook trade. In contrast, however, to attempts such as those of Luzeiro to adopt modern methods so that the publication of the traditional material for its traditional customers may continue to be commercially viable, we find in Brazil nowadays a number of anti-establishment intellectuals drawn to the traditional format as a type of "imprensa nânica" (alternative press). This produces what Manuel Diegues Júnior has called "literatura de cordel para-folclórica,"[34] really a special form of small-press activity. This phenomenon entails the noncommercial publishing of modern poetry by enthusiasts, a movement now firmly established in North America and Europe, and indeed in Brazil. We can best illustrate it by enumerating the similarities between cordel para-folclórica and small-press poetry publishing in general.

First, the poetry is seen as distinct from that of the literary establishment, which usually disparages it. Therefore the poets not only write poetry but they also have a missionary role in defending their type of poetry. They wish their achievements to be recognized by the establishment, yet they also wish to remain outside that establishment, as bohemian Zé Limeira/Charles Bukowski characters. Dedication and enthusiasm are prime qualities. In the words of the most active para-folkloric cordel poet, it is done "for love and cultural resistance."[35]

Second, the format is seen as an essential factor in distinguishing this poetry from that of the establishment. Crude production methods, such as mimeograph or the cheapest possible printing, are commonly and deliberately chosen. In Brazilian small-press poetry (sometimes called lixeratura, from lixo, trash), the stapling together of low-grade paper, smudging, and printing errors have a meaning (his emphasis) for the poets, according to Carlos Messeder Pereira.[36] One cordel para-folclórica publisher, José Rodrigues of Rio de Janeiro, notable for the extreme roughness of his chapbooks, "makes a point" of primitive production.[37]

There is in both types an ostensible lack of concern for financial matters. Such attitudes are intimately linked to a position of protest against capitalism. Publications are priced so cheaply that it is difficult even to recover costs. Franklin Maxado Nordestino, writing of himself in the third person,[38] explains that "he tries to live idealistically from his poetry and gets annoyed when asked 'Do you make any money at it?' He always replies that he could do so, because he believes in what he is doing, but that he really does it for love."

Enthusiasts are geographically scattered, and contact is chiefly by exchange of publications. Some individuals devote much of their time and energy to linking this loose network. In the world of cordel para-folclórica, Maxado is the most important such person.

This type of literature, being by definition a form of protest, has almost inevitably suffered repression: small-press poetry chiefly for obscenity; intellectual cordel for its comments on poverty and other sociopolitical issues. There were numerous prosecutions of small-press poets in the 1960s, usually in such provincial towns as Cleveland, Ohio, or Blackburn, Lancashire. Repression in Brazil under the military regime affected both traditional cordel poets, as I have indicated, and the intellectuals. But the former, because of their humbler social status, could not afford to be deliberately provocative, and in many cases did not believe it their duty to challenge the established order.[39]

Small-press (and "intellectual" cordel) poets tend to be politically liberal, and sympathetic toward fringe movements such as ecology. Impatience with traditional norms of capitalization, punctuation, and orthography are also frequent. Maxado is a spelling-reform enthusiast--his real name is Machado--and he has written chapbooks in his own spelling system. Similarly, the Cleveland, Ohio, small-press poet d. a. levy refused to use upper-case letters in his name. He became famous in the 1960s for publishing books printed on, and bound in, offcuts rescued from printing-shop waste. He was also the subject of considerable official harrassment for obscenity.

Above all, small-press poetry is an activity of middle-class intellectuals, with teachers of literature prominent among them. In the case of cordel para-folclórica this frequently causes resentment on the part of traditional poets who are of humble origin, self-taught, and often barely literate. João Antônio de Barros made a folheto of his indignation in a (scarcely) veiled attack on Maxado (who, having a university degree, is in Brazilian usage a "doutor"): "Apareceu jornalista / e até advogados / estragando os recados / dos poetas repentistas / que antes eram artistas / tratados por menestrel. / Hoje um tal bacharel / quer lhe atrasar o pão. / Doutor é poluição / nos livretos de cordel . . ."[40]

Acquisition

Few Brazilian libraries acknowledge the existence of small-press publications, except as possible candidates for the local collection. Outside Brazil, cordel (whether traditional or intellectual) does not even qualify for that. A handful of libraries do collect extensively. However, although materials are cheap, acquisition is time-consuming and cataloging difficult. Poor-quality paper makes preservation a particular headache. Microfilming is one possible solution, but this requires a significant investment in labor, film, and equipment.

In the case of cordel, purchase is especially difficult. An individual enthusiast could, eventually, build up a collection by sending low-value dollar checks to producers of cordel, accompanied by letters in Portuguese, requesting chapbooks as a personal favor. Some letters would go unanswered. Some poets would write back asking for the check to be made out in their real names, rather than the name they use in their publications. A good proportion of the material received would be duplicated, as most poets distribute their friends' publications as well as their own. But, in time, a collection could be built up by a patient overseas enthusiast.

A major academic library, however, could hardly pursue so time-consuming, uncertain, and fiscally unorthodox a method. Most academic collections have been formed through on-the-spot purchasing. At England's University of Essex, where one of the authors was Latin American librarian between 1965 and 1977, a small collection was formed almost entirely from the purchases of an enthusiastic professor in the Portuguese section of the Linguistics Department. We know of only one bookseller specializing in cordel; she, because of the low value of each individual item, can only trade on the basis of assorted lots (like a stamp dealer in less expensive stamps). She does keep sufficient records to avoid sending duplicates to the same customer. She reports a very limited interest, with about ten library customers in North America and Europe, most of whom appear satisfied with token collections of about two hundred titles. She claims, however, to have supplied about two thousand titles—about five years' production—to each of her most assiduous customers.

Cataloging is complicated insofar as the copyright owner often substitutes his own name for that of the original author. The Casa de Rui Barbosa therefore organizes its collection of cordel by a code consisting of the initial letters of each line of the first verse. Many authors "sign" their work by ensuring that the initial letters of the lines of the last verse form their own name, often making this obvious by giving prominence to such letters in the actual printing (e.g., by having them at right angles to the rest of the verse). Piracy is, however, quite rare: the producers of traditional cordel are too old-fashioned, genuine, and unsophisticated to be dishonest.

Another problem is the reluctance of catalog departments to be bothered with such "ephemera." A series of tests with OCLC have only revealed entries from three libraries. The Universities of Florida and Illinois have their cordel entered under "Literatura de cordel," although the latter institution does provide sufficient further information to enable each piece to be identified. The Benson Library at the University of Texas appears to be the only library that has contributed full cataloging to OCLC, but we understand that this has now been suspended at the request of their cataloging department. The Library of Congress has a comprehensive collection for the post-1950 period, acquired by its Rio office, but very little earlier material. All this, we understand, is held—uncataloged—in the Folklore Division.[41]

Cordel, when cataloged, is perhaps inevitably treated as belles lettres. In many cases, though, what matters is the content, particularly when this is political, religious, or moral. That the work is in verse is no more important than its using the Portuguese language, or the Latin alphabet. For the sertanejo, verse remains a way of conveying narrative as normal as it was in the English of Beowulf or the Greek of Homer.

But why bother with such intractable material at all? We would argue that, in their different ways, both traditional and intellectual cordel can play a valuable part in aiding the outsider's understanding of Brazilian society. Nothing else can indicate to us so clearly the beliefs and attitudes of the otherwise inarticulate masses of the less-developed parts of the country. Spufford, in introducing her work on seventeenth-century English chapbooks, tells us:

> The attention of historians interested in pre-industrial communities and in non-élites within them has only recently slowly turned from the reconstruction of the economic framework of such communities to the much more nebulous and more difficult attempt to recreate the mental world and imagery which such people had at their disposal. One of the very limited ways in which this can be done is to describe the fictional world to which the men, or women, who could read but could not necessarily write could be admitted . . . if he, or she, had tuppence to spend on . . . a chapbook.[42]

Is not the mental world of the cordel reader just as significant?

NOTES

1. "Prefácio" to Maria José Fialho Londres, Cordel: do encantamento às histórias de luta (São Paulo, 1983), p. 20.

2. With regard to format only; hardly with regard to content, when one thinks of Britain's Sun or the American National Enquirer.

3. Charles Nissard, Histoire des livres populaires . . . (Paris, 1854).

4. Sylvio Romero, Estudos sobre a poesia popular . . . (Rio de Janeiro, 1879-80).

5. Her Small Books and Pleasant Histories (London, 1981), pp. 11-13.

6. Her Stories on a String (Berkeley, CA, 1982), p. 10.

7. Hence violeiro. Other synonyms of cantador include repentista and poeta popular.

8. Who sold them after a family quarrel to spite her son-in-law Pedro Werta. See Franklin Maxado's O que é literatura de cordel (Rio de Janeiro, 1980).

9. Presumably no relation. Silva is the commonest surname among the poorer classes of the Northeast, closely followed by Santos.

10. The Brazilian movement has nothing but the accident of its name in common with the Spanish American modernismo of a generation earlier.

11.   "Whoever speaks to thee of 'cordel' is a student or tourist who regards our chapbooks as manifestations of art" (José Soares da Silva, O cangaceiro da roça quoted in "A vocação irresistível e penosa de Dila," Jornal do Brasil, April 10, 1979, p. B1.

12.   Aurelio Buarque de Holanda Ferreira, Novo dicionário da língua portuguesa (Rio de Janeiro: Nova Fronteira, 1975).

13.   V Encontro Nacional de Professores de Literatura. See "Ganhando status," Veja, 529 (Oct. 25, 1978), 151.

14.   "That depends . . . In the field of literature, it is growing. Where it is losing ground is in readership" (Manoel Camilo dos Santos, interviewed in O Norte (João Pessoa), March 21, 1979, 2, p. 1.

15.   "So I started changing my life story: the new version was a tremendous success" (José Soares da Silva, interviewed by Homero Fonseca, "A vocação irresistível e penosa de Dila," Jornal do Brasil, April 10, 1979, p. B1.

16.   His O folheto popular: sua capa e seus ilustradores (Recife, 1981).

17.   Robert Mandrou, De la culture populaire au 17e et 18e siècles (Paris, 1964), pp. 11-12.

18.   Spufford, Small Books, p. 259.

19.   "The Story of the Damsel Theodora, The Empress Porcina, The Fair Magalona, The Shipwreck of John of Calais, together with Charlemagne and the Twelve Peers of France, The Last Will of the Rooster and the Hen, and now, in recent years, the poems of the ballad writer João de Sant'Anna de Maria about the Paraguayan War" (Romero, Estudos sobre a poesia popular).

20.   (Brighton, Sussex: Harvester Press, 1985), chap. 7, pp. 162-182, "Classics and chapbooks."

21.   Slater, Stories on a String, pp. 147-148.

22.   Jornal do Brasil, April 10, 1979, p. B1.

23.   The cordel researcher Liêdo Maranhão de Souza claims to have a collection of this.

24.   The English popular press fascination with murder continues a preference well established in English chapbook literature. Henry Mayhew's London Labour and the London Poor, vol. 1 (London, 1851), pp. 302-303), instances two poor Norfolk families clubbing together to buy a penny broadsheet account of the execution of James Rush in 1849, which one old man read to the rest by firelight.

25.   Paulo Queiroz, "Os gêneros de cantoria segundo Bráulio Tavares," O Norte (João Pessoa), Aug. 21, 1977, Domingo: suplemento semanal, p. 1.

26.   "Cordel para tudo," Veja, May 11, 1977, p. 100.

27.   "We are already having to charge 500 cruzeiros for chapbooks of 8 to 16 pages and 700 for those of 32 pages when we have them--but they hardly exist any more" (Apolônio Alves dos Santos in private correspondence of Nov. 3, 1984).

28. Manuel Caboclo e Silva in private correspondence of Nov. 19, 1984.

29. Rodolfo Coelho Cavalcante in private correspondence of Nov. 5, 1984.

30. L. Hallewell, O livro no Brasil (São Paulo, 1985), p. 548.

31. "I found no chapbooks at all. So I have to get by with the small stock I have on hand. There is a marked falling off in production, due to high costs of labor and material such that small producers just cannot carry on" (private correspondence of Nov. 3, 1984).

32. His "Luzeiro Editora Ltda. e os trovadores da literatura de cordel," Brasil poético, 3:7 (Aug., 1976), 1.

33. Hallewell, O livro no Brasil, p. 539.

34. In a letter of June 21, 1977 to Maxado who quotes it in his O cordel televivo (Rio de Janeiro, 1984), p. 44.

35. Ibid., p. 96.

36. His Retrato da época (Rio de Janeiro, 1981), p. 74.

37. Maxado, O cordel televivo, p. 98.

38. Ibid., p. 96.

39. See Mark Curran, "Politics in the Brazilian literatura de cordel . . .," Studies in Latin American Popular Culture, 3 (1983), 115-126.

40. "You get journalists and even lawyers messing up the message of our popular poets, who formerly were artists, treated as troubadors. Now university graduates like these want to take the poet's livelihood away. [Chorus:] A 'doctor' is a form of pollution when he comes into the chapbook trade" (Barros's Doutor! que faz em cordel? [São Paulo?, 1976], cited in Maxado, O cordel televivo, p. 90.

41. How access to a chapbook collection, custom-made to scholars' probable research interests, could be provided, is demonstrated by Judith Endelman and Diane Bauerle's "Computerized Access to a Chapbook Collection," College and Research Libraries News, 46:7 (July/Aug., 1985), 340-342.

42. Spufford, Small Books, pp. 1-2.

31. REFLECTIONS ON THE FOTONOVELA

AND ITS READERS' RESPONSES

Renata Lellep Fernández

We have not systematically collected photonovelas
because our space is severely limited, we have to
make choices. After all, photonovelas are not
interesting, they are all the same.

Mr. Bill Blackbeard, Archivist
San Francisco Academy of Comic Art
March 27, 1985

Introduction

This conference has brought us together to consider what, if
any, works of popular culture to collect for libraries specializing
in Latin America. I am an anthropologist concerned with ecology,
health and the medical system, and social change. I have done
much of my fieldwork in Asturias, a province of northern Spain.
From this perspective I urge you to seriously consider adding
fotonovelas to your collection.

The epigraph does not accord with the action I urge. Why
should you collect fotonovelas? First, volume and readership: the
fotonovela incorporates an immense number of titles reflecting
virtually all literary formulas, and it also boasts the largest
readership of any genre.[1] It merits study for this reason alone.
Second, fairness: libraries undoubtedly have the critical literature
pertaining to this genre, but they lack the raw material which
would allow students to judge it for themselves. Third, history:
the fotonovela has evolved various subtypes under changing social
and economic conditions, and each of these in turn subsumes a
diversity whose range of expression is just beginning to be documented. The history of these types reflects social change.
Fourth, impact: most current analyses of the impact of the
formula upon the reader proceed as if this were a closed and
unilateral process. Interaction between the culture that produces
formulaic literature and its readership is surely more complex.
Agents who seek to influence economic, political, or cultural
change must understand the dynamic.

Author's Note. This paper was brought together for the
conference from materials gathered out of personal interest, with
little forethought for scholarly presentation. I have therefore
made little attempt to exhaustively document all of my statements
and speculations.

You can see then that critical and historical scholarship, as well as agents of change, requires access to the data. One might think the fotonovela's sheer abundance on the market would eliminate problems of access, but this is not the case. Disdain for the medium is such that even its publishers do not systematically preserve sample titles. Moreover, since profits are alluring but failure rates high, there is rapid turnover among publishers. Many fotonovelas are short-lived, or are treated as a negligible sideline by a more established publisher. This makes them hard to collect systematically. In Spain, where there is greater continuity of publication, libraries are few, underfunded, and understaffed. There, too, contempt for the genre often precludes its systematic preservation.

To illustrate: over my many years of fieldwork in Asturias, I had become accustomed to the ubiquity of the fotonovela and assumed that examples would not be hard to find. In 1980 I set out to survey the work of Corin Tellado, the best-known author of fotonovelas. I was able to obtain no more than ten issues, all privately held, spanning the seventies, and no examples of her production from either the fifties or sixties. The fotonovela may seem to saturate the newsstands. However, the cheap paper upon which it is usually printed, the many readers that thumb through a single copy, and the embarrassment of those found harboring it, all make it ephemeral. Readers in Spain for the most part feel ashamed of it. Interactions between the genre and the readership are, in consequence, difficult to trace.

How to Recognize a Fotonovela

Fotonovelas tell stories in photographs and printed words. The stories progress in frames, like comics, across the page and down. A frame presents the photograph, which is accompanied by speech and thought set off in balloons. Brief narrative comment is set off in boxes. Conventions guide the reader: the balloon points to the speaker; thought "bubbles" from her or him; the first speaker in a frame is assigned the topmost balloon. An outsized photo suggests intensity of feeling or duration of time, or invites the reader to pause. Photographic devices such as high contrast, or a deliberately softened image, provide variation and suggest a change of mood. Linked or overlapped frames suggest simultaneity. Zoom and collage are employed to focus or disperse attention. Crude conventions borrowed from comics also appear from time to time, but the enduring, authored fotonovelas employ such conventions only rarely. The fotonovela may limit invention, but it maximizes the reader's freedom. Fotonovelas allow the reader to choose her own pace and sequences, reread sections, and contribute unmentionable details to the story before her.

Fotonovelas are soft publications whose pages are usually stapled together. A story is told within a single issue, which rarely exceeds fifty pages. Some fotonovelas--I have seen these only in Mexico, never in Spain--contain several stories, serialized chapters, or fragments of stories. The fragments, interspersed with pages of complete stories, create a crazed effect. Those familiar with Latin American literary novels might interpret this crazing as intentional, but they may have merely been assembled in haste. Thick-backed glossy magazines, pitched at women, also sometimes carry pages of fotonovelas. I have heard that some, disguised to look like television guides, are directed at men and kept on hand in Spanish barbershops.

Advertising is not an important aspect. The single-author type--the most prestigious--carries advertising only inside the covers. These ads promote other fotonovelas, music, spectacles, and sometimes a television melodrama--in other words, they promote other media. Fotonovelas carrying several stories have more varied advertising, such as pitches for "sales opportunity, make a mint selling [plastic] jewelry." They also advertise cheap transportation to the capital, in effect paving the way to the alluring city depicted in some Mexican titles.

"Dear Abby" sections, horoscopes and homilies, and advice for feeding the baby or managing one's impulses are included in many fotonovelas, as if to balance expositions of temptation with those of prescription.

The plot assumed in Blackbeard's epigraph is a formulaic love story: lonely or unfulfilled female protagonist encounters a desirable partner, obstacles to legitimate love are overcome, a match is made. This formula does indeed characterize the original Spanish fotonovela but not, as we shall shortly see, all of its descendants.

The formula is subject to an evolutionary process. The fotonovela's formula at first reflected a cultural theme profoundly meaningful to people influenced by Catholicism. The same theme is recurrently expressed at First Communion, when a little girl dresses in white as a veiled bride. It is an attire and pose in which she remains fixed forever, framed as a photograph. Mutations of this thematic formula also arise, in some of which the original theme cannot be discerned. Mutations, however, survive only if the audience buys. Thus audiences, by means of market feedback, play a role in the fotonovela's evolution.

Types of Fotonovelas and Speculations about Their Effect upon the Reader

The formula felt to be so uninterestingly static by Blackbeard is the fotonovela rosa (rose-colored fotonovela), the first in the typology established by Flora.[3] Sentimental questions are resolved in the rosa within a moral framework inherited from Catholic traditions. The name rosa suggests the rose-colored glasses through which the reader, who is expected to identify with the female protagonist, is encouraged to see her world.

Temptations are strong, as are the forces opposing temptation; men are malleable, as demonstrated in the stories' strategies for shaping them; Cinderella and the Prince come from social and economic backgrounds that are alarmingly and enticingly disparate; fortitude and forgiveness lead to happy outcomes. This formula may be satisfying because it in part confirms the world the reader knows.

The fotonovela suave (soft fotonovela) resembles the rosa, but reduces the disparities of class. The suave sells in the neighborhoods of Mexico's materially more secure middle and upper classes. Its presumed readers find, reflected in it, the affluent living conditions and individualistic concerns of their class. It originated in Mexico in the early seventies.

The red fotonovela, fotonovela roja, appeared next. The red makes manifest the close relationship between sex and violence, love and death. It reflects social disintegration and the harsh economic realities pressing in upon the residents of barriadas (lower-class neighborhoods and shantytowns). According to Flora, reds employ the device that also makes Mexican cinema so popular: the unhappy ending.

Hill and Browner have lumped these three types into a single analytic group.[4] They expected, throughout, to find stereotypic women and men reflecting what the critical literature apprehends as the Marian and machista ideals. They found, to their surprise, that these stereotypes were absent from the fotonovela, though stereotypic views of class differences were indeed constant. This suggested to them that fotonovelas are read ritually, as if in consolation. Their study affirmed the reader's view that sex was of interest to all classes; that concerns with moral order preoccupied readers presumed to be of the lower class; and that only crass materialism concerned the upper class.

A fourth type identified by Flora is the picaresque fotonovela. Its story line is subordinate to sexually titillating adventures lived out in a fragmented social world. The Rosa's pictorial emphasis in face and gesture gives way in the picaresca to the female thigh photographed from a low angle. Flora believes that teenage boys make up the picaresca's readership.

The red and the picaresque type are recent phenomena that have, as yet, received little critical commentary. They had a previous existence, however, in the Peruvian radio serials of the fifties, as portrayed in Mario Vargas Llosa's 1977 La Tía Julia y el escribidor.[5] Fragmented, violent, and troubled lives become infinitely recursive upon each other, making it impossible to distinguish real life from the imagination. Indeed, Vargas Llosa's novel suggests that this distinction is illusory, as it is in the red and picaresca. Vargas Llosa's work leads me to speculate that fotonovelas may fill a vacuum that television, radio's multisensory successor, cannot. Graphics cannot be conveyed over radio, and sound and motion are missing from the fotonovela. In each case, the missing element leaves much to the imagination. This may be the fotonovela's strength.

Michèle Mattelart, the most vociferous critic of fotonovelas, does not consider this missing element a stimulus to imaginative freedom. She rather denounces fotonovelas as expressions of cultural imperialism intended to reinforce readers' passivity. She holds that fotonovelas mystify the relationship between the individual and society. They convince the reader that all that stands between her unfulfilled state and her happiness, her present poverty and her future material well-being, her degradation and her hoped-for satisfaction, are character defects, fate, or caprice. These obstacles, the reader is assured, can either be overcome through purification and personal effort, or circumvented by cleverness. Fotonovelas obscure the world system that is the true political cause behind the reader's troubled existence. The genre thus only postpones the apocalyptic day in which a solution will be found by collective, revolutionary means.[6]

A more appreciative critic, Fernando Curiel, maintains that there is no evidence that the writers and publishers of fotonovelas either intend or achieve such a systematic paralysis of spirit. Profit is what the producers aim for. In any event the genre--in which he takes delight--is too diverse to elicit such a uniformly passive response.[7] I would add that not every publisher of fotonovelas is even directly bent on profit. Certainly, publishers serving mission and development interests are not out to promote passivity. They are trying to identify the essence of the genre, and to then employ it for their own organizational, spiritual, or market goals.[8]

History of the Fotonovela in Spain

I became acquainted with the fotonovela and its history in Asturias, and have synthesized my view from the perspective offered by that province in its people. Corin Tellado, the world's most prolific author of novelas and fotonovelas, is a native of Asturias. She continues, despite her wealth and fame, to reside in the province and to vacation in its villages. Asturias is the historical region in whose northern mountain fastnesses, 1,200 years ago, a handful of Christians initiated the Reconquest. Except for that historic moment, the region is caricatured both in Spain and locally (in a defensive way) as the epitome of rusticity and backwardness. At the same time its image remains that of the innocent and sacred heartland of Christian Spain. Asturians, feeling inferior in the national hierarchy, try hard to cast off their dialect and rustic ways. The worldly success of their millionaire compatriot Corin Tellado is therefore a matter of substantial interest. Her success, by thrusting her and her genre into the regional news, has provided another local perspective on the fotonovela.

Fotonovelas originated in Mediterranean-Catholic Europe, implanted themselves abroad into the contexts into which they were exported, and, at least within the American continent, continue to generate new forms which cross national boundaries. The genre has become popular only in predisposed populations, populations that were missionized (by Spaniards and Portuguese) many generations ago with a pre-Reformation Catholic ideology. This suggests a core belief system underlying the original appeal of both fotonovela and the fictionalized radio serial. Important elements, which reappear in the fotonovela's suave and roja descendants, are confession, forgiveness, and personal trans-formation. The appeal entails a kind of "sanctification," says one of Vargas Llosa's characters.

In this larger historical sense, fotonovelas are perhaps an expression of cultural imperialism. But that imperialism stems from long ago. Moreover, the cultures that grew out of that contact are now so deeply rooted in the Americas that the suave, roja, and picaresca descendants of the original rosa European export must be appreciated as Latin American originals. The suave and picaresca have not reinserted themselves in their matria, Spain. This may be taken as evidence of their Latin American authenticity. I take them as an expression of "the grotesque reality which is ours," the central message of García Márquez' Nobel laureate address of 1982.[9]

The evolution and distribution of literacy, and consequently of high and low culture, play a role in the history of the foto-novela. Novels became popular in the nineteenth century, but they were at first only accessible to restricted circles which had both the literacy and leisure to enjoy them. More ordinary women "who did not know their place" also read novels, for which they were considered unsociable and slightly sinful. Rich and romantic oral traditions--fairy tales, verse, proverbs--had converged when rural migrants came to the industrial cities. But the migrant lost part of the social and cultural fabric that had supported the oral traditions in the countryside. New readers were thus eagerly receptive of story elements drawn from the leisurely paced works of the elite, even if these reached them only schematically and in inexpensive form. As duplication methods improved and repro-duction became cheap, pictures were added, permitting words to be schematized even more. A kind of industrial restricted code emerged by the early twentieth century, bereft of the details, time depth, complex characters, worldly institutions, and shifting perspectives so characteristic of the nineteenth-century novels of authors like the Asturians Leopoldo Alas and Armando Palacio Valdés.[10]

In this restricted code, words and pictures, whether sepa-rately or in combination, were purveyed to meet specific ends: sometimes to make a moral point, to reinforce religion, or to keep the masses quiet. The cromo given out at First Communions in

Spain, with its illustrations of the life of a Biblical figure or saint, exemplifies this production for the masses. One must not assume that these mass-produced words and pictures were received passively; they could serve as the stimulus for very personal transformations, as in the following example.

In the 1920s and 1930s, young rural Asturian women were prompted by inspired teachers to first copy the cromo in pencil, then enlarge it, transfer the design onto cloth, and embroider it in vivid colors. Through its several transformations it could hardly remain free of personal touches. The finished embroideries--for example a rustic-looking holy family, a Santa Lucia carrying her eyes on a plate--were hung over the bed, where I found them some forty years later.

The cromo, during its transformation, became closely linked to romance. The women, now old, told me how they invested their romantic dreams into that labor-intensive stitchery. Whenever I asked about the embroideries, their own tales of courtship emerged. They told me of how, as young women, they would bring chairs to sit together and work their stitches in each others' company, attracting young men as spectators. Courtship, under the influence of the cromo, thus assumed a new form and a new set of associations. The cromo worked like a kind of guardian angel, promoted courtship in the safety of a group, and was believed to guard against excess.

I should add, for those librarians concerned with archiving the popular arts, that I never found any of the original cromos printed on paper and do not know how faithfully the young women made their enlargements.

Historietas (illustrated storiettes) evolved out of the cromos. In Asturias they became associated with the Republican government of the 1930s. This regime had a mandate to improve literacy, widen education, and reduce the grossest disparities between rich and poor. Historietas were employed to these ends. While I have heard of the existence of these historietas, I have not seen them. But one expression of the flowering of local culture that took place during this time, villagers tell me, is that historieta story lines were used as the basis for rustic comedies produced in the parish. This is another example of a mass product taking on a personal or local expression.

The flow of mass-produced images of the Republican years soon ended. Civil War broke out, the Nationalists won, and Franco remained in office for the next thirty-nine years. During the forties he presided over autarquía, a period of extreme postwar scarcity. Autarquía meant that for more than a decade Spain had to provision itself from within, excluded as it was from cultural exchange and international trade. Censorship was imposed to keep down incipient countermovements. This repression was offset by broad programs to provision people with shoes, bread, and wine, keeping barefooted hunger and despair under

control.   Autarquía gave way to the somewhat less difficult
fifties, a decade of austerity.   This was a period during which
every effort was made to lift the nation by its bootstraps, without
however lifting the censorship imposed at the beginning of the
Franco administration.

Enter Corin Tellado, the Asturian photonovelist.   "Before a
man ever kissed me," she says, "I won a prize in an officially
sponsored writing contest with my first romantic story.   I was
seventeen."[11]   That was in 1951, a time when Franco welcomed
those who, within the strict guidelines of the Movimiento and the
very limited resources of the nation, might improve Spanish
morale.   By western European standards, Spanish literacy was
low.   Paper was also in short supply, and pulp forests were just
being planted.   Publications had therefore to be officially
approved and strictly limited in volume.   Franco found that
Tellado, in creating ilusiones, could make a few words go a long
way.

Ilusión is a word conveying multiple meanings.   My dictionary defines it as illusion, false show, counterfeit appearance,
smart lively irony, or apprehension.   But for Asturians, and
even more widely in ordinary usage, ilusión has a much more
positive sense that relates it to the life cycle.   To have ilusiones
means to believe in the future, to be motivated to work for
personal, practical, or visionary goals.   A young person bereft of
ilusiones is cynical or alienated, has lost his or her momentum or
motivation, and runs the risk of becoming a rootless drifter.
Young people without ilusiones are not considered normal.   Ilusión
is a companion of innocence and is appropriate to young people.
It tends to fade as people mature, but is partly restored when
parents nurture it in their offspring and, in turn, resorb it from
them.   Ilusión offers reason for one's existence.   A society in
which ilusión is not appropriately distributed is in despair.   The
novels of Corin Tellado helped Spain, during a period of extended
drabness, to restore ilusión.

It is not surprising then that paper was somehow authorized
to publish--in small print and tiny books, to be sure--the stream
of novelas that Tellado spun out.   Tellado's words were adapted
to fit animated figures in series, and in this way her ilusiones
began to reach a wider audience.   This, too, met state approval
because it meant that "gente sin cultura" were becoming culti-
vated, semiliterate.   Thus was born the romantic historieta, the
direct antecedent of the fotonovela.

In contrast to wartime historietas, those of the fifties
subordinated moral instruction to nurturing ilusión.   This is not
to suggest that Tellado sacrificed established morality for the
sake of profit.   Tellado was then, and continues to be, a member
of Acción Católica, a conservative quasi-religious organization
whose objective is to preserve Spanish traditions related to patria
and familia.   When, in post-Franco times, she was asked if ever

she was censored during her early years of writing, she replied
oracularly, "I didn't need to be. I was socially conditioned,
retarded. I still feel obliged to get myself home by 9 PM (as if I
were a young woman with a curfew)."[12] Her romances may have
explored the boundaries of approved social conduct, but they
always returned to moral center.

What Tellado published in the fifties was undoubtedly
compatible with national policy even if her publications were not
stamped by officialdom. Such endorsement tends, after all, to
undercut ilusión; in authoritarian regimes, it can be the kiss of
death.

Austerity gave way to a period of rapid economic development as the sixties approached. Trade relations, and cultural
and technical contact with other countries, were all resumed.
Spaniards began to migrate north, recruited as laborers in
northern European industries. Their remittances primed the
capital pump, and government-sponsored tourism brought in
foreign exchange. Economic growth meant that photography at
last ceased to be a luxury, and the romantic historieta
transformed itself into the Spanish fotonovela.[13]

The quality of photographs reproduced in Tellado's foto-
novelas was better than that of those in the Francoist daily,
ABC. Curiously, these two publications were cut to the same
size and toned equally in sepia. Tellado wrote the stories in
Asturias, and the remainder of the production took place in
Barcelona, a Mediterranean city with a long history of printing.
Her fotonovela, titled Corin Tellado, carried no dateline but was
numbered in series. A rival Selene came out in similar format.
These fotonovelas soon crossed the Atlantic. In the early sixties,
Latin Americans returning from visits to their ancestral Spanish
home created such a demand for Spanish fotonovelas that the
plates themselves were exported, to permit their mass production
in the New World.

Fotonovelas appeared also in Italy after World War II, whence
they spread to colonies of Italian immigrants in the Southern
Cone. There they were translated into Spanish, diffusing thence
across the continent. Both Italian and Spanish fotonovelas were
also translated into Portuguese for the huge Brazilian market.

Italian fotonovelas, in contrast with those of Spain, were
created in a democracy. Only after offensive sections had been
removed were they approved for publication in Argentina and
Brazil. "Political" material, rather than sexually provocative
features, tended to be excised. The former, for instance,
included passing references to collective labor movements: their
mere mention seemed to make South American censors queasy.
Had Italian fotonovelas entered Mexico directly, they might not
have been censored. Mexico's liberalism was, however, never
tested in this way, since the Italian products did not arrive, and

Spanish titles had already passed authoritarian scrutiny in Spain. This bit of history is significant. Those, like Mattelart, who deplore the fotonovela's omission of any signs of social solidarity, of labor movements, of neighborhood associations, or of cooperatives should keep this precedent in mind. While the Latin American type of fotonovela was set by authoritarianism, its anti-solidary posture is not inherent in the genre.

Economic and cultural changes in Latin America led to the decline of the imported fotonovela's popularity. The oil crisis, and the price escalation it set off, must have made the foreign product expensive relative to titles originating within Latin America. Tellado, for one, ceased in 1973 to be printed in the New World. Withdrawal of her work from Latin America's mass market undoubtedly accelerated the development of the suave, roja, and finally the picaresca genres. These descendants appeared in smaller format, bad print, and upon inferior paper, possibly putting the fotonovela within financial reach of people who had previously been unable to purchase the rosa. The Spanish fotonovela, however, has not disappeared from the Mexican scene. Some Mexicans consider it cursi to be seen with imported copies of Tellado. In present-day Mexico, Tellado apparently conveys status more than ilusiones.

The nomenclature of the fotonovela is evolving. On San Francisco's Mission Street, in the spring of 1985, I bought up a representative of every kind of fotonovela for sale. A Latina clerk insisted on selling me one without photographs. "Es una fotonovela de dibujo" (It is a fotonovela of drawings), she said. I bought it to compare with the fotonovela de verdad (true fotonovela). In its idealization of mother, it proved a reinvention of what I understand was the Spanish historieta. To a remarkable degree it also resembled "Mario," an animated television series popular in Spain during the summer of 1981. Both the novela de sábado" (Saturday afternoon TV novel) and the fotonovela de dibujo showed an orphaned, emotionally stranded boy trudging the world to find the mother whose death he could not accept. Feminists I knew then in Spain maintained that this TV novela was calculated to send dedicated career women back into the home. Despite their critical concern, they, their families, and the visiting anthropologist watched "Mario," enthralled. Afterward we would chide ourselves for weeping tears, for losing an afternoon to Mario's ilusión--and our own. We learned much later that the program was produced, not as we had thought, in Argentina--"a daughter of Spain" and hence a cultural offspring-- but in Japan. This provenance underscores the immense communicative power residing in these formulaic novels, whether on paper or video. They can be reproduced (and manipulated) across cultural boundaries, and they can be emotionally satisfying (or disturbing) to broad spectrums of humanity.

Fotonovelas in the Field

What, then, is a plausible relationship between the fotonovela or the formulaic text, the culture that produces it, and the culture that enjoys it? John Cawelti offers four hypotheses.[14] These should be kept in mind as we consider the specific types of fotonovelas.

First, formulas affirm the world that is felt to exist. Accordingly, fotonovelas must be a conservative force. When the fotonovela ceases to reflect the consensus it must either change its formula or lose its popularity.

Second, formulas resolve tensions and ambiguities. Accordingly, fotonovelas present a protagonist's dilemma, recognizing at once, for example, both her proximate desires and her own as well as society's long-range interests in orderly reproduction. The formula requires the harmonization of conflicting interest.

Third, formulas explore the boundary between the permitted and the forbidden. The fotonovela explores in fantasy and in a carefully controlled way the possibility—let us take recently observed examples—of a woman holding on to her career even while being courted (Tellado, about 1979), or of a woman forgiving the man who raped her on a date (Mexican fotonovela, 1985).

Finally, formulas assist in the process of assimilating changes. Fotonovelas, for example, have shown the reader that new legislation, such as Spain's recent legalization of divorce, need not threaten the survival of familial values.

We shall see, just as Cawelti holds, that the fotonovela has no single impact upon its readership. It is not, as Bill Blackbeard seems to assume, exclusively escape literature. Nor is it inherent in the genre to reduce its readership to passivity, or to evoke a univocal political response. The simple novel, however, because of its popularity, may be peculiarly suited to manipulating vast audiences.

At this point I drop my concern with the transnational aspects of the fotonovela to go very local. Let us travel to Escobines, a mountain village in Asturias, to observe the interaction of author, culture, and readership. Immediately striking in this regard is that Tellado, who has vacationed in this village and others like it, allows no local details to intrude into her work. The topical does not appear in Tellado, in an absence best understood in terms of her initial readership.

As I indicated earlier, Tellado was born and resides in Asturias, a region noted for peculiar rusticities of life-style and dialect. The mountains isolated Asturias for centuries. Asturians know that they appear backward, and that their local speechways are considered deficient. In this regard, Asturians are, of course, not alone; rural people in peripheral regions of many European countries feel such disregard. This disrepute may become thematic in "high" literature" (Quijote, Alas, Valdés, Marañón), but it is assiduously avoided by Tellado. Her formula positively omits either mention or depiction of anything regional or local.

Tellado thus omits reference to anything that might be considered rustic, backward, or distinctively Asturian. She also systematically avoids placing her stories in a specific time. Her couples, for example, walk on paved streets bordered by blank walls; street signs and license plates are unreadable or blanked out. She refuses to let such objects be markers of anything but what is generically modern, industrial, or cosmopolitan.

Mountains, so ubiquitous on the Asturian horizon, do not appear in the long shots. Shrines, typical destinations for a lovers' outing in Asturias or Spain, are neither mentioned nor depicted. Tellado's approach differs from high culture, where a premium is often set on portraying the particular.

The language Tellado employs in dialog is likewise remarkable. Her characters all speak standard Castilian. Their speech and her narrative are free of any class association, and free of words that do not translate uniformly into all Spanish-speaking countries.

This cannot be accident. I asked readers--young, single Asturian village women--about these characteristics. I posed the question in the early seventies, while Franco was head of state. This composite reply summarizes their comments:

> Tellado knows what we want. We've had the local up to here (fartucámosnos con lo de aquí). We don't want to mire ourselves in local stuff when we read for pleasure. Listen to the way we talk and denigrate ourselves. It would be mockery to see that on a printed page. Look at our pigs in the street, look at the wooden balconies on which we dry the livestock feed reminding us that we are country people and that animals must be fed. Look at the mountains that hem us in. Tellado vacations up here, enjoys herself in this village, as a change from civilized city life. While she's here she notices us, takes note of our ilusiones. She notices how we dress up on a Sunday for the men from far downriver who come to the weekly dances. She notices how we refuse to let the priest get us up in regional garb for the annual village fiesta. She notices how the Women's Auxiliary (Sección Femenina, affiliate of the National Movement) can't persuade us to practice the regional dances. Asturianina, bah! That activity is for girls already of the city. Tellado has us in mind, readers like us.

These replies came from fifteen-year-old girls. They had already finished school and were on the threshold of mocedad,

youthful bloom, the courtship years. This is the idealized period
of youth during which the family of origin recedes in importance,
courtship becomes the dominant theme, and a girl lives, almost,
for the moment. The future family has not yet assumed importance. Mocedad is a golden time of life. Indeed, marriage is put
off as long as possible so as to prolong this golden period.

During mocedad, premature pregnancy is to be avoided
because it triggers marriage. And with marriage come the
responsibilities of adulthood: raising children, tending a store, or
managing a farm. Mothers encourage the girls to make the most
of mocedad, for to them it is a future resource. Memories of
these "golden years" will be drawn upon and relived during the
years of heavy responsibility. Memories, the mothers know, will
lighten the burdens of maturity.

The mothers of the girls did not, however, agree that reading Corin Tellado was a way to intensify or extend la mocedad.

> We throw them out, those magazines, burn them.
> Daughters hide them from us, but we find them behind
> the stack of firewood, under the cushions of the
> kitchen bench, and even up under the bed of hay in
> the herding huts. What's bad about those stories is
> not that they show the flesh but that they inflame it.
> Es la picardía. They incite interest where the girls'
> interest doesn't belong. Those fotonovelas accelerate
> ripening. Look, we weren't even mozas until at least
> age eighteen, now girls barely out of school start going
> out at fifteen or even sooner. They start dressing up,
> sneaking into dances. All that stimulation, all that
> concentrated attention upon love starts them going off
> in pairs too soon. Courtship becomes serious . . .
> prompts early marriage, and curtails la mocedad.
> Married so soon they'll get tired of each other and even
> be wanting divorces. Tellado offers them ilusiones, but
> those ilusiones as Tellado offers them undermine
> mocedad, cut it off too soon.

I have no reason to think that the village matrons who spoke
like this would study for any length of time a fotonovela found
behind the kindling. Reading, they said with few exceptions,
was for schoolchildren. Reading was for the local justice of the
peace who daily displayed his Francoist allegiance sitting on a
chair outside his house, perusing the Official State Bulletin.
Reading was for spinsters. Reading novels was not appropriate
for the woman who manages a household, a husband, offspring,
and a farm. "Tengo que vivir mi propia novela" (I've got enough
to do living out my own novel). (Some village women, counter to
this ethos, did however read novels. They baptized their
daughters with names like Floripes, Azenor, and Azucena--names
that, contrary to custom, were not repeated with the grand-
daughters.)

Urban Asturian women--shopkeepers, teachers, unemployed housewives, middle-class friends of mine--did read novels from time to time. But most of them preferred light material that did not drag. If church literature was not to their taste, and if Hola's stories on the love lives of the aristocracy, reported through all the decades of Francoism, did not please them either, they acted as Tellado herself suggested: "Fotonovelas. It's the servant girls who buy them and their mistresses who read them" (Una literatura que compran las criadas y leen las señoras).[15]

Middle-class women who admitted to familiarity with foto- novelas were unconcerned that they did not reflect Asturian particularities. In fact, in their eagerness to blend their fantasies with those of what they assumed to be the larger world's, I doubt that they noticed the systematic reduction.

No middle-class woman described herself as a regular reader of fotonovelas, but copies were available in the beauty shops and always looked well thumbed. I saw them there, being read very often by middle-class women toward the close of their reproduc- tive years, in a period of the life cycle shadowed by insomnia, chills, headaches, hemorrhages, marital difficulties, self-doubt, and depression. I have never succeeded in getting one of these readers to read a fotonovela with me and comment upon it.

But these same women spontaneously and repeatedly during this stressful period of the life cycle tell me about their mocedad: how they and their husbands met, encountered and overcame obstacles, and eventually married. These personal stories repeat elements that are stock themes in the fotonovela rosa: shyness, longing, hesitation to speak, fleeing from contact, age or status differences, misunderstanding, fear of future in-laws, the long trip to the strange city. The major difference is temporal: the matrons look back to their own youth, while the fotonovelas are atemporal.

The astonishing repetition of these details convinced me that mocedad was indeed a resource. In drawing upon it (rememorar), a woman resolves to assume again the disposition she had during mocedad, and to discard the nagging, strident, nervous, or over- bearing disposition that has overtaken her. It is a way, the women say, of restoring happiness to the marriage.

I am sure my friends are not exceptional in this regard. The revivification of youth is a solution endorsed widely in Hispanic culture. The woman's page in the dailies usually carries an advice column, such as "Dicta el Corazón" in La Nueva España. Prescriptions in such columns for the midlife crisis include the same kind of remembering as the women practice when they tell me about mocedad. I can imagine that a woman lacking an intimate friend with whom to review her mocedad or noviazgo (engagement) might turn to a fotonovela as a substitute. I speculate that the middle-aged imagination fills in the schema with personal detail from youth and courtship, possible precisely because the Tellado fotonovela is unencumbered with detail or complexity.

From this report of my Asturian field experience it becomes clear that the fotonovela interacts differently with the various segments of the readership. The sociopolitical context in which it is read also affects the readership's response. After Franco died in 1975, Spain experienced an abrupt relaxation of censorship, especially in regard to sexually provocative materials. By the summer of 1976, newsstand magazines displayed the novelty of buttocks and breasts as if human skin were major news. In this new context, the fotonovela ceased to attract the attention of village girls as before, or to draw flak from self-righteous mothers.

Television had for some years been showing city ways to the country people, and whatever titillation youngsters once got from the fotonovela was now available from the skin magazines. The fotonovela, without changing much at all in that half year, had become tame--for the context had changed. The "R" rated Emanuelle I and II played for months on end in the provincial capital, and consistently attracted a full house of spectators who entered the theater largely as singles. In the village, The Joy of Sex became a standard item in the young marrieds' bureau drawer, and even got put away in the dowry chest. In this context Tellado became almost a nostalgia piece, a remnant of the Francoist past.

The context does not change uniformly, however. If Tellado is still producing fotonovelas, it may be because girls in the mountainous hinterland, without movies or TV, still demand and read copies as their lifeline to the modern world. It may also be because there still are middle-aged, middle-class women who retrieve some part of their youth in them, or who by reading them recapture a youthful attitude. Only from these former was I able to get the back copies that spanned the decade.

The fotonovela, in sum, is a vital, varied, evolving form which provokes an equally complex relationship with its audience. The form has much to show us, and is well worth including in our research collections.

NOTES

1. According to the Spanish press of the nineteen-seventies, U.N. statistics listed the novelist and photonovelist Corin Tellado as the most widely read author in the world. She had surpassed Mao Tse Tung sometime early in the decade--and she is still producing today.

2.   My impressions of the fotonovela are gathered from the following sources. I surveyed Spanish fotonovelas of the seventies, wrote up notes, and afterward discarded the issues of <u>Corin Tellado</u> and <u>Selene</u> I had used. In March, 1985, I purchased several examples of every available fotonovela in San Francisco's Mission District. Overlapping with these were a few purchased in April, 1985, in the Hispanic stores of New Brunswick. These American and Latin American publications extended over the following range:

<u>Capricho</u>, March 28, 1985, "Delincuente."

<u>Cárcel de Mujeres</u>, no. 1249, "Doble Asesinato," Editormex.

<u>Chicas Fotonovela</u>, no. 718002, "Vive hoy, un rojo atardecer," ELE, México, DF.

<u>Cita</u>, no. 718001 80817, "Señora Pecadora," ELE, México, DF.

<u>Libro Sentimental</u>, April 9, 1985, "Llévame contigo mamita," Novedades Editores.

<u>Novelas de Amor</u>, April 8, 1985, "Ese Hombre no te Conviene," Novedades Editores.

<u>Vanidades</u>, no. 7, "Yo no soy tu juguete," by Corin Tellado.

3.   Cornelia Butler Flora, "The 'Fotonovela' in America," <u>Studies in Latin American Popular Culture</u> [hereafter <u>SLAPC</u>], 1 (1982), 15-26.

4.   Jane Hassler Hill and Carole Browner, "Gender Ambiguity and Class Stereotyping in the Mexican 'Fotonovela'," <u>SLAPC</u>, 1 (1982), 43-64.

5.   Mario Vargas Llosa, <u>La Tía Julia y el escribidor</u> (Barcelona: Seix Barral, 1977).

6.   Michèle Mattelart, <u>La cultura de la opresión femenina</u> (México, DF: Editorial Era, 1977), reviewed by Ellen McCracken, "Toward an Interdisciplinary Semiotics: Michèle Mattelart's <u>La cultura de la opresión femenina</u>," <u>SLAPC</u>, 1 (1982), 237-245.

7.   Fernando Curiel, <u>Fotonovela rosa, fotonovela roja: una historia de Fernando Curiel</u>, 2d ed. (México, DF: Difusión Cultural, Universidad Nacional Autónoma de México, 1980), reviewed by Jayne H. Hill, <u>SLAPC</u>, 1 (1982), 252-257.

8.   Ronald Parlato et al., <u>The Use of Popular Graphic Media in Development</u> (Washington, DC: Office of Education and Human Resources, Development Support Bureau, Agency for International Development, 1977), reviewed by William A. Smith, <u>SLAPC</u>, 3 (1985), 192-196.

9.   Gabriel García Márquez, "Text of Nobel Lecture Delivered in Stockholm in December by 1982 Literature Laureate Gabriel García Márquez," <u>The New York Times</u>, Feb. 6, 1983, p. 17.

10. See, for example, Leopoldo Alas, La Regenta (Barcelona: Biblioteca "Arte y Letras," 1884-1885), or Armando Palacio Valdés, La Aldea Perdida: Novela-poema de costumbres campesinas (Madrid: Hijos de M.G. Hernández, 1903).

11. Vicente Gracia, "Corin Tellado: Paso de todo, tío," Interviú (ca. 1981, p. 68)--sent me as a clipping without further reference.

12. Ibid., pp. 68-69.

13. Photography was such a luxury in the Spain of the 1940s that the Asturian General Hospital hired an artist to copy X-rays by hand (Tolívar Faez, M.D., personal communication).

14. John G. Cawelti, Adventure, Mystery, and Romance: Formula Stories as Art and Popular Culture (Chicago, IL: University of Chicago Press, 1976), pp. 35-36.

15. Asturias Semanal (Oviedo, Spain), n.d., a weekly magazine that appeared for a few years in the 1970s.

III. *New Approaches to the Literate Elite*

32. THE SOCIAL HISTORIAN AND THE HISTORY OF OPERA IN LATIN AMERICA

Ronald H. Dolkart

Opera has firm roots in Latin America's colonial past. It began as an imported phenomenon, with most of the compositions and their interpreters coming from Europe, although there were also always local imitators of these foreign models. The early operas appeared in the viceregal capitals of Mexico City and Lima. La púrpura de la rosa, performed in Lima in 1701, is considered the very first opera composed in the Spanish colonies; La parentrope followed in Mexico a decade later.[1]

The rapid rise of opera's popularity in Latin America coincided with the nationalistic fervor that followed independence. It may seem paradoxical that Latin Americans would embrace a cultural form so closely associated with Europe when they had just fought to throw off Old World colonialism. But opera was identified with the French, Italian, and even German traditions, and symbolized liberalism and progress instead of Iberian reaction and stagnation.

Soon after the new nations proclaimed their independence, in the 1820s and 1830s, the popular operas of Europe began to be staged in the capital cities of Latin America. These performances were given by traveling companies from Europe, mainly Italy, and secondarily from Spain (but using Italian texts) and France. Such enterprise presented clear opportunities for financial gain: as with similar activities in Europe itself, opera production in Latin America lay in the hands of an entrepreneur, the impresario.[2] A contract would be negotiated between the theater, which might be municipally owned, and the impresario. The latter would offer a defined repertoire, usually dangling the bait of recent European successes before the benighted Latin Americans. Then the company, often named for the impresario, would leave from a port like Genoa during the Northern Hemisphere's summer months, when no European theaters were open. Its destination would be the Southern Hemisphere's winter season of opera, or tropical mountain cities where the climate remained temperate through the entire year. Singers, chorus, orchestra, and scenery would all have to be transported on the month-long voyage across the Atlantic. They would then remain for three to five months in one or two cities such as Buenos Aires and Montevideo, Rio de Janeiro and São Paulo, Mexico City and Guadalajara, or remoter places.

Except for rare occasions, most of the singers who went on these voyages were second-rank or worse, and they were forced to perform in a variety of roles for which their voices were often ill-suited. The opportunities for substantial remuneration remained a potent, but often chancy, attraction. Most companies claimed that they lost money, perhaps so the impresario could reduce salaries at the end of the tour. On the other hand, the artists received a much more enthusiastic reception from the opera-hungry patrons of Latin America than they could ever have earned in Europe.

Latin America's audience for opera grew larger and more sophisticated as the nineteenth century progressed, largely as a result of the influx of European immigrants. Italian arrivals identified opera as the most significant form of public display of their culture; the Germans and French, although fewer in numbers, insisted on musical drama in their vernacular. Thus opera, which tended in Latin America to be given in the language of its original form, reflected the pluralistic nature of Latin America's urban society and formed an important aspect of its popular culture.   o

Argentina demands primacy among Latin American nations producing opera, and indeed it has evidenced a deeper and longer attachment to opera than any other country in the region. Opera in Argentina, of course, meant opera in Buenos Aires. As that city grew as a center for international immigration and trade, porteños felt the need to construct a major opera house: the first Teatro Colón opened in 1857. This "primitive" Colón was torn down in 1888 when the elite insisted on a grander auditorium. The Teatro de la Opera, which served as the principal site for opera until the new Colón could be completed, witnessed glorious days of fin-de-siècle opera. So did several other locations, offering a multiplicity of productions. The present Teatro Colón began its activities in 1908, and represents the one opera theater in Latin America to have achieved world renown.

Brazil preceded Argentina as a focus for the European operatic explosion of the eighteenth century, and enjoyed a brilliant period of activity with the Jesuits' founding of the Casa Opera in the 1760s. The great decades for nineteenth-century opera in Rio de Janeiro extended from Pedro II's accession, in 1840, to the outbreak of the Paraguayan War in the mid-1860s. Opera was not only the diversion of choice for the now numerous bourgeoisie of a cosmopolitan city, it became an obsession in the cafes and newspapers. Brazil produced its own notable group of opera composers, including Carlos Gomes, whose Il Guarany gained worldwide fame. While the appearance of many great figures of European opera in Rio on their tours of South America provoked a continued interest on the part of the public, by the late nineteenth century enthusiasm was on the wane. Rio de Janeiro (in 1909) and São Paulo (in 1910) opened magnificent opera houses after the turn of the century. Both locales were called the Teatro Municipal, and each has hosted many famous performances over the past seventy-five years.

Mexico was described as a nation in which "opera ruled like a goddess." Italian opera, especially opera buffa, won the hearts of the Mexican public from its earliest presentations in the first decade of the nineteenth century through midcentury. The bel canto style of Rossini, Donizetti, and Bellini remained most fashionable. The period of the Restored Republic saw a more varied program, including Verdi operas put on by major singers from Europe. The Teatro Nacional could never keep up with the demand for tickets. The Porfiriato's wealth provided increased funding for longer and better seasons, and sometimes several companies appeared during the year. Mexico only lacked a world-class opera house, which Don Porfirio intended to provide for the centennial celebration of 1910. The Revolution interfered, and what is today the Bellas Artes did not open until 1934. This lack of a home for opera did not make much difference, since such European diversions were scorned by the revolutionary ideals. Opera made few subsequent appearances in Mexico until the 1940s, but it has since enjoyed growing popularity.

That opera appeared in the larger, Europeanized cities of Latin America should come as no surprise, although its extent and significance may be somewhat unexpected. Yet opera was not limited to a Buenos Aires, Mexico City, or Rio de Janeiro. It spread to almost every capital city in larger nations, and well beyond to the more remote frontiers. Opera had a mission in Latin America, the goal of bringing civilization to those dark corners which so greatly desired to be like a France or an Italy. And what better way to emulate them than by seeing and hearing the highest expression of their culture.

Brazil had opera not only in Rio de Janeiro. São Paulo offered its first full season in 1874, and the schedule quickly grew to a dozen different operas. This development coincided with the city's upsurge of coffee wealth and the influx of European immigrants. Furthermore, São Paulo's location made it possible for companies and singers on the Atlantic coast to stop on their way between Rio and Argentina. Impresarios found that they could make another stop in Porto Alegre, where the Teatro São Pedro provided a primitive location for performance. The Northeast and the Amazon Basin even got their own taste of the lyric stage, with Bahia's Teatro de São João presenting a full company in 1845 and with several visits thereafter. And then there was the Teatro Amazonas in Manaus on the Amazon River. This unique building, constructed with the wealth of the rubber barons, was inaugurated on December 31, 1896. It seldom presented opera, despite the posturing of the protagonist in Werner Herzog's film, Fitzcarraldo.

The Southern Cone, aside from Argentina, includes Uruguay, Chile, and Paraguay. Montevideo of course shares a riverine boundary and a cultural affinity with Buenos Aires. It attracted many companies across the Plata to Uruguay's Teatro Solís, opened in 1857. Santiago de Chile finished the construction of its Teatro Municipal in the same year. Chile seemed to prefer the French over other European cultures. After a French company's 1876 visit, something of a polemic arose between the partisans of French opera, which they found more refined, and the followers of Italian opera, which they insisted had better music. The Italian repertoire nonetheless dominated, if only because most of the visiting companies came from Italy. Even Asunción in Paraguay saw and heard some opera from time to time after the Olimpo Theater opened in 1887. Paraguay was a prime target for the type of foreign companies best labeled "musical-theatrical troupes," which would present farces and truncated versions of opera in the same evening.

The Andean nations of Venezuela, Colombia, Ecuador, and Peru constituted one of the lesser, although by no means negligible, regions of operatic activity. Caracas, because of its easy accessibility from Europe, fared best. With a new opera house after the middle of the nineteenth century, European companies stopped off almost every year. Venezuela thus established a solid operatic tradition; after the turn of the century, many of the best singers began to appear. Bogotá, on the other hand, demanded a formidable journey into the higher reaches of the mountains. Thus the initial presentation of operas came as late as 1848, and the next group of artists only arrived a decade later. They stayed an entire year, as they kept delaying their departure. Not until the very last decade of the nineteenth century did Bogotá construct a substantial opera house, the Colón. The productions of opera, if any, in Lima and Quito have remained undocumented.

The Caribbean region and Central America took up opera with enthusiasm in certain countries, notably Cuba and Guatemala. Havana offers the unique case of an early permanent opera association. A group of singers arrived from Spain in 1811, and they remained for some two decades. Cuba was soon receiving a better class of artists than usual outside of Buenos Aires or Rio de Janeiro, due to its continued connection with Europe through Spanish colonial control, and because the sugar plantocracy was willing to pay for good performances. Independence after 1898 brought about a declining interest in opera, although an occasional "star" like Caruso would stop off for a concert. Guatemala City completed a major theater, the Teatro Nacional--ordered and paid for by the government--in 1859. The Guatemalan government often subsidized impresarios who would bring in a set number of singers, and public enthusiasm remained high well into the twentieth century.

Over the nineteenth century, thus, opera in Latin America grew in terms of numbers of performances given, and spread in

terms of location of productions. Most significant was the power
that opera came to exercise over the worldview of Latin Americans: they accepted a concept of opera as the highest expression
of the European culture they sought to emulate. The pinnacle of
export-oriented prosperity, generally attained in the first two
decades of the twentieth century, led to the construction of great
opera houses and the importation of famous singers and con-
ductors. Then the world depression of the thirties initiated a
decline in resources which no longer permitted Latin Americans to
afford the best opera. Two other considerations also helped
account for opera's decline: the revolutionary mentality which has
identified opera as a decadent Western imposition; and the pervasive influence of the cinema. This inexpensive and ubiquitous
entertainment soon became the popular choice.

     Historical research has changed radically during the past two
decades with the rise of a persuasive and now pervasive group of
scholars in the United States who have referred to their work as
the "New Social History." The origins of this perspective lie with
the French historians associated with the journal Annales. The
topics emphasized are not the great events brought about by
famous leaders but the everyday life of the masses. French
historians thus focused on rural existence in the Middle Ages and
the Early Modern Period.[3] American historians have proceeded in
two directions, combining this perspective with insights from the
social sciences. One trend has centered on quantification, the
need to use clear statistics as evidence in a process greatly
aided by the computer. Another has emphasized the culture of
groups during large blocks of time, providing an anthropological
perspective in history.
     This "New Social History" places particular importance on
"the informal, the unarticulated, the daily and ordinary manifestations of human existence, as a vital plasma in which all more
formal and visible expressions are generated."[4] Research has
focused on the average or marginal individuals in history, the
so-called anonymous or inarticulate. However, the everyday
activities of elites are also a part of this social viewpoint.
Consequently, "any branch of history can be converted into social
investigation by turning attention from its usual main object of
study, whether laws, ideas, or events, toward the people who
produce them."[5]
     Until very recently, the history of opera has been
unaffected by any such social analysis. The work of musicologists has quite properly looked at the composers and their works,
comparing them as to their musical features and influences.
Sociologists of music have considered the manner in which musical
compositions reflect the characteristics of any given society.
From their standpoint, it is important to examine the "functional
relationships of the style and contents of an opera, with its

actual social surroundings and with certain sociomusical groups."[6] As a result, we know a great deal about the operas and their performances, and speculation abounds about what special temporal and social factors influenced musicians and producers. Such literature has often seemed highly specialized and remote on the one hand, or rather simplistic and anecdotal on the other.

A few examples may suggest the direction of the new social history of music and opera. One emphasis is on the business of producing opera. Opera was a widely dispersed phenomenon. It took place not only in the great theaters of European capitals but also in small towns throughout the world. It required investments in singers, orchestra, scenery, costumes, and transportation. Rosselli's appropriately titled The Opera Industry in Italy from Cimarosa to Verdi: The Role of the Impresario is a model for such monographs.[7] He first shows the reader how opera production worked in terms of the many provincial theaters in Italy: contracts had to be negotiated with the municipality, and then the impresario had to form a company that he hoped would please the public. In short, this activity was very risky entrepreneurship. So many individuals went bankrupt that a new system eventually arose in which opera houses had permanent resident managers.

Professor Rosselli's major strength lies in his methodology and data. One appendix discusses problems of the comparability of evidence. The old, anecdotal history of opera tended to repeat stories about the salaries of singers or the fees of composers. Rosselli instead turned to the sources most useful for solid figures, the contracts of the impresarios and the court cases that often grew out of them. Certainly, Rosselli has broken new ground in the history of opera, and his study is highly suggestive for those who want to delve into the lyric theater's past from this social perspective.

William Weber's Music and the Middle Class concentrates on concert performances in major European capitals during the nineteenth century in order to see "what the classical tradition has meant in the lives of its devotees."[8] He writes social history in terms of patrons of concerts, and the groups from which they came. The rise of the middle classes forged a new relationship between musical production and its financing. The result was the "entertainment world" of the concert hall. This analysis clearly applies to opera on an even more grandiose scale, and Weber's careful look at the archives of musical institutions shows the road that researchers will have to follow.

The social history of Latin America has lagged behind that of Europe and the United States, although there have been significant efforts to trace the formation of new societies under colonial Spanish rule. For the nineteenth and twentieth centuries, "popular culture" has been an important area of interest to social historians. This concern has produced a number of monographs, as well as a journal committed to its study.[9]   The social rituals of elites, however, have been largely ignored.   The opera, as one of their principal passions, and opera theaters, as one of their major gathering places, deserve a close look.   Specific questions include the production of opera in Latin America, its operatic consumers, and how opera fitted into the developing urban culture of the nineteenth and twentieth centuries.[10]

The new social history presents special research problems and, consequently, special challenges to librarians who serve its practitioners.   The archives used by historians have clustered in special collections of primary documents concerning particular issues.   These source materials are then verified through the use of newspapers, reports, and other contextual resources.   Social history, however, also requires more imaginative resources, often disparate and obscure, which must be fitted together in order to portray some aspect of society.   The starting place is often government records, from which statistics can be extracted for computer analysis.   Then the search is on for a myriad of contemporary (to the period being studied) books and pamphlets, in order to establish the mentality and ethos of the society. Finally, the testimony of historically neglected or unrecorded participants is sought in judicial proceedings or diaries and letters.

The new social history of opera, with its emphasis on productions and on audiences, looks principally to three major archival sources.   First, and foremost, are the records maintained by the principal opera theaters.   These provide dates and casts of opera performances, but more importantly give the names of boxholders and subscribers, ticket prices, and forms of administration.   Second come official papers, especially those of municipalities, because the opera houses belonged to city governments.   Local debates about the policies and politics of opera help situate it within the broader social context.   Third are the documents of individual impresarios and opera companies, which include much information about production costs and public tastes.   The contents of periodical literature are also indispensable.   Reviews by critics often have lengthy commentary on operagoers, the reactions of audiences, and the social relationships reflected in the opera house.   Popular magazines offer pictorial essays on the opera season, and interpret what the performances meant for the cultural climate of the city.

The social historian of opera faces one significant problem: should he or she work in the music library or the research library?   Most major universities have established a separate music facility, originally to house scores and other performance-related materials, and subsequently supplemented with books and journals.   Research in social history may begin here, to establish basic chronologies from published monographs and reference

works.   Traditional musicological studies of composers and
countries must also be consulted for their useful bibliographic
information.   Detailed histories of opera houses, listing performances and casts over the years, are readily available.
However, music libraries rarely house the special collections
needed by music historians concerned with social history.   The
researcher must move on to the principal research facility, with
its collections of government documents, periodical reviews, and
personal memoirs, in order to complete the picture of changing
economic conditions and public tastes.

I mention this division of libraries in order to raise an issue
central to the social history of opera: the need to systematically
collect musical, and especially operatic, materials.   This problem
is especially acute with regard to Latin American materials.   Music
bibliographers focus on the traditional languages of musicological
scholarship: German, French, and English.   They possess little
interest in or knowledge of Spanish and Portuguese sources.
Consequently, music libraries seldom contain much in the way of
Latin American books or journals.   Most large Latin American
cities issued weekly or monthly periodicals on musical life, but
these are seldom found in North American university collections.
Latin American bibliographers usually concentrate on general
research collections, and leave music to their colleagues on
another part of the campus.   The hope of this social historian of
opera is for the most coordinated approach possible in establishing significant collections of Latin American music materials.

NOTES

1.   The acknowledged authority on early opera in Latin
America is Robert Stevenson.   Works of particular interest to
opera include the articles "Lima," in the New Grove Dictionary of
Music and Musicians (London, 1980), X, 861-862, and "Mexico
City," in ibid., XII, 240-242; and the volumes Music in Mexico
(New York, 1952) and Foundations of New World Opera (Lima,
1973).

2.   See the excellent analysis of the "business" of opera in
John Rosselli, The Opera Industry in Italy from Cimarosa to
Verdi: The Role of the Impresario (Cambridge, England, 1984).

3.   For an interesting summary of the "new social history"
see Elizabeth Fox-Genovese and Eugene D. Genovese, "The
Political Crisis of Social History: A Marxian Perspective," Journal
of Social History, 10:2 (Winter, 1976), 205-220.

4.   James Lockhart, "The Social History of Colonial Spanish
America: Evolution and Potential," Latin American Research
Review, 7:1 (Spring, 1972), 6.

5.   Ibid., p. 6.

6.   Alphons Silbermann, The Sociology of Music, trans.
Corbet Stewart (London, 1963), p. 137.

7.   Cited above, n. 2.

8.   William Weber, Music and the Middle Class: The Social
Structure of Concert Life in London, Paris and Vienna (London,
1975).

9.   Studies in Latin American Popular Culture (Las Cruces,
NM), 1982--.

10. For an example, see Ronald H. Dolkart, "Elitelore at
the Opera: The Teatro Colón of Buenos Aires," Journal of Latin
American Lore, 9:2 (1983), 231-250.